Geology of the Lower Hudson Valley *(overleaf)*

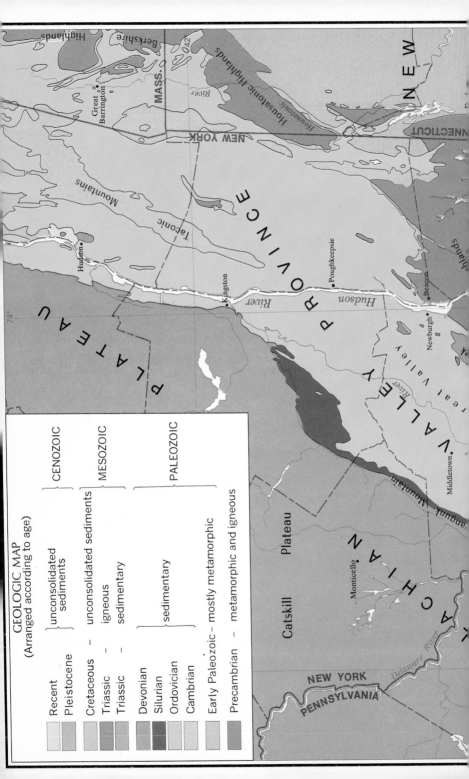

GEOLOGIC MAP
(Arranged according to age)

Recent — unconsolidated sediments — CENOZOIC
Pleistocene

Cretaceous — unconsolidated sediments
Triassic — igneous — MESOZOIC
Triassic — sedimentary

Devonian
Silurian
Ordovician — sedimentary — PALEOZOIC
Cambrian

Early Paleozoic – mostly metamorphic

Precambrian – metamorphic and igneous

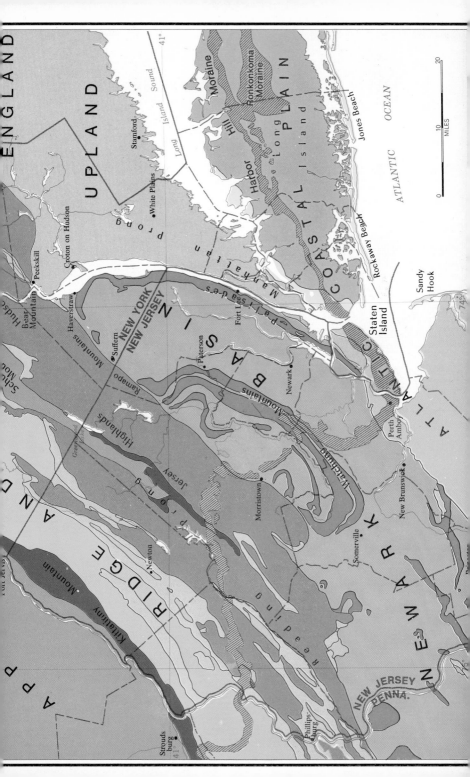

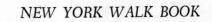

NEW YORK WALK BOOK

NEW YORK

Pen sketches by ROBERT L. DICKINSON
and RICHARD EDES HARRISON

With an Introduction to the Geology of the Region by
CHRISTOPHER J. SCHUBERTH

WALK BOOK

FOURTH EDITION

COMPLETELY REVISED
UNDER THE SPONSORSHIP OF THE
New York–New Jersey Trail Conference
AND

The American Geographical Society

DOUBLEDAY/NATURAL HISTORY PRESS
Garden City, New York

FOREWORD

This is a book for all who live in the great metropolitan area of New York and feel the need to get away from its frantic pace and commercial engulfment. The American Geographical Society is delighted to join with the New York–New Jersey Trail Conference in making available this fourth edition of the *New York Walk Book*. First published in 1923, it has become a fundamental source book for veteran hikers and neophyte trailblazers alike.

The Society's contribution to the text of the publication was directed by Wilfrid Webster, Editor of Special Publications, whose keen editorial resourcefulness was indispensable in shaping a uniform whole from the individual parts provided by numerous authors and field workers.

The maps have been entirely redrawn and updated by the Society's Cartographic Department under the supervision of Miklos Pinther, Chief Cartographer. We are especially indebted to those members of the New York–New Jersey Trail Conference whose intimate knowledge of trail and terrain greatly aided in the onerous final checking of the maps.

AMERICAN GEOGRAPHICAL SOCIETY

PREFACE

In presenting this fourth edition of the *New York Walk Book,* the New York–New Jersey Trail Conference hopes it will introduce the joys of walking as a hobby and a pastime to those in the metropolitan region who may be unaware of the green space and even wilderness tracts within fifty to a hundred miles of the city, accessible by bus and car. For the thousands of hikers who already know this, it is designed to reflect the changes in trails and shifts in hiking areas which have occurred since the last edition, and as a reminder of regions yet unvisited.

The sketches of Dr. Robert L. Dickinson, one of the three authors of the original *Walk Book,* so well conveyed the nature and flavor of the region that they have been retained in each edition. Thanks to the generosity of Mrs. George B. Barbour, Dr. Dickinson's daughter, who made the original drawings available to us, we have also been able to include a few previously unpublished. They have been supplemented by the drawings of Richard Edes Harrison. In the same spirit of interpreting our hiking country he has added illustrations for regions which were unavailable or beyond a day's trip twenty years and more ago.

The genesis of a fourth edition of this book occurred in 1964. A committee was thereafter appointed and the task of mobilizing a large group of volunteers began. From their field notes the manuscript and maps began to take form. Supervising and directing this vast effort was an indefatigable trio: Elizabeth D. Levers, Elizabeth Snyder, and George M. Zoebelein.

What can walking do for you? It will provide exercise in whatever degree you desire. It is available everywhere, in all seasons, and requires little equipment. It can be enjoyed alone or with friends. Over twenty-five years ago Dr. M. Beckett Howorth, a hiker who was also a physician, described the art of walking:

You know as much of the art of walking as I do. It consists of walking in rain, fog, or snow, as well as on clear days or by moonlight. Some of its most beautiful moments are in storm. It consists of knowing what to eat and drink, and how to prepare and consume it, alone or with others; how to make or erect a shelter; how to find comfort in a sleeping bag; the names of flowers, their structure, their odors, and how they grow. The names of birds, their flight, their songs, their eggs and young, their virtues and their vices. How the earth is made, its hills and valleys, its rocks and soil. Streams, a trickle on a rock face high on a cliff, or a Valley of a Thousand Falls; a cool drink from a spring, a hot face washed in a tiny brook, or a tingling bath in a mountain stream or glacial pool. Fire, for a cup of tea, or a full meal at the end of day, a fire for warming, or a big campfire with tales and song, and even the dread forest fire. Scenes, big, little, at all angles and all distances, with snow, or the greens of spring climbing uphill, the great flower beds of summer, evergreen forests, glaciers, ice in chimneys, the colors of fall; and clouds, all kinds, never two alike, never a sky the same; and pictures, with their memories. Last, and most important, companionship, all sorts, cheerful or glum, bright or dull, active or lazy, skillful or clumsy, bold or timid. Of all such is the art and pleasure of walking.*

Trails, similar to the proverbial wife, are fickle. Their routes and conditions are apt to change quite drastically and without warning. Thus, in addition to whatever else the hiker wishes to carry, he should also take along a good supply of common sense and use it whenever and wherever necessary.

This book, therefore, like the previous editions, endeavors to be more than a guide to the trails. Schunumunk, Doodletown, Bashbish Falls, the Wharton Tract, *Clepsysaurus manhattanensis,* Claudius Smith, Wittenberg, skunk cabbage, and striped maple—here they are —and many more.

Solvitur Ambulando
NEW YORK–NEW JERSEY TRAIL CONFERENCE

---

* This quotation is from an article written by Dr. M. Beckett Howorth for *Consumers' Research Bulletin* in March 1944. It was reprinted as a chapter in a collection of essays written by members of the New York Chapter of the Appalachian Mountain Club, published in 1945 under the title *In the Hudson Highlands.* The article was based on the author's experiences as a walker in the mountains. It is republished here with his permission.

ACKNOWLEDGMENTS

This edition of the *Walk Book* would not have been possible without the generous assistance and helpful advice of: Warren Balgooyen, Naturalist, Kitchawan Research Laboratory, Brooklyn Botanic Garden; Harold J. Dyer, former Regional Parks Manager, Taconic State Park Commission; Jack J. Karnig, Superintendent, Black Rock Forest, Harvard University; John C. Orth, Palisades Interstate Park Commission; Charles E. Pound, Commissioner, Westchester Department of Parks, Recreation and Conservation; James M. Ransom, author of *Vanishing Ironworks of the Ramapos;* and Samuel Yeaton, Trustee, Long Island Chapter of the Nature Conservancy. The section on the Pine Barrens was contributed by Lester S. Thomas of the New Jersey Division of Parks, Forestry and Recreation. Christopher J. Schuberth, of the American Museum of Natural History, has checked the geological statesments in all the chapters.

The unstinting cooperation of the following members and friends of the New York–New Jersey Trail Conference in walking miles of trails, and gathering and checking facts, history, and legend is gratefully acknowledged:

Jacob Abele
Grace J. Averill
Richmond S. Barton
Arthur C. Beach
Ivan Brooks
Mrs. Paul Brugger
Wilma Brugger
Al Butzel
William B. Cocks
Mary E. Coen
Andrew De Maio
Robert Deming
John A. Dierdorff
Edward Di Gangi
Mrs. Walter B. Ellwood

Fred Ferber
Robert M. Gage
Robert Gasser
Everett E. Gilbert
Donald C. Gordon
Rosa Gottfried
Peter Hannan
Ruth G. Hardy
Irma H. Heyer
William Hoeferlin
Mr. and Mrs. Norman Jette
Mr. and Mrs. Thomas Joyce
Abe Kaplan
Theodore Kazimiroff
William P. Kent

Lee Lefcourt
Nat Lester
Elizabeth D. Levers
Mr. and Mrs. Nathan Levin
Hedy Linsmeier
Dr. and Mrs. Julian R. Little
Frank J. McAdam
Stewart Manville
Carolyn C. Meyer
Julian M. Miller
Sumner Miller
David F. Moore
Harry F. Nees
Mr. and Mrs. Frank J. Oliver
Lore Oppenheimer
Robert Parnes
Lawrence Paul
Francis W. Penny
Marie Reith
Regina Reynolds
Mr. and Mrs. Eric P. Richter
Ruth Robinson
Albert P. Rosen
Carolyn Small Ruda
Emma Rutherford

Mr. and Mrs. Charles Sanders
Edna Schmidt
Robert Schulz
Richard B. Sichel
Donald Simon
David Sive
Mr. and Mrs. Daniel Smiley
F. I. Smith
Harry J. Smith
Elizabeth Snyder
Mr. and Mrs. John J. Stankard
Stanley C. Steckler
John W. Strahan, III
Harris H. Tallan
La Verne Thompson
Gardner Watts
Mathilde P. Weingartner
Walter G. Wells
Robert L. Wendt
Samuel Wilkinson
Mary Louise Wise
Helen Q. Woodward
Henry L. Young
Gerhardt E. Zauzig
George M. Zoebelein

CONTENTS

Appalachian Trail

Arden-Surebridge Trail

Blue Disc Trail

Breakneck Mountain Trail

Conklin's Crossing Trail

Crown Ridge Trail

Deep Hollow Shelter Trail

Diamond Mountain Trail

Dunning Trail

Hillburn-Torne-Sebago Trail

Hurst Trail

Kakiat Trail

Lichen Trail

Long Mountain–Torne Trail

Long Path

Major Welch Trail

Nurian Trail

Pine Meadow Trail

Popolopen Gorge Trail

Raccoon Brook Hills Trail

Ramapo-Dunderberg Trail

Red Cross Trail

Reeves Brook Trail

Seven Hills Trail

Sherwood Path

Skannatati Trail

Stony Brook Trail

Suffern–Bear Mountain Trail

Timp-Torne Trail

Tower Trail

Triangle Trail

Tuxedo–Mt. Ivy Trail

Victory Trail

White Cross Trail

NEW YORK WALK BOOK

THE LOOK-OFF
(from the first edition)

OIL that was ever Indian can never lose all of that impress. Our Island of Islands, borne down at one end by the world's biggest burden of steel and stone and pressure of haste and material gain, still holds, on the primitive sweep of its further free tip, the Redman's cave and the beached canoe, tall trees, steep cliffs, and airs of the Great Spirit. The magic of the moccasin still makes good medicine. Fortunate are we that in civilization lurks the antidote to civilization—that strain in the blood of all of us, of caveman and treeman, of nomad and seaman, of chopper and digger, of fisher and trailer, crying out to this call of the earth, to this tug of freefoot up-and-over, to the clamor for out-and-beyond. Happy are we, in our day, harking back to this call, to be part of an ozone revival toward lucky finds in this wide fair wilderness and toward breakaway into Everyman's Out-of-doors.

The order and fashion of the revival were somewhat in this wise. Our seniors remember the days of swift expansion, when the sole concern was the building site. "Blast the scenery," said the seventies and proceeded to do it. Railroads and roads and money returns from quarries and lumber had full right of way. Into our towns one came, through the ugly suburbs, into uglier urbs. And then, when hope was least, a messenger of the new-old freedom appeared. The bicycle swung us, a generation now white-haired, round a wide radius of country roads, and gave back to us the calves and the leg gear of our patroon saint, Father Knickerbocker, and with the legs two eyes for environs. When the time came for supplanting tandem tired by a rubber quartette, and a touch of the toe leapt past all two legs could do, a motor radius that swept a circle almost infinitely wide gave new concepts of the countrysides. Still attention was focused on the roadway, and the new driver saw even less over wheel than over handlebar. Next golf arose, and the well-to-do strolled upon greenswards, ever watching a ball. Then scout training arrived to set the young generation on its feet and to teach it to see what it saw and to care for itself in the open. With it came nature study to fill the woods and fields with life and growth. And then the fashion for walking was upon us—walking, with its leisure to observe the detail of beauty; walking, organized and planned, imparting impetus to safeguard and preserve the best of the countryside: walking, the only simple exercise, at once democratic, open-air, wide-eyed, year-round.

It has been amusing to watch New York, which is hardly in other ways hesitant, waken by degrees to the idea that as a center for exercise on foot she may claim variety and advantage and adventure surpassed by few cities. You can choose your walk along the sweep of the beaches of the Atlantic, of the deep hill bays of Long Island, or the rocky coves of Connecticut; over ridges showing fair silhouettes of the citadels and cathedrals of commerce—or where beavers build; on the looped, mile-long bridges that span an estuary—or across a canal lock; above precipices overhanging a mighty river and through noble community forests between lonely peaks and little lakes—or just in lovely common country, rolling and wooded, meadowed, and elm-dotted, interlaced with chuckling brooks. To and from these multitudinous footways and camp sites transportation is provided with an expedition and diversity possible only to a large city. And, last of all, the chance at this will be under the variegated stimulus of our particular climate and around the only great capital that is within easy reach of the second color wonder of the world—Indian summer in steep-hill country.

Truly with the "Englysche Bybels" that antedate King James's we may say:

Blessed of the LORDE is this land,
    for the sweetnesse of heven, and of the scee vnderliende;
    for the sprynges;
    for the precious thinges off the Sonne;
    for the sweetnesse of the toppes of the oold mounteynes,
      and for the daynties of the hillis that last foreuer.

RAYMOND H. TORREY
FRANK PLACE, JR.
ROBERT L. DICKINSON

Spring 1923

METROPOLITAN NEW YORK:
ITS GEOLOGIC SETTING
CHRISTOPHER J. SCHUBERTH
The American Museum of Natural History

New York's prominence in cultural, financial, and industrial affairs often obscures further one little-known fact: that this thriving metropolis, as well as its immediate environs of eastern New Jersey, southeastern New York and Long Island, and southwestern Connecticut, is from the geologic viewpoint one of the most diversified in the world. While New York may not present the topographic grandeur of a city such as Denver or Zürich, a careful examination of the rock record quickly reveals the Metropolitan New York region to be most unusual in at least two other respects. First, an unprecedented barrage of one dynamic geologic process after another affected this portion of eastern North America—submergence beneath marginal seas; sedimentation and crustal subsidence; volcanism; mountain-building; metamorphism and plutonism; more mountain-building; long-term and deep erosion; more sedimentation, volcanism, and crustal instability; more erosion; resubmergence beneath newer marginal seas; continental glaciation; and finally, during a most recent episode of postglacial change within the past five thousand years, the development of barrier islands by the turbulent action of Atlantic waves along the New York and New Jersey shores. Indeed, New York's terrain has been molded and remolded into its present and very transient form over the past one and a half billion years of documented earth history by all the agents responsible for bringing about surface change. In addition, few, if any, urban areas of comparable size can surpass in number the more than 170 different mineral species recovered from the twenty-square-mile area of Manhattan Island alone, or match some of them in size, color, or perfection of their crystal form.

To the inexperienced eye, the broad physical appearance of the terrain may seem to be a confusion of many kinds of topographic elements; no unifying pattern in the distribution of landscape features or in their geological foundations may be evident. But not so to the careful observer. To him, all the diverse elements in the landscape—the ridges, the valleys, the plains, the mounts, the islands, the seemingly diverse geology—can, within a hundred-mile radius of midtown Manhattan, be organized into five clearly distinguishable physiographic provinces. Easily identified on the front end-paper map, these provinces are the: (1) Atlantic Coastal Plain (orange and green), (2) New England Upland (mostly dark brown and gray), (3) Newark Basin (light green and red), (4) Ridge and Valley Province (mostly purple), and (5) Appalachian Plateaus (blue). With the exception of the Atlantic Coastal Plain, the other provinces are part of a much larger regional section of Eastern America, the expansive Appalachian Highlands.

A physiographic province is a natural division of the earth's surface that, on the basis of a distinctive regional topography, can be contrasted with adjoining provinces. General altitude, relief, topographic form, and the spatial distribution of the individual landform features present are some of the important landscape elements of any province. But these elements, in turn, are inextricably related to the types of bedrock the province contains, which further document the distinctive kinds of events that had occurred during the early, formative stages in the geologic evolution of the province.

Geologic processes, such as erosion and crustal uplift, that subsequently have operated on this bedrock throughout the long course of earth history, also play vital roles in shaping the individual province into its present visual configuration. Whether the rocks have undergone a complex deformational history and so are generally of the intensely deformed metamorphic type, or, whether the deformation elements are less complex, or, whether the bedrock shows little evidence of deformation other than a broad uplift in relation to sea level, describe an additional feature of a province, namely, its structural framework. Yet, when all is said and done, regardless of how complex the geologic structure may be, or how involved has been its geologic history, or at what stage in its ongoing development it may happen to be in, no two physiographic provinces are alike. When contrasted with an adjoining region, the individuality of a physiographic province can be most simply and directly expressed in terms of its broad regional topography, the major rock types it contains and their relative ages, and the integrated pattern of the individual landform features present.

With these necessary introductory remarks, let us examine more closely the geological characteristics, as well as the regional extent, of each of the five provinces. Since the Atlantic Coastal Plain is topographically the simplest and geologically the youngest, let us consider the physical nature of this province first.

The Atlantic Coastal Plain extends without interruption along the East Coast, from Florida to Long Island. All of southern New Jersey southeast of a line connecting Trenton with Staten Island in New York City, for example, is included in this province, as is also eastern Staten Island and all of Long Island. Northeast of Long Island, the Coastal Plain, as the continental shelf, lies completely submerged beneath the relatively shallow waters of the Atlantic. Unconsolidated and variously colored layers of gravel, sand, and clay are the materials of this province, and, with elevations rarely exceeding three hundred feet and with no significant relief, these flat-lying strata slope gently downward to the edge of the sea.

Laid down within the past 75 million years, during the Cretaceous and Tertiary periods, the sediments of the Coastal Plain reflect a complex history of changing physical environments; of marine transgressions and regressions; of sluggish-flowing streams spreading their flood-plain and deltaic sediments seaward as they meandered through extensive marshes and swamps; of estuaries slowly fingering landward with rising seas. The complexity of the Coastal Plain deposits is strikingly documented by the fossils they contain. On the one hand, hundreds of different species of plant fossils have been recovered, including the remains of cycads, conifers, ferns, and such flower-bearing plants as magnolia and sassafras—all clearly suggestive of a nonmarine history of deposition. On the other hand, the fossil evidence indicating periodic marine invasions includes abundant sharks' teeth, fragments of extinct cephalopods, and plesiosaur bones, those now-extinct long-necked marine reptiles that once roamed what were shallow coastal waters, 70-odd million years ago.

While the Coastal Plain sediments are visible to all in eastern New Jersey, on Long Island they lie completely buried beneath an extensive cover of Pleistocene materials. Glacial deposits, laid down about thirty thousand years ago, near the "end" of a Late Pleistocene Ice Age, effectively conceal almost all of Long Island's pre-Pleistocene sediments. Two moraines, lines of hills composed of unsorted and unstratified boulders, cobbles, gravel, sand, and clay of all sizes and compositions, and torn away by the ice sheet from the New England landmass to the north, mark its farthest positions. The southern, or Ronkonkoma Moraine, extends westward from Montauk

Point, where it dramatically lies exposed to wave erosion, through
Lake Ronkonkoma, to Lake Success in western Nassau County. The
northern, or Harbor Hill Moraine, extends westward from Orient
Point, along the heads of such bays as Cold Spring Harbor, Hempstead Harbor, Manhasset Bay, and Little Neck Bay. West of Lake
Success, only a single moraine, a single line of hills that identifies
the Harbor Hill Moraine, makes up all the high ground of Queens
and Brooklyn—Forest Hills and Bay Ridge, for example. At The
Narrows, by Fort Hamilton in Brooklyn, this moraine crosses the
waters of New York Bay and enters Staten Island at Fort Wadsworth.

Meltwater streams carrying sand and gravel beyond the edge of
the terminal moraines laid down their sedimentary load as a gently
seaward-sloping outwash plain. Once extending many miles farther
to the south, a postglacial rise in sea level flooded most of the
southern part of this plain. In fact, at Montauk Point, all of the
outwash plain lies completely submerged by the sea and only the
moraine stands face to face with the sea. But with stabilization of
sea level some five thousand years ago, Atlantic storm waves reworked much of this glacial sand and gravel to develop the spits
and barrier islands—Southampton Beach, Westhampton Beach, Fire
Island, Jones Beach, and so on—the prized resort areas to which
many a New Yorker retreats during sweltering summer days.

Elsewhere along the Atlantic coast, it is the Coastal Plain sands
that were reworked in the same way as were the outwash sands of
Long Island by the surging sea to form a spit such as Sandy Hook,
or the barriers of Island Beach or Long Beach, along the Jersey
shore. Shifting constantly under a relentlessly attacking surf, these
fragile outposts are all that stand between a seemingly all-too-
aggressive sea and the mainland. Although they are the most recent
addition to our ever-changing landscape—and a vital element in the
coastline's protection—they are the most vulnerable and transitory
of all the present landforms.

North and west of Long Island lies an expansive region of old
and deeply worn-down mountains, the recently glaciated New England Upland. Hills, mostly of resistant gneiss, schist, granite, and
some quartzite alternating with valleys of less resistant slate and
marble, are all that remain in southeastern New York and north-
central New Jersey, or in Connecticut, Massachusetts, Rhode Island,
Vermont, New Hampshire, and Maine, to document the numerous
episodes of crustal upheavals that affected this region in the distant
geologic past. For some one billion years—between one and a half
billion and 500 million years ago—eastern North America was sub-

jected to periodic episodes of intense deformation. In the process, the crust deep below the surface underwent compositional and structural changes. Molten masses of liquid rock, commonly called magma, subsequently invaded the newly formed metamorphic basement to solidify into widespread bodies of granite, gem-bearing pegmatite, and other granitoid rocks. Rising ever higher, the magma-invaded crust was crumpled into mountain systems of pronounced topographic grandeur. Long cycles of erosion followed—rain, sleet, and hail whittled away at the craggy peaks over the next hundreds of millions of years and reduced these once majestic mountains to their very metamorphic and igneous core. By about 200 million years ago very little, if anything, of these mountains remained. Only their complex crystalline roots stand as a monument to these crustal events.

In southeastern New York, in the vicinity of Peekskill along the east shore of the Hudson, the New England Upland separates into two distinct south-pointing projections, the Manhattan and the Reading prongs. While the Manhattan Prong east of the Hudson terminates at the southern tip of Manhattan Island (northern Staten Island to be more precise), the more westerly projection, the Reading Prong, extends across the Hudson into north-central New Jersey and terminates at Reading, Pennsylvania, about 140 miles distant.

Because of their geographical separation, these two sections of the New England Upland are easily identified south of Peekskill. But to the north, the sections, although blending into one continuous region, persist as two identifiable geologic terrains. These may be distinguished on the basis of at least one important fact: the geologic age of the crystalline bedrock. While the Reading Prong is composed of a complex of high-grade metamorphic and some igneous rock of unquestionable Precambrian age (the oldest have been radiometrically dated at a little under 1.2 billion years and the youngest at about 800 million years), the metamorphic bedrock of the Manhattan Prong, as well as the rest of the New England Upland, is considered to be about one half this age. As a further, and perhaps somewhat more graphic distinction, the Precambrian terrain exhibits greater relief than do the other portions of this province. Its extent can readily be traced along a zone of "highlands" northeast from Pennsylvania into New Jersey, where the designation "Jersey Highlands" is applied. The Ramapo Mountains behind Suffern, for example, are a local, familiar range within the Jersey Highlands, while their continuation into New York State, the historic Hudson Highlands, form an imposing landscape through which the Hudson has carved a truly spectacular gorge. Storm King, Bear Mountain, Breakneck, and Dunderberg are only the more well-known mounts and ridges within the Highlands that rise over one thousand feet above the waters of the Hudson.

East of the Hudson, in western Connecticut, the continuation of this Precambrian terrain is identified as the Housatonic Highlands; in western Massachusetts, as the Berkshires. All are elements of the New England Upland, but are distinguishable from the rest of the province on the basis of a known Precambrian geology and a considerably more rugged topography.

In the Manhattan Prong of the New England Upland, which extends southward into northern Staten Island from a line connecting Peekskill with Danbury, Connecticut, some question still remains regarding the age of its metamorphic bedrock. Two facts, however, have emerged. One is that an initial episode of metamorphism occurred some 480 million years ago; a second episode of primarily granite and pegmatite emplacement occurred some 120 million years later. These two dates, arrived at through careful radiometric studies made on numerous rock samples collected from the Manhattan Prong, are not in dispute. Nor is the conclusion questioned that prior to metamorphism the original rock types were sedimentary.

The dispute, instead, centers around the age of the pre-metamorphic sedimentary terrain. Some geologists consider it to have been Precambrian, others Early Paleozoic, probably Cambrian to Early Ordovician. Still others consider a part of the sedimentary record to have been Precambrian and the remainder Early Paleozoic. With the exception of a few echinoderm fragments recently found in a quarry at Verplanck Point a few miles below Peekskill that suggest an Early Paleozoic age, any fossils that may have been present in the original sedimentary strata to clearly establish their geologic age have long since been destroyed during the metamorphic episodes. Therefore, although the age of metamorphism is Early Paleozoic, it is preferable to indicate the geologic age for the Manhattan Prong and its northeasterly extension as being uncertain.

The dates of metamorphism and magmatic emplacement—480 million and 360 million, respectively—coincide closely with two well-known and completely documented orogenies, or mountain-building periods, that affected eastern North America early in the Paleozoic Era, the Taconian near the end of the Ordovician Period, and the Acadian near the end of the Devonian. Today, the Taconic Mountains in eastern New York State, the metamorphic bedrock of the

Manhattan Prong, and the semiprecious gems and other rarer minerals of the emplaced pegmatites—beryl, tourmaline, garnet, spodumene, or rose quartz, to mention five—are the striking products of these ancient crustal crises.

Much more could be said about the complex geology of the New England Upland, but instead, let us examine the region between the Reading Prong—or the Jersey Highlands—to the west and the Manhattan Prong to the east (the Coastal Plain, south of Staten Island). Here is found the Newark Basin, the third province of Metropolitan New York's geologic setting.

As the northern section of a 300-mile long and up to 50-mile wide lowland that extends from Haverstraw, New York, through Rockland County and central New Jersey, southeastern Pennsylvania, and southwest to the vicinity of Fredericksburg in northern Virginia, the Newark Basin was of importance to New York City, as well as other large eastern cities for that matter, because it provided (and still does so in one instance) two well-known rock materials. Red sandstone quarried at the turn of the century and sent across the Hudson was for many years one of New York's most fashionable building stones. Although neither used nor quarried any longer, the sandstone can still be seen in the "brownstone houses" in many of the older and once-prestigious neighborhoods of Manhattan and Brooklyn. So also did the Palisades, the Hudson's western rampart and New York's finest scenic attraction, provide for many years, particularly during the 1850s, the "Belgian bluestone" when a rapidly growing "lower" Manhattan set out to pave its thoroughfares and a few of its sidewalks. The compact nature of the Palisades rock gives it great wearing power. Although no longer used for street and sidewalk paving, it is still valued for use as riprap, very large blocks used in revetments to protect bluffs and other landforms exposed to intense wave erosion, or as aggregate, crushed gravel-sized stone used in concrete required for heavy-duty service. Indeed, were it not for the farsighted plans in the early 1900s to create an Interstate Park along the Hudson's west shore, the Palisades would have been so extensively quarried by now that only a much reduced remnant would be standing today. Two quarries still operate in the Palisades, one at West Nyack, the other at Haverstraw, and their products, carried on long strings of tug-pulled barges, can be seen almost daily heading slowly down the Hudson toward New York.

The geological history of the Newark Basin begins late in the Triassic Period, about 190 million years ago, when giant crustal blocks were lifted and tilted to form mountains, and the blocks between them became basins. Thousands of feet of sediments, re-moved from the surrounding fault-block mountains, were deposited in these intermontane basins as nearly flat, broadly coalescing alluvial fans. Only the remnants of one of these basins, the Newark Basin, with its westward-tipped thick sequence of stratified sandstones and shales, is preserved in the Metropolitan New York region.

Fossils recovered from Newark Basin strata reveal a fascinating population of creatures, mostly reptiles and freshwater fishes, that once roamed about what is today the preserve of the New Jersey and Rockland County commuter. *Clepsysaurus manhattanensis,* an extinct crocodile-like phytosaur, and perhaps New York's first verte-brate inhabitant (he is over 190 million years old), was discovered along the west shore of the Hudson at Fort Lee, in 1910, about a half mile south of what is now the west pier of the George Wash-ington Bridge. Numerous fossil fishes have been found in black shales of an abandoned quarry at North Bergen, New Jersey, be-hind the Palisades. Exceedingly common is the freshwater fish, *Diplurus newarki,* member of a unique suborder of fishes called coelacanths which, today, is represented by only one living form, recently discovered in deep waters off the east coast of Africa. During the Late Triassic, the coelacanths were abundant in ponds, lakes, and swamps. Then came the black mud that buried and preserved them.

It was in the same North Bergen quarry that three New Jersey high school boys uncovered, in the fall of 1960, the almost complete remains of a unique reptile. Particularly distinctive were the ex-ceptionally elongated ribs apparently attached to a membrane used by the creature for gliding. Since the fossil represented an organism hitherto completely unknown to science, paleontologists were naturally excited by this discovery. *Icarosaurus* still stands as the earliest-known winged vertebrate.

Elsewhere, in the vicinity of Newark, near the South Mountain Reservation, over one thousand footprints, clearly those made by dinosaurs, have been uncovered since late 1969 by two particularly dedicated and conscientious high school boys. Just who the dino-saurs were that left behind their distinctive three-toed tracks for us to discover still remains to be determined. No skeletal fragments have yet come to light.

Late in the Triassic, as the Newark Basin became filled with thousands of feet of westward-sloping sediments, many of them stained bright red with hematite, deep-reaching faults became the passageways for escaping magma. While some of the liquid rock, in moving upward from subterranean reservoirs, failed to reach the surface before solidifying, much of it spilled out as widening sheets of lava across the sediment-chocked Late Triassic landscape. Today, the Palisades and the Watchung Mountains, with their near-vertical, east-facing erosional escarpments and gently west-sloping dip surfaces, are the most striking products of these episodes of igneous activity.

Both the igneous rock of the Palisades, a diabase, and the Watchung Mountains, a basalt, are similar in composition; both are durable and resistant mixtures of interlocking pyroxene and plagioclase feldspar. But in the diabase of the Palisades, the minerals are easily observed without magnification, and the dark-colored pyroxene and light-colored plagioclase, arranged in a particular three-dimensional pattern, gives the rock a characteristic mottled appearance. Forcibly injected deep underground as a sill between the already deposited sedimentary strata, slow cooling of the magma permitted the development of visible minerals. Continued erosion subsequently has exposed this intrusive rock mass to view. Extending southward without interruption from near Haverstraw, the Palisades ridge gradually decreases in elevation until it finally disappears underground in Staten Island, forty-five miles from Haverstraw.

Where the ridge, because of its differential resistance to erosion, is boldly exposed, the long, almost continuous diabase columns give the Palisades the appearance of a colonial stockade, or palisade, hence the name. Indeed, the Indian name for the Palisades seems to have been Weh-awk-en—awk, the middle syllable, meaning "rocks that resemble trees." Closeup, one sees that the roughly polygonal, often hexagonal, columns, several feet wide, are formed by gigantic vertical fissures. Extending up through the entire thickness of the diabase, these fractures were produced by the cooling and subsequent contraction of the solidifying magma. Horizontal fissures often intersect the vertical contraction fractures that form the columnar pattern. With subsequent weathering and erosion, the diabase tends to break down into distinct masses that resemble stairways. It is not strange, therefore, that the term "trap" should become so popular to describe the diabase. It is derived from the Swedish *trapp,* meaning stairs.

About twenty miles to the west of the Palisades, the several ridges of the Watchung Mountains, like the Palisades, stand out as conspicuous topographic elements in an otherwise comparatively uninviting lowland. Escarpments over four hundred feet rise above their surroundings at Preakness and High Mountain near Paterson, or South Mountain near Millburn. But unlike the Palisades, the Watchungs stand as erosional remnants of once-extensive lava flows rather than the remnants of an intrusion, and so are composed of dense, fine-textured black to blue-gray basalt, in which the minerals, because of a rapid cooling history, are not visible. As further evidence of their extrusive origin, numerous vesicles are often present along the upper surfaces of the basalt, a consequence of the rapid expansion of the dissolved gases rising and escaping into the cooler atmosphere. The basalt flows subsequently were buried beneath additional sedimentary layers and still younger lava flows, only to be re-exposed by the combined forces of weathering and erosion.

The basalt of the Watchung flows, like the intrusive diabase of the Palisades, contains abundant pyroxene, a common iron-bearing mineral which, when exposed to the atmosphere, oxidizes into limonite. The limonite imparts the characteristic yellowish-brown surface coating to both dark rock types. Also, because of a similar history of fissure development, the basalt exhibits the same step-like pattern as does the diabase. Today, most of the trap quarried for industrial use is obtained from several active and large quarries in the basalt of the Watchung Mountains rather than from the two quarries still operating in the diabase of the Palisades.

Two last provinces, the Ridge and Valley Province and the Appalachian Plateaus, still remain to be discussed. Extending some twelve hundred miles, from the lowland of the St. Lawrence River to Alabama, the Ridge and Valley Province varies in width from about fourteen miles at the New York–New Jersey border to eighty miles along a line between Harrisburg and Williamsport, Pennsylvania. Sometimes called the "Folded Appalachians," thirty to forty thousand feet of Early Paleozoic sedimentary strata, all deposited as originally horizontal layers in ancient marginal seas, were extensively folded and faulted—but not metamorphosed—near the end of the Paleozoic Era during an orogeny known commonly as the Appalachian Revolution. Differential erosion between the uptilted edges of resistant sandstone, quartzite, and conglomerate and the less-resistant shale and limestone has resulted in a series of near-parallel, alternating ridges and valleys.

Most of the Ridge and Valley Province can be divided longitudinally into an eastern part, which is dominantly a valley, the Great Valley, and a western, much narrower part characterized by linear, northeast-trending sandstone ridges separated by equally linear, northeast-trending valleys of shale and limestone. North and west of the Highlands, the Hudson and Wallkill rivers occupy the

Great Valley, hence the oft-used names, Hudson and Wallkill valleys, for this portion of the Ridge and Valley Province.

Two major ridges of the province in this immediate region are Shawangunk Mountain in New York State (it continues into New Jersey as Kittatinny Mountain) and Schunemunk Mountain. Shawangunk-Kittatinny Mountain is underlain by resistant conglomeratic sandstone, strikingly white in color, laid down as an originally horizontal layer in an ancient sea, during the latter part of the Silurian Period some 420 million years ago, and then uplifted during the Appalachian Revolution. The few minor ridges to the west of Shawangunk Mountain are supported by Late Silurian and Early Devonian sandstone and somewhat more resistant sandy shale layers, all rich in fossil marine invertebrates; the intervening valleys are underlain by equally fossiliferous, but less durable, shales and limestones. Thus, the influence of alternating strong and weak strata upon the topographic forms is most conspicuous in this province.

Schunemunk Mountain, on the other hand, does not occur in the western part of the province along with the other linear ridges. Instead, it lies along the eastern edge of the Great Valley, a rather peculiar position for it to be in. Its bedrock is composed not of the predominantly shale layers of Ordovician age that underlie the floor of the Great Valley, but rather of downfolded Silurian and Devonian conglomerate, sandstone, and shale identical to those of Shawangunk Mountain, the minor ridges behind it, and the eastern portion of the Appalachian Plateaus some twenty miles to the west.

How could such a peculiarity in the geologic relationships take place? Why are the rock types of Schunemunk Mountain, such as the distinctive quartz-pebble conglomerate of Middle Devonian age, and similar to the coarse, Middle Devonian sandstone in the Catskills, so far removed from their main occurrences? The answers to these questions are not easy, nor can a justifiable comment of the possible explanations be attempted in one or two sentences. Nevertheless, it appears that the uplifted and upturned sedimentary strata of the western part of the Ridge and Valley Province, and the uplifted and unfolded strata of the Appalachian Plateaus, once extended much farther to the east. How far? At least to the present position of Schunemunk Mountain, and possibly still farther to the east. Following the mountain-building episodes late in the Paleozoic Era, some 300 or so million years ago, long-term erosion subsequently removed all the intervening post-Ordovician strata between Schunemunk Mountain and Shawangunk Mountain to the west. Because of the pronounced durability of the quartz-pebble conglomerate at

the top of Schunemunk, this formation served as a protective cap
rock for the less resistant strata underneath. Why at the present site
of Schunemunk Mountain, and not at some other position just to
the west? A tough question to answer.

To the west of the Ridge and Valley Province lie the Appalachian
Plateaus, a broad terrain of mostly Middle to Late Devonian conglomerate (like that at the crest of Schunemunk Mountain), sandstone, and shale, much of it locally fossiliferous. Unlike the Ridge and
Valley Province to the east, however, the Appalachian Plateaus have
not been subject to the same intense deformation so characteristic of
other regions in the Appalachian Highlands. Although elevations
exceed four thousand feet, the flat-lying strata have been uplifted
to this considerable height with minimal deformation. They have
also, because of their great elevation above sea level, undergone considerable stream dissection. This dissection is so pronounced near the
eastern margin of the province, particularly in the section we know
as the Catskills, that the topography is commonly misnamed as
mountains. Extensive upland tracts viewed from a distance do suggest
a gently rolling plateau, but it is not possible to travel far across the
uplands without coming to a deeply incised stream valley which may
be a few hundred feet deep if a minor valley, or up to two thousand
feet if a major one. Thus, the Catskills of New York, or the Poconos
of Pennsylvania, are mountains only in the erosional sense. They are,
in fact, deeply dissected plateaus. But because they have been called
mountains for so long it is understandable that because of their visual
appearance they will not be known by their proper definition—deeply
dissected plateaus—by the general public.

No discussion of the Lower Hudson Valley's geology would be
complete without a further comment on one last geologic episode, one
that witnesses drastic changes in the climate and brings arctic conditions to this region. Some thirty thousand years ago, late in the
Pleistocene, an ice sheet more than a thousand feet thick crept southward across eastern Canada and New England, and went on to cover
all of Manhattan island and the Bronx, most of Staten Island, and
the northern portions of Brooklyn and Queens in New York City
and, to the east, Nassau and Suffolk counties of Long Island. The
maximum extent of this continental glacier is defined by the terminal
moraine that snakes across the Lower Hudson's landscape (see front
end-paper). Parallel scratches that mark the direction of glacier flow
abound. As the ice melted northward again, some thirteen thousand
years ago, it left behind its rock debris, often composed of exceptionally large and conspicuous boulders, or erratics, spread unevenly

over the land, so that much of the bedrock is concealed by this glacial till. In many of the broader valleys, particularly in the Great Valley, can be found low, relatively steep-sided hills of stratified sand and gravel. These glacial kames, occurring either as isolated mounds or in clusters, were formed by the material collecting in openings in the ice sheet during a stagnant phase. Today, these have become a valuable resource for the local farmer whose open borrow pits in the kames can be seen dotting the landscape.

To the casual observer, the geological setting of the Metropolitan New York region, long in the making, often appears fixed and unchanging. It is clearly evident, however, that despite this seeming permanence the landscapes of the Lower Hudson Valley are but a momentary scene in the grand design of change. A late afternoon walk along the crest of Schunemunk Mountain, for example, permits one, under the long rays of a setting sun, to reflect on the topographic variety of the surrounding region, and perhaps to consider how these landscapes and their underlying bedrock foundations came into being. To retreat before a turbulent, wind-driven sea during a midwinter storm along the barrier coast and to observe firsthand the struggle between sand and surf brings one face-to-face with geologic reality. With shoreline processes serving as a bridge into the past, namely, showing that all geologic processes are ongoing, one can grasp more fully, and place into better perspective, the bigger scene: of primordial seas periodically flooding vast regions of Eastern America; of ancient mountain systems slowly rising in response to profound forces operating deep within the crust; of flows of molten lava and immense sheets of glacier ice reshaping the region we today call the Lower Hudson Valley. Energy values and time spans differ, but their effect is one of continued change which, according to the rock record here in this vicinity, began some one and a half thousand million years ago.

SUGGESTIONS
FOR NEW HIKERS

If you can walk, you can hike. You will need little or no training, and age is no obstacle. To learn more about the trails and to gain experience in how to enjoy them, write to the New York–New Jersey Trail Conference, G.P.O. Box 2250, New York, N.Y. 10001, for a list of hiking clubs. Whether you walk with an organized group or with friends, some knowledge of the area to be hiked is necessary for safety and valuable for enjoyment. Such knowledge can be obtained from highway maps, topographic maps, and trail maps. From these one can learn the nature of the terrain, and where to find the trails. Highway maps are free at gas stations, and the "Yellow Pages" phone books list stores which sell topographic and trail maps. Also, see *Suggested Readings*, pages 306–308, for titles of trail guides.

Hiking Alone

If you haven't had trail experience, you should not hike alone— and even an experienced hiker always lets someone know the area he will be hiking in.

Equipment

Use what you now have, as far as possible. Avoid investing in expensive equipment until you have seen what other hikers use, have heard their opinions, and have decided what will suit you best.

Clothes

1. Sturdy, comfortable, waterproofed shoes with nonskid soles. Shoes should preferably be ankle high and large enough to wear one or two pairs of wool socks. In hot weather, many hikers prefer sneakers.
2. Slacks or jeans, or in winter wool pants. On hot days, shorts can be worn on clear trails.
3. Extra wool shirt or sweater.
4. Rainproof parka or nylon poncho.
5. Gloves, hood, etc., according to the weather.
6. In winter, start "cold," with warm clothes in your pack. You may feel chilly, but you'll soon be warm and won't perspire. Put on the extra sweater or other heavy clothing at the lunch stop.

Pack (Knapsack)

Lightweight, but large enough to carry the extra garments; lunch and beverage; extra socks if your shoes are not waterproof; small first-aid kit, a flashlight, compass, map, matches in a waterproof case, and a sturdy jackknife.

Food

High-protein foods in concentrated form; fruits and juices will supply energy without weight. A hot beverage refreshes, even on a warm day.

Water

In the area covered by this book, except in the Catskills, do not drink from springs, streams, or ponds, as they may be polluted. There is no dependable water supply at the shelters along the trails, except in the Catskills as noted. Water may be carried in a small plastic bottle.

You want to travel light, but not at the cost of being hungry or cold or wet. Remember, you're supposed to be enjoying yourself!

Safety and Comfort

Hike Plan

Before leaving your home consult your map and the *Walk Book* to determine the time and effort involved. If you are not going with an organized group, tell someone of your plan. On smooth level ground your pace may be three to four miles an hour; on trails, two to three. The pace will be slowed by rough terrain, snow, rain, heat, and the effort of ascents and descents. Consider available hours of daylight, so as not to have to finish your hike in darkness. If you are not an experienced trail hiker, it might be wise to limit yourself, at first, to distances of five miles or less if the ground is level. On hilly terrain, three miles would be a safe upper limit for an over-twenty-five neophyte hiker.

Blazes and Cairns

The clubs belonging to the New York–New Jersey Trail Conference mark and clear over six hundred miles of trails in the metropolitan area. A system of painted "blazes" placed on trees and sometimes on rocks makes these trails understandable to any hiker. A double blaze indicates a change in direction. The trail descriptions explain the colors used on each trail. Where a paint blaze is not practical, watch for a pile of stones, obviously man-made, which indicate the direction. This is a "cairn."

Escape Routes

Before starting, note routes which may be used to shorten the hike in case of storm, illness, or accident, or an overambitious hike plan.

Lost—You or the Trail?

1. Stop, look around, then go back to the last blaze or cairn seen.
2. If no blaze or cairn is in sight, look at the ground for a trace of the path. Perhaps a turn in the trail was missed.
3. If no trail is in sight, sit down and relax. Think about where you have been. Look at your map.
4. If you are with a group, wait a reasonable time for your

absence to be noted, and for someone to come back. Three of anything—shout, whistle, flash of light—is a call for help.

5. If alone, consult your map and compass, and decide on the most direct route *out* to the nearest road. Remember that the top of the map is North. Use the compass to follow the route decided upon. In the Catskills follow any stream downhill.

6. If darkness falls, stay put and keep warm with those extra garments in the pack and with a fire. Build the fire in front of a rock, because its heat will be increased by reflection. But be careful not to let the fire spread.

First Aid

For a one-day hike, carry band-aids and an antiseptic for cuts and scratches, and moleskin for blisters. Put the moleskin on irritated spots *before* the blisters form. Other items useful and certainly necessary on longer trips are: ace bandage with clips, for sprains; gauze pads; eye cup and ointment; adhesive tape; safety pins; aspirin; ammonia inhalants; snake bite kit. These items, plus a pencil and paper, should be carried in a metal box or waterproof case, in the knapsack.

NATURAL HAZARDS

A good outdoorsman knows the possible hazards of the trail, and what to do about them. But he doesn't worry about them.

Thunderstorms

A thunderstorm is dangerous only because of lightning. If you are on an exposed ledge or on a mountain peak, get off quickly. If you are on the trail, among trees, avoid taking shelter under a tall tree.

Wild Fruits and Mushrooms

Do not eat any without positive identification.

Poison Ivy

The sap of this plant is probably the principal trail hazard, for it can cause intense itching and a weeping rash. Poison ivy, easily identified by its groups of three shiny green leaves (red, in the fall), is prevalent along fences and stone walls, on tree trunks, and along stream banks. It bears white or green berries, which also should not be touched. Even in late fall, the bare vines exude enough sap to be dangerous if the hiker comes in direct contact with them.

Poison Sumac

This shrub, found mostly in the swampy areas, has thirteen pointed leaflets, six or more inches in length. Although not considered as virulent as the sap of poison ivy, the sap of the poison sumac is capable of provoking a rash.

Insects

Long sleeves, long pants, and insect repellent are the best guards against insects. Ticks, sometimes prevalent on Long Island, are more insidious. Sometimes they can be plucked off, or their grip loosened with a match flare.

Snakes

A good trailsman soon learns to identify the small and harmless garter snake. This snake, quite common in our region, is beneficial to man and should be left alone. Rarely encountered are the region's two poisonous snakes, the rattlesnake and the copperhead. A rattlesnake is most quickly recognized by the rattle on its tail; its markings are not uniform, varying in coloration from yellow or tan to nearly black. When suddenly disturbed, a rattlesnake will rattle, and as a rule will try to get away rather than attack. The copperhead is pale brown with reddish blotches on its body and a coppery tinge on its head. It is not a specially vicious snake, preferring to escape rather than to attack. But it is a slow-moving reptile, and this sluggishness increases the chance of an unexpected encounter.

These two poisonous snakes are not found on Long Island. When walking trails in other parts of our region during the "snake season" (May to October), the best protection is always to be alert when climbing rock ledges and over logs. Look before placing your hand on an overhead ledge, for support. If you are bitten, don't panic. Get out your snake bite kit, follow directions, stay quiet, keep warm, and send a companion for help.

Take Care of the Trails and Woodlands

Smoking

Never smoke when hiking—smoke only when sitting down. Be sure your match is out, then bury its head in gravel or dirt. Be sure your cigarette stub, cigar stub, or pipe dottle is completely out, then cover with gravel or dirt.

Fires

On day trips use a fire only for warmth, if needed, and build it in stone fireplaces provided at shelters and campsites. If necessary, in a real emergency, build a small fire and only on rock or sandy soil; never near trees or on dry leaves or pine needles. Brush away leaves, twigs, etc., for an area of five feet around the fire. For best results in building a fire, use standing dead wood such as branches from dead trees, or bare twigs from evergreens. Do not cut green wood; it won't burn. Before you leave, put out the fire completely, then douse with water or cover with earth; in fireplaces, do not use water because it cracks the heated rock.

Litter

Whatever you have not used up, carry home. Do not attempt to burn or bury refuse; there is no space for this in our heavily used woodlands. Leave the trail and lunch stop and campsite as if no one had been there. "Leave nothing but footprints."

Property

Many of the trails cross private land, with the owner's permission. Respect this privilege and build no fires, leave no litter, and stay on the trail. Leave plants, animals, and other property alone for others to enjoy.

Closing of the Woods

When the woods are dangerously dry from lack of rain, parks and other public areas may be closed to hikers. The New York–New Jersey Trail Conference urges complete cooperation with park commissions and others who must make these decisions. Stay out of the woods and request others to do the same.

Part I

Column near
Greenbrook
above the
dock at
Lambiers

The Palisades Interstate Park

Dickinson

1 · THE PALISADES

All but the northern tip of the Palisades lies in New Jersey. This is the original section of what is now Palisades Interstate Park. The fall between precipice and beach is well wooded except on the talus slopes at the base of the cliffs. An attractive addition to the native species there are the Empress trees (*Paulownia tomentosa*), imported from Asia for the old estate gardens along the present route of the Palisades Parkway. Around Memorial Day they startle the visitor with their exotic masses of bluebells. Actually, along this narrow strip between beach and cliff, where most of the mileage is on edge, there is a surprising variety of trees, shrubs, and flowering plants.

HISTORY

Some early voyager up the Hudson named the cliffs of the lower river the Palisades, probably from the likeness of the giant pillars of trap rock to the palisaded villages of the Indians. There has been much debate as to whether the first European to see the Hudson was Giovanni da Verrazano, a Florentine in the service of the King of France, or Estévan Gomez, a Portuguese in the service of the King of Spain. The controversy hinges on a famous letter which the Verrazano supporters claim he addressed to Francis I of France on July 8, 1524, in which he relates his entry in March 1524 into what, from his description, his opponents as well as his supporters agree could have been none other than the Upper Bay. However, there seems to be no question as to the authenticity of Gomez's voyage along the east coast of North America in 1525 and his entry into New York harbor. The opponents of the Verrazano claim contend that the Verrazano letter, including the date, is pure fiction, whether or not Verrazano wrote it; that there is no official record that Verrazano ever made such an expedition for the King of France; and that the descriptions of the east coast of North America contained in the letter were plagiarized from Gomez's report.

Well-documented events begin only with Henry Hudson in 1609, when the *Half Moon,* on September 13, made its second anchorage of the day opposite the present location of Fort Lee. Hudson ascended the river as far as the site of Albany in search of the Northwest Passage and returned on finding no outlet up the river. He was attacked by the Indians of Inwood on the point now under the George Washington Bridge.

We think of the Palisades as wooded and inaccessible cliffs. But the Hollanders peopled this strip in such numbers that no part of northern New Jersey, except Hackensack, had as many inhabitants as "Under the Mountain" in the days of uniformly bad roads, when the river constituted the highway. Although Indian names rarely remain, the Dutch left many names, some not altogether simple to recognize when given English sounds. The hollows where Greenbrook Pond is located have always been known as the "Kelders"; this is readily seen to mean the "cellars." It requires study, however, to trace "Bombay Hook" to "Boomje," meaning "little tree." "The Miraculous," the name of the glen south of Englewood Landing, is puzzling. It is not derived from its neighbor, Englewood Cliffs College, operated by the Order of St. Joseph of Newark, which did not arrive until long after the place was named.

On the terraces "Under the Mountain" one little farm crowded another; several of these lasted until the Park bought them out. At the beginning of the twentieth century descendants of the original settlers were still tilling the ground and gathering famous French pears from tall and ancient trees. These families became rich, their prosperity due to the shallows of the river and the rocks on the shore. The river swarmed with shad in season. The swamp-edged island of Manhattan required docks and bulkheads and here by the Palisades were blocks of extreme hardness ready-shaped for wall building, and soft stone for house construction.

In the days when river steamers burned wood, it was cut on top of the Palisades and pitched down where the water was deep in-

Rockmans, where the cliff is 520 feet above the river and 280 feet sheer drop. A stid pillar Dobbs Ferry: the country back of Tarrytown Sleepy Hollow and Irving's country. Below Forest View Basin ©

shore; hence High Gutter Point at the state line. When fireplaces heated houses, wealthy New Yorkers bought sections on top of the plateau, each with a convenient "pitching place." The spot chosen for throwing down the wood had to have beneath, not huge rocks where logs would wedge or smash, but a smooth or small-stone slope, or a cliff edge overhanging the river, with a fair landing place below. One was at Allison Point; the DePeyster pitching place was north of Clinton Point; another, belonging to the Jeffries and having a stone dock, was north of Greenbrook. Up to 1895 there were 11,000 acres of unbroken forest on the top of the Palisades, providing some of the finest timber in New Jersey.

The Revolutionary history of this region is a rich one. In 1776 General Hugh Mercer built Fort Lee to control the river. On top of the cliff a redoubt guarded the sunken ships and chained logs stretching across to Jeffries Hook on the Manhattan side, where the little red lighthouse now stands under the George Washington Bridge. To the north the highest land within Manhattan was crowned by Fort Washington, supposed by some of Washington's officers to be impregnable. Southeast, the location of the battle of Harlem Heights may be seen through the dip at 125th Street to Columbia University; Barnard College stands on the famous buckwheat field. After this fight the Americans marched along the east shore of Manhattan to dig in at White Plains, and the British army marched south over the same road to attack Fort Washington. From the west shore, General Washington watched that disaster and surrender and, as Cornwallis crossed at Alpine with six thousand men, had to order Fort Lee and all its stores of war material abandoned in such haste that the British found kettles on the fires.

The beginning of the Palisades Park dates from the time when New York City was slowly aroused to the devastations of the quarrymen blasting along the cliffs for trap rock. About the middle of the nineteenth century much of the loose and easily accessible talus was pushed down to be used as ships' ballast. The real menace to the Palisades came with the demand for more and more concrete to build skyscrapers and roads. Quarries were opened from Weehawken to Verdrietige Hook above Nyack. To check this activity the Palisades Interstate Park Commission was created in 1900 jointly by New York and New Jersey. Enabling legislation was pushed in New Jersey by the New Jersey Federation of Women's Clubs, whose memorial is the charming Women's Federation Park with its "castle" near Alpine. In New York, Andrew H. Green, "Father of

Greater New York" and founder of the American Scenic and Historic Preservation Society, worked for the necessary legislation with
the cordial support of Governor Theodore Roosevelt and other
conservation-minded officials. Land was acquired and developed as
parks with all needed facilities.

In the early days most of this development was accomplished with
gift money received from the Commissioners and interested individuals, but in recent years funds for development projects have been
provided by the two states. Of the many individuals who contributed
generously of time, talents, and money in creating the system of
parks, special recognition must be given to George W. Perkins, Sr.,
who was the Commission's first President and the organizing genius
of its development. With the story of his leadership should be
coupled the generous action of J. Pierpont Morgan at a critical time,
and many notable gifts of land and funds, private and public in
about equal proportions. As one result, quarrying of the river faces
of many mountains in Rockland County was stopped. Later the
Park Commission was also charged with the preservation of the
natural beauty of the lands lying in New York State on the west
side of the Hudson, including the Ramapo Mountains as well as
state park lands in Rockland and Orange counties and those in
Sullivan and Ulster counties outside the Catskill Forest Preserve.

In 1933 John D. Rockefeller, Jr., offered to the Park Commission
certain parcels of land on top of the Palisades which he had been
assembling for some time. He wrote to the Commission: "My pri-
mary purpose in acquiring this property was to preserve the land
lying along the top of the Palisades from any use inconsistent with
your ownership and protection of the Palisades themselves. It has
also been my hope that a strip of this land of adequate width might
ultimately be developed as a parkway. . . ." In that year there
seemed little likelihood of finding funds for a parkway, but various
lines were explored and legislation passed which enabled the Commission, in December 1935, to accept the deeds to the land offered.
Additional properties were donated by the Twombleys, and by the
trustees of the estate of W. O. Allison. The Parkway, completed to
Bear Mountain in 1958, is an attractive limited-access drive for non-
commercial traffic only.

Since 1937 both the New York and New Jersey sections have
been administered by a single Palisades Interstate Park Commission
under a compact which legally cemented a uniquely successful cooperation between two states. The land in New Jersey, and in New

York to a point 0.5 mile north of the interstate boundary, is now officially Palisades State Park; the remaining acreage is wholly in New York.

GEOLOGY

The contrast between the red sandstone, in horizontal strata, at the bottom of the cliffs, and the gray vertical columns above it, may interest the hiker and perhaps puzzle him. By what geological processes was this area built of such contrasting rock types?

The rocks of the Palisades section of the Park are almost exclusively of two kinds: sedimentary sandstones and shales, and the igneous intrusive diabase of the Palisades. Both were formed during the Triassic Period, some 190 million years ago. For millions of years, sand and mud had washed down from surrounding highlands and had spread out over wide areas in sedimentary layers thousands of feet thick. Consolidated partly by pressure, but in greater degree by the deposition of mineral matter which penetrated the porous mass and cemented particles together, these deposits are today identified as the Newark Series. They can be seen exposed both beneath the igneous rocks of the Palisades and beneath the Hackensack meadows farther to the west.

While these sedimentary strata were being laid down, molten rock was forced upward through rifts to form a single, prominent sill, the Palisades, about a thousand feet thick for some forty miles along the Hudson. At the contact of the hot magma and the adjoining sandstone and shale layers, some of the thermal metamorphic rock—hard quartzite and baked shale (hornfels)—are visible in many places. As the molten mass cooled underground, contraction fissures broke the sheet into crude vertical columns, often hexagonal or pentagonal in outline. After the diabase became exposed, these contraction joints were lines of weakness and were further affected by frost and rain, causing blocks to be pried off and fall into heavy talus slopes at the base. Because of this, the diabase often has a step-like appearance and so it is popularly known as trap rock, from the Swedish word *trapp*, or "stairs." Since it is much resistant to weather and water than is sandstone, the crumbling away of the sandstone has left the diabase exposed in the monolith we admire today. This igneous body ends in Rockland County, near Haverstraw, curling westward to two summits, High Tor and Low Tor.

Newark sandstone forms the walls of most of the old Dutch farmhouses in New Jersey, and the brownstone fronts of many of the older private homes in Manhattan. At a number of localities in New Jersey, footprints and other fossils of land animals of the Triassic Period have been found. Huge reptiles wandered over the mud flats then. The oldest inhabitant of the New York region of whom any authentic relics have been found curled himself up, lay down to die, and turned into stone in what is today the borough of Fort Lee, along the shore near Dupont Dock. He was discovered there in 1910, in the sandy shale hardened by the overhanging trap rock, about twenty feet below the basalt. As the American Museum of Natural History pictures this first fossil of our region, he looks something like a narrow-nosed, long-legged alligator, twenty-three feet from his slender snout to the tip of his tapering tail. He is a phytosaur, and his name is *Clepsysaurus manhattanensis*. There are also mud cracks and fossils of freshwater fish that testify to the continental origin of the sediments. The reddish ledges of Newark sandstone are exposed in many places along the shore path. The rock occurs chiefly near the river level and is often hidden behind the talus. Not far from the state line, however, it rises as high as 180 feet above the water.

An ice sheet that subsequently covered the New Jersey region, with its tools of sharp rock fragments borne along under the glacier and pressed against the underlying rocks by the enormous weight above, left its indelible imprint on the bedrock surfaces. Glacial striations are found in great abundance on the top of the Palisades ridge, in places several inches to one foot deep and five feet wide, as at Englewood. The polish produced by fine glacier-borne materials on the hard bedrock surfaces may be seen also all along the top of the diabase ridge, as, for example, north of the administration building at Alpine. Where the ice scoured off loose earth and even rocks of immense size (and differing compositions) west of the Palisades, erratics can be seen scattered all through the Park. Some came from as far to the west as the Highlands; others, such as Sampson's Rock in Englewood Cliffs, and Hering Rock, on the western slope of the Palisades, north of East Clinton Avenue in Tenafly, are the familiar Newark sandstone, glacially transported from a short distance to the west to their present sites.

TRAILS OF THE PALISADES INTERSTATE PARK IN NEW JERSEY

The Palisades State Park covers 2446 acres, of which 16 are in New York. Between cliff top and water the Park width averages under one-eighth mile; the maximum elevation at the front, 530 feet, is at two spots west of Forest View. The highest clear cliff is 330 feet.

A broad and level path follows the water's edge the length of this section, about 12.5 miles (no blazes). Fishing and crabbing are allowed in the stretch between Ross Dock and Englewood, and from the shore at Alpine. Bathing, for many years a feature of the shore, is now prohibited due to the pollution of the Hudson. Good paths lead at intervals to the top, and at Englewood and Alpine fine driveways descend to the river and the parking areas; these are connected midway by a motor road built in 1909, which is closed to walkers.

On top, the blue-blazed Long Path runs between cliff edge and Parkway (see pages 37–39). Also on top, but outside the Park, is a series of trails marked in 1942 by Alexander Jessup and later maintained and improved by William Hoeferlin.

A tilted column undermined, near top of cliff at the north end of Ross Dock.

olivene under trap rock

Allison Trail. Length: 8.5 miles. Blazes: yellow.

Allison Trail runs from the George Washington Bridge bus stop to Ruckman Road in Alpine. Several side paths lead to Tenafly and Cresskill in the valley to the west. It crosses the entrance to the Greenbrook Sanctuary and connects with

Little-Chism Trail. Length: 1.5 miles. Blazes: red.

This runs west of Rt. 9W from East Clinton Avenue in Tenafly to Alpine, past the entrance to Greenbrook Sanctuary. It passes a ruined dam once used for drainage control and through several ecologically interesting areas.

The Greenbrook Sanctuary is a wild, rugged area in the center of the Park, with about 6 miles of trails, along the cliff edge and around a 6.5-acre pond—the Kelders. The Sanctuary is open only to members but membership information is available from the Palisades Nature Association, P. O. Box 155, Alpine, New Jersey 07620.

SHORE PATH

Fort Lee to Englewood Boat Basin. Length: approximately 3 miles.

From the bus stop at Bridge Plaza, walk south a short distance to Main Street. At the triangle, turn left, then right on Monument Avenue to reach Fort Lee Battle Monument, by Carl Tefft, showing soldiers of the Revolution scaling the crest of the Palisades. From the east side of the park note the slight rise of land to the north; this was the site of Fort Lee. Follow narrow Palisade Road, the oldest street in the area, downhill to Bluff Point, for a view south to the Statue of Liberty and Staten Island. In 1776 there were earthworks on the southern tip, a redoubt about in a line with Main Street. The redoubt guarded the barriers placed in the river to prevent passage by the British, and an abatis of trees and brush farther north. It was here in November that General Washington watched the flag being hauled down at Fort Washington, across the river, as the colonials surrendered to the British. This point will be developed as Fort Lee Historic Park with reconstruction of batteries, a museum, and picnic areas.

Return north (and note the hundreds of scattered cavities left by quarrymen), then follow Hudson Terrace downhill to the park entrance, descend the steps to the shore, and walk north past the remnants of DuPont (Powder) Dock to the boat launching ramp under the Bridge. Passing former beaches at Hazards and Carpenters

note that the absence of talus at the base of the cliff is a consequence of the quarrying done here. At 2 miles Carpenters Trail
leads to the top; the finest cliff faces for petrified design are the
walls of rock seen from the middle section of this trail. On the
shore, water and refreshments are available at Ross Dock. Then for
more than a mile north, terraces and open groves are arranged as
picnic places. Beyond a rocky stretch is Englewood Boat Basin.

To reach Rt. 9W, where buses run to New York, walk 20 minutes
up the approach road from the Boat Basin. From the sidewalk along
the road the grade is easy and the views fine, but there is little
shade. A pleasant alternative is the shaded footpath rising near a
cascading stream.

Englewood Boat Basin to Alpine Landing. Length: 5.5 miles.

Englewood Boat Basin has an immense parking space, which
makes it an ideal starting point for those who come in cars. The
path north crosses picnic grounds at Bloomers Dock, passes Frank's
Rock, a huge boulder hanging between path and shore, and winds
past Undercliff Dock. All this stretch was a farming settlement
"Under the Mountain" in the old days before the park began. South
of Undercliff, on the upper level, is a cemetery, a relic of this settlement. The point above is High Tom. At Canoe Beach (1.5 miles)
is another picnic place with Hopkins Grove above. Above Powder
Dock, look up at Clinton Point between the trees. After crossing
Lost Brook, which loses itself flowing under the talus, arrive at
Lambiers Dock. From the tip of the dock there is a fine profile of
several headlands as far as Man-in-the-Rock, the northern column of
Bombay Hook.

In 0.3 mile, cross Greenbrook Falls, a trickle in August and an ice
mass in January, but in spring, after rain, impressive as seen from
the river bank. All this section is finely wooded. From the Falls the
path follows the river to Huyler House (3.8 miles). The old house,
built about 1840 and now empty, was an important transfer point
for goods and passengers between interior New Jersey and the city.
For the remaining mile to Alpine Boat Basin the path is full of
variety and charm. Beyond a fine growth of laurel is a big boulder
called Hay-Kee-Pook ("His Body") where legend has it that an
Indian lover committed suicide, despite the shallowness of the water.
On reaching the grassy level, do not fail to look north to see the
slender curved pinnacle of Bombay Hook. This highest, most isolated, and conspicuous pillar of rock in the Palisades literally curves

70 feet high between two mighty slides. The northern approach road enters here, but has no sidewalk; the walker continues past the boat basin to Cornwallis' "Headquarters," once a tavern where the British spent a night and are said to have scaled these cliffs by the Revolutionary Trail, which the present path to the top follows in part. The tavern was the first headquarters of the Park and is now a museum open in the summer months. The ascent takes about half an hour to reach Closter Dock Road for buses to New York.

Alpine to Forest View. Length: about 2.5 miles.

Northward from Alpine Boat Basin follow a wide path behind the former Riverview bathhouse and past fine hemlocks, a brook, and some mature deciduous woods to a stairway, then through picnic grounds to reach the shore before Bombay Hook. Bear right at a fork to pass Excelsior Dock and the grassy expanse at Twombleys. The name is that of the former owner who gave the grounds to the Park. Because of the layers of oyster shells found here, Twombleys is believed to have been the site of Indian camps. Around Bombay Hook (1.3 miles) are the highest cliffs of the Palisades. When beyond a stand of white birch, a tree seldom seen so far south, look up to the two vast bastions called Ruckman Point, and look north to Indian Head, where the best aspect of its face comes out—not the Indian or the patroon, but the Yankee pioneer. Here a path ascends, the upper part steep steps with high rises; turn left to see a stone castle commemorating the work of the New Jersey Federation of Women's Clubs in securing the first lands of the Park. Turn west on a footbridge over the Parkway to the Scout Camp where buses to New York stop.

Forest View to State Line. Length: less than 2 miles, but allow an hour and a half.

The final segment of the store path includes its most striking scenery. This walk along the foot of the five-hundred-foot cliffs of Indian Head and past the rough talus of the Giant Stairs, where the falcon hawk is sometimes seen, is preserved in its natural state, accessible only to hikers. From Forest View head north, either on the grass or on the upper path, to see some of the immense rock masses. After making a long traverse over slide and talus, begin the descent of the Giant Stairs at 0.8 mile. In another 0.5 mile, close to shore, the path crosses a slough which marks the state line; take the left fork up on a well-built trail to the front at High Gutter Point. Continue through Skunk Hollow, on the lands of the

The Giant
Stairs
north of Forrest
View, opposite
Hastings, in
the Autumn

R. L. Dickinson
"1925"

Lamont Sanctuary, to join the blue-blazed Long Path to Rt. 9W, where buses to New York stop opposite the main entrance to Columbia University's Lamont-Doherty Geological Observatory.

THE LONG PATH

When the Palisades Interstate Parkway was built, the accessibility of the cliff top renewed interest in the larger trail project of the Long Path, originally proposed in 1931 by Vincent J. Schaefer of the Mohawk Valley Hiking Club of Schenectady. He thought New York, like Vermont, should have a "long trail" from New York City to Lake Placid. With W. W. Cady of New York assisting in the region south of the Catskills, some marking was undertaken but the only portion completed was the present Northville–Lake Placid Trail. In 1960 Robert Jessen of the Ramapo Ramblers urged a Path from George Washington Bridge to the Adirondacks; the new plan makes Whiteface Mountain the terminus of the trail.

Fort Lee to Englewood Cliffs. Length: 2 miles. Blazes: blue.

The most popular approach, and the most scenic, is on foot across George Washington Bridge; an alternative is by bus to the Bridge Plaza in Fort Lee. From the Bridge a wide, level path swings toward the cliff. View lower New York from the farthest projecting cliff near the bridge tower. Downhill about 0.3 mile a square promontory shows one of the best of the southern rock faces; here Carpenters Path descends to the shore path. The Long Path continues north by an overpass leading to a hollow where skating is possible in season, then comes again to the front at a mounted cannon in the former Coytesville Park. After passing the walls of several former estates it enters (1.3 miles) a small park, now maintained by the Park, which was built as a memorial to W. O. Allison. It is open most of the year; water and rest rooms are available.

The Miraculous is the gully to the north of Allison Park. The Path swings to the shoulder of the Parkway past the campus of Englewood Cliffs College and enters a small woodland, bypassing Allison Point, then crosses Palisade Avenue. Here the shore may be reached either by a zigzag path or by the sidewalk along the road. For a short side trip cross Rt. 9W and walk north along Floyd Avenue, one block west, to reach Sampson's Rock, a glacial erratic.

Englewood Cliffs to Alpine. Length: 5.5 miles.

Any bus along Rt. 9W stops at Palisade Avenue; walk east to

the edge for the path which follows a level but scenic route to Alpine. The Path north soon traverses the former Dana estate; note an exotic Oriental pine near the Parkway. In the woodland beyond watch for the rock promontory, High Tom, with views north and down to Undercliff Grove and cemetery. Next cross Rockefeller Overlook (1 mile); opposite is Spuyten Duyvil and the northern tip of Manhattan. After passing the ruins of the Cadgene estate the Path follows undulating terrain through woodland to a meadow and a depression, Devil's Hole. The slight rise beyond is Point Clinton (1.5 miles), a favorite viewpoint from the time of the first settlers. A little farther it crosses the entrance road from 9W into Greenbrook Sanctuary. Buses on 9W stop here. The Path continues north along the fence, with short steep stretches, then across the Alpine Outlook of the Pathway (4 miles) and reenters the woods past a house foundation. Descend to cross Walker Hollow, a long open swale with views of downtown Yonkers across the river, and ascend past the foundation of the Zabriskie House (4.8 miles); the dry cellar may be used as an emergency shelter. Passing several other foundations, the Path goes through an underpass to Closter Dock Road, where buses to New York stop. To reach the shore, continue on the path 0.3 mile and turn down the trail to Alpine Boat Basin.

Alpine to Scout Camp. Length: 2.5 miles.

There is little parking at the bus stop at Closter Dock Road and 9W. North from the underpass it is an hour's walk on level paths to the Scout Camp. After another underpass, Alpine Approach Road, the Long Path turns left past the Headquarters Building of the Palisades Interstate Park (the former Oltman House). Note the tower west of the Parkway, the site of the first FM station, built by Major Edwin Armstrong, the radio pioneer. The Path traverses woodland, then the former Ringling (circus) estate, and 1 mile from Closter Dock Road swings to the cliff edge and passes the largest separated section of rock in the Palisades, Grey Crag, some 300 feet long and 10 to 20 feet wide, accessible by a bridge. In winter and early spring look for 300-foot ice columns where water plunges over the cliff.

The Long Path passes Bombay Hook (1.5 miles) on another ridge and then crosses an area recently ravished by drought and fire and ends abruptly at Ruckman Road, at the edge of the cliff. The rock wall here is 520 feet high. The Path turns left on Ruckman Road, then turns north and parallels the Parkway along a

fence to reach an overpass to a bus stop on Rt. 9W at the Scout
Camp entrance. The white circular radar dome of Mt. Nebo, several miles north, is visible.

Scout Camp to State Line. Length: 2 miles.

From the east end of the overpass the Path approaches the cliff
edge, and passes the weird-shaped buildings of the former Burnet
property behind the fence on the right, and Maisland (Corn-lot)
Hollow on the left, the location of Federation Park. Far below are
the remains of Forest View pier. The trail goes north, then east
down a steep slope. Before the Path turns down very steeply, to
continue to Forest View at the shore, there is a stone stairway to
the north. The trail bears left to the Park Road at the top of the
cliffs, crossing a brook which rises in Maisland Hollow. Here turn
right on the road to Point Lookout, where water and refreshments
are available in summer.

The trail continues on a wide wood road to the state line, marked
by a fence and a six-foot shaft erected in 1882, then descends, near
the cliff edge, through a gate to High Gutter Point. This name
recalls the early wood-burning river steamers which came into the
bank at the foot of a chute for their fuel. Here there are good views
over Hook Mountain, the old mile-long pier at Piermont, and
Tappan Zee. A staircase of natural stone leads down and west, joining the path from the river, into Skunk Hollow. This area is the
Lamont Sanctuary; the path right leads to the cliff edge. The area
below is not open to the public. The main path goes left (west) to
9W, where buses stop at Lamont-Doherty Geological Observatory
entrance. Several cars may be parked near the boulders on old 9W,
or at the parking area at Point Lookout up the old highway. If
returning to Point Lookout, when passing Skunk Hollow on the
old highway, turn right on a wood road near a brook bed (this is a
former bridle path abandoned thirty years ago). In about a half
mile, as the trail begins to descend, turn right on a level wood road,
cross the brook, and shortly turn left to Point Lookout.

2 · THE PALISADES RIDGE
IN NEW YORK

Map 2

ORTHWARD from the Palisades in New Jersey are eight relatively small state parks on the diabase ridge reaching almost to Bear Mountain Park. All were created, at various times, to save the areas from destruction. Two are tiny beach areas once developed for swimming and now awaiting the end of river pollution. The other six form an almost continuous chain on the river or circling on the hills west of the villages along the bight of Nyack. From south to north they are:

Tallman Mountain State Park (687 acres).

This park lies on the jutting headland near Piermont and the cut of Sparkill. Part of this park was acquired in 1929 after a ten-year legal battle to save it from quarrying. A proposed "oil tank farm" set up on its south side in 1923 would have developed the area into another Bayonne. Squat tanks, a pipe line, loading pier, and related facilities were partially in operation when public outcry forced its termination. These 540 acres were added in 1942.

The park area is mostly a broad wooded plateau, from whose two higher "peaks" there are good views over the Hudson. Most of Tallman is developed as a picnic area with roads and parking areas; in the northwest corner are sports facilities and near the river a swimming pool, and marshes that provide good "birding." The Long Path traverses it, passing some of the abandoned relics of the oil project.

Blauvelt State Park (590 acres).
Blauvelt lies on the west ridge some two miles north through land still partly in private ownership or in local park projects. The first 212 acres of the park were the gift to the Park Commission in 1911 by the heirs of Stephen Rowe Bradley of Nyack. It included the popular Balance Rock, destroyed in 1966 by vandals. In 1913 the Commission received the former Blauvelt Rifle Range. This facility had been designed to replace the National Guard Range at Creedmoor, Long Island. After nearly a half million dollars were invested in plant and equipment, however, it became readily apparent that the people of South Nyack, on the east side of the mountain, were receiving more than raindrops from the firmament. After numerous, but fruitless, attempts to make the range safe, it was abandoned less than three years after its construction. The Long Path follows along part of the concrete wall built then.

Summer camp programs made use for some time of the almost-new buildings. At present the area is undeveloped as a park. Numerous hiking and bridle trails go in every direction. The western part is quite level, but the northern and eastern areas are rugged.

Hook Mountain State Park (661 acres).
North of Nyack, Hook Mountain juts into the river to match Tallman, but it is higher and wilder, with fine views. The name is derived from the Dutch, "Verdrietige Hoogte" (Hook), meaning tedious or troublesome point, because of the contrary winds which navigators encountered off the point. It is literally a hook, however, when viewed from the air or on a map.

In the last quarter of the nineteenth century, the quarrying which started at the Palisades spread upriver, threatening the defacement of Hook Mountain on the Tappan Zee, and the entire river front. The landings, such as Sneden's, Tappan Slote (Piermont), Rockland Landing, and Waldberg (or Snedeker's), where ferries plied across the river or where steamers docked en route to New York, could expect to see a bustle of new activity, and some did.

In 1872 the erection of a stone crusher at Hook Mountain signaled the beginning of large-scale operations. By the turn of the century, this and thirty-one smaller quarries between Piermont and

Nyack were in vigorous operation; blasting was going on furiously. Sentiment was growing to stop this defacement, as had been done on the Palisades. George W. Perkins, President of the Park Commission, had the greatest part in stimulating this opinion among philanthropic men and women of wealth. He believed the forested hills of the Highlands of the Hudson, famous for their scenery and their Revolutionary strongholds, would be an outlet for the people of the metropolitan district. In addition to various bond issues, the Commission was aided in its plans by generous givers, including members of the Harriman, Perkins, and Rockefeller families, who have been adding to Park holdings even up to the present time.

The first of the purchases at Hook Mountain was in 1911, with the acquisition of the large quarry at the south end of the mountain. By 1920 the last of the quarries ceased operations and the public had a 6-mile-long park along the river where once such a park seemed only a dream. (In 1906 the jurisdiction of the park had been extended to Stony Point.) Hook Mountain Park is still largely undeveloped, but the trails are among the finest for ruggedness and views. At its south end is the tiny Nyack Beach Park, today a picnic area; at the north end is Haverstraw Beach Park, now almost entirely unused.

Rockland Lake State Park (1078 acres).

The other great industry which broke the serenity of the river front developed from the harvesting of Rockland Lake ice from 1831 to 1924. The discoverer of the superiority of ice from spring-fed Rockland Lake is unknown, but its renown became widespread to the point where the better New York restaurants would accept no other. In 1711 John Slaughter purchased land at Rockland Landing, including Trough Hollow, the gap in the ridge where a narrow and precipitous path leads to the river. A dock was built and gradually there was some commercial traffic, but Nyack and Haverstraw had better natural facilities. As ice was harvested it was conveyed to Rockland Landing by a sort of "escalator" and loaded on river boats. Later the giant Knickerbocker Ice Company was formed, at one time employing four thousand men. Icehouses over 350 feet long and 50 feet high, each with a fifty-ton capacity, were situated at the northeast corner of the lake. In 1860 a cog railway was built through Trough Hollow, connecting lake and dock. A spur line of the West Shore Railway also ran to the icehouses. But the growth of mechanical refrigeration permanently halted ice harvesting operations in 1924. Thereafter Rockland Lake became a popular,

privately owned recreation center for summer swimming and picnicking and winter ice-skating.

In 1958 the Commission acquired 256-acre Rockland Lake and
surrounding upland areas. Later, additional acreage was purchased
so as to include the entire "bowl." This is now one of the most
intensively developed and heavily used of the parks, with pools,
golf courses, and huge parking areas on the level plain with a
sweeping view of the gentle hills around and toward the Hudson.
In the northwest corner a nature museum and trail has been set
up. Fishermen are welcome, as are skaters when conditions permit.

High Tor State Park (492 acres).

The northern end of the Palisades turns west from the Hudson
with two high points: High Tor (832 feet) behind Haverstraw, the
highest headland in the Palisades, and Little Tor (710 feet), 1 mile
farther west. High Tor, one of Rockland County's most striking
landmarks, was once used as a signal point by colonists during the
Revolution. Long cherished as part of the Van Orden farm on its
south side, High Tor was theatened by quarrying for its trap rock,
as Elmer Van Orden grew older without descendants. Maxwell
Anderson's picturesque play, *High Tor,* and local love for the little
peak aroused the Rockland County Conservation Association, the
Hudson River Conservation Society, and the New York–New Jersey Trail Conference to action. Their campaign resulted in the
purchase of the ridge and its presentation in 1943 to the Commission.

The gift in 1943 of the adjoining property by Archer M. Huntington, writer and philanthropist, included the ridge west of High
Tor, the almost equally famous and impressive Little Tor, and
much of the south slope. But the slope facing the Hudson all the
way north from Long Cove is still in private hands and in danger
of being developed. The Commission has recently built a small
swimming pool on the south side of Little Tor and plans to maintain most of this park as a bird and game sanctuary with facilities
for hikers.

Stony Point Reservation (83 acres).

It is somewhat isolated but well worth exploring, both for its
beauty and its historic associations. It is a rugged promontory jutting some 2000 feet into the river east of Rt. 9W about 3 miles
north of Haverstraw. At its widest point it is about 1500 feet. The
site of the old lighthouse is about 150 feet above the river, afford-

ing beautiful views up and down the valley. For many years it was administered by the American Scenic and Historical Preservation Society, but it has been under the jurisdiction of the Commission since 1946.

Stony Point is closed in winter. In spring the whole Reservation seems covered with white dogwood blossoms. Shaded walks lead past the various historical markers; and there are picnic tables and a military museum, built in 1936. There is good parking and in every way it is a pleasant place to spend a day of easy walking and a picnic, or to undertake some study of Revolutionary history.

THE LONG PATH

State Line to Piermont, about 3 miles.

From the bus stop at the entrance to Lamont-Doherty Geological Observatory to the foot of the long pier at Piermont is a walk of about 1½ hours, on smooth trails. Northward it follows 9W a few yards, then turns into the woods downhill on a dirt road, the last remaining portion of the "boulevard," forerunner of the modern highway. The Long Path leaves the dirt road for 9W again, just south of intersection with Oak Tree Road. At this crossroad (traffic light) Oak Tree Road leads east to Sneden's Landing, the western end of a ferry route established in 1719, and made famous during the Revolution when Mollie Sneden, whose house still stands under the cliff (private), rowed the boat across. On this road is the site (also on private land) where the American flag received, by order of Parliament, its first salute from the British in May 1783. The British fleet had used the anchorage below since 1776.

Oak Tree Road left (west) leads through the village of Palisades to the village of Tappan, about 2 miles, now established as a historic site. As it is a road walk, take a bus from the intersection west on Oak Tree Road to Tappan and return the same way. Until 1798 Tappan was, alternately with Goshen, the county seat of then undivided Orange County. In the center is the '76 House (Mabie's Tavern, still a restaurant) where the British spy, Major John André, was imprisoned after his capture at Tarrytown. It was also the site of a meeting on July 4, 1774, which adopted the Orangetown Resolutions, seeking by non-importation to force the repeal of the Stamp Act.

To the south, on Livingston Lane, is the entrance to the grounds of the deWindt House, now a national shrine open to the public, with a museum in the former carriage house. Built in 1700, this well-preserved example of Dutch architecture was Washington's headquarters during the trial and execution of André and again when it was the scene of the conference for the British evacuation of New York. It it maintained by the Masons in memory of Wash ington. The church north of the '76 House is the third building on the site. Opposite is an outstanding example of a Jeffersonian town house (private); on the left is the church "manse," built in 1726, the oldest parsonage in continous use as such in the United States. Between is the five-acre village green where the Orange County courthouse and jail stood until destroyed by fire in 1774. West along Old Tappan Road is André Hill crowned by the André Monument near the gallows' site where André was hanged and buried on October 2, 1780; in 1821, his body was removed to Westminster Abbey. The monument was erected in 1879 by Cyrus W. Field, the projector of the Atlantic cable.

The Long Path, from the intersection of 9W where it was left for these side excursions to Sneden's Landing and Tappan, continues about one block on the highway, passing an old flagpole and antique shop on the left and the handsome "Big House" (private) on the right. In a few yards the Path turns right (east) off 9W onto a dirt road (Palisades Interstate Park property). In a half mile it turns left (north) near several concrete structures, passes through a clearing and then follows an unbending, shaded road. Here and there, rectangular berms are scattered through the area. These berms are long, elevated mounds of earth at right angles to each other. Originally intended to retain oil seepage from the tank farm which once stood here, some are now filled with rainwater and, although shallow, make good "birding" sites. At the road's end (1.5 miles) the Path swings right toward the river and follows an old farmers' road, long abandoned, which leads to a picnic area in the Tallman Mountain section of the Park, where water and a comfort station are located. A network of motor roads from the main park entrance on Rt. 9W circles the recreation areas and brings the motorist to any one of several well-arranged picnic places. It is little used except on weekends.

From the comfort station the blue-blazed Path descends across a ravine and past the swimming pool (2.3 miles) near the river. At the traffic circle, the road going downhill runs along the river to rejoin the trail at Piermont. The trail itself goes past the circle to the top of Tallman Mountain, where there are fine views east across the Hudson and to the north. Below (to the north) is the village of Piermont, once the New York terminus of the Erie

Railroad, where passengers transferred to a steamer at the pier's end. It is said that the railroad's original charter required the line to be located entirely within New York State. When this was modified, the railroad was then able to use a tunnel through the trap rock of Bergen Hill to reach Jersey City.

From the mountaintop the Path descends steeply to the town, crossing Spar Kill and the marshes. The bus to New York will stop at a small park on the creek in Piermont.

Piermont to Nyack, about 7.5 miles.

The walk north (about 4½ hours) hugs the western slope of the Palisades ridge from the bus stop at the long pier on the Spar Kill. Where the railroad spur crosses the road the Path heads uphill on a side street, up a stairway to the upper highway. After crossing 9W it follows Highland Avenue (Tweed Boulevard) north. This "boulevard" was built, beginning in 1871, to connect Sparkill and the village of Rockland Lake and was so-named because local politicians tried to emulate the notorious "boss" Tweed and his New York City boulevards. Beyond a bend in the road (1 mile) the path climbs the embankment to a corner of Rockland Cemetery, established in 1847 by Eleazer Lord, a founder of the Erie Railroad, as a National Cemetery. Here on a rise nearby is the grave of John C. Frémont, "The Pathfinder," and just to the south that of Henry Honeychurch Gorringe, whose exploits in bringing Cleopatra's Needle to America are depicted on his monument, a replica of the obelisk in Central Park. (As an alternative, little used Tweed Boulevard may be followed along the crest of the ridge.)

From the cemetery the trail proceeds north on a wood road along the ridge; above, out of sight, is the Mt. Nebo radar installation. This Clausland Mountain area is largely county park, acquired with the help of Nature Conservancy. The trail descends to cross a brook (1.8 miles), climbs, then descends across another brook to Clausland Mountain Road (2.8 miles). North of this, the trail passes a water impoundment, once part of the former rifle range, now a park of Orangetown, and crosses the brook into somewhat dense undergrowth. After passing a huge red oak, it reaches a broad wood road which is the southern boundary of Blauvelt State Park (3.3 miles).

The yellow-blazed Piermont Trail from the post office in Sparkill, which has crossed and recrossed the Long Path, now turns along this boundary, but later twice meets the LP blue blazes. The Long Path turns right at the park boundary, then follows a series of wide paths through a reforestation project, across a park road to a broad expanse of flat rock outcroppings. Beyond, a turn to the right in the woods leads to a concrete wall. This was the wall which supported the targets of the former rifle range. The trail now follows a generally northeasterly direction along various paths, crosses a brook and follows the north side of the ravine with stands of hemlock, to reach Tweed Boulevard. The road turns uphill to the crest of the ridge (4.8 miles), the site of the once-famous Balance Rock, destroyed by vandals in 1966. From the crest are excellent views of both the Hudson and the Hackensack valleys.

In a few hundred yards down the road the trail bears right on a gravel route, past a water tank and impressive rubble of talus, to a good view of the Tappan Zee and Bridge, then past Nyack Missionary College. At Bradley Hill Road the trail jogs left, climbs over a small wooded knoll and proceeds along a hard-surfaced road to Rt. 59 and the Thruway at the traffic lights. The route ahead continues up to a plateau before descending east along the next crossroad, Christian Herald Road, to reach Rt. 9W for a bus to New York. An alternative is to turn right along Rt. 59 down into Nyack for a return bus.

Closer to the river, and below the Long Path, the branch line of the Erie Railroad from Piermont to the Nyacks has been abandoned and the right-of-way is for sale. It has been urged by conservationists in Rockland County that this level and fairly wide tract can best be used to make a bicycle way that may also be walked from Piermont to Hook Mountain, continuing on the shore path. The villages of Piermont and Grand View have already acquired the right-of-way within their boundaries. It is hoped that the County Park Commission will sponsor this, though they have no funds now.

Nyack to Long Clove Along the Ridge, about 6 miles.

This is a summit walk on trails and wood roads over several steep areas (time about 4 hours). From the bus stop at Rt. 9W and Christian Herald Road, in Upper Nyack, walk north on 9W toward the base of Hook Mountain to pick up the old location of 9W on the right, now a path at a lower level. (To make a circular trip, see the section on "Nyack Circular," below.) The path climbs first the south, then the west side of Hook Mountain. Its summit is the second highest in the Palisades rampart (729 feet) and commands a view in a complete circle. To the north is the circle of ridges to be traversed, with Rockland and Congers lakes in the bowl behind the ridge; the rampart of the Ramapos and Highlands to the west and north; to the east, the long slope of Westchester County with Tarrytown and other villages along its front; the Tappan Zee Bridge and Nyack to the south, with the broad fields of the estates of Upper Nyack in the foreground.

The trail slopes down Hook Mountain, then ascends along the ridge close to the edge of an abandoned quarry. On the next summit the remains of a chimney is the last remnant of the Gerard Cottage (1.3 miles). There are fine views across the Hudson to Ossining and Croton Point and beyond to Croton Dam. Downhill, in 0.3 mile, a wood road branches left to the park golf course below, where a good flowing spring is located 200 yards along the fairway. The trail stays on Tweed Boulevard along the ridge, turns uphill to pass the "dark pond" (2.3 miles) near the summit, then descends to Rockland Landing Road. The last few hundred feet are over rocks so steep that they should not be attempted in winter or on slippery days. To avoid the precipitous path, turn abruptly to the left on an overgrown wood road, then west past the old village school to the former crossroads of Rockland Lake village near the gap in the ridge. To find a bus for an early return, follow the road from this three-way corner and a path downhill past Rockland Lake to the small nature museum at its northwestern shore. The museum trails are catwalks over a swamp, through red maples; a solitary Atlantic white cedar may be the only one in the county. Various caged animals are on exhibition. The Grove, a picnic area located where the museum now stands, was opened in 1873 and drew crowds who came by special trains on the West Shore Railroad. From the Park entrance it is a ten-minute walk on Lake Street to the bus stop on Rt. 303.

The Long Path along the ridge continues across the Rockland Lake village crossroads, past a family cemetery on the right up a steep slope. The next descent along the face of an abandoned quarry is to Trough Hollow (3.3 miles), once the main road from the village to the river landing. Past a stone wall near the refreshment building for the golf course, the trail crosses wooded knolls to the top of a cliff, the site of another former quarry. There are views east across the Hudson and west to Rockland, Swartwout, and Congers lakes. Cement markers indicate the boundary of Hook Mountain State Park, the land between the ridge and the river. The trail climbs to the highest point on the ridge (5.3 miles) to a view of Lake DeForest, a large reservoir on the Hackensack, then descends, crosses a power line over a West Shore Railroad tunnel to reach a large open area and Rt. 9W. This is the Long Clove, a natural cleft in the Palisades ridge. Buses will sometimes stop here.

Nyack Circular: Long Clove to Nyack by the Shore Path, about 6.5 miles north to south.

To reach the shore path from the parking area near Long Clove, take the wood road which descends and follows the railroad south to a tunnel under it. At the Park gate, near a small parking area, scramble down to a wood road leading north to a rocky point and walk downstream a few hundred feet to see a granite boulder on which is carved: "André the spy landed here September 21, 1780." On returning to the Shore Path, come to Haverstraw Beach State Park (0.5 mile), now unused. Here was once a thriving settlement, known at various times as Waldberg or Snedeker's Landing or as Red Sandstone Dock. The broad path was opened early in 1932 to connect the playgrounds and recreation center at Rockland Landing with Haverstraw and Nyack. Now little used, it is a charming way through abundant ferns and tall trees, with large stands of striped maple.

At low tide (about 2½ hours later than at Sandy Hook) a walk along the river's edge is well worth taking for the geological exhibit it provides. Sandstone and shale, overlaid with trap rock talus, appear in the cliffs; pebbles and boulders range in age from mostly Precambrian granite and gneiss through red Triassic sandstone and shale to Pleistocene clay sand and gravel, with gravel planing and erosional features for good measure. The low land projecting from the opposite shore almost to the middle of the Hudson is Croton Point; Teller's Point is its southern tip. This was the delta of the old Croton River, formerly at river level but now elevated to a height of eighty feet. The crust of the earth gradually rose with the disappearance of the last glacier and the removal of the tremendous weight of ice. Beyond are the Westchester hills of a more ancient metamorphic terrain; in the distance is Long Island's terminal moraine.

The Shore Path passes a watchman's cabin to the first of the abandoned quarries in Hook Mountain State Park and continues along the level which marks the contact between the red sandstone beneath and the trap rock which overlays it. The Empress tree (*Paulownia tomentosa*) grows here on the diabase talus slopes resulting from old rock slides. The common tree of the upper level is the box elder, and along the path are many hundred-year-old hemlocks. On the terraces above are old Indian oyster-shell middens. At the end of the second quarry a path bears left to Rockland

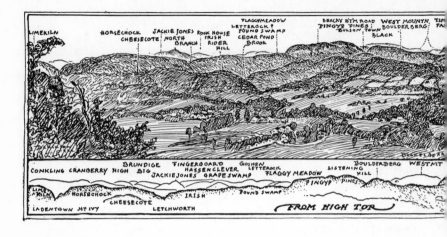

Landing North (2.8 miles). Immediately beyond, a wood road bends up the ridge to Trough Hollow. Next is the third quarry, somewhat larger than the others, and once landscaped as part of the park development. The columns of the cliff face reveal Triassic intrusive diabase (trap rock). The automatic navigation beacon on a reef in the river (3.3 miles) is Rockland Light. A quarter mile farther are the remains of Rockland Landing South. The Path turns north and upward past a police cabin onto a road to the top of the ridge and the largest of the quarries. This road may be followed to return to Long Clove over the tops, or across the ridge to Rockland Lake and the highway. The cliffs here rise four hundred feet or more with columnar flutings noticeable at the south end.

The Path south, now a road, descends to the river, where there may still be old hulks of ice boats and remains of the "escalator" by which the ice was once lowered to the river. The Path then runs close to the sandstone cliffs where a park lean-to (4.3 miles) was built of the plentiful talus, then around a headland to the Tappan Zee. Below the last of the quarries is Nyack Beach State Park, now only a picnic area (5 miles). South of the Park's entrance follow North Broadway in Upper Nyack 1 mile and turn right uphill on Old Mountain Road past Rockland County's oldest cemetery and soon reach Rt. 9W where the hike from Nyack began. (A few blocks further south on North Broadway is Old Stone Church, the oldest church building in the county. The next street is Castle Heights Avenue, with a bus stop for the trip back to New York.)

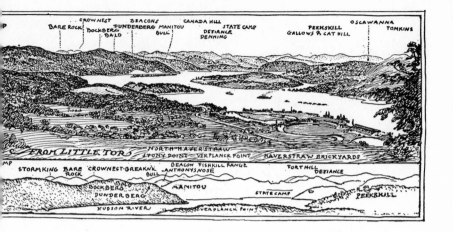

The labels in the upper panorama, from left to right:

BARE ROCK · CROWNEST · DOCKBERG · BEACONS · DUNDERBERG · BALD · MANITOU · BULL · CANADA HILL · DEFIANCE · STATE CAMP · DENNING · PEEKSKILL · GALLOWS & CAT HILL · OSCAWANNA · TOMKINS

MP FROM LITTLE TOR · NORTH HAVERSTRAW · STONY POINT · VERPLANCK POINT · HAVERSTRAW BRICKYARDS

The labels in the lower panorama:

MP · STORMKING BARE ROCK · CROWNEST · BREAKN'K BULL · BEACON FISHKILL RANGE · ANTHONYSNOSE · FORT HILL · DEFIANCE
DOCKBERG · DUNDERBERG · MANITOU · STATE CAMP · PEEKSKILL
HUDSON RIVER · VERPLANCK POINT

Long Clove to Mt. Ivy (south to north), about 6.3 miles.

For those who did not hike the "Nyack Circular," the Long Path continues northward and climbs the southeast side of High Tor in a series of natural steps in the diabase. Near the base of High Tor, in a shallow hollow, the white-blazed Deer Path leads steeply down to meet Rt. 9W opposite a bar about a half mile south of the old Haverstraw railroad station. On the summit of High Tor (1.8 miles) is the foundation of an airplane beacon, now removed, surrounded by the polygonal pattern of the diabase column ends, like a honeycomb in stone. High Tor is the highest point on the Palisades-Tor ridge (827 feet). The tower on the horizon to the south is at Alpine; the one to the north is Jackie Jones in the Ramapos. The view to the west shows the curving range yet to be traveled. Straight below is the village of Haverstraw and the river.

A scramble, short but steep, brings the Path down to a fire road leading through the woods. It is a good half hour's walk to Little Tor. Just south of Little Tor is a brook that hardly ever runs dry (3.5 miles). A path downhill to the left leads to the base of the mountain near the swimming pool; to the right a branch leads in less than 0.3 mile to the north side ledge and then 100 yards to the summit of Little Tor (710 feet), a fine viewpoint. Garnersville, West Haverstraw, and some of the clay banks once used in brick-making lie below. One mile north, is the New York Reconstruction Home, built on the site of the Hett Smith house where Arnold and André met on September 21, 1780, to arrange the delivery of West Point to the British. To the right is Grassy Point, where a town marina has been built, and farther north, Stony Point Reservation. Beyond, Dunderberg rises from the river, with Bear Mountain looking over the saddle and the summit of The Timp to the left.

The path along South Mountain, as the ridge from here west to Mt. Ivy is named, leads in another 0.5 mile to the white-blazed Little Tor Trail, leading right to Haverstraw's Doud Street, off Rt. 202. At 4.3 miles is a highway, Central Avenue, crossing the ridge, which marks the end of the Park ownership. The mile or so to Mt. Ivy is privately owned and in danger of being developed. The trail now runs pretty much along the crest through red cedars and other second growth. Northward, west of Thiells, the buildings of Letchworth Village, a state institution named in honor of the philanthropist William Pryor Letchworth, are visible. At the end of the ridge is the grassy opening on the summit of Mt. Ivy above the long-abandoned Gurnee quarry; ahead is a panorama of the Ramapo Mountain rampart. In the middle is Cheesecote Mountain, so-named from the original patent for the land; it is now a Haverstraw town park. The trough-like hollow running back into the mountains opposite is File Factory Hollow, with Horse Chock Mountain to the north of it and Lime Kiln Mountain to the south. Mt. Ivy is the end of the Palisades trap rock above ground. The trail swings down around the quarry to reach Rt. 202 (6.3 miles); here a local store can usually furnish refreshments.

3 · BEAR MOUNTAIN—
HARRIMAN STATE PARKS

HISTORY

THESE two jointly operated state parks constitute more than 75 percent of the Palisades Interstate Park acreage. The name Harriman Park perpetuates the name of Edward H. Harriman, the railroad builder, who conceived the idea of establishing a park in the Highlands, and of his widow, Mrs. Mary A. Harriman, who carried out his intention by giving ten thousand acres to the state in 1910.

In 1908 the State of New York had secured Bear Mountain for the incongruous purpose of erecting Sing Sing prison at that location, and had established a stockade between Popolopen Creek and what is now Hessian Lake, where hundreds of convicts were put to clear the timber for the prison site. There was much public objection to this use for an area which possessed not only such scenic and recreational values, but sacred historical associations as well. It was on this natural terrace above the Hudson that Fort Clinton and Fort Montgomery had been built during the Revolution, and the militia of Orange and Putnam counties had fallen in fruitless defense of them in 1777. Mrs. Harriman, however, insisted that in exchange for her gift the Palisades Commission's jurisdiction be extended to Newburgh and that the state discontinue its plan to use Bear Mountain as a prison site.

The immediate years after the Harriman gift saw funds for park extension and development raised by private subscription. On this, Mrs. Harriman worked closely with George W. Perkins, then President of the Commission. In a sense, the whole park is a memorial to Mr. Perkins. His interest for twenty years, until his death in 1920, his enthusiasms and his capacity for enlisting men and women of wealth in the support of what he saw as a necessary recreational outlet for the metropolitan district were of vast benefit to the park in its formative years. In the 1930s, the road to the summit of Bear Mountain and the tower were constructed as a special memorial to his service.

In subsequent years, further large gifts were made by nearly all the well-known philanthropists and the extension of both the area and the engineering works was pressed under the able supervision of the late Major William Welch, General Manager and Chief Engineer from 1910 to his retirement in 1940. He may well be remembered by all who use the roads and the lakes which he created. Appropriately, Lake Welch, the newest of the large artificial bodies of water in the park, was named for him in 1947. Since 1922 the Bear Mountain Inn has been open and a Trailside Museum, established by special gifts in 1927, has greatly increased the interest of visitors in the knowledge of regional history and wild life.

The postwar years saw the construction of convenient, although at times distressing, new parkways to and through Harriman State Park. These are replacing the former picturesque roads that cannot handle the crowds wishing to use new facilities such as those at Anthony Wayne, Lake Welch, Sebago Beach, and Silvermine. In 1963 over 3000 additional acres were joined to Harriman State Park, particularly in the area north of Suffern. Two years later the Commission acquired Iona Island, a 118-acre rocky promontory jutting out into the Hudson just south of Bear Mountain. The island has a colorful history—as Indian camp ground, strategic point in Revolutionary War activities, farmland where the Iona Grape (which gave the island its name) was developed, summer resort and excursion playground, and finally, beginning in 1899, as an "off-continental United States" base of the U. S. Navy operated as an ammunition depot.

A new role was given to the Commission in 1966 when it was charged with the responsibility of State Historic Sites in its region. These included a cluster of sites in and near Newburgh. A year later its jurisdiction was again extended to assume responsibility for all state parks as far north as the Catskill Mountains.

Of chief interest to the walker, however, is the great expanse of wild park property which neither the motorist nor the picnickers who crowd the "developed" areas ever see. In the early years of the park the walker had many dirt roads and miles upon miles of the wood roads built by the iron workers to follow, or he could choose his own way through the thickening woodland according to the topography, his taste, and his compass. As the park administration began to build roads and enlarge the ponds into lakes, the walker blundered into them, to his wrath, even when he had been able to keep himself fairly well oriented on his map. Many are the amusing stories old-timers can tell of coming out in unexpected spots, perhaps uncomfortably late in the day. With a job that must be reached on Monday morning there are limits to the pleasures of exploration. More unsatisfactory still was the difficulty of getting to the real tops of the wooded slopes or of finding the splendid views from cliff and ledge in which the region abounds. Now the blazed trails through the park have sought out these objectives for the hiker to enjoy but still many other "undiscovered" gems have been left for the experienced to find by himself.

PLACE NAMES IN THE HUDSON HIGHLANDS

Some place names on the Highlands, especially those of Dutch derivation, may seem quaint but their origins are part of our history. One of these is the name of the hamlet of Doodletown which, until recently, was located in the valley between Bear Mountain and Dunderberg. A picturesque story connects the name Doodletown with the song "Yankee Doodle," claiming that the town was named after the British passed through it in October 1777, playing that march while on their way to attack the forts on Popolopen. It is disproved by the fact that Governor George Clinton, in his report to General Washington on the loss of the forts, tells of sending, a few hours before the British stormed the American works, a half company out to "the place called Doodletown" to scout the British advance. The name, therefore, was a familiar one before the battle. According to Cornelius C. Vermeule of South Orange, the New Jersey expert on place names, "Doodletown" is derived from two Dutch words, "dood" meaning dead, and "del," meaning dale or valley. He suggests that when the Dutch skippers put into the mouth of Doodletown Brook for wood and water, they noticed some aspect of the hollow—possibly dead trees standing after a forest fire, or perhaps a dark, forbidding look which lead them to call it "Dooddel" or Dead Valley. The suffix "town" was added later, probably, by English settlers. Another word of Dutch origin is "clove," used in early days to refer to certain valleys in the area. This comes from the word "kloof," meaning a ravine.

Among the quaint names in the area the oddest are "Timp," and "Pyngyp." The cliffs at the west end of the Dunderberg massif and the pass between it and West Mountain were called "Timp," Mr. Vermeule believes, from an obscure Dutch word, "timpje," a colloquial diminutive, meaning a small cake or bun, although the older form, "timp," is almost forgotten. Perhaps some early Dutch skipper, looking across Haverstraw Bay at Dunderberg and noting the general shape of the Dunderberg-Bockberg-Timp massif from Jones Point to Timp Pass, thought of it as a loaf of bread or cake taken out of the baking pan and laid upside down for frosting, with slightly slanting ends and a flat top. From the Dutch-settled farmlands to the south this appearance is even more marked. "Pyngyp" is another colloquial name, and good sailor's slang, according to Mr. Vermeule. "Pijngjip," pronounced "pingyp," is an onomatopoeic marine term in the language of the Zuyder Zee, which means the slatting or cracking sound as the boom of a fore and aft rigged vessel, schooner or sloop, comes around on a tack. Pyngyp is the name of a rocky knob on the Palisades Interstate Parkway at Tiorati Brook Road. Its bare cliffs served as a steering point for Dutch skippers tacking across Haverstraw Bay against a head wind. As they neared Grassy Point on a westerly beat, and came in range of those cliffs up the valley of Tiorati Brook, they were due to "pijngjip" or go about with the usual slatting of sails and booms which sounds like the word. This explanation sounds probable and nothing better has been offered.

Animal names have been given to many places in the area. There is a Catamount Mountain, a Panther Mountain, and a Wildcat Mountain. Turkey Hill, behind Queensboro Reservoir, is called that because wild turkeys—now extinct in the Highlands—once were plentiful on it. Bear Mountain is thought to have received its name because bears once lived there, and one of the earliest mentions of it, the Richard Bradly Patent of 1743, refers to it as "Bear Hill." So also do maps used by both the Americans and British in the Revolutionary War. However, S. W. Eager in his *An Outline History of Orange County* (1847) writes that it "had its name from its bald crest." If Eager is correct, then perhaps the person who drew up the Bradly Patent, on having the name communicated to him verbally, interpreted it to mean the animal and not the condition of the mountain, and spelled it accordingly. To complicate the situation further, the people across the Hudson in Peekskill knew it by still another name—Bread Tray Mountain.

Orange and Rockland counties were occupied by Indians, who left many relics of their residence in that area, some of which are to be seen in the Bear Mountain Museum. Place names in this region may have their origin in these pre-Columbian settlements. The word Ramapo is regarded as an Indian name meaning "formed of round ponds" and hence applicable to a river where potholes occur. After the river had been so named, it would be only natural to refer to the adjacent hills as the Ramapo Plateau or more specifically the Ramapo Torne. Mr. Vermeule, however, believes it may be a corruption of a Dutch name. "Tuxedo" is a word that may be of Indian origin. It is said to be derived from *P'tauk-seet-tough,* which means "the place of bears." But it may perhaps come from "Duck Cedar," a name found on old maps of the area.

A few of the place names which the hiker will encounter, and their meanings, are:

Askoti	One side
Cohasset (Upper & Lower)	Place of pines
Kanawauke	Place of much water
Massawippa	Huron Indian maiden
Menomini (Now Silver Mine Lake)	Wild rice
Minsi	Place where stones are gathered together
Nawahunta	Trout
Oonotoukwa	Cattails
Sebago	Big water
Skannatati	The other side
Skenonto	Deer
Stahahe	Stones in the water
Te-Ata	The dawn
Tiorati	Sky-like
Wanoksink	Place of sassafras

Scattered all through the Bear Mountain—Harriman Park are lakes with Indian names. These lakes are artificial and of very recent origin and their names have no connection with or relationship to the former Indian inhabitants of the Hudson Highlands. Often these arbitrarily selected names replaced earlier Anglo-Saxon names. For example, after Cedar Pond and Little Cedar Pond had been converted by damming into one much larger body of water, it was given the name of Lake Tiorati. Similarly Little Long Pond became Lake Kanawauke and Old Car Pond was renamed Lake Stahahe.

DUNDERBERG SCENIC RAILWAY

This uncompleted and abandoned scenic venture is one of the curiosities of the Highlands. Walkers over Dunderberg Mountain, on the Ramapo-Dunderberg Trail, or on old roads that climb the

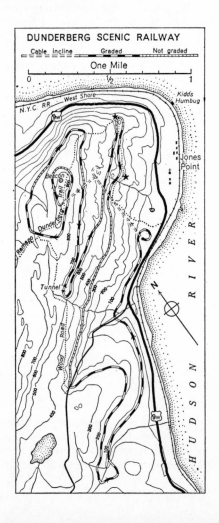

sides of the mountain, come upon sections of the grade of a railway which can be followed for stretches as long as a mile. But each section ends abruptly and gives the casual walker little impression of a unified scheme. The whole "railway" can be explored in a day by bushwacking from one section to the next, once the general plan is understood (see the illustration). The "railway" was to have consisted of a cable incline starting from the level of the Hudson River at a point about a half mile south of Jones Point and rising in two stages to the summit (926 feet), where a hotel and summer colony were projected. The descent was to be made by gravity on a winding course with gentle grades over the face of the mountain, some 10 miles in all. The southernmost of these loops approaches the road to the "Mott Farm" west of Tomkins Cove.

William Thompson Howell seems to have been the one who discovered and mapped it for the twentieth century. George Goldthwaite located the original prospectus and description in engineering journals of 1890, when the work started, and Priscilla Chipman filled out the account from other contemporary sources. An enterprising promoter, H. J. Mumford of Mauch Chunk, Pennsylvania, who was doing well operating a similar switchback there, conceived the scheme as another moneymaker, nearer New York, and, to quote his prospectus, "the toiling millions who take an outing in the summer." A company was incorporated in 1889 and work went on during 1890 and part of 1891. But these years were the beginning of a grave depression and money gave out. The work was stopped suddenly. Those who had put their money into the venture lost it. Workmen rioted when payrolls were not met. Thus the "railway" remains as we see it today, grown up to trees.

The map was compiled by plotting the details from Howell's map on the Peekskill sheet of the Army Engineers map, 1:25:000. Note in the upper right-hand corner of the map "Kidd's Humbug." This refers to the supposed landing place of Captain Kidd, when he and his men came ashore to bury treasure in the hills to the west. The so-called Spanish Mine near the Ramapo-Dunderberg Trail on the west side of Black Mountain is reputed to have been the location of this treasure. The story continues that it was removed later by a few men who left the bones of one of their number behind them.

GEOLOGY, FAUNA, AND FLORA

The Highlands of the Hudson and their extension southwesterly into the Ramapo Mountains along the New York–New Jersey border, in which 51,000 acres of the Park are now located, constitute one of the most picturesque topographic features of the eastern states. The bedrock is among the oldest of geological record, all Precambrian in age, and includes greatly metamorphosed sandstones, shales, and limestones known as the Greenville Series, but is mostly composed of high-grade metamorphic rock, known as the Highlands Complex. Subsequent invasions of granitic magma late in the Precambrian, some 700 to 800 million years ago, have considerably complicated the geology. The banded gneisses display extreme metamorphism of the older sedimentaries, and, in part, flow structures in the invading molten rock. The Highlands probably were once more than 10,000 feet high but most of their mass has since eroded away within the past 600 to 700 million years. The present hills are the remnants of what was a mountain system comparable to the present-day Rockies. Standing above the sea since the close of the Precambrian, the Highlands constitute one of the oldest land masses in North America.

Among the striking evidences of the most recent episode of continental glaciation in Harriman Park are the abundant glaciated rock surfaces, which are polished, scratched, and grooved, and the many immense erratic boulders transported by ice from the Catskills and elsewhere to the north.

The Bear Mountain and Harriman parks harbor a wide range of plant and animal life. Twenty-four species of reptiles, two hundred and forty-six species of birds, and thirty-nine species of mammals have been recorded. Ninety-four species of birds nest in the area.

Among the larger mammals deer, raccoon, woodchuck, and squirrel probably are the most often seen, although otter, mink, beaver, and wildcat are present in limited numbers. Because of the varied habitat —the brackish Iona Island marsh at sea level in the Hudson River to the mountainous interior reaching 1400 feet, with twenty-eight lakes and numerous swamps, open fields, hemlock forests, and hardwood ridges—amateur students of ornithology, botany, and ecology find the area of great interest.

Of the five hundred kinds of trees in the United States, many are found in the Park. Some of the principal evergreens are cedar, spruce, hemlock, balsam, and pine. The deciduous (leaf-bearing) varieties include oak, maple, hickory, ash, tulip, beech, tamarack, sour gum, and sweet gum. Among the shrubs are laurel, rhododendron, witch hazel, spice bush, wild azalea, sweet pepper bush, alder, blueberry, and sumac. In addition to the well-known flowers of meadow and forest, the watchful hiker will find many others less known and even rare. Numerous ferns, mosses, and lichens grow throughout the Park.

IRON MINES IN THE HUDSON HIGHLANDS

The abandoned shafts, pits, and dumps of old iron mines are among the most fascinating features of the Highlands and the Harriman Park today. There were over twenty mines that were worked at one time or another. The iron is of probable igneous origin, having been possibly a part of an upwelling of molten rock that affected the older rock formations. Mining began in Colonial times, about 1730, and at the height of the industry, at the time of the Civil War, the industry controlled the life of the region and supported a sizable population.

With all the historical emphasis that has been given to the Boston Tea Party and the stamp taxes, it is not always realized that one of the chief reasons for dissatisfaction in the Colonies was the policy of the ministers of King George III, who permitted the mining of iron but refused to allow Americans to manufacture it into articles of common use. The law required that the iron must be shipped to England in pigs as they came from the charcoal furnaces, and there made into bars, cutlery, nails, pots, pans, and so forth, then reshipped to America, with duty being collected both ways. Iron manufactures, therefore, were "bootlegged" in hidden "slitting mills," as they were called, and a source of graft enjoyed by colonial administrators was to conceal these mills, when properly "fixed," against discovery by agents of the Crown and consequent forced demolition or confiscation.

The largest and by far the most important mine was the Forest of Dean, which was first opened about 1754 by Vincent Mathews. On land now belonging to the U. S. Military Academy, and with the opening filled in, the mine can no longer be located. It was last worked in November 1931.

Another mine, with a name going back to the operations of one of the most remarkable characters of our colonial history, is the Hasenclever, south of Lake Tiorati on the wood road leading south toward Welch Lake. It is named for "Baron" Peter Hasenclever, a German industrial adventurer. Backed by English capital, Hasenclever came to America in 1764 looking for opportunities for profitable investments, and decided that iron ores offered the best field. He obtained patents or grants of forest and ore lands covering over 100,000 acres from the colonial governments of New York, New Jersey, and Nova Scotia. Between 1764 and 1768 he brought to the area—from Germany—hundreds of iron miners and artificers, charcoal burners and other workmen, with their families. They settled around his mines and furnaces, and some of their descendants remain in these regions today. Starting at Ringwood, New Jersey, Hasenclever extended his operations to Charlotteburg, New Jersey, and to Long Pond (Hewitt), New Jersey, and into New York in the Hudson Highlands and the Mohawk Valley.

Hasenclever was soon making plenty of iron of good quality and shipping it to England; if his luck had held he might have become a Colonial Andrew Carnegie. His works were all of the best and he introduced the newest English and German methods, which greatly improved output. He built sturdy roads to his mines, some of which survive in present-day highways, while others, long abandoned and hidden in the forest, attest his expansive operations. He damned streams to make lakes and changed the face of nature considerably. He put a dam at Greenwood Lake (formerly Long Pond) to supply power for operating his furnaces in that area. He dammed Tuxedo Lake and made it overflow south into Ringwood Creek for a time, to add to his water power at Ringwood Manor. In the Highlands he dammed what were the two Cedar Ponds into one, although after his failure they reverted to two. (A century and a half later Major Welch, as General Manager and Chief Engineer of the Palisades Interstate Park, dammed them again on the same line as Hasenclever's dam of 1767, to form the present Lake Tiorati.)

Difficulties caused by overextension of his business, failure to receive payment from England for his iron, and the general disturbance of international trade as unrest grew in the Colonies led Hasenclever to suffer one of the biggest "crashes" of his time. He returned to England in 1769 and later to Germany. While in London he was declared an absconding bankrupt, but that he was not severely blamed by intelligent public opinion here is indicated by Benjamin Franklin's effort after the war to persuade him to return to America to redevelop the iron industry.

While in London, Hasenclever wrote a pamphlet defending his course in America, a copy of which is in the New York State Library in Albany. Robert Erskine, a Scottish civil engineer, was brought over by Hasenclever's creditors to try to straighten out his iron business at Ringwood. He operated the mines there and built the first Ringwood Manor House. When the Colonies revolted Erskine took sides with his adopted country. Ringwood became one of the chief "munitions works" for the Americans and much of Washington's maneuvering in northern New Jersey after the fall of New York was designed to defend Ringwood and keep it hidden in the forests. The second of the great iron chains across the Hudson, that at West Point, was made of metal from the Long Mine near Sterling Lake.

In 1777 Erskine was appointed Surveyor General to the American Army and made the first good maps of the Highlands of northern New Jersey and southern New York. A full set of these is preserved in the library of the New York Historical Society.

After Erskine's early death the property passed to others; in 1853 it was purchased by Peter Cooper, the New York philanthropist, and from him it passed to his son-in-law, the great ironmaster, Abram Hewitt, whose descendants, Erskine Hewitt and his nephew, Norvin H. Green, gave the Manor House, and later 579 acres around it, to the State of New Jersey. It is now maintained as a public park— Ringwood Manor State Park. The Manor House and the fine formal gardens developed by Mrs. Hewitt are a fascinating museum of life from 1775 to the 1930s and of the early iron industry. It is most easily reached by road up Eagle Valley, about 4 miles west of Sloatsburg, just over the state line into New Jersey.

About 1 mile east of the Manor House at Ringwood are located the Ringwood group of mines; the largest and most prominent were the Peters and the Cannon. The Peters was probably opened shortly after Cornelius Board moved to Ringwood in 1740 and erected the first ironworks there. The shaft was last worked in 1954, after having been reopened and reconditioned by the government during World War II. There were over fifteen mines in the Ringwood group. Today some of them are being filled in and will soon disappear.

WALKS IN THE MINES REGION

A separate section of the Park is located about 4 miles westward on the Wanaque River, close to Hewitt. Going west through Hewitt on the highway to Greenwood Lake, turn off to the right on the dirt road that lies a few yards past "Ye Olde Country Store" building, and soon turn right again after passing over a little stream. At the dead end of this dirt road is the location of the old Long Pond iron furnace, first developed by Hasenclever and continued by Erskine, and those of two later furnaces erected by Abram Hewitt just prior to and during the Civil War. The ruins of the latter two furnaces have been standing for years plainly visible, as have the two 25-foot water wheels, burned by vandals in June 1957 and now mere skeletons compared to their original appearance. The ruins of the Hasenclever furnace were discovered in a mound covered with leaves in 1956 and were excavated in 1967.

Famous now for its gardens, Sterling Forest is a region known for its place in the history of early mining and smelting. A considerable part of this property is owned by the City Investing Company (permission for hiking may be granted to a group on request). Long abandoned and overgrown roads cross it. The remains of over twenty old mines and several furnaces are on the Sterling property. Several of the mine shafts have been filled in and closed. Sterling Mine, one of those that can no longer be seen, was opened in 1750 and closed shortly after 1900; its shaft sloped nearly 1000 feet under Sterling Lake. Just to the north of it can still be seen the water-filled opening of the lake mine shaft which goes down a distance of 3800 feet on the slope, far out under the lake. This was the principal producer from 1900 to 1921 when it closed down along with the other Sterling workings. The concrete headframe still stands at Scott Mine. Near the Red Back Mine, whose ore was high in sulfur, may still be seen the ruins of the huge cast-iron roaster, twenty feet high, in which the sulfur was burned out. Still farther north near Rt. 17A lie the extensive workings of the Alice Mine. Southwest ridges are faced on their west sides by steep rugged cliffs, hidden in dense forest and invisible from any outside point but striking to come upon in this little visited region.

The northern part of this country west of the Ramapos is best entered from Rt. 17 (by bus from Port of New York Authority terminal to Southfields), then west along the Orange Turnpike past the ruins of the old Southfields iron furnace and north toward Mombasha Lake and Monroe. Two old roads, closed to vehicles, lead south (left) from this to Rt. 17A on the northern boundary of the closed area. The Appalachian Trail in this region goes almost east-west, and the Orange Turnpike and each of its two branches to the north (right) cross it at convenient distances for circular walks from Southfields and Arden. The Southfields furnace had a high double arch supporting the charging bridge. The furnace was erected during 1805–1806, and was dismantled and rebuilt in 1839. This second furnace had its last blast in 1887. It was owned by Peter Townsend, who with his sons also owned the Sterling Ironworks for a long period.

The great dark chamber of the Bradley Mine, on the south face of Bradley Mountain about 6 miles east of Arden station on the Erie or 2 miles west of Lake Tiorati, is impressive both in summer, when it is filled with black water in its lower shafts and hung with mosses and liverworts, and in winter, when its entrance is barred with a palisade of thirty-foot icicles and its frozen water surface is studded

Queensboro Furnace

with eerie ice stalagmites. The Surebridge Mines (two great open pits in the woods south of Upper Cohasset Lake), the Pine Swamp Mines on the south side of Fingerboard Mountain (the largest left as a slanting chamber), and the Hogencamp Mines on the east side of the mountain of that name, north of Kanawauke Lake, are among the largest of these old workings. Others are scattered throughout the region. One of the largest, Bull Mine, east of Schunemunk, is described in Chapter 5.

The Greenwood Ironworks, at Arden, consisted of the Greenwood charcoal furnace built in 1811 by James Cunningham, and the Clove anthracite furnace erected by Robert and Peter Parrott in 1854. The Greenwood furnace lies in ruins in the ravine at the outlet of Echo Lake, and the Clove furnace is about 200 yards east of the Arden railroad station and the New York Thruway. Tens of thousands of tons of magnetite ore from the Bradley, Surebridge, Hogencamp, Pine Swamp, Garfield, Boston, and other mines east and west of the Ramapo valley were smelted in these furnaces during the Civil War. The pigs were shipped by rail to Cornwall-on-Hudson where they were ferried across the river to the West Point foundry at Cold Spring to be made into the famous Parrott guns and shells. The two Parrott brothers were Peter, who operated the mines and furnace, and Robert, who designed and made the guns and projectiles.

During the period 1861–1865, Arden was a little Pittsburgh with a population of over two thousand engaged in the mining of ore, the production of charcoal fuel, and the smelting and shipping of pigs and blooms. The woods in the western part of the Highlands were filled with the homes and hamlets of the workers. There was a village of twenty houses and a school at the Hogencamp Mines. Foundations of a considerable number of houses can still be traced near the Pine Swamp Mine by the side of the Dunning Trail.

Another center of the early iron industry which will interest walkers in the Highlands is the old Orange (or Queensboro) Furnace built about 1784, on the dirt road leading north from Queensboro Circle on the Seven Lakes Parkway. About three quarters of a mile downstream from the furnace is the site of the Queensboro Forge. The furnace was last worked in 1800, whereas the forge was active as late as 1843. The Orange Furnace is the center of a remarkable network of old roads, which may still be traced. Ore and charcoal were conveyed to the furnace by ox team over considerable distances.

Smelting with coal replaced smelting with charcoal. The iron deposits of Pennsylvania and the Great Lakes region, so much more easily mined than those in the Highlands, although not so rich in high quality metal, were exploited. Thus the New York–New Jersey industry declined and by 1890 had almost completely disappeared. The inhabitants drifted away from the region where there was no more work, leaving houses to fall into the cellar holes still visible along many old roads now overgrown. Apple trees, lilac bushes, and old-fashioned flowers remain as occasional mementoes of these homes. The orange-red day lily (*Hemerocallis fulva*) is one of the most common of these garden relics and has survived longest, although it was an importation from Europe which originated in Asia. It is strange to find the lily, perhaps a last survivor of this vanished horticulture, defiant after other adventitious species have been suffocated by the increasing density of the shade of the persistent native trees and shrubs which are recapturing the ground the pioneers cleared.

TRAILS IN THE BEAR MOUNTAIN– HARRIMAN PARKS

Anthony Wayne Trail. Length: 2.7 miles. Blazes: white.

This trail, a loop from Popolopen Gorge Trail at Turkey Hill Lake to Timp-Torne Trail on the west end of West Mountain, is named for "Mad Anthony" Wayne, a hero of the American Revolution. The trail does not follow the route over which Wayne and his troops marched to attack Stony Point in 779, but it does cross it on the Palisades Parkway at the Anthony Wayne Recreation Area. Before the construction of the Parkway in the early 1950s it was possible for a walker to follow the old road used by the soldiers. Now, however, almost all traces of it have vanished.

Hikers from Bear Mountain may walk this trail in a circular trip. Auto travelers can park at the small picnic area just south of Long Mountain traffic circle on Seven Lakes Drive, which the trail passes. The trail between Seven Lakes Drive and Turkey Hill Lake is fairly level. East of the Drive the trail goes down and over Palisades Parkway and then through the Anthony Wayne Recreation Area to an old road, which it follows to the left a short distance; it then turns off to the right over the shoulder of West Mountain. The Timp-Torne Trail here comes in from the right and the two coincide to Seven Lakes Drive, where Anthony Wayne Trail ends. The Timp-Torne continues on.

Appalachian Trail. Length: from Bear Mountain to Rt. 17, 16.3 miles. Blazes: white.

This section of the AT connects with the following trails in the Park: Major Welch, Suffern-Bear Mountain, Timp-Torne, Ramapo-Dunderberg, Fingerboard-Torne, Hurst, and Arden Surebridge. For details, consult the *Guide to the Appalachian Trail in New York and New Jersey.*

The Appalachian Trail extends two thousand miles from Mount Katahdin in Maine to Springer Mountain in Georgia. The proposal for such a trail was made by Benton Mackaye in 1921. It was completed in 1937, through the efforts of hiking clubs and other volunteers from Maine to Georgia. By act of Congress in 1968 it became one of the first of two National Scenic Trails, to be kept forever as a footpath. (The second trail included in this act is the Pacific Crest. Others are under consideration.)

In the Park the AT crosses nine summits. The diamond-shaped metal marker that is sometimes seen along the trail was designed by Major Welch, General Manager and Engineer of the Park.

Arden-Surebridge Trail. Length: 5 miles. Blazes: red triangle on white.

This trail extends from Arden station on the Erie-Lackawanna Railroad to Seven Lakes Parkway near the southwest corner of Lake Tiorati. It connects with the Appalachian Trail, Long Path, Lichen, Ramapo-Dunderberg, Dunning, and Red Cross trails. A perusal of the map will show that several circular walks can be combined from these trails.

The A-SB runs southward from Arden station to New Arden Road, the route paralleling the railroad tracks. This road is the Harriman Entrance to the Bear Mountain–Harriman Park from Rt. 17. Cars may be parked in a rough clearing south of the road and east of the bridge over the Thruway. Buses from the Port Authority terminal will discharge passengers at the Harriman Entrance. Across the tracks from the station is the old Greenwood Furnace.

After crossing the railroad and the bridge over the Thruway, the AT diverges to the right (southeast over Green Pond Mountain) and the A-SB continues along the paved road until, opposite a farm gate, it leaves the paved road and follows an old track to the right into the woods for about a half mile before it once again meets New Arden Road, which it crosses; it then goes over a short stretch of rocky swamp, crosses the road once more, and, after crossing the rather obscure "Crooked Road," begins the steep ascent of Island Pond Mountain. On the summit (a fine view), it joins the AT again. Here also is the route of the Long Path. This is the only place in the Park where three trails coincide for any distance. All three follow this route southwesterly over the mountain to, and through, the curious rock formation known as the Lemon Squeezer. Sometime during the last great continental ice sheet, or after it melted approximately eleven thousand years ago, the rocks cracked and tumbled. One, coming to rest on the parent body, formed a triangular tunnel; another, parting slightly from the bedrock, formed a narrow crevice.

Once through the Lemon Squeezer the Arden-Surebridge Trail turns left (east). The trail now goes over faint old wood roads and in a short distance crosses the southern end of Dismal Swamp, a grassy clearing with dead trees here and there. Further on it passes the northern end of the Lichen Trail, in a dense growth of rhododendron. It then continues through a picturesque arching tunnel of rhododendron and through a stand of hemlock to the Surebridge Mine Road, over which, during the Civil War, ore was hauled by horses and oxen to the Greenwood Furnace at Arden. Here it turns right and shortly crosses the Ramapo-Dunderberg Trail at a trail junction identified by a stone fireplace beside a boulder. Care must be taken to stay on the chosen path, since both trails are marked in red. About a half mile farther on, the A-SB crosses a brook. Dunning Trail (yellow blaze) begins here. Continuing past the tailings and pits of several abandoned mines, the trail follows a fire lane to its eastern terminus at Seven Lakes Parkway, crossing Pine Swamp Mountian's northern shoulder on the way. The Red Cross Trail begins on the opposite (east) side of the Parkway.

Blue Disc Trail. Length: 3.8 miles. Blazes: blue.

This trail connects Pine Meadow Trail (at Seven Lakes Parkway and Johnstown Road) with the Ramapo-Dunderberg Trail at the foot of Black Ash Mountain. The first blaze is on a telephone pole at the junction of Seven Lakes Parkway and Johnstown Road. It goes along Johnstown Road to the first road diverging left. Here the trail leaves the road and climbs up Sleater Hill to a power line, which it briefly follows. Leaving the power line, it crosses Kakiat Trail and ascends steeply, skirting the hill known as Almost Perpendicular; continues north along a ridge, descends gradually to squeeze between two boulders and under a small cliff to reach a stream. The trail follows the stream up and past a swamp and crosses the Tuxedo– Mt. Ivy Trail at Claudius Smith's Den, then continues north to its terminus at the place known as Tri-trail Corners. Here three trails meet: Victory, Ramapo-Dunderberg, and the Blue Disc.

Breakneck Mountain Trail. Length: 1.6 miles. Blazes: white.

Connects the Tuxedo–Mt. Ivy Trail and the Long Path south of Breakneck Pond with the Suffern–Bear Mountain Trail on the ridge east of the north end of the pond. The beginning of this trail is 0.1 mile east of Pine Meadow Road east on the Tuxedo–Mt. Ivy Trail. It climbs and winds gradually over Breakneck Mountain and, in 0.2 mile, passes a large boulder called West Pointing Rock. A sharp projection on its west side accounts for its name. A short distance beyond there is a fine view north. The radio relay tower on Jackie Jones Mountain also can be seen. Here, on the exposed bedrock, rests a boulder split in two, a reminder of the great ice sheet that once covered the land and left many such rocks in its wake as it melted back. From this point the trail descends steeply, then continues north to its terminus at the S-BM Trail and Red Arrow Trail. Big Hill Shelter is 0.8 mile north on the S-BM Trail. There is no water at the shelter.

Conklin's Crossing Trail. Length: 0.65 mile. Blazes: white.

A short cutoff from the Pine Meadow Trail to the Suffern–Bear Mountain Trail. The chief value of this trail is to shorten the distance from Pine Meadow Lake to Suffern for anyone using the S-BM Trail south to Suffern. From the Pine Meadow Trail near the eastern end of Pine Meadow Lake, turn right and cross a fairly level woods to the S-BM Trail on the crest of the rampart near a tremendous boulder. Left (north) on S-BM 0.3 mile is the E. D. Stone Memorial Shelter. The S-BM right (south) leads to Suffern.

Crown Ridge Trail. Length: about 5 miles. Blazes: blue.

This trail branches north from the Timp-Torne Trail near the summit of Popolopen Torne and runs along the crest of scenic Crown Ridge to Rt. 9W west of the town of Highland Falls. Nearly all of the trail lies within the West Point Military Reservation; for this reason, the public was excluded during World War II and for many years thereafter. In 1966, however, the trail became available to groups on request. (Write to: Office Services, Engineering Dept., U.S.M.A., West Point, N.Y. The permit must be picked up on the day of the hike.) The area is covered by the U.S.G.S. "Peekskill" and "Popolopen Lake" sheets, though the trail is not delineated.

The Crown Ridge Trail affords a succession of fine views of the Hudson Valley, extending from the Fishkill Range in a northerly direction to the Dunderberg massif in the south. For the most rewarding views, the trail is best walked in seasons when the trees are bare. Although the trail traverses many completely open ridges and summits, there are considerable stretches where views may be obscured by leafy growth in the growing season. At the same time, a winter traverse in snow is to be discouraged, as the footway is steep and rough in places. Drinking water is scarce at any season.

The southern end of the Crown Ridge Trail is best reached by ascending the steep eastern flank of Popolopen Torne, using the Timp-Torne Trail. (This trail may be picked up either at its terminus on Rt. 9W just north of Popolopen Bridge, or, to make the walk 1 mile shorter, at the point where it crosses the blacktop Mine Road which runs west from Fort Montgomery.) At the crest of the ridge, the first blue blazes of the Crown Ridge Trail will be found leading to the right (north), just where the Timp-Torne makes a left turn (south) to climb the few remaining feet to the top of the Torne. It is recommended that this short side trip be made before starting north on the Crown Ridge Trail, for the sake of seeing the sweeping panorama from the summit.

Returning to the beginning of the Crown Ridge Trail, follow it north along the ridge crest, which dips briefly into a notch; the trail then climbs about 300 feet to a wooded summit, and passes an open ledge with extensive views. Note the occasional masonry piers along the trail in this section, marking the eastern boundary of the West

Up the Hudson from West Point with snow on the Highland slopes

Point Reservation. A short descent brings the trail to an old roadway, which it follows to the right (east) for a few paces before leaving it to turn uphill to the left (north) once more. The trail now continues north, almost immediately making two crossings of a bulldozed military track (watch for the blazes), after which there are no further roadways or branch trails. A series of small summits are passed, with occasional view points.

A 250-foot ascent from a swamp leads to the summit ridge of Bare Rock Mountain, 1 mile long and largely open ridge, offering spectacular and constantly changing views. This is the exhilarating finale of the Crown Ridge Trail; a sharp descent to the right (east) from the last open ledge leads to a wood road, along which the trail turns left (north) to its terminus at Rt. 9W.

The entire walk, starting from Popolopen Bridge and including the side trip to the top of Popolopen Torne, with time out for lunch, rests, and views, can be done in six hours without undue effort. Public transportation is available via bus, from the Port Authority Terminal in Manhattan, to Bear Mountain Inn and Highland Falls Village, the nearest access points by this means of travel. An extra mile of road walking must be added at each end of the trip to make connections. Groups using private cars may park on a side road just north of Popolopen Bridge ("Old 9W"), forking west from 9W, or on Mine Road near the Timp-Torne Trail crossing. Parking may present difficulties eventually, as more residences are erected along the road. The northern end of the trail offers no convenient parking spot, since barrier fences prohibit use of the shoulders of Rt. 9W. A satisfactory solution, however, is to park in the town of Highland Falls (turn sharp right from 9W approximately 4 miles north of

Bear Mountain Bridge, and follow the blacktop road 0.8 mile to Highland Falls, passing Highland Falls Water Co. installations). Park at the first available curb location. Route 9W, and the end of the Crown Ridge Trail, are now immediately above, up a steep wooded embankment which can easily be negotiated on foot.

Deep Hollow Shelter Trail. Length: 0.7 mile. Blazes: white.

A loop from and to the Long Mountain-Torne Trail on Long Mountain, this trail coincides with the Long Path from its junction with the Long Mountain–Torne Trail to the shelter (latrine and pipe spring water supply). It then climbs steeply right (east) straight up to terminate at the Long Mountain–Torne Trail.

Diamond Mountain Trail. Length: 0.4 mile. Blazes: white.

Connects the Pine Meadow Trail with the Seven Hills Trail and Hillburn-Torne-Sebago Trail. It starts west of the Pine Meadow Lake dam and coincides for a short distance with the Pine Meadow Trail, leaving the latter after crossing Christy Brook where Tower Trail diverges north. The trail then ascends steeply up Diamond Mountain with views over the country to the east. The trail ends on top of the mountain at the point where Seven Hills Trail and Hillburn-Sebago-Torne Trail coincide.

Dunning Trail. Length: 3.4 miles. Blazes: yellow.

From the Nurian Trail on Stahahe Mountain to the Arden-Surebridge Trail at the crossing of Pine Swamp Brook. Also connects with Ramapo-Dunderberg Trail, Long Path, and Skannatati trails.

This is as interesting and varied a trail as any in the park. It was opened and blazed by Dr. J. M. Dunning, a member of the New York Chapter of the Appalachian Mountain Club. It gives access to several of the old mines and can also be used in combination with several other trails to form a circuit. From Southfields follow the Nurian Trail for two miles to the top of Green Pond Mountain. Here the yellow marking begins, going southeast from the summit to touch Green Pond, a small body of water with a rocky, precipitous north shore over which the trail winds. Most of the pond's shoreline it rimmed with thick vegetation. From Green Pond the trail goes east, and, just before reaching Island Pond Road, crosses the Nurian Trail. It then follows Island Pond Road left (north) 100 yards, turns east 50 yards to Boston Mine, which is a water-filled cavern, climbs up the north side of the mine opening and then goes eastward

0.5 mile to the Long Path, with which it coincides for 0.3 mile. The old wood road that is followed is the "Crooked Road." The Long Path north to the AT also follows this old road. The Dunning Trail leaves the Long Path where the latter turns north (left). About 0.5 mile farther on, Ramapo-Dunderberg crosses on the ridge of Hogencamp Mountain. Dunning continues slightly downward and northeast. It suddenly turns right and down to a washed out old mine road in a ravine, which it follows a short distance south and then turns sharp left around a large rock in the rear of which is a cave. Here the trail, still following the ravine road, goes along the steep south slope of the mountain. Here, too, it passes over one of the shafts of Hogencamp Mine. Be careful! The shaft is close to the trail! A few hundred feet beyond may be traced foundations of buildings from the mining days. In a few hundred yards, the trail descends to another old road (where Skannatati Trail turns to the right) and goes left (northeast) on it, passing the west side of Pine Swamp, which it follows for 0.5 mile. Pine Swamp Mine is on the left, but the mine entrance cannot be seen from the trail. Look for a pile of mine tailings to the left of the trail, from which it is a short climb to the entrance. The trail continues to follow the old road past the mine for about 0.3 mile until it reaches its terminus at the Arden-Surebridge Trail.

Hillburn-Torne-Sebago Trail. Length: 4.7 miles. Blazes: white.
From the T-MI Trail at Lake Sebago dam to Ramapo Torne. The trail follows the brook south from the dam, crosses TMI and joins Stony Brook Trail, with which it coincides for some 400 feet, and then turns east (left) up Diamond Mountain in a steep and rocky climb. Near the top is a good lookout over Lake Sebago. On top the Seven Hills Trail joins it and the two coincide for 0.3 mile, past the junction (left) of Diamond Hill Mountain Trail, to the high point of Diamond Mountain. It then descends 200 feet, turns sharp right (west), leaving the Seven Hills Trail, and continues over Halfway Mountain to Pine Meadow Brook, joins Kakiat Trail, turns left with it a few feet and crosses the brook on a bridge above the Cascade of Slid. About 300 feet upstream (left) it meets the Pine Meadow Trail, coincides with it for a few hundred feet, then turns right, uphill to where Seven Hills comes in from the left. The two coincide a short distance and then divide, the HTS diverging left to cross the Raccoon Brook Hills Trail. After rounding the steep east slope of the mountain, the trail passes the rock formation known as the Russian Bear and descends into a hollow where it crosses a brook. Ascending the opposite slope, HTS rejoins the Seven Hills Trail.

The two coincide left (south) 0.3 mile to where Seven Hills diverges right and HTS continues along the ridge top about a 0.3 mile to its terminus at Ramapo Torne.

Hurst Trail. Length: 0.5 mile. Blazes: blue.

Connects Seven Lakes Drive with AT and R-D trails, where the latter coincide on Fingerboard Mountain. Fingerboard Shelter is at its western end (no water supply). This trail once extended west of Fingerboard Mountain to New Arden Road, but that section is no longer maintained. The entire route is uphill from Seven Lakes Drive, on the west shore of Lake Tiorati, being a gentle climb of about 200 feet from the Drive to the Shelter, with good footing most of the way.

Kakiat Trail. Length: 7.2 miles. Blazes: white.

Although this trail, from Tuxedo railroad station to Rt. 202, touches no high or open viewpoints, there is a considerable variety of terrain along its route. It is named from one of the oldest land grants on the east side of the Ramapos. Kakiat is a corruption or contraction of the Indian word "Kackyacktaweke," which appears on the land grant patent of 1696, referring to the land purchased from the Indians and confirmed by patent from King William III.

Leave Tuxedo by crossing the Ramapo River on a footbridge 250 yards south of the station and, crossing under the Thruway, turn south through Tuxedo's eastern suburb. In about 100 yards, at the end of the paved road, the trail leads off into the woods and soon follows a wood road eastward around Daters Mountain, crossing Blue Disc Trail at the base of Almost Perpendicular. At about 2.3 miles the trail crosses Seven Lakes Parkway and circles to the south around a ridge and down to a bridge across Stony Brook. It then turns left on the old road along the brook up to Pine Meadow Brook, crosses on another bridge, and makes a sharp right along the north bank of Pine Meadow Brook, while the Stony Brook Trail goes straight. The going here is quite rugged, over and around very large boulders along the ravine.

At the Cascade of Slid watch for the Frank Place memorial tablet on a tree overlooking the cascade. (Place was a pioneer trail walker and one of the authors of the first edition of the *New York Walk Book.*) A little farther on is a junction with the Hillburn-Torne-Sebago Trail, and shortly after that a junction with the Seven Hills Trail. Here the Kakiat Trail and Seven Hills Trail cross Pine Meadow Brook over a bridge, the former turning sharp left and the latter (marked blue) going straight. Kakiat continues east and then southeast up a tributary stream, passes Raccoon Brook Hill Trail (black on white blaze) twice and winds about until it crosses the Suffern–Bear Mountain Trail on Cobus Mountain at the 6-mile mark, then goes down the mountain through a hollow to cross the Mahwah River and terminate at Rt. 202 at the crossing of the gas pipeline and clearing.

Lichen Trail. Length: 0.5 mile. Blazes: blue.

This trail connects Arden-Surebridge and Ramapo-Dunderberg trails. Its southern end is 6.1 miles from Tuxedo on the R-D Trail; the northern end is 3.1 miles from Arden on the ASB. The trail was marked by Frank Place in 1933, and is named for the lichens found on the rocks along its route.

Starting from the north end at the A-SB Trail, the Lichen climbs Hogencamp Mountain, through a hemlock grove, ascending about 100 feet in elevation before leveling off somewhat on the summit. It then follows the mountain top, over ice-smoothed ledges and between clumps of pitch pine, dipping and climbing slightly until it meets the R-D Trail on a flat area of exposed bedrock. Along the way are wide views over the country to the west, including Island Pond and the hills beyond the Ramapo Valley, toward Greenwood Lake. It is convenient as a short cut between the R-D and the A-SB.

Long Mountain–Torne Trail. Length: 3.2 miles. Blazes: blue.

From Popolopen Gorge Trail near Deep Hollow Shelter to Popolopen Torne. This trail follows the northern section of the discontinued Fingerboard-Torne Trail. Only the first quarter mile is on Park property, the remainder being mostly on the grounds of the United States Military Academy, and permission is required to walk there. Because of this restriction, and because rerouting of the trail on the Reservation may be necessary in the near future, no description of the section in the Reservation is given here. From the junction of the Popolopen Gorge Trail and the Deep Hollow Shelter Trail, Long Mountain–Torne Trail goes north up the slope of Long Mountain, with at least one good outlook southward, and, after attaining the ridge, soon passes the Torrey Memorial, from which spot there is a fine view east. (Raymond Torrey was one of the authors of the original *New York Walk Book.*) Continuing along the ridge, the trail dips into a saddle and passes the Deep Hollow Shelter Trail coming up the hill from the west. This connecting link may be followed to the shelter and the Long Path. A short distance beyond this point the Long Mountain–Torne Trail crosses the wide firebreak that marks the military reservation boundary. As already stated, permission is required to continue east of this point.

Long Path. Blazes: blue.

The section of this trail considered here is that which runs from Mt. Ivy on the Park's eastern border west and north to Route 293 and Long Mountain Parkway. The distance between these two points is 25.5 miles. The total length of this trail, when the northern end in the Adirondacks is completed, will be 416 miles. The southern terminus is the George Washington Bridge.

From Mt. Ivy the route of this trail and the Tuxedo–Mt. Ivy Trail coincide to Dutch Doctor Shelter. The first two miles are over paved roads. Follow the blazes west along Route 202 until, in about 0.8 mile, they diverge to the right down another road. In about 1 mile, at Ladentown Church, the trail swings right down Mountain Road toward the hills. In a short distance the pavement ends and the trail continues on through the woods and up the mountain. Near the summit the Red Arrow Trail meets it on the right (begins here) and the Long Path and Tuxedo–Mt. Ivy Trail begin a swing southwestward and shortly cross the Suffern–Bear Mountain Trail. About 1 mile farther on the Breakneck Mountain Trail branches off to the right (begins here) and, a hundred yards or so farther west, the Long Path and Tuxedo–Mt. Ivy Trail cross Pine Meadow Road East, beyond which they wind over low ridges and through rocky hollows for about 0.5 mile, cross Pine Meadow Road West and skirt the slope of Conklin Mountain, ascending gradually. Shortly after crossing Pine Meadow Road West, they pass near Monitor Rock, continue on, gradually climbing, until they cross Seven Hills Trail. Beyond this point the way is downhill to Seven Lakes Drive, where the roadway is used to cross the dam of Lake Sebago. The trails then turn westward into the woods, follow the shore of the lake, cross a wood road, and climb over the hill to Dutch Doctor Shelter. At this point the T-MI diverges left (west) and the Long Path from here north to the Appalachian Trail at Island Pond follows the route of the former White Bar Trail. The White Bar is no longer an official trail. It was once part of a series of trails laid out in 1920–23 around the Boy Scout camp at Lake Kanawauke.

From Dutch Doctor Shelter, the trail winds north and northwest, skirts some swamps, crosses Victory Trail and White Cross Trail, then continues on for about 0.5 mile and crosses Ramapo-Dunder-

berg Trail, and, shortly beyond, joins the Triangle Trail, with which
it coincides for 0.2 mile. It then diverges right and goes over Hemlock Hill to Rt. 210, which it crosses. It now follows Island Pond
Road a short distance and then turns right and goes along the edge
of a ravine through which flows Stahahe Brook.

Soon the Nurian Trail comes in from the right and coincides
with the LP about 100 ft. before diverging to the left. The LP
continues north to the Dunning Trail, which comes up from a
hollow on the left. The two trails coincide for about 0.2 mile. The
Dunning then heads east and the LP leaves it to go north over
fairly level ground to its junction with the Appalachian Trail northeast of Island Pond. (Brien Memorial Shelter is 0.5 mile west on
AT.)

The LP and the AT coincide from here to Fingerboard Mountain.
The LP-AT heads east from Island Pond, climbs to that remarkable
rock formation, the Lemon Squeezer, where the Arden-Surebridge
Trail joins them from the east. The three trails then coincide to
go through the Squeezer and up Island Pond Mountain. At the top,
the A-SB diverges left and goes steeply down the hill toward Arden;
the LP-AT descends east, skirts around the north end of Dismal
Swamp, and crosses Surebridge Mountain to the old Surebridge
Mine Road and the Surebridge Mine diggings—two water-filled
holes. The old road is followed north a few hundred feet and then
the trail goes east up the steep slope of Fingerboard Mountain to
meet the Ramapo-Dunderberg Trail on the ridge.

The three trails coincide north, pass Fingerboard Shelter and the
Hurst Trail (starts here) and, about 0.5 mile north of the shelter,
the LP diverges left from the AT-RD, descends to New Arden
Road (Bradley Mine 0.1 mile left on this road), crosses it and
follows a wood road north around Bradley Mountain and along the
ridge. Shortly before reaching Stockbridge Shelter, 2.7 miles north
of New Arden Road, the curious Hippo Rock is passed. This is a
large overhanging boulder that seems to be ready to topple over.
The shelter commands a fine view south.

About 0.2 mile farther north are two small cave shelters located
in a rocky hollow. From there the trail continues north, and in
another 1.8 miles crosses the Long Mountain Parkway, a short distance beyond which it meets the junction of three trails: Deep
Hollow Shelter, Long Mountain–Torne, and Popolopen Gorge, all
three of which begin here. The LP now coincides with the Deep
Hollow Shelter Trail to the shelter, and beyond goes off on its own,
crosses the brook and follows the military reservation boundary west

up over the steep slope of Howell Mountain, named for William Thompson Howell, a pioneer trail walker of the Highlands. There is a fine view from the summit. After a descent into Brooks Hollow the trail crosses the brook and a short way beyond that passes on the right a cave large enough to shelter one or two persons during a shower. The trail then climbs steeply up over Brooks Mountain and descends to Rt. 293 in the valley.

Major Welch Trail. Length: 3.3 miles, including loop. Blazes: red.

This trail, from Bear Mountain Inn to the summit of Bear Mountain, was named in honor of Major William A. Welch in 1947.

This trail ascends Bear Mountain's north slope. It starts behind the Inn and follows the asphalt path along the western shore of Hessian Lake nearly to its north end before turning sharp left (west) into the woods. It climbs gently for a short distance, then makes another sharp left turn and begins a steep, steady ascent of about 800 feet to the summit. There are several excellent vistas along this stretch. Before reaching the summit, the trail crosses Perkins Memorial Drive. At this point the trail divides: one branch follows the drive west, then turns back to the summit over a weathered bedrock ridge. The other branch leads straight across the road to the summit. The last-mentioned is the shorter route, but less scenic.

Nurian Trail. Length: 3.3 miles. Blazes: white.

From Southfields station of the Erie-Lackawanna to the RD Trail (junction about 0.8 mile north of crossing of Rt. 210); Dunning Trail intersects at two points. Nurian Trail is named for Kerson Nurian, a member of the New York Chapter of the Adirondack Mountain Club, an indefatigable worker and walker who laid it out as a connection with the RD Trail to make an interesting 8-mile walk, with considerable climbing, from Southfields station to Tuxedo station. Although there is but one outlook point, and that with limited view, the climb up the ravine of the Island Pond outlet brook (Valley of the Boulders), past numerous falls, is one of the most attractive sections of trail in the Park.

Follow the railroad tracks north of station for about 100 yards, watching for markers leading east (right) into the woods. Shortly cross the Ramapo River on a footbridge and, a little farther on, cross the New York State Thruway on an overpass. (While the Thruway was under construction, it appeared that hikers would have access to the Park only at Arden and Tuxedo. Members of hiking clubs in the metropolitan area, under the leadership of Robert P.

Stephenson, an active member of several of these clubs, succeeded in convincing the state highway authorities that additional access was essential for fullest use of Park trails.)

On the far side of the Thruway the trail turns sharp left (north), following a dirt road for about 0.3 mile, then turns off sharply to the right (east), to begin the long ascent up the west side of Stahahe Mountain (formerly called Green Pond Mountain and still so named on some maps), passing through, on the summit, a long hollow formed by faulting of the bedrock ages ago. After descending to the north end of Lake Stahahe, and circling that end of the lake on an asphalt road, the trail makes a sharp left turn into a wood road (filterbeds to the left, in woods), which it follows about 200 yards, then turns right (east) up the ravine of the Island Pond outlet brook, climbing through an area covered with large rocks. This ravine extends for approximately 0.2 mile, and a few spots are difficult to negotiate, especially in winter. The trail turns right (south) near the head of the ravine and goes up along a rock ridge, passing an outlook point. Just beyond it meets the western terminus of the Dunning Trail (yellow blaze). The Nurian bends left and passes down and through a small valley, crossing the Dunning again, to a fire lane (Island Pond Road), which it intersects. It then leads right (south) over rolling ground for about 0.5 mile, crosses a brook and climbs the west slope of Black Rock Mountain to meet the RD Trail.

Pine Meadow Trail. Length: 6.2 miles. Blazes: red.

A cross trail from Sloatsburg to the Suffern–Bear Mountain Trail along the scenic Pine Meadow Brook. Connects with Seven Hills, Reeves Brook, Kakiat, Hillburn-Torne-Segabo, Tower, Diamond Mountain, Conklin's Crossing, and Sherwood Path trails.

From the Sloatsburg station of the Erie-Lackawanna the Pine Meadow Trail follows the tracks north for about 400 feet, then veers toward the right (east) and continues along a dirt road a short distance to Seven Lakes Drive. Here it follows the Drive east toward Lake Sebago until it turns right into the woods, parallels Seven Lakes Drive to Reeves Brook Trail, passes a clearing and swings eastward, with Stony Brook close on the left. In a couple of hundred yards it passes a spring on the right. A half mile farther it meets the former Quartz Brook Trail on the right. About here the trail leads uphill on a wood road, leaving Stony Brook to the left, and in 0.3 mile comes close to Pine Meadow Brook, here 100 feet down in a ravine. The trail continues to climb along the south bank of the brook to the splendid waterfall known as the Cascade of Slid. Above the falls the Hillburn-Torne-Sebago Trail comes in from the left, coincides with the Pine Meadow Trail for 100 yards, and then leaves at the right.

Two miles from its start, the Pine Meadow Trail, now at the level of the brook, turns left and crosses on the same log bridge which the Kakiat and the Seven Hills trails use, and then turns right and follows the north bank of the stream, curving around Diamond Mountain to pass the large boulders called Ga-nus-quah or Stone Giants, by the Indians. Here there is a rock gorge with a small cascade. Here, also, the Tower Trail begins and coincides with the Pine Meadow until the latter turns sharp right. At that point the Tower Trail goes straight ahead up the ridge. Diamond Mountain Trail starts here, too. Pine Meadow Trail continues east and crosses a gravel fire lane 50 yards north of the dam of Pine Meadow Lake. It then follows the north shore of the lake. Near the lake's eastern end it passes the site of Ramsey Conklin's cabin. This structure, built in 1778, stood until 1935. Ramsey Conklin, the last of his family to live in it, died in 1952. Beyond the cabin site the trail turns away from the lake, slightly uphill. Conklin's Crossing Trail branches right (begins here). In another quarter mile Pine Meadow Trail crosses a fire lane, Pine Meadow Road East. Sherwood Path begins here, branching right. Pine Meadow Trail then continues east across Many Swamp Brook 1 mile to the Suffern–Bear Mountain Trail.

Popolopen Gorge Trail. Length: 4.3 miles. Blazes: red vertical stripe on white.

Begins 0.2 mile north of the Bear Mountain traffic circle on Rt. 9W north of Bear Mountain Inn, generally following the southern bank of Popolopen Brook to Turkey Hill Lake. Use the asphalt footpath along the east shore of Hessian Lake to the traffic circle. Proceed north on 9W beyond the traffic circle. The trail enters woods on left (west) of Rt. 9W and leads gently downhill along a wood road to Roe Pond, where there is an old dam and falls and, across the creek, the foundation of what once was a mill. The trail continues to follow the steep southern side of the gorge, passing the area called "Hell Hole," where rocks in the brook are very picturesque in early spring, with water dashing over and around them, until a steep climb of about 100 feet brings the hiker to the Bear Mountain Aqueduct path, which it follows. After about 1 mile, the trail diverges left from the aqueduct path, crosses several drainage brooks and then the wooden bridge over Popolopen Brook. The trail soon follows a dirt road to a junction with Fort Montgomery Road. The latter is the route of the Timp-Torne Trail. Turn left and follow red blazes down Ft. Montgomery Road (blue blazes of Timp-Torne also here). In about 0.3 mile, Popolopen Gorge Trail diverges right on an old wood road, passes Queensboro Lake, then swings north-westward to the dam at Turkey Hill Lake. The trail passes the dam and climbs some rocks to the lake shore which it follows to the north end of Anthony Wayne Trail. It then veers west, uphill, away from the lake. After passing through a small hollow, it comes to its terminus at the junction of Long Path, Deep Hollow Shelter Trail, and Long Mountain–Torne Trail.

Raccoon Brook Hills Trail. Length: 2.3 miles. Blazes: black.

The trail runs from Seven Hills Trail to the Kakiat Trail. It heads east from Seven Hills Trail, descending into a hollow where it crosses a brook that flows along a fault line, on the other side of which rises the steep rock wall called a fault scarp by geologists. Climbing up around the eastern end of the scarp, the trail passes the rock formation known as The Pulpit, and goes northeast over Raccoon Brook Hill to cross the Kakiat Trail, after which it makes a wide loop over the bare ledges of two low, flat-topped hills with fine views of the country around Pine Meadow Lake. Eventually it returns to the Kakiat Trail, where it ends at a point 0.3 mile west of where it crossed.

Ramapo-Dunderberg Trail. Length: 20.8 miles. Blazes: red on white.

This trail, from Tuxedo to Jones Point, is the oldest of the park trails built by the walking clubs. Generally speaking, it is a ridge trail, through different types of forest and with many view points.

The trail starts from its western terminus at Tuxedo station, heads over the Ramapo River on a footbridge, follows the road left on the other side to an underpass of the Thruway, and turns left on the road beyond. In a few hundred feet, it turns right into the woods in a northeasterly direction, climbing around Horse Pond Mountain, and passing, in 0.1 mile from the road, the terminus of the Triangle Trail (yellow blaze). About 0.5 mile farther the Tuxedo–Mt. Ivy Trail begins, diverging to the right. The RD is the *left* branch. This must be emphasized, both trails are blazed with red. The RD continues northeast to the crossing of Black Ash Swamp Brook. Here is a natural rock dam formed by the last glacier, that melted off about eleven thousand years ago. Here also is Tri-Trail Corners, where three trails—the RD, the Blue Disc, and Victory—meet. The RD climbs northward to the summit of Black Ash Mountain, with a good view from near the top over the swamp to the south. The Long Path crosses the RD in the dip between Black Ash and Parker Cabin mountains.

The RD continues north up to the top of Parker Cabin Mountain, where, on the level summit, Triangle Trail comes in from its western loop, coincides with the RD for about 150 feet and then bears east (right). The RD descends the north side of Parker Cabin Mountain to a gap where it crosses Victory Trail (blue blaze). From the gap, the RD ascends steeply up Tom Jones Mountain. Near the stone shelter on the summit there is a fine view to the east and south. The trail descends steeply down the northeast slope to Tom Jones Gap, where it crosses a brook just before reaching Rt. 210. North of this road, the trail climbs gradually up Black Rock Mountain, named, it is said, for the many charcoal burners' pits that were once found there. At the top of the first ridge, between rock walls, the Nurian Trail (white blaze) begins at the left and the RD bears right over a rock ledge. From this point to its crossing of the Arden-Surebridge Trail it is easy walking, and easy to miss the trail. The Bald Rocks Shelter is a half mile from the junction with the Nurian Trail. The water supply is a small brook 100 yards downhill east of the shelter, but it is not reliable in dry weather.

Beyond the shelter the RD crosses the Dunning Trail (yellow blaze) and continues north over Ship Rock. The bright red leaves of the sour gum trees (*Nyssa sylvatica*) in the swamp below the west side of the Rock give the Park its earliest fall color. A tablet set in a rock beside the trail here is a memorial to George Goldthwaite, erected in 1964 by the Fresh Air Club. Goldthwaite was a pioneer trail walker who, although famous for his speed on the trail, is better remembered by his friends for his complete knowledge of Park trails and old roads and for his skill and consideration as a walk leader.

A short distance northward the Lichen Trail (blue blaze) begins, meanders northwest over ledges and offers a shortcut to the A-SB. The RD then winds through the woods and down to a crossing of the Arden-Surebridge Trail at a stone fireplace beside a boulder. Remember, both trails have red markings, so take care not to choose the wrong path! From the crossing the RD begins the climb of Fingerboard Mountain around a low cliff and beneath a glacial pothole 6 or 7 feet high on its face, geologically one of the most remarkable features of the route. As the mountain levels off at the top, the Long Path (blue blaze) and the Appalachian Trail (white blaze), which coincide here, come in from the left, and the three trails continue northward together, passing, about 1/10 mile beyond the junction, the Fingerboard Shelter and the western end of the Hurst Trail (blue blaze). A half mile farther on, the Long Path diverges left. The RD and AT continue on to New Arden Road, where they turn east (right) and follow the road past Tiorati traffic circle and lake to turn into the woods about 0.3 mile east of the circle.

The two trails travel east over Goshen Mountain and up along Letterrock Mountain. At a crossing of an unmarked wood road, in the saddle of this mountain, is Letterrock Shelter. The trails mount the steep southwest ridge of Black Mountain by switchbacks, and wind along the top. There is an open view south, including the unfinished dam at Owl Lake, abandoned since the 1930s. From the summit the trails descend gradually down the east slope to Beechy Bottom, crossing first a wood road and then the Palisades Parkway.

It was through this valley that General Anthony Wayne and his soldiers marched on their way to storm Stony Point on the night of July 15, 1779. The valley and the road that they followed changed little until 1933–34, when three camps of the Civilian Conservation Corps, each with two hundred young men, were established here. Two were near the RD Trail where the old Wayne road crosses the Beechy Bottom Brook, and the third on the former site of the farm near the Mica Mine below the steep west face of West Mountain. The site of this camp is now covered by the Anthony Wayne Recreation Area. Under the direction of Park foremen the CCC boys living here, and those in eight other camps located in the Park, accomplished an immense amount of work of permanent value in building new lakes, roads, fire lanes, etc. But even this activity did not disturb the character of Beechy Bottom itself, for until the construction of the Palisades Parkway in the 1950s, the grassy road along the west side of Beechy Bottom took the hiker past the foundations of farmhouses, clumps of lilac, and old apple trees remaining from the days when this valley was the route from Central Valley to the river. A segment of this road still exists in the gap between West Mountain and the Pines. This was formerly used as a part of the Horn Trail. (See S-BM Trail description.)

Beyond the Parkway and the brook the AT diverges northeast (left) and the RD ascends steeply to the southern crown of West Mountain, past the holes of an old iron mine, where a faint road diverges east. On the open ledges near the top, the RD meets the

Suffern–Bear Mountain Trail (yellow blaze) just above the Cat's Elbow. All of the viewpoints enjoyed from here were once the posts of Continental, Tory, or British scouts.

After coinciding a short distance, the S-BM turns north (left) and the RD swings east across the summit and descends into Timp Pass, where it meets the Timp-Torne Trail (blue blaze). Here also is the eastern terminus of the Red Cross Trail. Rising above is the Timp, a striking cliff with a pronounced overhang at the west end of the Dunderberg massif. It is one of the most picturesque rock faces in the Park. The overhang is due to the fact that the Timp is another of the southwest-facing uplifted ends of fault blocks, common in the Highlands, and weathering has split off the granite on its ancient joint planes. From Timp Pass the RD ascends by what was once known as Six Chins Trail, over a rough talus slope, up under the overhanging cliff. The RD turns right at the top, but the best overlook is from the open summit a few steps to the left. (Unfamiliar with the road in the brook valley to the west, Sir Henry Clinton's army, in 1777, toiled over Dunderberg to the east to storm Forts Clinton and Montgomery at Bear Mountain and Popolopen Creek.)

The trail continues east, enters the saddle between the Timp and Bald Mountain, where it crosses two fire lanes, then climbs steeply up Bald Mountain to the summit, where there is a panoramic view west and north. A little farther east, and to the left of the trail, is the Cornell Mine, named for a family once numerous hereabouts. The mine is a small vertical hole, and should be approached with care. The RD continues east, and at a "five corners" of wood roads and trails turns onto a wood road and then to a path. A few feet east of this junction it crosses part of the grade of the Dunderberg Scenic Railway. As the RD descends over ledges to Jones Point on the Hudson, it crosses several times the graded embankments of the uncompleted railway.

After crossing Rt. 9W, the trail ends at Jones Point, named for the family who for several generations owned this land, including Dunderberg. Captain Thomas Jones, the founder, came to America in 1692. Jones Beach on Long Island also is named for this family.

There is ample parking space at the trail terminus, which is opposite the dock of the Hudson River Reserve Fleet. Buses from the Port Authority Terminal to Bear Mountain will stop to discharge or pick up passengers on Rt. 9W where the road to the Fleet dock turns off 2 miles north of Tomkins Cove.

Red Cross Trail. Length: 7.6 miles. Blazes: red cross on white.

From Timp Pass to Seven Lakes Drive near the south end of Lake Tiorati, where it connects with eastern terminus of the Arden-Surebridge Trail. The eastern end of this trail was once at the entrance to the Allison Boyce Girl Scout Camp on Mott Farm Road, but now begins at Timp Pass where the Ramapo-Dunderberg and Timp-Torne trails cross. To reach it, follow the directions for Timp-Torne Trail.

The Red Cross Trail starts by heading down from the Timp Pass in a southerly direction for about 0.3 mile, bends around to the southeast for a short distance, then swings south for about 0.3 mile more, where it turns westward and climbs gradually. This is the longest climb on the trail, and the footing is good. The climb is about 400 feet in elevation on this stretch. Near the top the old Beechy Bottom road crosses. (Look for a geological survey marker on a rock by the road.) This road was used by General Anthony Wayne and his troops when they marched to attack Stony Point on the night of July 15, 1779. A little farther on, the trail crosses a small brook. In 0.3 mile Suffern–Bear Mountain Trail comes in from the left and the two trails coincide for a short distance in a northwesterly direction, following a well-defined wood road until the Red Cross diverges left (west) and the S-BM goes right (north). In a short distance, the trail reaches the Palisades Parkway, which it crosses and continues west. About 1.5 miles beyond, it passes the site of Burnt House on the right. Many years ago a woodcutter lived there until he was burned out. The cellar hole is all that remains. From Burnt House to Tiorati Brook Road the route is still over fairly level terrain, except for a short climb over the slope of the old Orange Furnace. (It is said that some of Washington's soldiers had a camp on the site of the present ball field.) This wood road and the present Tiorati Brook Road going west from this point to the lake are the remains of an old road of Revolutionary War days. Tiorati Brook Road, east of where the trail crosses, was not in existence then. The trail follows the wood road past Hasenclever Mine, then circles to the northwest around the south end of Hasenclever Mountain, crosses a power line, and ends at Seven Lakes Drive directly across the highway from the eastern terminus of the Arden-Surebridge Trail, and beside a private road.

Reeves Brook Trail. Length: 1 mile. Blazes: white.

From Pine Meadow Trail at Seven Lakes Parkway to the Raccoon

Brook Hills Trail. The area over which this trail passes is rather uniform in forest cover, but interesting geologically. Several fault lines are crossed, as the brook flows down over natural steps of rock. The rock formation called "The Pulpit" is about 0.1 mile north of the eastern terminus of this trail on the Raccoon Brook Hills Trail.

Seven Hills Trail. Length: 6.8 miles. Blazes: blue.

This trail, from Sloatsburg to Monitor Rock, connects with Hillburn-Torne-Sebago, Raccoon Brook Hills, Pine Meadow, Diamond Mountain, Tower, Long Path, and Tuxedo–Mt. Ivy trails. It begins east of the New York Thruway at the junction of the first road on the south side of Seven Lakes Drive, follows beside the Thruway a short distance, then swings east around South Hill, following an old wood road. The Seven Hills Trail crosses Beaver Brook and begins a long but gradual ascent of Ramapo Torne. There is a junction with the Hillburn-Torne-Sebago Trail at a saddle in the ridge. Seven Hills Trail goes left onto H-T-S and the two coincide for about 0.3 mile to where H-T-S diverges to the right and Seven Hills swings left, passing first a junction with Reeves Brook Trail, then with the former Quartz Brook Trail, and, after a mile, again coincides with the H-T-S. The latter soon diverges left and the Seven Hills continues downhill to cross Pine Meadow Trail and Brook. It then climbs steeply up to the summit of Diamond Mountain, where there are fine views of Sebago Lake. Here, also, the H-T-S comes in from the left, coincides a short distance, and diverges again to the left. On the summit the Diamond Mountain Trail and the Tower Trail lead off to the east. About 100 yards along on the Tower Trail there is a fire tower (erected in 1966). About 0.5 mile beyond, the Seven Hills Trail crosses the Tuxedo–Mt. Ivy Trail and then a wood road, after which it climbs steeply to its terminus at Monitor Rock. The story is that the rock was named years ago by members of the Fresh Air Club, when they found beneath it a copy of the *Christian Science Monitor*.

Sherwood Path. Length: 1.9 miles. Blazes: red.

This trail connects Rt. 202 with the Suffern–Bear Mountain and Pine Meadow trails. It begins on Rt. 202 about 5 miles north of Suffern (parking for about two cars beside road), follows a dirt road that runs north to the Mahwah River, crosses the river on a bridge and turns sharp left (south) downstream. In a short distance, where the road branches, continue straight ahead, passing a pipe spring beside the trail just beyond the fork. About 0.3 mile from the starting point, the Sherwood crosses a gas pipeline clearing and Pittsboro Hollow Brook. An unmarked wood road diverges to right at this point. Watch the markers. The trail bears westerly up the side of Horse Stable Mountain, crossing a power line opening with a brook on the right. At a fork at 0.7 mile, the unmarked wood road to right is the Pittsboro Hollow Trail, which, after crossing the brook via an old bridge, continues north past the site of Gill Pitt's cabin to the Suffern–Bear Mountain Trail. Sherwood Path follows the left fork uphill. In about 100 feet turn left (south) on a fire lane then uphill to the E. D. Stone Memorial Shelter. This shelter was erected in 1935 in memory of Edgar D. Stone and his wife, Tessie, founders of the Tramp and Trail Club of New York. Just before reaching the shelter watch for a pipeline spring (reliable at all seasons). The Suffern–Bear Mountain Trail crosses at the shelter. The Sherwood Path bends toward north for a short distance over fairly level ground, then west, crossing Many Swamp Brook, to its terminus at the Pine Meadow Road where Pine Meadow Trail crosses.

Skannatati Trail. Length: 4.8 miles. Blazes: white.

Connects Dunning Trail near Hogencamp Mine with the S-BM at Big Hill Shelter. This is a low-level route for most of its length, much of the trail being over sections of old wood roads.

Starting at the Dunning, south of Pine Swamp, the Skannatati leads steeply downhill and follows an old wood road along the lower ridges. Winding downhill further, past a massive rock wall, the trail bends left and soon ascends another hill where it merges with a wood road coming down the hill from the left. The two coincide downhill about 200 feet and then the trail turns sharp left, then right, crossing Pine Swamp Brook on steppingstones. It twists around among the trees and rocks to the shore of Lake Skannatati, which it follows to Seven Lakes Parkway, where it turns right for a few hundred feet then left into a wood road that goes past the south shore of Lake Askoti. It soon turns sharply south, crosses the shoulder of Rock House Mountain to Rt. 210 on which it travels right for about 100 feet and then turns left into the woods again on another wood road. Swinging around swampy areas, it climbs the west slope and follows a wood road crossing Lake Welch Parkway to St. John's Road. Left, 1000 feet on this road is St. Johns-in-the-Wilderness, an Episcopal chapel. Crossing the road, the trail first proceeds straight, then turns left, crossing a boulder-strewn hollow, and climbing a rather steep, low hill. It bears right and descends to a wood road, which it follows to the right. In about 0.5 mile, it crosses Beaver Pond Brook on stepping stones. A short distance beyond, it turns left on the paved road and follows the old turnpike (dirt) northward for 0.5 mile until it turns right uphill to its terminus at the Suffern–Bear Mountain Trail and Big Hill Shelter.

Stony Brook Trail. Length: 1.6 miles. No blazes; signs at each end identify it.

Connects Pine Meadow Trail with Lake Sebago dam at Seven Lakes Drive. This is a low-level trail with easy footing. Much of the way is over an old wood road. The Stony Brook is a very beautiful stream—particularly in spring when it is flowing high and fast with melt water from the winter's snows.

Suffern–Bear Mountain Trail. Length: 24.3 miles. Blazes: yellow.

This trail from Suffern to Bear Mountain is quite rugged in many places. It is not recommended for the novice, or anyone without proper footwear. One terminus is on the east side of Rt. 59 at Suffern, a few hundred feet north of the Thruway overpass. It goes steeply up a ravine to a fine view point on the slope of Nordkop Mountain. Joining a wood road for a time, it follows north along the ridge of the Ramapo Rampart. The wood road is soon left behind and the trail winds over the fairly level mountaintop until, about 1.5 miles from Suffern, it climbs a rock formation known as the Kitchen Stairs. Beyond this the going becomes more rugged, through an area littered with giant boulders of all sizes and shapes. This area, located in a hollow through which flows the Os-sec Brook, is called the Valley of Dry Bones. After climbing the next hill the trail runs along the eastern edge of the Rampart through the long-abandoned Sky-sail Farm (which, it is said, was the highest farm in the Ramapos), with westerly swings around the streamheads, to two big boulders called Grandpa and Grandma, a little beyond which it meets the Kakiat Trail (white blaze).

The trail continues north over Cobus Mountain or Cobusberg, named for Jacobus Smith, brother of Claudius (see Tuxedo–Mt. Ivy Trail). On the next hill, the trail leads along a cliff overlooking the glacial cirque behind Horse Stable Mountain, and, over it, the valley to the east, then descends to Conklin's Crossing Trail (white). Further along downhill it crosses Many Swamp Brook and continues up the steep slope to the north of the brook to the Stone Memorial Shelter. About 100 feet east of the S-BM, on the Sherwood Path, is an excellent pipe spring.

The S-BM continues northward over Hawk Cliff, and soon bends sharp left and descends to its junction with the unmarked Pittsboro Hollow Trail, which comes up from the valley to the east. At this point stands a large white oak tree, on the north side of the path where the two trails meet. This is the Witness Oak, used as a surveyor's landmark in early days.

The two trails coincide for about 0.3 mile, then the Pittsboro trail diverges left near the place where the Pine Meadow Trail begins. The S-BM continues a bit eastward, bending north and descending to Gyascutus Brook in the hollow. The trail climbs steeply over Panther Mountain, descends over a field of boulders in the bed of a lost brook (it can be heard beneath the rocks), and again climbs steeply up to the crossing of the Tuxedo–Mount Ivy Trail (red blaze), where there is a stone fireplace. Further along, atop Circle Mountain, the Ladentown benchmark gives the elevation as 1199 feet above sea level.

As it ascends the farther slope, S-BM joins the former Red Arrow Trail. The two coincide northwestward across File Factory Brook, cross the old Woodtown Road just beyond the brook, and continue together 0.5 mile to Reservoir No. 3. Climbing Breakneck Mountain, the S-BM Trail turns northeast, where it meets the beginning of the Breakneck Mountain Trail just before the old Red Arrow Trail diverges left. The S-BM follows the crest to Big Hill Shelter. There is a fine view from the shelter. Water from a brook to the east is uncertain. The trail then descends the ledges, crosses a wood road, and enters another wood going northeastward. It crosses the Old Ramapo Turnpike and reenters the woods, climbing gradually up the south side of Jackie Jones Mountain (1276 feet) to the radio relay tower. It then descends to a narrow asphalt road on which it goes left a half mile to Rt. 210, turns right to cross the brook via Rt. 210's bridge, and north into the woods along an old wood road. Then, after crossing Irish Mountain, it winds down to Tiorati Brook and Tiorati Brook Road, which it follows to the Palisades Interstate Parkway. The trail crosses the Parkway (watch for traffic) and immediately begins the steep ascent of the ledges on the south side of Pyngyp Mountain. Halfway up is a memorial tablet, erected by his friends in the walking clubs, to Harold Scutt, who found the route for the S-BM up these ledges and was killed in an airplane accident soon after.

The trail bears eastward near the summit, crosses the highest point (1016 feet), and then descends to a wood road in the notch beyond, and on down to Stillwater Brook at the old road from

Bulsontown. It follows this road right 100 yards then turns sharp left across the brook and up the elevation of The Pines. From the ledge on the west side of this summit there is a fine view north and northwest. The trail drops off The Pines by faint wood roads to a more open one, where it meets the Red Cross Trail and then turns left with it about 200 yards. The S-BM leaves the road sharp right, crosses a rough and broken area of small swamps and steep ledges, crosses a telephone line and then a brook, and meets the old road through Beechy Bottom, which was the Revolutionary route of "Mad Anthony" Wayne. The trail climbs the steep slope beyond (with a detour to the left to a good view south from the top of a ledge) and through open oak woods to a stony road built by the CCC as a fire road. This was formerly part of the old Horn Trail, a valley route to Tomkins Cove, and is now abandoned. The S-BM crosses this road and climbs over the knobs of the southern spur of West Mountain.

Just beyond a turn called the Cats Elbow, on the open ledges near the top, the S-BM meets the Ramapo-Dunderberg Trail. The two coincide for a short distance, then the RD swings east, while the S-BM takes the left fork northward, past fine views, into the hollow between West Mountain and the Timp. Here it follows an old wood road to the right for several hundred feet and then, at a curve, leaves it to climb the cliff to the north by a zigzag route called the Fire Escape. Near the top, the Timp-Torne Trail crosses. (On the latter trail, a little way to the east, is the West Mountain Shelter, from which there is a fine view south toward New York City. Water is available at the brook in the hollow.)

The S-BM heads northeasterly over a shoulder of West Mountain that rises above the now-abandoned hamlet of Doodletown. From the shoulder, the trail bends left down on a steep rock talus to a ravine, where, crossing the brook, it follows its left bank to a wood road. It goes left on the wood road and makes a loop around the western end of the Doodletown valley, coming up the north side of the valley to cross Seven Lakes Drive. Beyond the Drive the trail climbs over a low shoulder of Bear Mountain, at the top of which the Appalachian Trail joins from the left. It coincides with the S-BM to the terminus of the latter near the ski jump at Bear Mountain Inn.

Timp-Torne Trail. Length: 9.9 miles. Blazes: blue.

This trail extends from Rt. 9W 1 mile north of Tomkins Cove to Fort Montgomery on the same road. It starts near a turn-off on

BEAR MOUNTAIN   STORMKING CROWNEST BREAKNECK BEACONS CLOVE CREEK GARRISONS ANTHONYS NOSE
BULL   WEST POINT

Popolopen valley

VIEW NORTH
FROM THE TIMP
TO BEAR MOUNTAIN
AND WEST POINT
UP THE HUDSON RIVER

PARK ROAD

THE INN

DOODLETOWN   Dickinson

Rt. 9W, where there is parking for cars. This is 1.5 miles north of Mott Farm Road, uphill from a gas station. It heads west into the woods following an old wood road for about 0.5 mile, then leaves the road and continues to wind westward, crossing a fire lane at 0.5 mile, beyond which it turns north and goes up through Timp Pass. At the top it meets the Ramapo-Dunderberg Trail and the beginning of the Red Cross Trail. From here it climbs West Mountain to the shelter, with a fine view south. The water supply is a brook that the TT crosses on the way up to the shelter from the RD. A little past the shelter, the Suffern–Bear Mountain Trail comes in from the north and the two trails coincide for 200 feet out to the top of the Fire Escape. The S-BM drops down left and the TT turns right and climbs a little to the highest point of West Mountain (1260 feet) and along the narrow ridge, with fine views over the park. In 0.3 mile it is joined by the Appalachian Trail ascending left from Beechy Bottom. The two are identical for nearly 1 mile. The trails go northeast and then east, with a good view of Bear Mountain, and begin to descend, bending northeast. At about 900-foot level, the AT diverges right and the TT heads west down over the ledges of the ridge to Seven Lakes Drive. Just before reaching the drive, watch for the beginning of the Anthony Wayne Trail.

The TT crosses Palisades Interstate Parkway via the bridge and turns right onto the Old Fort Montgomery Road. This road is part of the route used by General Anthony Wayne and his soldiers when they marched on Stony Point. It was also used by the left wing of the British force that attacked Forts Clinton and Montgomery in 1777. A quarter mile after leaving the drive, the Popolopen Gorge Trail comes in from the left and the two trails coincide for a few hundred feet, when the PG Trail turns sharp right onto another old road. The TT continues north on the Fort Montgomery Road

past the old Queensboro Furnace, then turns sharp left into the
woods, uphill, and shortly crosses the paved Forest of Dean Road,
beyond which it climbs to the summit of Popolopen Torne (941-foot
elevation). From the summit of the Torne, the trail drops down the
east side of the mountain coming again to the Forest of Dean Road,
which it crosses, and descends a short distance through woods to
an aqueduct which it follows east for 0.5 mile. Then, descending
to the bottom of the gorge, it climbs out after another 0.3 mile,
and terminates at Rt. 9W, a little north of the bridge that carries
that highway over the Popolopen Gorge.

Tower Trail. Length: 0.8 mile. Blazes: yellow with black T.
This trail connects Pine Meadow Trail and Seven Hills Trail and
provides access to Diamond Mountain fire tower. It starts at two
large boulders known to the Indians as Ga-nus-quah, or Stone Giants,
at an open spot on Pine Meadow Brook, reached via Pine Meadow
Trail. It coincides with the Pine Meadow Trail for about 0.3 mile,
where the latter diverges to the right (east) and the Diamond
Mountain Trail (white blaze) goes uphill to the left. The Tower
Trail ascends diagonally to the open eastern ridge of Diamond
Mountain. The junction with the Seven Hills Trail (blue blaze)
is 100 yards beyond (west) the fire tower at the summit.

Triangle Trail. Length: 4.9 miles. Blazes: yellow triangle.
The Triangle is an easy loop from the Ramapo-Dunderberg Trail
near Tuxedo to the joint route of the Tuxedo–Mt. Ivy Trail and
Long Path near Dutch Doctor Shelter. It connects with R-D Trail
again on Parker Cabin Mountain, and with Victory Trail near Lake
Skenonto. The trail leaves the Ramapo-Dunderberg Trail 0.6 mile
from Tuxedo station, branching left on a wood road up Deep Hollow Brook. On the slope of Parker Cabin Mountain it joins the
Long Path for a short distance, until the latter turns off the wood
road to the right (south). The Triangle Trail continues straight
ahead, climbing steadily to the top of Parker Cabin Mountain by
an easier route than does the Ramapo-Dunderberg Trail, which it
meets again at the summit. About 100 feet north, it diverges right
to the sharp eastern edge of the mountain, starts down steeply and
then continues more easily over low ridges and levels, crossing the
Victory Trail, to a point where it meets the Long Path again. The
trail ends here. To the right (south) 0.1 mile is Dutch Doctor
Shelter. The Tuxedo–Mt. Ivy Trail may be followed back to Tuxedo.

Tuxedo–Mt. Ivy Trail. Length: 10.3 miles. Blazes: red on white (horizontal dashes).

Extends from the Ramapo-Dunderberg Trail near Tuxedo to Mt. Ivy. To reach the beginning of this trail, follow the R-D from the Tuxedo station. In about 1 mile the T-MI starts, going off to the right (east). The markings of both trails are red on white, but differ in their shapes: those of the R-D are round, and those of the T-MI are horizontal dashes. About 0.3 mile from its western terminus, the T-MI passes the rock known as Claudius Smith's Den. Smith was a colorful Revolutionary War Figure. He and his band of outlaws used these caves as a hideout. From them they made raids on the farms in the valley to the west, stealing horses and cattle, and spreading terror through the surrounding hills. A party of Continental soldiers eventually captured Smith, and he was hanged at Goshen on January 22, 1779. It is said that Smith covered the fronts of the caves with boulders to better conceal them, small and secret entrances being left in the rocks.

A few feet east of the caves the Blue Disc Trail crosses and not far beyond the White Cross Trail ends. The T-MI then goes over Blauvelt Mountain and down into the valley of Spring Brook, which it crosses to Dutch Doctor Shelter, located in an old farm clearing. Here, near the brook, a German herb doctor named Wagner lived long ago. There is a good water supply at this shelter, in the form of a pipe spring near the brook. Here, also, the Long Path comes in from the north and coincides east with the T-MI. The two trails head southeast from the shelter a short distance, then turn east and go over the ridge and out to the service road leading to the camps on the west side of Lake Sebago, cross it, and, skirting the south shore of the lake, soon come to Seven Lakes Drive and the dam at the foot of the lake. The trails turn left onto the Drive, crossing the dam via that road, and then turn sharp right down the embankment to Stony Brook. Here they cross the Stony Brook Trail and the north end of the Hillburn-Torne-Sebago Trail and climb the north side of Diamond Mountain, angling left to the saddle. They cross the Seven Hills Trail only 100 yards south of Monitor Rock, a large white boulder which was formerly on the T-MI Trail and is now the northern terminus of the Seven Hills Trail.

The two trails continue on in a northeasterly direction down to Pine Meadow Road West, an unpaved firelane, cross it, and 0.5 mile farther on cross Pine Meadow Road East. A few hundred feet east of this road the Breakneck Mountian Trail begins, branching to the left. The T-MI and LP turn east along the long-abandoned road that once lead to Christie's Mill to the junction of this road with the Woodtown Road. Here they turn, go south for 100 yards, crossing the head of File Factory Brook, where once Tim's Bridge stood, turn abruptly east, and go out to the front of the Ramapo Rampart, skirting small swamps.

As it begins the descent from the Rampart, the trail crosses the Suffern–Bear Mountain Trail and follows the old Two Bridges Road downhill, past the end of the Red Arrow Trail, to the hard-surface end of Mountain Road, and across the Mahwah River on that road to old Rt. 202, on which the trails continue eastward to Rt. 202 and Mt. Ivy, where the T-MI ends. The Long Path continues south to George Washington Bridge.

Victory Trail. Length: 3 miles. Blazes: a blue "V" on white.

A loop from the junction of the Ramapo-Dunderberg and Blue Disc trails at the Black Ash Swamp (a spot called "Tri-Trail Corners," because of the three trails meeting there) to the R-D in the pass between Parker Cabin and Tom Jones mountains. It also connects with White Cross, Long Path, and Triangle trails.

Victory Trail follows a wood road for most of its length. At the eastern end of Black Ash Swamp the White Cross Trail and the Long Path cross. Farther on, near Lake Skenonto, the Triangle Trail crosses. After passing the lake the Victory Trail leads to Sebago Lake. This it follows a short distance, then turns left (north) into the woods. There is a gradual but steady climb up through the pass where the trail ends at Route 210. This last section is the remnant of a road of Revolutionary War days from Johnsontown to Southfields.

White Cross Trail. Length: 1.9 miles. Blazes: white cross.

The White Cross connects the Ramapo-Dunderberg Trail at the south side of Parker Cabin Mountain with the Tuxedo–Mt. Ivy Trail at Claudius Smith's Den. It crosses Victory Trail and Long Path.

This trail follows a low-level route, passing several swamps, and its chief interest is the opportunity it offers for observation of swamp growth and birds. It goes south from the Ramapo-Dunderberg Trail at the base of the steep slope of Parker Cabin Mountain. After descending to Parker Swamp, it goes along the west side of the swamp to the Long Path, crosses that and then the Victory Trail, and continues over level, rocky ground covered with mountain laurel, around the south side of Black Ash Swamp, then left (southwest) uphill to its terminus at the T-MI near Claudius Smith's Den.

4 · STORM KING—
BLACK ROCK FOREST
(Map 5)

INTRODUCTION

ONATED to Harvard University in 1949 by Dr. Ernest Stillman, Black Rock Forest, in the northern part of the Highlands west of the river, is a preserve of unusual interest for hikers. It includes about four thousand acres of a high rugged granite plateau, with a dozen summits over 1400 feet above sea level. Dr. Stillman, a New York physician whose father assembled the main tract, owned the land until his death. In 1922 Dr. Stillman gave about seven hundred acres in Storm King Clove to the Palisades Interstate Park to insure the preservation of the scenic surroundings of the old Storm King Highway. This tract now forms the foreground for the fine eastward view from the present Storm King Highway (9W) before it turns westward for its descent to Cornwall. Studies and experiments in forestry have been made in the Black Rock Forest for many years, and the reservation is still being used for research demonstrations and graduate instruction, which hopefully will insure the permanent care of this forest tract.

In 1963, however, the Consolidated Edison Co. of New York filed an application for a license to build a hydroelectric plant on the west shore of the Hudson River at the base of Storm King Mountain. This was to be the largest hydroelectric plant in the world with a generating capacity of 2000 kilowatts. It would require

a reservoir of 240 acres, flooding a portion of the water supply of
the Town of Cornwall, and would take, in all, 200 acres of the
Forest. Connected with the reservoir by a tunnel 40 feet in diameter
blasted through the heart of Storm King, the powerhouse would
include three chambers, 80 feet wide, fifteen stories high, and two
football fields in length. A recreational complex would be constructed above ground fronting directly on the Hudson. The tail
race, where water is drawn in and discharged, would require a
sheer cut from the face of the mountain 60 feet long and 200 to
300 feet deep, and behind this, likewise fronting the river, a rock
and graded slope reaching 65 feet above the river. Transmission
lines would cross under the river and then run overhead on towers
as high as ten-story buildings, cutting a wide right of way from
Nelsonville across Putnam County.

Some local people in Cornwall were in favor of the plan because
of the expected tax revenues, but the proposal created widespread
protest, not only from those who wished to preserve the natural
beauties of the Hudson Gorge, but also from those with an economic
viewpoint. The fish eggs of the shad and striped bass which spawn
in the Hudson could be destroyed by being sucked against the filter-
ing screens, thus affecting both commercial and recreational fishing
off Long Island and Connecticut. The high tension wires would
destroy scenic and property values on the land they crossed, and
would interfere with local community planning. The excavation and
drilling inside the mountain would be within 180 feet of the New
York City Aqueduct, with potential damage to New York City's
water supply, as this was an area which caved in during the original
construction of the Aqueduct, due to geologic faults. If there were
to be seepage of briny and polluted water through the earth dams
and surrounding soil it would threaten the wells and ground water
of Cornwall's local water supply, as well as plant life. It became
known, also, that Cornwall proposed to draw upon the New York
City water supply, which in those drought years was already strained
to the point of rationing. When the Aqueduct was built, existing
municipalities under which it was constructed were given rights to
tap this source at a rate not to exceed the per capita consumption
of New York City residents. Normal population growth would soon
have required Cornwall to tap this supply, but Con Ed hastened
this event by financing the project as partial replacement for the
anticipated destruction of the Upper Reservoir.

The protests were coordinated by the Scenic Hudson Preservation
Conference, sparked by Leo Rothschild, who for many years had

been attempting to interest people in the preservation of green space in the metropolitan area. Organized by private citizens, the Conference gradually attracted sponsorship and funds from other private conservation and outdoor groups. As a result of proceedings brought by the Conference, the U. S. Court of Appeals in December 1965 rescinded the license to build the plant that the Federal Power Commission had granted to Con Ed the previous March and ordered the proceedings remanded to the Federal Power Commission. Hearings resumed and proceedings have continued through 1970. Final decision, probably of the Supreme Court, is not expected until 1972. Meanwhile, in March 1965, Governor Rockefeller appointed the Hudson River Valley Commission, which by August 1966 became a permanent Commission to preserve the Valley, treating Storm King and much of the Hudson Highlands as park land. The Governor's action followed that of a number of Congressmen, beginning with Representative Ottinger in 1965, who introduced bills for the preservation and improvement of scenic, historic, recreational, and other natural values along the riverway.

The decision on the Con Ed case will be felt not only along the Hudson River but throughout the nation, for this is a case testing whether a commercial developer can be permitted to ignore comprehensive planning for an area; whether the development to meet one need, electric power, for example, should be carried out at the expense of other human needs.

Black Rock Forest is bounded on the east by a line which approximately follows the old military road over the mountains from West Point to Cornwall. East of this boundary, to the Hudson River, lie Palisades Interstate Park and land of the West Point Military Reservation. On the north the Forest extends out to the front of the hills overlooking the lowlands, and in part actually borders these lowlands. On the west it extends down the slopes overlooking the valley of Woodbury Creek and Mountainville. On the south it includes a part of the rugged Mt. Rascal, overlooking Cat Hollow north of Popolopen Lake, and continues down near Round Pond and thence around the northern edge of Bog Meadow Pond and eastward toward Crows Nest. Except for the small area of water-supply land around Bog Meadow Pond, the U. S. Military Reservation adjoins Black Rock Forest on the southeast, south, and southwest.

The preserve is named for Black Rock, a prominent pitch-pine-clad summit south of Cornwall, which is one of the most conspicuous in the area, with grand views to the north, east and west. It includes the highest summits west of the river in the Highlands proper, that is, in the old Precambrian rocks (Schunemunk Mountain to the west is a somewhat higher ridge but of a younger geologic age). The highest summit, Spy Rock, is 1464 feet above sea level and gives a wide circle of views, including an outlook, through clefts in the hills southward, to the Hudson at Peekskill and Haverstraw. From this outlook sentinels from Washington's camp at Newburgh watched British vessels sailing up the Hudson to Haverstraw Bay.

Access to the Forest by bus is from the Port of New York Authority to Mountainville (on the west side), or to Cornwall-on-Hudson (on the east side). If going by car, see the trail descriptions below for access from Rt. 9W, Angola Road, Mine Hill Road, and Mineral Spring Road. From Rt. 9W cars also may be driven to the Upper Reservoir in the Forest: take the first right turn coming down the west side of the ridge, from Storm King parking space; turn sharp right under 9W; bear right around the hill, then left to the Reservoir. On the east side the access is via Round Pond Road, turning right on the dirt road past the gate to Little Bog Meadow Reservoir, where there is a parking space for two cars. This is the eastern end of Continental Road.

TRAILS IN BLACK ROCK FOREST
AND ON STORM KING

Black Rock Forest is open for hiking, but fires, bathing, and camping are not permitted. For maps, use the "West Point" and "Schunemunk" quadrangles of the United States Geological Survey or write to the Harvard Black Rock Forest, Cornwall, N.Y. 12518, for the official Forest trail map.

The Forest has a network of trails, some blazed and some unmarked. There are two main trails, running approximately southwest to northeast: the Stillman (yellow blazes) and the Scenic (white blazes), as described below. The Sackett Mountain Trail (yellow circles), approximately parallel to these, is a ridge trail with outlooks to the west and north. Crossing these trails from approximately north to south are a number of short trails which can be combined in a variety of long and short walks. The experienced hiker will find many additional possibilities in exploring the wood roads which survive from the days when this area was settled by families scattered on small farms, from pre-Revolutionary days to the beginning of this century. Around that time these woods were logged, but have now grown back. The Continental Road was originally the only route across the mountains to West Point, Highland Falls, etc., and was used until the "New Road," leading past the Upper Reservoir, was built. The latter is now known as the "Old West Point Road," and is itself a hundred years old.

Stillman Trail. Length: 10.5 miles (eastern portion of Schunemunk-Storm King Trail), from Rt. 32 in Mountainville to Rt. 218 in Cornwall-on-Hudson. Blazes: yellow.

This trail is a continuation of the Jessup Trail (yellow blaze) from Monroe over Schunemunk Mountain, connecting at Mountainville. At the junction of Rt. 32 with Angola Road (bus stop), the Stillman branches northeast. (Parking is permitted at the Angola Roller Rink, on Angola Road 0.3 miles east of where the trail leaves the road.) In just under 2 miles the trail leaves the road on the right, and goes southeast uphill until it joins a wood road and follows that to the right for a short time. It then bears left, still uphill, following a ravine. It continues to climb steeply to the top of the hill (994 feet). Here is a splendid view down the valley to Schunemunk, and, in the opposite direction, to the Hudson River, Breakneck Ridge, and Mt. Beacon. In descending, the trail runs south, turns sharp right across a field to the west, and climbs a stone wall to an old wood road. A gravel road passing through a field beside the trail is on private property and should not be used. At a fork, south of this point and within sound of a brook, the Stillman Trail bears right, and the old wood road bears left, uphill. The trail crosses the brook, soon ascends a ridge with views of Schunemunk, and then swings east, entering the lands of Harvard Black Rock Forest. It climbs steeply, heads north as it slabs a long ridge, and reaches the western terminus of the Sackett Mountain Trail (yellow circles). At this junction the Stillman Trail turns sharply right (east) and subsequently reaches a dirt road running north and south. This is Hall Road. Continuing south, the trail turns left into another wood road and climbs to the eastern end of the southern saddle of Sackett Mountain (1290 feet). From this point to the Continental Road it is called the Sutherland Trail (see below). There is an outlook over Sutherland Pond and the hills to the south from a short side trail at the top of the saddle. Here also the Compartment Trail (blue blaze) crosses. The Stillman (Sutherland) Trail continues along the ridge, crosses the Continental Road, and climbs up to Black Rock (1410 feet), an open rocky summit with good views to the west, north, and east, then leads down to Aleck Meadow Reservoir, passing the southern terminus of the Black Rock Hollow Trail. Crossing Aleck Meadow Road, it continues east to the foot of Mt. Misery, where the Scenic Trail (white blaze) comes in from the Hill of Pines. The Stillman then climbs steeply to the top of Mt. Misery, with more fine views, and descends, crossing the brook which is the outflow of the Upper Reservoir. The Reservoir Trail leaves at the brook crossing to continue north. Here the Stillman Trail briefly uses the Old West Point Road, which may be followed north to Rt. 9W and Mountain Road in Cornwall. The trail goes east for about 200 yards, turns into a wood road (here leaving the Black Rock Forest), then cuts through the woods over the eastern saddle of Whitehorse Mountain, northward to Rt. 9W. Turning left on this highway, and crossing it, the trail then climbs the rampart over Butter Hill and on to Storm King (1335 feet). Outlooks to the north, west, south, and east from various ledges along the trail provide views of the Hudson River, Mt. Taurus, and Mt. Beacon, and West Point Military Academy. The trail then descends steeply, crosses the property of the Five Point Mission, and arrives at Rt. 218 through the Mission gate. Parking is permitted behind the Mission house. To reach the bus stop at the center of town in Cornwall-on-Hudson, the hiker should walk north (left) about 0.5 mile.

Sutherland Trail. Blazes: yellow.

This trail is in effect a section of the Stillman Trail, extending from the western end of Sutherland Pond to the Continental Road. Its most interesting feature is the view of the Pond and hills beyond from Echo (or Split) Rock, only about 100 feet south of the trail at its western end.

Scenic Trail. Length: 7.2 miles from Rt. 32 to Mt. Misery. Blazes: white.

Access to the Scenic Trail is from Rt. 32, 0.8 mile south of the bus stop in Mountainville, which is at the junction of Rt. 32 with Angola Road. The trail crosses the Forest more or less parallel to the Stillman Trail (yellow blaze) until it joins it, and ends at Mt. Misery. Entrance to the trail from Rt. 32 is between a double row of maples on the east side of the road. After a little over 1 mile through the woods, it crosses Mineral Springs Road about a mile and a half south of the junction of the latter with Angola Road. The trail uses the road for about 100 yards, then follows a stony dirt road diagonally southeast into the woods to Green Falls, a triple cascade flowing over a series of ledges through a dark hemlock grove. Permission for groups to hike through the Falls area, which is on private property, should be obtained by calling Merrill Gardner, Cornwall, N.Y.

The trail turns sharply left at the Falls to climb out of the gorge into open woods, crossing a red gravel private road. Shortly beyond, a side trail blazed in blue leads to a rock ledge for a close-up view of Schunemunk Mountain, and long views to south and north. The trail then follows another red gravel road between houses before passing the boundary of the Black Rock Forest. Several crossings of Mineral Springs Brook, interspersed with occasional boggy spots, make the next mile a wet walk. In a plantation of red pine and yellow poplar the Scenic Trail turns south. At this junction is the southern terminus of the Compartment Trail (blue blaze) and the northern terminus of the Huber Trail (blue blaze). The Scenic Trail continues south on Jim's Pond Road until it turns sharply east, coincides for a short distance with the Arthur Trail (yellow blaze), then continues east. Less than 0.3 mile beyond, the Scenic Trail meets the Chatfield Trail (blue blaze) connecting across the Forest with Chatfield Road. Shortly beyond, a blue-blazed side trail leads to Eagle Cliff, overlooking Jim's Pond. The next junction is with the Ledge Trail (yellow blaze), another connection across the Forest to Chatfield Trail. A 5-minute bushwhack beginning about 190 paces north of junction with the Ledge Trail, and after passing a laurel thicket, turning directly north into the woods and following the ridge (rock outcroppings), leads to the summit of Spy Rock (1461 feet), marked by one pitch pine. The views are especially fine north toward the Catskills and northwest to the Shawangunks. Across the Continental Road the Scenic Trail continues northeast on Bog Meadow Road and in less than 0.5 mile leaves the road as a trail to meander up Rattlesnake Hill (the turn off the road is abrupt and rather obscure). As the trail continues north over the hill it crosses Carpenter Road, then goes up and over Hill of Pines to its junction with the Stillman Trail in a swamp at the southern base of Mt. Misery. Here it crosses the Swamp Trail (blue blaze).

Sackett Mountain Trail. Length: 1.5 miles along the crest of Sackett Mountain. Blazes: yellow circles.

Cleared in the summer of 1967 by Jack J. Karnig, Superintendent of the Forest for Harvard University, this trail is an attractive addition to the various combinations now possible in planning a walk in the Black Rock Forest. Leaving the Stillman Trail a little over

0.3 mile east of Mine Hill Road, it continues north, then east, and jumps two brooks before arriving at the crumbling walls and chimney of the old Beattie cabin. (Dr. Beattie visited his patients by horse and buggy, up and down these mountain roads. His descendants still live in the family home on Angola Road. The cabin was built as a family camping retreat before Dr. Stillman owned the Forest.) The trail then uses the Hall Road for about 150 feet, leaves it from the east side, winds around a hill with rocky outcropping, and heads east and uphill to the Continental Road. At its junction with Hall Road the Compartment Trail (blue blaze) takes off southwest. (The Hall family formerly lived at the junction of the Continental Road and 9W.)

Beginning from the south side of the Forest, the following are the connecting trails:

Ryerson Trail. Blazes: yellow.
Branches right (south) from Scenic Trail just inside the Forest boundary, and ends at Jim's Pond Road.

Huber Trail. Blazes: blue.
Cutoff from Ryerson Trail north to end at Jim's Pond Road, where it coincides with Scenic Trail.

Arthur Trail. Blazes: yellow.
From Jim's Pond Road north across the outlet of Sutherland Pond, briefly coinciding with Scenic Trail and rejoining Jim's Pond Road at the junction with Scenic Trail and Compartment Trail. (Jim Babcock was the first forester and caretaker of Black Rock, a woodsman and a rattlesnake hunter. The pond was named for him, and the Arthur Trail for his son.)

Stropel Trail. Blazes: yellow.
From Black Rock Forest boundary corner, across Jim's Pond Road and up ledges to Scenic Trail, east of side trail to Eagle Cliff outlook.

Compartment Trail. Blazes: blue.
From the junction of Scenic Trail with Jim's Pond Road north to Hall Road at its junction with Sackett Mountain Trail, crossing Stillman Trail en route.

Chatfield Trail. Blazes: blue.
From the Scenic Trail northeast to connect Secor Trail and Chatfield Road, near Tamarack Pond. (The trail is named for a hamlet which is now a part of Cornwall.)

Secor Trail. Blazes: yellow.
A short cut from Chatfield Trail to Chatfield Road. (Named for a family residing in Cornwall.)

Ledge Trail. Blazes: yellow.
A connecting link between Scenic Trail and Chatfield Trail.

Black Rock Hollow Trail. Blazes: white.
From Stillman Trail north, following Black Rock Brook as it flows out of Aleck Meadow Reservoir. Terminates at the chlorinater building on a dirt road leading north to Rt. 9W. (The dirt road is closed to motor vehicles.)

Reservoir Trail. Blazes: blue.
From Stillman Trail just west of Upper Reservoir, where Stillman turns sharply right (east) to Old West Point Road. Follows a brook which is the reservoir outlet down to the chlorinater building on a dirt road leading north to Rt. 9W. (The dirt road is closed to motor vehicles.)

White Oak Trail. Blazes: white.
A pleasant short cut which avoids the road walk from Continental Road around the north end of Arthur Pond, to connect with White Oak Road to the northeast. Turn northeast on the road to pick up Stillman Trail (yellow blaze) to Black Rock, or southwest to join the trails leading off Aleck Meadow Road on the east side of Aleck Meadow Reservoir.

Swamp Trail. Blazes: blue.
From Aleck Meadow Road east between Mt. Misery and Hill of Pines to Old West Point Road, crossing the Scenic Trail about halfway.

Hill of Pines Trail. Blazes: white.
A loop trail from Carpenter Road north to meet the Swamp Trail shortly before it emerges on Old West Point Road. Avoids the climb over top of Hill of Pines to reach Upper Reservoir.

CROWS NEST (STORM KING SECTION OF PALISADES INTERSTATE PARK)

The northernmost area of the park system between West Point and Storm King Mountain is relatively little frequented and contains no marked trails. Although a favorite of the early Highlands walkers, highway construction and the encroachment of the Military Reservation have tended to make it less accessible to the casual hiker.

One of the most famous of all Hudson Highland landmarks, Crows Nest Mountain, forms the southern boundary of this section. Although the main summit is situated within the limits of the Military Reservation and permission must be secured to walk here, subsidiary peaks lie within the park and are well worth investigation.

The hiker who is experienced in the use of a compass and who enjoys bushwhacking can gain access to the general area from Rt. 9W at the height of land just south of Storm King Mountain. By using the "West Point" quadrangle of the United States Geodetic Survey as a reference, one can follow the ridges in an easterly direction out to the precipitous rocks overlooking the Hudson. Although the elevations here are not much over 500 feet the slope falls off so sharply to the river below that one has a feeling of real exposure. Across the river lies the protruding bulk of Mt. Taurus (Bull Hill), its flank gouged by the stone quarry which runs down to Little Stony Point on the shores below.

From the old Storm King highway (Rt. 218) the cliffs can be gained by a steep and rather arduous climb up the ravine which is located about 0.6 mile north of the Lee Gate entrance to the Military Academy. A little searching on the southerly side of the stream running down the ravine will disclose an old logging road which winds up to the backbone of the main peak. From here a scramble through the brush and up the rocky slope brings one out on top of the cliffs.

Immediately to the south, and within the Military Reservation boundaries, a small brook which drains the easterly slope of Crows Nest plunges over the precipice and forms an impressive waterfall as it tumbles below. Several hundred feet up the left, or southerly side of the brook, is the Grotto, a shallow cavern in the granite uplift of rocks. The Grotto finds frequent mention in the diaries of the early Highlands walkers as a refuge and dining place in time of stormy weather. One of the most avid of these hikers, William Thompson Howell, mentions that a cache was established at the Grotto as early as 1887.

The deep ravine on the southerly side of Storm King Mountain, called Storm King Clove, is another section worth exploring. From the parking lot at the highest point on Rt. 9W a well-defined wood road leads down into the clove and eventually out to the old Storm King highway. From the wood road the adventurous hiker may undertake a variety of scrambles up the south side of Storm King, which looms above. For the less daring it is possible to bushwhack across the floor of the valley and up the slopes of the so-called North Peak of Crows Nest. Again there are fine views of the river and an excellent outlook toward Breakneck Ridge and the Beacons. One can return to 9W by following the ridges which lead back from the river toward the west.

Throughout the area, overgrown wood roads and faint paths appear at random, and occasionally a series of rock cairns betoken someone's private trail. In view of the lack of marked trails it is necessary to rely on the topographical map for orientation. As mentioned above, the "West Point" quadrangle of the U.S.G.S. is the appropriate reference for the entire section.

NEW WINDSOR CANTONMENT

A recent addition to the Interstate Park system is the historic site of the last winter encampment of the Continental Army, occupied during the final year of the American Revolution. Some seven hundred log buildings were erected in the winter of 1782–83; only one original building still stands.

Although fighting supposedly had ended at Yorktown, the British main army was still in New York City. The Americans, therefore, could not disband. The Continental Army had to be kept at full strength. The waiting, following seven years of hardship, tried their spirits. Worse than the discouragement of the men was the dissatisfaction of the officers, with little to do but worry about arrears in pay and no promise of pensions. A conspiracy to defy disbandment by force unless Congress met their demands was overcome by a personal appeal from General Washington.

The tavern, the shops, and the Publick Building have all been restored and furnished with authentic maps, uniforms, arms, and other appropriate equipment. Restoration was undertaken in 1933 by a group of private citizens to tell the story of the ordinary soldier in the Revolution, to re-create the conditions under which he lived. Muzzle-loading contests, pipe and drum music, demonstrations of bullet-making, horseshoeing, and eighteenth-century cooking bring the times vividly to mind.

Overnight camping and picnicking may be arranged for groups. Modest fees are charged for parking and admission to the buildings. The Cantonment may be reached from the Thruway via Rt. 17 to Harriman, then north on Rt. 32 to Vail's Gate; or from 9W west from New Windsor.

5 · SCHUNEMUNK MOUNTAIN

(Map 6)

INTRODUCTION

EST of the Black Rock Forest in the northern Highlands, on the opposite side of the valley through which run Woodbury Creek, Moodna Creek, the Newburgh branch of the Erie-Lackawanna Railroad, and the New York State Thruway, and extending southwest, lies Schunemunk Mountain—an impressive ridge, double-crested on its north end, nearly 1700 feet high. It is more than 8 miles long from its southwestern end near Monroe, on the main line of the railroad, to its northeastern point, near Salisbury Mills. On a map it does not seem topographically different from the gneiss and granite Highlands eastward, but geologically it is much younger, being composed of sandstones, shales, and conglomerates of Devonian time, with Silurian as well as Ordovician strata at its base. It is part of a long ridge of similar strata extending forty miles southwestward into New Jersey, past Greenwood Lake and Green Pond, and ending at a point near Lake Hopatcong. It was formed as sediments in a narrow sound of the ancient sea. At the beginning of Silurian time this sea surrounded the "Old Land," Appalachia, in which was included much that is now New England, eastern New York, and northern New Jersey, together with land now covered by the Atlantic.

The conglomerate ledges, composed of the highest and youngest of the Schunemunk strata, are conspicuous on the long level summit, with a reddish purple matrix enclosing white quartz pebbles up to six inches in diameter—the remnants of erosion of streams

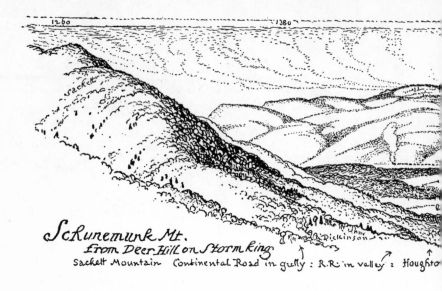

Schunemunk Mt.
from Deer Hill on Storm King
Sackett Mountain   Continental Road in gully : R.R. in valley : Houghto

from the hills of the "Old Land." Subsequent lateral pressure has folded the formation into a U- or V-shaped trough, with the strata on the east limb dipping to the west and those on the west limb dipping to the east. It has also undergone extensive longitudinal and cross faulting which has further confused the original sedimentary relations. This crush zone led to the cleft in the middle of the northern end, making a double-crested effect, with the densely wooded Barton Swamp in the depression between the crests.

On the other side of the valley to the west, and topographically associated with Schunemunk, is a line of wooded knobs of Precambrian gneiss extending from Woodcock Hill (over 1000 feet), west of the north end of Schunemunk, southwest to Sugar Loaf (of Orange County). Their position, surrounded on the east by Devonian and Silurian formations and on the west by Ordovician slates and limestones of the Walkill valley, has caused much geological speculation. Earlier interpretations held that these knobs were parts of a syncline, or a structural downfold, and were at the original western border of the Highlands, and that the Schunemunk strata had been laid down in this trough. Later studies suggest that these knobs are gigantic overthrust blocks, shoved from the western front of the Highlands when the great push of the Taconian Orogeny occurred, some 480 million years ago. Their relative hardness caused them to stand up as knobs, while softer formations around them wore down

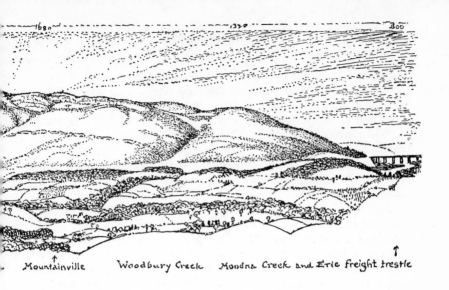

1680   1370   800

↑
Mountainville   Woodbury Creek   Moodna Creek and Erie freight trestle

into the valleys. Woodcock Hill is made up of both Precambrian gneiss abutting the Ordovician formations on its west foot and Schunemunk strata on its eastern slopes.

The views from the ridge of Schunemunk are impressive and extensive. Usually pronounced skun-uh-munk, the name means "excellent fireplace" in the Algonquin tongue. This name was given to the palisades village that once existed on the northern spur of the mountain, in which lived the Indian tribe that originally owned the land. Today the northernmost half of the ridge is owned by the Star Expansion Company, of Mountainville, New York, whose owner has permitted hikers to tramp this region over the years.

Useful maps for this region are four U. S. Geological Survey maps: "Popolopen Lake," "Monroe," "Maybrook," and "Cornell." Access by car is by the Thruway to Harriman exit (16), then north on Rt. 32 to Highland Mills, Woodbury, or Mountainville, or by Rt. 17 to Monroe. Short Line Buses service Central Valley, Highland Mills, Mountainville, and Monroe.

Jessup Trail (first section). Length: 8.1 miles. Blazes: yellow.

This trail is described in two sections to facilitate making short one-day round trips. Use the map to plan trips. From the northeastern end of the mountain, near Mountainville, this first section is a moderate climb (850 feet) of about an hour to Taylor Hollow, a high clove divided by Baby Brook, the only source of good water that seldom fails and probably the only one on the mountain in dry weather.

Access to the Jessup Trail is from Rt. 32 opposite Angola Road in Mountainville. Go downhill, following yellow blazes on the road marked Mountainville 0.1 mile to Taylor Road, and proceed on this about 0.3 mile, crossing the bridge over the Thruway. A grassy area on the left is maintained for hikers by the Star factory and cars may be parked here.

Continuing on Taylor Road about 0.4 mile, enter a field on the left and follow a faint dirt road for about 0.5 mile northwest across the field into the woods. There the Jessup Trail joins a clear dirt road in a hemlock grove, and rises alongside a set of pools interspersed with cascades. The trail then leaves the dirt road and crosses the Erie freight line. It climbs about 700 feet in 0.8 mile, arriving at Taylor Hollow alongside Baby Brook.

Here the Jessup turns left up the central ridge to the summit, about 500 feet higher. As an alternative, follow the Barton Swamp Trail straight ahead, or the Western Ridge Trail to the right. For a short day's walk, return to Mountainville by either of these two trails.

Jessup Trail (second section). Jesuit Home to Taylor Hollow.

The access to the southwestern end of the Jessup Trail is on Seven Springs Road about 0.1 mile southeast of the Jesuit Home. It may be reached by car or taxi from Highland Mills or Monroe. In about 0.5 mile the trail climbs about 300 feet and commands a fine view. The ridge here is rather narrow and when the trees are bare there are views down into the valleys to the east and to the west. Continuing through several notches for over a mile, the trail passes a strange white boulder. This is a glacial erratic of dolomitic limestone originating somewhere to the north and deposited on Schunemunk by the last great glacier to grind south across the land, some 20,000 years ago. The trail then goes under a telephone line to an extended area of bare rock that provides an excellent viewpoint looking northwest over Round Hill, one of a line of wooded knobs composed of Precambrian gneiss that march parallel to Schunemunk for most of its length. After winding briefly through a swamp patch, the trail meets the terminus of the Forrest Trail coming in from the southeast.

A little beyond, the Jessup passes a path leading west to a bog where water occasionally may be fresh enough to drink. The mountain gradually widens in the next 0.5 mile to a high spot where a radio relay tower and TV antennas have been built for communities in the valley northwest of the mountain. The trail briefly follows a dirt road, then ambles on for over 0.5 mile toward the widest part of the mountain.

Here the trail changes underfoot to the marvelous and unique conglomerate rock that makes Schunemunk so fascinating. This rock, sometimes called "pudding stone," has, because of the hematite present, a gray or reddish-purple matrix of hard quartzite enclosing a kaleidoscopic assortment of pebbles up to six inches in diameter, many of them white quartz. It was originally a bed of mud, sand, and abrasion-rounded gravel on the shores of an ancient inland sea, material which was deposited about 350 million years ago, during the Devonian Period, by fast-flowing streams descending from highlands that existed farther to the east. Later, the mixture was gradually cemented together and compacted by pressure into solid, hard conglomerate. At the top surface of this rock the pebbles have been neatly ground flat by the same massive layer of slowly moving ice that deposited the white boulder farther back on the trail.

The Long Path (blue blaze) coming from High Knob enters from the southeast and, after a few steps, departs to the northwest. Surmounting a series of ledges through clefts in the rock, the Jessup Trail attains an elevation of 1662 feet where good views are obtained to the east and to the west. Beyond an unusual arch formed by the downgrowing limb of an old oak tree, there is sometimes water to be found at the foot of some small ledges on the trail. Nearby, the Western Ridge Trail (blue on white blaze) comes in from the west, terminating at a cairn on the Jessup Trail.

A few minutes more walking leads to the highest point on the mountain. At a cairn on a gently sloping table of conglomerate, the elevation is 1664 feet, higher than any of the neighboring summits in Harriman State Park, Black Rock Forest, and the Hudson River area from Storm King to the Beacons. Splendid views of these mountains are seen from this vantage point and the hiker with sharp eyes may count at least four fire lookout towers and two radio relay towers in this panorama, as well as the Perkins Memorial Tower which juts above the outline of Bear Mountain to the southeast. On a clear day the higher peaks of the Catskills are identifiable across the horizon to the north: Slide, Cornell, Wittenberg, Plateau, Sugarloaf and Indian Head. To the west, the tall monument at High Point State Park at the Kittatinny Mountain in the northwestern corner of New Jersey can sometimes be discerned. In between, from west to north, stretch the Shawangunks past Sam's Point to Mohonk.

A short distance farther along the trail there is a path leading northwest to a group of large blocks called "The Megaliths." From their tops one may look across Barton Swamp to the Western Ridge. In less than 0.5 mile the Dark Hollow Trail (white on black markers—individually maintained) goes east down the mountain to the railroad tracks, where it joins the Sweet Clover Trail (white blaze). A short distance down this trail is a hole containing water if the weather has not been too dry. After another 0.5 mile on the Jessup Trail, the Sweet Clover Trail enters from the east, coincides with the Jessup Trail for about 0.3 mile, and then branches off to the west.

Here and for the next 0.5 mile on the Jessup Trail there is a continuous series of magnificent views, particularly in the late afternoon when the sun illuminates the Hudson River and the Beacons. Fine views of the Western Ridge also abound and it is easy to see that the rock surface there slopes down to the southeast while that underfoot slopes to the northwest. This downfold in the rock formation is a result of lateral pressure acting on the crust during the major mountain-building episode some 250 million years ago, near the end of the Paleozoic Era. Later erosion, some additional crustal uplift, and further erosion left the hard conglomerate layer in the same concave shape, and, because of its different resistance to erosion, it stands now high above the surrounding valley.

The Jessup continues among the clumps of gnarled pitch pines and drops into Taylor Hollow.

Western Ridge Trail. Length: 2.3 miles. Blazes: blue on white.

This trail runs along the Western Ridge, generally parallel to the Jessup Trail. Access is from Mountainville by the Jessup Trail to Taylor Hollow, alongside Baby Brook. The trail ascends up steep ledges to the Western Ridge and its splendid views of the Hudson River, North and South Beacon mountains, Storm King Mountain, and the nearby slope of the central ridge of Schunemunk. It is said that somewhere here on the northern spur of the Western Ridge was the Indian village whose fireplace gave the mountain its name. The trail turns southwest along the relatively narrow ridge overlooking the Washingtonville valley with its peaceful pastoral scenery. About 0.8 mile from Taylor Hollow is the terminus of the Sweet Clover Trail from the east. In another 0.8 mile the Western Ridge Trail reaches a bare ledge sloping eastward, where there is an excellent

view of the central ridge and of Barton Swamp in the trough between the two ridges. Here the trail goes steeply downhill into
Barton Swamp (past one end of the Barton Swamp Trail) where
it turns right, joins the Barton Swamp Trail for a short distance,
then left, climbing steeply to the southeast over ledges with views
of the Western Ridge and the distant mountain ranges beyond.
Continuing southeast, the trail ends at a cairn on the Jessup Trail.

Barton Swamp Trail. Length: 1.6 miles. Blazes: red on white.

This trail follows the wooded trough between the central and
western ridges, providing a quick, sheltered exit to Taylor Hollow.
Barton Swamp Trail begins where the Long Path rises out of Barton Swamp to cross the Western Ridge. Going northeast, it is soon
joined by the Western Ridge Trail coming in from the right. The
Western Ridge Trail turns left and the Barton Swamp Trail goes
down through trees, paralleling the headwaters of Baby Brook, crosses
to its west side and in less than a mile crosses the Sweet Clover
Trail. The trail crosses back to the east side of Baby Brook and
descends gently through hummocks covered with mountain laurel.
In less than 0.8 mile the trail meets the Jessup Trail alongside Baby
Brook in Taylor Hollow. The Jessup Trail offers an exit route northeast to Taylor Road in Mountainville.

Sweet Clover Trail. Length: 2.8 miles. Blazes: white.

This trail is a good east-west approach to the highest points. From
the hiker's parking area on Taylor Road (see Jessup Trail) follow
an asphalt private road past a barn. Turning west into the meadow
the trail becomes a dirt road, turns south, then west into the woods.
The trail leaves the dirt road to cross the Erie freight tracks about
1 mile from the start. A short detour south along the tracks leads
to the start of Dark Hollow Trail (see Jessup Trail).

The Sweet Clover Trail climbs steadily, across a slope of flaggy
sandstone that plunges down to Dark Hollow Brook far below to
the south, then switchbacks up past the northernmost branch of
Dark Hollow Brook, across a swampy stretch, then uphill again.

At about 1450 feet the trail meets the Jessup Trail and runs
north with it about 0.3 mile on magnificent conglomerate rock,
yielding splendid views. It then turns west and drops steeply into
Barton Swamp and crosses the headwaters of Baby Brook. Reaching
the Barton Swamp Trail, it climbs steeply up the Western Ridge
to terminate at the Western Ridge Trail.

The Long Path. Length: 5 miles. Blazes: blue.

Crossing Schunemunk at its widest part, the Long Path uses some previously abandoned trails. This section leaves Rt. 32 at the railroad trestle about 1.6 miles north of the Highland Mills bus station. From the west side of Rt. 32, follow the trestle to the top, walk north along the tracks of the Erie freight line about 0.4 mile and turn left on a dirt road. Follow this 0.2 mile to a gravel pit, turn right over a small stream, and enter the woods.

The trail climbs steadily west, then north, again west, for over 0.5 mile, then turns north up a rocky defile to the top of Little Knob (1000 feet). The trail ascends a wooded incline, then to the right up a talus slope, up the rising edge of a cliff bordered with twisted pitch pines, then right again to the summit of High Knob (1383 feet). Here are excellent views to the east, north, and south.

From the western side of High Knob the LP descends north along the top edge of the high pine-bordered cliff above an impressive ravine. At the saddle of this ravine the trail turns left across a double notch, turns right and climbs steeply to the top of another rock wall. High Knob and its cliffs are visible from here.

The trail then goes northwest, ascending gradually for less than 0.5 mile to a high point with á view to the north. It then drops a bit, bends left, then sharp right to cross a headwater of Dark Hollow Brook. From this headwater it climbs steadily northwest for less than 0.3 mile where it joins the Jessup Trail on the conglomerate rock at an elevation of 1600 feet. There are views east and west.

The Long Path continues northwest down a gentle slope, enters the woods, and descends a series of ledges overlooking Barton Swamp and the Western Ridge; the last ledge is steep. Then the trail plunges down a talus slope into Barton Swamp, across a brook, turns right into a wood road leading northeast about 0.8 mile through terrain which is likely to be soggy underfoot.

Passing the end of Barton Swamp Trail on the right, the Long Path bends to the left and rises over a saddle in the Western Ridge to a rapid descent of the mountain for over 0.8 mile. Crossing under a telephone line and passing just left of a hidden pond, the trail continues downhill to the north for almost 0.5 mile, and joins Clove Road next to a white house opposite a small lake about 1.8 miles south of Salisbury Mills. The Long Path continues 2 miles farther over Woodcock Hill to Rt. 94 west of Salisbury Mills.

Forrest Trail. Length: 2.3 miles. Blazes: white.

This trail is an easy approach to the southern half of the Jessup

Trail from Rt. 32 north of Highland Mills. Access is at the beginning of Ridge Road, 0.7 mile north from Highland Mills bus station. The trail follows Ridge Road uphill to the northeast for 0.9
mile, then turns right into Schunemunk Road. Winding past a large
red barn, a reservoir. and a horse-training stable, the trail continues
on this road for 0.7 mile, then enters the woods to the right on a
well-defined wood road. A car (or a taxi from Highland Mills) may
be driven directly to this point.

The wood road leads northwest 0.3 mile to the base of a steep
slope of loose sandstone slabs that split into distinctively flat plates,
commonly called "flagstone" but identified as graywacke. A 400-foot
scramble up this slope leads to better footing near the top, where
the trail meets the Jessup Trail at 1400 feet and ends.

BULL MINE

One of the largest and most interesting magnetic iron mines in
the New York area is Bull Mine, last worked in 1884. Most of the
Ramapo mines are water filled, but Bull Mine is unusual in that it
can be penetrated approximately 1000 feet before reaching water.
It is located about 1.5 miles north-northwest of the junction of
Route 208 and Route 17 on the top of Bull Mine Mountain. This
junction is just north of the town of Monroe.

To find the mine, use the "Monroe" topographical quadrangle. A
good flashlight, or carbide lamp, per person is absolutely essential.
For a sample of magnetite ore, take along a magnet; magnetite is
the only common mineral that can be picked up with one. If the
trip is made in winter or early spring, a rope and an ice axe may
also be necessary. Only experienced rock climbers should attempt
exploration under winter conditions.

Take the bus or drive to Monroe. From there walk, drive, or take
taxi to Oxford. It is possible to follow dirt roads and an old mine
road to reach the top of the hill, and the mine. Beware of an un-
protected vertical shaft on the right near the top of the hill.

An alternate route can also be taken, using the government
topographic map. Follow Rt. 208 about 1.5 miles north of its junction with Rt. 17. At this point, the topographic map shows a
cemetery. Take the minor road to the left for about 0.4 mile from
Rt. 208, going downhill and passing north of a pond. Park along
this dirt road just north of Bull Mine Mountain. Walk south, across
open fields to the woods at the base of the hill. Cut through the

woods to a grove of hemlocks on the northeast side. With a little luck, find a path which will lead to the top and the mine. Otherwise, bushwhack to the top. At the mine there are excellent views of the Shawangunks and of the Catskills to the northwest.

The main entrance is a vertical cut about 100 feet wide. It is possible to scramble down this entrance on the southwest corner, but a far easier entrance is from the northwest corner, outside the cut. Descend west about 20 feet down the mine dumps. Here is another, smaller entrance, which can be crawled into with little difficulty to the bottom of the vertical cut. Beyond this point, lights are necessary. Descend eastwards from about the middle of the cut, being very careful not to roll the loose rocks down on your friends in front of you. After reaching the first large pillar, which supports the roof, go promptly to the left side of the passage. Beware of continuing on the right side, where there is a sheer drop. Just past the pillar, ice is frequently encountered in the winter and early spring and a rope and an ice axe may be necessary. If ice is present, practice extreme caution. Hug the left wall and continue down, and beware of loose rock underfoot. A short distance beyond, if there is no ice, an easy 7-foot scramble leads to a large room. Two small ponds fill the bottom of this room. To the west, two other chambers can be explored. Here and there on the ceiling, little brown bats can be seen sleeping. Please, do not disturb!

The mine entrance is an excellent place to have lunch after returning to the surface. If it is raining, the mine itself affords dry accommodation.

6 · THE SHAWANGUNK MOUNTAINS

(Maps 7 and 8)

INTRODUCTION

HAWANGUNK (pronounced "shon-gum") is the name of a mountain ridge with a topographic feature somewhat unique to the New York area. A typically narrow ridge composed of extremely durable conglomerate—the Shawangunk Conglomerate of Late Silurian age—it stands as a striking example of the process described as differential erosion. The shale layers that lie both above and below the conglomerate are much softer and do not readily resist the forces of weathering and erosion; they are more rapidly reduced to lower elevations. The resulting linear Shawangunk ridge, with its striking talus slopes of downward-tumbled boulders, is different in character from the Catskills, the Adirondacks, or the Highlands, and, as a topographic feature, always comes as a surprise to those who see it for the first time.

At its northern end, the ridge rises gradually from the Hudson River Valley near Kingston as a series of low hills, suddenly dramatized by the "table rocks" and "ice caves" of High Falls and by the spectacular Mohonk escarpments of Bonticou Crag, Sky Top, and Eagle Cliff. The first of the five successively higher lakes, Mohonk (1250 feet), is cradled between the latter two cliffs. From this point southward, the ridge grows higher and broader, and at Gertrude's Nose it bends to the west toward Ellenville. The lakes, in order are Minnewaska (1650 feet), Awosting (1875 feet),

Haseco, (known locally as Mud Pond (1850 feet), and Maratanza
(2250 feet). Near the last is Sam's Point, the highest elevation of
the range (the widest point is near Haseco Lake). Beyond Sam's
Point, the ridge settles again into lower, less wild, and less spectacular hills until it reaches the Delaware Water Gap and New
Jersey border at Port Jervis, where it is known as Kittatinny Mountain. The entire range will be traversed by a marked trail to connect
with the Appalachian Trail.

The Shawangunk Mountains are mapped on the U. S. Geological
Survey's "Rosendale," "Mohonk Lake," "Gardiner," "Napanoch,"
"Ellenville," and "Wurtsboro" quadrangles (1:24,000). These maps
are helpful in locating approach roads but are not useful for hiking
because the trails are not shown; the scale does not permit an ade-
quate representation of the cliff-riddled terrain. For walks on the
Mohonk and Minnewaska estates, the detailed maps available from
the hotels are essential; these may be obtained from Lake Mohonk
Mountain House, Mohonk Lake, New Paltz, N.Y. 12561, and
Lake Minnewaska Mountain Houses, Inc., Lake Minnewaska, New
Paltz, N.Y. 12561, respectively.

The shale layers that underlie the Shawangunk and Kittatinny
mountains also make up the floor of the broad valley, the Great
Valley, immediately to the east. Laid down originally as mud deposits in an extensive marginal sea during the Ordovician Period
some 500 million years ago, they were subsequently folded, uplifted,
and then eroded during a crustal upheaval near the end of the Ordovician. Submerged again beneath a warm, shallow sea during the
succeeding Silurian Period about 450 million years ago, wave action
laid down an almost beach-like layer of sand and fine gravel, the
"white stone" of the Shawangunks. Another episode of crustal
deformation about 280 million years ago tilted all these strata into
their present position—but differential erosion alone is responsible
for the present-day relief. Most recently, glaciers that crossed this
region into New York City left their marks, too, as the north-south
trending faint striae, seen most often along the ridge top. These
should not be confused with the abundant "slickensides," sections
of highly polished and deeply grooved rock caused by friction
between sliding masses subjected to the ancient crustal upheavals.

The large number of pre-Revolutionary stone houses to be found
throughout the Shawangunk region attests to the early attractiveness
of the fertile Wallkill and Rondout valleys alongside the range.
The Dutch settlers in particular left their trace in the place names.
Even the slopes of the mountains were farmed for many years,

although they never were considered high-production fields; old family records indicate that sons who received their share in bottom land got less acreage than those who were given the slopes. Today the once-open land is returning to forest.

Trails often run through unmarked and frequently unrecognized charcoal pits, for charcoal was an important product one hundred years ago, when the tanbark industry moved into the area (as well as into the Catskills), stripping it of most of its hemlock trees. Two notable stands survived—the Palmaghatt on the Minnewaska estate, which later received extensive damage during the 1950 hurricane, and Glen Anna at Mohonk.

For many generations, and possibly even during the time of the Indians, the Sam's Point—Cragsmoor area was famous for its huckleberries. Rather than permit the berries to be shaded out by competing vegetation, fires were set periodically. The pine which characterizes the region survived, as did some other interesting species, and the huckleberry crop flourished.

The early commercial berry pickers spent the summer in shacks along the entrance road to Ice Caves Mountain. Some of their homes still exist as unattractive mementos of the past. Remains, too, may still be seen of a network of trails, marked by cairns, leading to favored picking areas.

The occurrence of rare flora in the region (locations are a carefully guarded secret) was perpetuated by the burning out of competing species, and this fragile environment, famous among botanists, is sufficiently important that part of it recently received national landmark recognition. The practice among responsible hikers, to "leave nothing but footprints, take nothing but pictures," should be observed meticulously in this "fire climax."

No history of the Shawangunks could be complete without mention of the Smiley family. To them the hiker owes the preservation of much of the range, unscarred by blatant commercialism. Albert K. Smiley acquired the original 300-acre parcel, comprising Mohonk Lake and the surrounding land, from John Stokes in 1869. To maintain the character of the property, adjoining farms and other private holdings were added to the estate as they became available. The property was originally conceived as a summer home for Albert K. and Alfred H. (his twin brother) and their families. However, their salaries as schoolmasters would not support the luxury of such extensive acreage, and they found themselves in the hotel business. In 1879 Alfred H. Smiley opened his own hotel, the Lake Minnewaska House. This establishment now consists of two buildings: Cliff House east of the lake and Wildmere at the north. Both estates expanded until Mohonk reached 7500 acres, Minnewaska more than 10,000 acres. Over the years the carriage roads, paths, and trails as we now know them were constructed. The Smileys of Mohonk pioneered in road-building techniques, conservation, and land management practices, to the ultimate benefit of the hiking public.

At the present time 6000 acres of the Mohonk estate are in the process of being transferred to the Mohonk Trust, a charitable trust set up by the Smiley family in 1963 to work in the areas of man's relationship to himself and to his environment. All the land will continue to be open to the public; trust ownership, it is felt, will help to preserve the land from the incursions of highways and commercial development.

In 1970, the State of New York, with the help of Nature Conservancy, created Minnewaska State Park. The tract centers about Lake Awosting but also includes Lake Haseco and Stony Kill Falls. The remaining portion of the Minnewaska Estate, under 3000 acres in size, will still be privately managed. This area contains Lake Minnewaska and Awosting Falls. The New York–New Jersey Trail Conference has been invited by the state to establish a system of trails in the new state park.

Fees are charged at Mohonk, Minnewaska, and Sam's Point for day trips, and Mohonk for camping. This has become necessary because of the ever-increasing cost of maintenance, patrol, taxes, and insurance. The cooperation of users in curtailing litter and vandalism will help to prevent further escalation of such costs.

THE MOHONK ESTATE

The Mohonk estate extends for 8 miles, roughly from Bonticou Crag to Millbrook Mountain. For hiking, the usual points of access are Mountain Rest and the Trapps; camping facilities are available at a number of points and walks could also be started from these areas. Walking at Mohonk ranges from easy, though scenic, strolls on the 45 miles of carriage roads to rough scrambles over boulders, through crevices, and across open ledges (aided where absolutely necessary by strategically placed ladders). Only a brief indication of the possibilities can be made here; the hiker must go, map in hand, and make his own discoveries.

Mountain Rest.

From New Paltz (Exit 18, New York State Thruway), follow the main street (Rt. 299) through the village, and take the first right after the Wallkill Bridge. At the next fork bear left, keep straight ahead at the next intersection, and continue uphill to the Mountain Rest Gatehouse, the entrance to the Mohonk property. Parking facilities and information are available here. The Adirondack Trailways bus serves New Paltz; take a taxi to Mountain Rest. To the northeast, several carriage roads lead to Bonticou Crag; a trail (blue blaze) climbs up the talus slope to the crest. To the southwest, carriage roads lead to the hotel and the central part of the estate. Close to Mountain Rest are Glen Anna, the Rock Rift Crevices, and the Cave of Aeolus. One of the most popular objectives is Sky Top, a prominent cliff whose stone tower (the Albert K. Smiley Memorial Tower) is visible from as far away as the Thruway. The map in the fire observer's room will help identify the features of the distant landscape. The Crevice at Sky Top and the adjoining Labyrinth Path are noteworthy, and the western escarpment with Eagle Cliff, Humpty Dumpty, Cope's Lookout, Arching Rocks, and Giant's Workshop amply repays exploration. Rhododendron Swamp, via Laurel Ledge Road and the Old Minnewaska Road, affords much of botanical interest. The Oakwood Drive circles through groves of dogwood which are spectacular both in spring and fall. Signs identify road and trail crossings and terminals; the rougher trails have painted marks and arrows to show the way.

Gateway-Kleinekill Area.

Stay on Rt. 299 out of New Paltz until in view of the stone Gateway building, with its circular arch. This area is at present leased to the Mid-Hudson-Catskills Museum, which has constructed nature trails. From here, walk to Kleinekill Farm along Lenape Lane, the carriage road which was for many years the main approach to Mohonk Lake, and then by various roads to Rock Spring Bridge and the Sky Top region. At the farm a road to the left leads to Duck Pond, also known as Kleinekill Lake, where camping is permitted by prior arrangement; campers may drive all the way in. There is a fine view of Sky Top Tower, and many trails and woods roads go off in various directions.

The Trapps.

From New Paltz, stay on Rt. 299 to its end at Rt. 44-45. Turn right, up the mountain; after the hairpin turn, at the point where

the road bends to the right through the pass, there is a large parking area on the left, with excellent views. Just beyond is Trapps
Bridge, easily reached from the left side of the road. This steel
bridge carries the carriage road between Mohonk and Minnewaska
and is the starting point for walks in this area. To the north, there
is soon a fork, the Undercliff Road going to the right, the Overcliff
Road to the left. The two roads meet again at the Rhododendron
Swamp, providing a circular route of 4.5 miles around the Trapps
(the name is believed derived from the Dutch "treppen," for steps).

In the spring and fall Undercliff Road resounds to the clank of
pitons and carabiners and the calls of climbers on the cliffs, for
this is the prime rock climbing area in the East. The climbing is
strictly regulated and is not to be attempted by the uninitiated:
fatalities have occurred here. Those who feel the urge should join
one of the climbing groups for proper training.

To the south from Trapps Bridge the carriage road takes its
winding way to Lake Minnewaska, with views (to the right) of the
cliffs of Dickie Barre across the Coxing Kill Valley. This is the
region of the annual hawk watches. Great numbers of bird watchers
gather each fall to see the huge variety of birds which funnel into
the thermal currents of the ridge as they begin their southward
migration. From the carriage road there is an unmarked trail which
goes constantly up over the huge rock slab to the observation point.
A blue-marked trail, taking off to the southwest (left) from the carriage just before Coxing Kill is crossed, leads by easy stages
(the last portion is marked by cairns) to the red-marked Minnewaska Trail between Lake Minnewaska and Millbrook Mountain, a
spectacular cliff with the highest sheer drop east of the Mississippi.
From here a trail continues to Gertrude's Nose. At Trapps Bridge
another blue-marked trail goes to the left through a small camping
area and, following the cliff edge for the most part, also leads to
Millbrook Mountain.

Coxing Camp.
From Rt. 299, follow Rt. 44-55 to the right, as described above.
After passing Trapps Bridge, take the first right (Trapps Road)
and go right at the next fork (Clove Road). The camp is on the
right. Swimming, picnicking, and overnight camping are available
here. Across the stream is a blue-marked trail which follows along
the northwestern edge of the estate; after some distance, a red trail
to the right (Clove Path) leads to the hotel area.

The Log Cabin.

This is a camp on Mossy Brook Road, to the left off the public road continuing past Mountain Rest (see above). Advance arrangements must be made and the key obtained at the Gatehouse. A cutoff path leads to Birch Turn on Mossy Brook Road, from which the central part of the estate is readily accessible.

THE MINNEWASKA AREA

The Minnewaska area fits end to end on the ridge with Mohonk and extends some 6 miles farther to the southwest, from Rt. 44-55 to Millbrook Mountain to Lake Awosting. The main access point is from the hotel entrance, but the area may also be gained from the Trapps (see above) and from the Wallkill Valley. As at Mohonk, carriage roads lead to almost all points of interest; extended trail walks through heavily wooded areas can also be made here.

From New Paltz take Rt. 299 to its end at Rt. 44-55; turn right and continue across the gap to the Minnewaska entrance, on the left. From northern New Jersey and Port Jervis take Rt. 209 to Kerhonkson, then Rt. 44-55 to the entrance. Kerhonkson may also be reached by bus. Parking is available near the entrance or at the lower parking area at Wildmere.

Close at hand are trails to the Crevices, Beacon Hill, and Awosting Falls. The complete circuit of Lake Minnewaska provides an interesting scramble. From the lake, trails and roads radiate out to Millbrook Mountain, Gertrude's Nose, the Palmaghatt, Castle Point, and Lake Awosting. These may be combined in various ways to make up circular trips.

SHAWANGUNK ESCARPMENT *from* MOHONK
FROM PHOTO BY MARY LOUISE WISE

Gertrude's Nose.

From the southeast corner of Wildmere House at Lake Minne-waska it is possible to follow marked carriage roads which lead, in about 4 miles, to Millbrook Mountain, the end of the road. A little beyond the end of the road is a sign to Gertrude's Nose via the Ledge Trail. The trail (faint orange markers) follows along the cliff edge south with spectacular views to Gertrude's Nose, about 1.8 miles. About 0.5 mile from the start of the Ledge Trail, and just before a descent into a low divide, there is a faint trail which leads west, back to the carriage road, if a shorter walk is desired. At Gertrude's Nose the trail turns sharply back toward the north, still following the cliff edge. It crosses a brook where good water is available, climbs steeply, and leads back to the carriage road in approximately 1.8 miles.

The Palmaghatt.

The Palmaghatt Ravine contains two of the Shawangunk's many waterfalls, and, although the ravine itself is territory only for dedicated bushwackers, trails around its perimeter offer fine views for a moderate one-day walk. Located about 1 mile south of Lake Minnewaska on the eastern front of the range, the ravine is surrounded by steep cliffs and talus slopes which extend to Gertrude's Nose on the east and Hamilton Point along the west. For many years the Palmaghatt contained a treasured stand of virgin hemlock, now sadly depleted by hurricane and ice storms. The Dutch name means "Laurel Glen." Both Upper and Lower Palmaghatt Falls are about 45 feet high and consist of a series of cascades over shale. The Lower Falls are steeper. For views down into the Palmaghatt, it is possible to approach from Lake Minnewaska on the hotel property's network of carriage roads and trails leading to Gertrude's Nose or Hamilton Point. For a circular trip starting in the Wallkill Valley, leave cars at the base of the road to the Bergen County Girl Scout Council's Camp Ridge-Ho, north of Tillson Lake. From the camp a trail (white blaze) leads to the east cliffs near Gertrude's Nose; an alternate route from the camp (red blaze) offers views of the Lower Falls and, via a dead-end spur (blue blaze), the Upper Falls before rejoining the main trail.

Atop the cliffs, from the Gertrude's Nose side, the rim of the ravine can be followed first on a trail (marked variously in orange and red) and then on carriage roads. Shortly after the road, now diminished to trail proportions, reaches Hamilton Point, a faintly marked trail, Shirley Path, descends toward the valley but soon dwin-

AWOSTING FALLS IN WINTER R.E.H '70

dles away so that it is necessary to bushwhack down to Palmaghatt
Kill and across to Camp Ridge-Ho again.

Lake Awosting.
The carriage road from the southwest corner of Wildmere
House at Lake Minnewaska to Lake Awosting, 5 to 6 miles, passes
along the west side of the Palmaghatt. In 1967, however, a new road
was constructed to the lake from the Minnewaska entrance on Rt.
44–55. It is planned to use this area for day guests as a place for
swimming, hiking, picnicking, and boating. As at Minnewaska and
Mohonk, motor boats are prohibited on Lake Awosting. Activities
are on a moderate fee basis.

It is also possible to reach the lake from Ellenville, leaving from
behind the town dump via an old road known as Smiley or Napanoch Road, usable as a footpath only. This road passes Napanoch
Point with superb views, crosses Fly Brook, and eventually reaches
the northwest shore of the lake, in all a distance of about 6 miles.

Another rather poorly marked trail leaves the south end of Lake
Awosting and proceeds southwest along the summit of the ridge to
Haseco Lake (Mud Pond), where the evidence of former beaver
dams is still visible; eventually the trail reaches Verkeerder Kill
Falls and Sam's Point, a distance of 4 miles one way. A sphagnum
bog to the north of Haseco Lake has all the plants usually associated with this type of land.

Lake Awosting can be reached from the north via Stony Kill Falls. Follow Rock Haven Road which leads off the old route of the present Rt. 44-55 (a road that makes a loop off the present road, about 1.5 miles east of its junction with Rt. 209) to where a chain bars further passage by car. Continue on foot past old slag deposits, cross the brook to its east side, and bushwhack up to the falls. These are a charming sight in their rock amphitheater. It is then necessary to retrace a few yards and go further to the left to find a route up the steep cliff and again rejoin the brook. Follow up the bedrock slabs of the brook and join an old carriage road which leads southeast to Fly Brook and the trail from Ellenville to Lake Awosting.

Sam's Point.

The area from Lake Awosting southwest to Sam's Point is the broadest, highest, least "cultivated," and yet most traversable section of the range. It may be approached by the new road to Lake Awosting at the Minnewaska gate or by way of Ice Caves Mountain, through Cragsmoor, off Rt. 52.

The Sam's Point–Lake Maratanza–High Point section of the ridge is owned by the village of Ellenville. In 1967, part of this section, including an area containing one of the famous ice caves, was leased for a twenty-year period to a group which calls itself Ice Caves Mountain. These lessees have created a nature trail that points out various ecological, geological, and botanical items of interest. A Committee from the Mid-Hudson Catskill Museum, headed by Daniel Smiley, acts as consultant for conservation and natural history.

Sam's Point (2255 feet) is the most accessible and the most striking of the view points and consequently has suffered the most from vandals with paint cans. It is named for Sam Gonzalez, a hunter who was reputed to have jumped off the cliff to avoid being captured by Indians in hot pursuit. He survived by landing in a clump of hemlocks.

The ice caves consist of vertical crevices in the Silurian conglomerate in which melted snow and rain collect during the winter in sufficient quantity to freeze into ice 3 to 10 feet deep, which lasts well into the summer. The resultant cool air creates a microclimate which encourages the growth of plants with northern affiliations and with different blooming dates from those outside the caves. Mountain laurel blooms four to six weeks later down in the caves than on top; dwarf dogwood has been observed blooming two

Crevice
and
steps

Road

Sams Point

Dickinson

months later at the bottom than at the top. In 1967 the ice caves on this part of the ridge were declared a national natural landmark, and fees are charged.

Aside from the ice caves with the developed nature trail, another series is accessible in about 1.5 miles by a red-blazed trail which leads to the west from the parking lot near the fire lookout tower. The crevices are from 50 to 100 feet deep and from 10 to 50 feet wide. It is possible to go down into some of them, but great caution should be used because the trail is difficult and treacherous. The red-blazed trail continues on down the mountain to Ellenville and terminates on Rt. 52 on the north side of a stream and gorge (North Gully) which lie east of the village.

SHINGLE GULLY, *fault crevices*   ELLENVILLE, N.Y.

Verkeerder Kill Falls.

On the east side of Maratanza Lake is a small parking area and the well-marked start of a red-blazed trail leading off to the east to the top of Verkeerder Kill Falls and continuing past the falls to Haseco Lake and Lake Awosting. The walk to the falls is downhill and takes about forty-five minutes. It is a refreshing spot and shows a spectacular view of the sheer rock face carved by the stream.

The falls can also be reached from the south by following the light-blue blazed Long Path through Crawford. An alternate, but unmarked, route follows the charming small pools of the stream, and with the help of deer trails the base of the falls can be reached. From there, by skirting to the right to the end of the rock face, the top can be reached by a steep climb.

The Long Path.

The southern end of the LP can be reached by car from Rt. 52 in Walker Valley. Drive north along the Oregon Trail to the town of Crawford. Cross the bridge over the Verkeerder Kill, and here pick up the light-blue blazes of the LP. Turn sharp left just after crossing the bridge, and follow blazes along the road for about 1 mile. Park the car on the black-top road, not on the lumber road, which is privately owned. On foot follow the new lumber road on the left. Soon the trail leaves the road and follows along the stream until it reaches the top of the falls. Here it joins with the red trail to Lake Awosting.

When the trail reaches the top of the ridge, turn sharp left (west), and follow the escarpment with fine views to the east and the south. Follow the trail to the High Point lookout tower, and continue along the main western ridge; cross Smiley Road, and make a long gradual descent partially along a power line to a road near the base of the mountain. Turn right on the road for about ½ mile to Rt. 44-55, then turn left and reach Rt. 209-55 at Kerhonkson. The total distance from the lumber road in Crawford is 11.2 miles.

7 · THE CATSKILLS
(Maps 12, 13, and 14)

ORTH OF the more familiar Metropolitan hiking areas are the Catskills, whose higher areas can provide especially rewarding hiking. The construction of the New York Thruway and improved roads mean that any of the summits can now be climbed on a one-day trip, although it may at times be a long day. The many paved roads through the mountains are well populated with hotels, boardinghouses, and homes but the higher, more rugged and remote parts are unspoiled. From the summits and other vantage points the views are magnificent. To the east, below the escarpment, the Hudson Valley is spread out against a backdrop of the New England hills and in other directions are the fir-topped peaks with little or no sign of man's intrusion.

Acquisition by the State of New York during past years of about 250,000 acres to form the Catskill State Park has forever protected, as wild forest lands under the State Constitution, most of the highest summits as well as some lower areas which were cut over years ago or were difficult to exploit. There are thirty-four peaks and ridges with elevations of 3500 feet and over, about one third of which are trailless to the top, and almost a hundred are over 3000 feet high. Marking and maintenance of official trails are performed by the New York State Department of Environmental Conservation.

In addition to the trails maintained by the State there are many usable wood roads and hunters' and fishermen's trails, some blazed, others not, that may be followed by hikers experienced in the use of topographic maps and compass. These lend considerable interest and variety because they penetrate the more remote areas.

GEOLOGY

The Catskills include the highest topography in the Appalachian Plateaus Province, where altitudes occasionally exceed 4000 feet. The drawing shows a panorama front west to east. Mountainous only in the erosional sense, the Catskill region is structurally a plateau that has undergone a long cycle of stream denudation. Cutting deeply into the near-horizontal strata, the divides between adjacent valleys are often high and sharp-crested; thus the mountainous appearance.

The bedrock of the Catskills is almost entirely of sandstone, shale, and some conglomerate laid down during the Devonian Period some 380 million years ago in a complex delta-type environment. Elevated in a series of comparatively gentle uplifts to a height perhaps thousands of feet above the present highest elevations, the land experienced a long period of extensive erosion. This long interval of erosion cut down the deep valleys and wore out the broad Hudson Valley, removing still younger Catskill rock formations which once extended east of the river, and left the highest summits topped by more resistant late Devonian strata of hard conglomerate. This formation can be seen on the top of Slide Mountain (4150 feet). The loose pebbles of milky quartz so generally distributed there and on other high summits resulted from the physical disintegration of the conglomerate. Variations in resistance of individual sedimentary layers are responsible for a series of cuestas, or unsymmetrical ridges with one slope long and gentle and the other a steeply sloping near-precipitous scarp. The boldest of these cuesta scarps is that which forms the eastern margin of the Catskills and overlooks the Hudson Valley to the east, and stands as much as 3000 feet above the valley.

This geological history of the Catskills can be read in their gentle curves, curves that are modified on some slopes, notably on the eastern fronts of Overlook, Kaaterskill High Peak, and the Black-heads, and on Cornell and Balsam Cap. Here are terrace-like cliffs and shelves where the level strata have been cut back vertically, probably by ice erosion. But there is relatively little bare rock in the form of flat ledges or high, exposed cliffs, as in most mountains. The effects of the glaciation of the Pleistocene Ice Age are not as prominent as in the Adirondacks and Hudson Highlands. It is probable that the higher Catskills were not covered very deeply by the ice sheets, for foreign material is scarce above 3500 feet. Even

where ice smoothing occurred, the soft nature of much of the sedimentary rock permitted postglacial weathering to roughen it and break it down into residual soil which has been covered by dense vegetation. The forest cover often mantles cliffs 50 to 100 feet high, unsuspected until they are reached because of the dense trees.

Although the Catskills are higher than the summits of the Taconics or those of the Hudson Highlands, they have no areas where there are typical above-timberline alpine flora, such as is found on more open mountaintops that are no higher and that are even much farther south. Above 3000 feet the Catskill flora is northern in associations but hardly as boreal as might be expected. The heavy residual soil from the soft sandstones has encouraged the invasion of southern or lowland species and "boreal islands" of subarctic plants are infrequent. Up to 3000 feet the vegetation is that of the beech-birch-maple-hemlock zone and above that of the northern spruce-fir. The Hudsonian or subarctic relicts are absent except for small stands of *Potentilla tridentata* on the ledges of Overlook Mountain at 3000 feet and on North Mountain east of Haines Falls.

HISTORY AND MYSTERY

The perceptive hiker finds much of interest in the Catskills—the geology of the mountains, the variety of the forests and, of course, the many wildflowers and birds. But he soon comes to realize that the land, now tree-covered, has been lived on and worked over. Following a trail or compass bearing, it is not unusual to come upon an old stone wall or the remains of a chimney or foundation, evidence that someone tried to farm a piece and raise a family. And

here and there a cemetery will tell a story, in its stones, of sickness and death. Many old roads, faintly distinguishable, climb to overgrown clearings around vanished lumber camps. Above them there is no path to the fir-clad summits, where timber is so dwarfed and inaccessible that it has never been cut, and where the ledges are covered several feet deep with a humus made by centuries of decaying fir and spruce needles.

Much has been written about Indians, dwarfs, and Rip Van Winkle, making the Catskills a land of mystery and fancy—and beauty. The Hudson and Mohawk valleys were well traveled by Indians long before Henry Hudson sailed up the Hudson (which he named the North River). They lived in the Catskill valleys, they hunted in the mountains, and went through them when on war expeditions and, later, on forays against the Dutch settlers in the Hudson bottom lands. One of their routes was the valley of Esopus Creek, and they also attacked from the gulf of Peekamoose and Watson Hollow. But for the Indians as well as the colonists the Catskills were not inviting. Until the end of the eighteenth century these mountains remained a largely broken wilderness of primeval hemlock. It was the need for this hemlock that finally brought men into the wilderness to destroy it.

Tanning of hides had been carried on in the United States to a limited extent prior to the Revolution. One tannery was established in Athens, New York, in 1750, but rapid growth came after the War of 1812, when Americans were free to engage in world trade without interference from the British. The two processes employed were based on the use of oak bark for sole leather, and hemlock bark for uppers and other uses. Since one cord (128 cubic feet) of bark was required to tan ten hides, it was more economical for the tannery to be near the woods. With its ready supply of hemlock and water, the Catskills soon became a center for the industry. In 1817 Jonathan Palen established a tannery at the base of Kaaterskill Clove. Others followed in Prattsville, Edwardsville (now Hunter), Phoenicia, and later in Tannersville. Some of the present town names came from those of the proprietors of these tanneries. By 1825, Greene County was producing more leather than any other county in the state, with Ulster not far behind.

Raw hides were received in compact bales from South America, brought by boat from New York City and by wagon to the tannery. For Hunter the route was from Kingston via Woodstock, Bearsville, and Mink Hollow. Catskill was the docking point for Palenville and Prattsville. A tannery was not a complicated setup—usually a series of tanks set on a flat stone foundation, with some sort of roof. The hides were spread out in layers, alternating with layers of ground bark, and covered with water. They were allowed to soak for weeks, then moved from one tank to the next until the process was complete.

Bark was cut only during May and June, when the sap was rising and peeling could be done readily. The hemlock trees were said to be 7 to 11 feet in diameter. A gash was cut around a tree as close to the ground as possible, and then another gash was cut 4 feet above this. Vertical cuts were then made 12 to 16 inches apart and the sections stripped off. The tree was felled and additional strips removed until the lower branches were reached. Above these it was considered that the pieces were too broken up to handle economically. Some trees were cut for lumber, but, as hemlock is a coarse-grained wood that splits readily, it had use only for large beams and planks for the tanning vats and for the enormous ice houses that once lined the Hudson River above Catskill. Most of the trees were left to rot. The tanning industry in the Catskills hit its peak during the Civil War and declined rapidly thereafter when the supply of hemlock was exhausted. By 1867 most tanneries had closed down, although the Simpson tannery in Phoenicia operated until 1870. Some idea of the consumption of bark may be gained from the report that the Pratt tannery turned out over two million hides during its existence, which would have required over 200,000 cords of bark.

Cutting down these tremendous trees opened the land to sunlight and conditions more favorable to growth of birch, maple, oak, and other hardwoods. As these took over, a new industry was born—the making of barrel hoops by cutting saplings with a draw knife. This industry began about 1848 and lasted until about 1890, when machine-sawed wooden hoops and steel hoops replaced hand-hewn hoops. Another wood industry that existed for a time was the making of furniture, the "chair factories" as they were known locally. This industry accounted for some of the vacant buildings still seen in Catskill towns.

Still another industry that operated in the Catskills was the quarrying of bluestone, a hard, dense, fine-grained sandstone of gray-blue color. This industry flourished in the latter part of the nineteenth century and provided "curbstone" and "flagstone" for the sidewalks of New York until the development of Portland cement brought large-scale quarrying to an end. The largest quarry still operating is near the eastern end of Ashokan Reservoir in West Hurley. Piles of rejected stone may be found at many places where there were workings or exploratory openings, as in Shandaken or Phoenicia. In the western Catskills there are still working quarries that supply bluestone for veneer and for walks and patios, but the demand is much smaller.

What puzzles the hiker are the remains of farmhouses or indications of cleared land in the most unlikely places. He wonders why anyone would think of farming on such terrain. To transport bark, lumber, and hides took many horses—thousands when the industry was at its peak—and horses require feed. So, as the land was cleared of hemlock, it was plowed where possible and sown to hay on the steep slopes, to corn and oats on more level areas, with some better space given to potatoes and wheat or buckwheat for the men. After tanning ceased, some farmers attempted general farming, but the soil was poor and the conditions too difficult. Left now are the fallen chimneys and sometimes an apple tree bearing misshapen, wormy fruit that is enjoyed only by the bears and deer. The views from some of these old high-valley farms have prompted purchase by summer residents.

Railroad construction did not begin until 1866. Four years later the Ulster & Delaware Railroad began service from Weehawken to Phoenicia, to Stamford in 1879, and through Stony Clove to Tannersville in 1882. Passenger service has been discontinued on all lines, but bus service is available to many points.

Catering to summer visitors is a continuing business. It began with the Catskill Mountain House, built high on an overhanging ledge above Palenville between North and South mountains, a house with ten guest rooms when it opened in 1824. Patrons were transported by stage from Catskill up through Sleepy Hollow, which took the better part of a day. So popular was the view from its porch that "The Mountain House" grew to more than three hundred rooms and was visited by the prominent and the great until after the turn of the century. Among its frequent guests were Thomas Cole and other painters of the Hudson River School, many writers and educators, as well as society leaders and politicians, including President Grant.

In 1878 the Overlook House was built on Overlook Mountain, then Mt. Tremper House in Phoenicia, the Grand Hotel in Highmount, the Laurel House at Kaaterskill Falls, and in 1881 the Hotel Kaaterskill on South Mountain. This was said to have twelve hundred rooms and to be then the largest mountain hotel in the world. Not one of these hotels has survived. Many smaller establishments serve guests in this area, but the very large ones were in the western Catskills. The Hotel Kaaterskill burned down in 1924, and the property was acquired by the state. Other later acquisitions by the state were the Laurel House and the Catskill Mountain House, the old structure of which was cleared away by burning in 1963. This whole area, including North and South lakes, and the network of trails built by these hotels to provide a series of panoramic views for their guests, is being maintained for public use by the State Department of Environmental Conservation.

CLIMATE

Traveling from the New York area one soon comes to realize that the climate of the Catskills is different. A gentle spring day in New York City may be a day of snow flurries or freezing rain in the Catskills. The temperatures are generally lower, and in the remote and higher sections snow may accumulate in November and last through April. For that reason more and more hikers are taking to snowshoes for the winter months and finding the country even more beautiful. In summer or winter, weather conditions may change rapidly, and it is well to be prepared for sudden changes with extra clothing and suitable equipment. Moreover, winter climbing, though exhilarating, is more strenuous and may be exhausting. Do not attempt too much, and travel in groups of four or more. Also, although the main roads are plowed, many of the side roads on which there are no winter residents are not cleared. Conditions may be right for snowshoeing, but the hike as planned may be too long for available daylight hours.

TRAILS AND BUSHWHACKING

As mentioned before, many miles of trails in the Catskills are maintained by the State Department of Environmental Conservation. These trails are designated with official metal markers, blue for trails that run generally north and south, red for trails running east and west, and yellow for trails running diagonally. Light blue paint blazes will be found elsewhere. These are the temporary markings on the Long Path (LP) which, it is expected, will eventually be a connected trail from the George Washington Bridge in New York City to the top of Whiteface Mountain, near Lake Placid. At present, it crosses the Catskills from Kerhonkson north to Vernooy Falls, around Samson Mountain, over Peekamoose and Table mountains to Denning. From there it utilizes Conservation Department (CD) trails over Slide, Cornell, and Wittenberg mountains to Phoenicia, then down to Mt. Tremper, where it again picks up the CD trail to Mink Hollow and over Sugarloaf, Twin and Indian Head mountains to Platte Clove. A connection to Haines Falls via High Peak is yet to be worked out. From Haines Falls it uses the CD Escarpment Trail to East Windham. LP markers are used only where the state markers do not appear.

The marked and maintained trails are described below. In addition, there are many usable wood roads and hunters' and fishermen's trails, some of which are blazed, usually with paint. Trails indicated on the topographic maps, especially the earlier issues, are often so overgrown as to be difficult to follow. Although the walker can explore a great deal of the wilderness forest land in the Catskills by using the marked trails, it is only by getting off the beaten path that he can really find out for himself what the wilderness is like. Trail-less travel, or "bushwhacking," leads to many interesting discoveries—a little-known waterfall, perhaps a bear den, a balancing rock, or one of the remains of the mountain industries of the last century. Best of all, bushwhacking permits the hiker to be more keenly aware of his environment. Such adventures, however, should be sought only by hikers experienced in the use of map and compass, in groups of 3 or more.

To provide incentive for visiting mountain peaks and areas not usually seen by the average hiker, the Catskill 3500 Club was founded in 1962. This club has stimulated a great deal of interest in the thirty-four Catskill summits over 3500 feet in elevation. Roughly one third of these peaks have no trails to the top, so the hiker is on his own and must use map and compass to make these ascents. He should not, however, blaze or otherwise mark his route. This is not only illegal, but defaces the wilderness. To leave the least trace of his passing, he and his friends should avoid walking in a file.

Using the main highways as dividing lines, Catskills trails may be considered in four area groups: Southern, Central, Northeastern, and Western.

Southern—south and west of Rts. 28A and 28 (West Shokan, Phoenicia, and Big Indian);

Central—north of Rts. 212 and 28 (Woodstock and Phoenicia); east of Rt. 42 (Shandaken and Westkill); south of Rt. 23A (Lexington, Tannersville, and Kaaterskill Clove);

Northeastern—north of Rt. 23A; south of Rt. 23 (Cairo, Windham, and Prattsville);

Western—west of the West Branch—Big Indian Road; west of Rts. 42 and 23A (Shandaken, Lexington, and Prattsville).

SOUTHERN CATSKILLS

Slide Mountain, Cornell, and Wittenberg.

The best-known trails in the Catskills are those that reach the summit of Slide Mountain (4180 feet), the highest point in the region. These trails were originally blazed by private clubs and individuals but are now included in the State Department of Environmental Conservation system and are well marked and cleared. Most popular of the approaches to Slide Mountain is through Woodland Valley, one of the deepest valleys in the Catskills. The road leaves Rt. 28 one mile west of Phoenicia. (This point can be reached by bus from New York via Kingston.) It follows Woodland Creek and is marked with yellow disks. In 4 miles it meets the red-marked trail for Wittenberg Mountain, with parking 100 yards beyond. The yellow trail continues 6 miles to Winnisook Lodge and a second junction with the red trail, as mentioned below.

The red trail crosses the creek and starts to climb Wittenberg (3780 feet), an ascent of 2800 feet in about 3 miles. It is steepest at the beginning (where the trail was widened in 1934 by the CCC as a downhill ski run) and again near the top. The gentler grade is across the "Terrace" from which there are excellent views to the north and east and down the valley. The Terrace lean-to is passed at 1.45 miles. From the summit there are splendid views east and

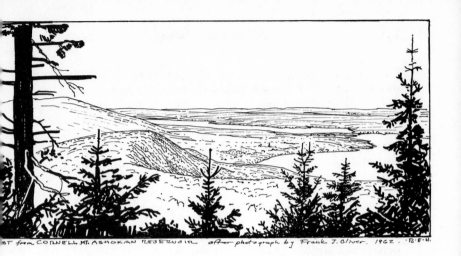

ST from CORNELL MT. ASHOKAN RESERVOIR after photograph by Frank J. Oliver, 1962. · R·E·H·

south over Ashokan Reservoir. Views to the north are cut off by the growth in recent years of a good stand of evergreens. (Also noticeable over the years, the dense growth of hardwoods on the Terrace and above has eliminated much of the azalea, the trout lilies, and Dutchman's breeches that older hikers remember, a reminder that the woods are changing, constantly if not rapidly, as the cycle advances.) Shelter may be found in a cave just off the summit which has long been a refuge of climbers and porcupines alike. There is a small spring nearby but a canteen is more certain.

From Wittenberg the trail goes south and, just before the low point of the next notch, reaches a junction with a trail (red blazes) that leads down steeply to Maltby Hollow above West Shokan. Continuing on the main trail there is a spur trail (blue blazes) to the summit of Cornell Mountain (3865 feet) with views through the trees to the south. The main trail turns right and descends into the deep notch between Cornell and Slide through an isolated stand of virgin spruce. It then climbs steeply to the summit of Slide Mountain, where there are two lean-tos with fireplaces but dubious water supply. Just below the open rock top is a tablet in memory of John Burroughs, naturalist and poet.

In Memoriam
JOHN BURROUGHS
*Who in his early writings introduced Slide
Mountain to the world. He made many visits to
this peak and slept several nights beneath this
rock. This region is the scene of many of his essays.
Here the works of man dwindle in the
heart of the southern Catskills.*

Burroughs climbed from the end of Woodland Valley, following the west branch of Cornell Brook, then through brush and up the slide north of the summit. This slide, said to have occurred about 1820, is now covered with forest growth and seems stabilized. Both this and the similar, smaller slide on Cornell Mountain above the east branch of the brook may be climbed by those interested in bushwhacking. They are steep and require a detour around private land at the base.

The return to Woodland Valley may be made by continuing on the red trail to Winnisook Lodge (a private residential club of long standing) on the West Branch—Big Indian road, and then by the yellow trail. This is longer but almost entirely downhill through woods. The distance is 8.6 miles, a total of 14.65 miles for the loop. From the top of Slide the red trail descends easily westward along the northern front of the mountain on what was a bridle path from Winnisook Lodge. In less than a mile the blue-marked Curtis-Ormsby Trail turns left on an old road to the East Branch of Neversink Creek. This trail was cut and maintained for some years by members of the Fresh Air Club of New York in honor of "Father Bill" Curtis, a famous athlete, sports writer, and club official who, with a companion, perished in a summer snowstorm on Mt. Washington. At the junction is a granite monument erected as a memorial to Curtis by former (State) Supreme Court Justice Harrington Putnam of Brooklyn, an ardent outdoors man who had a farm at Denning.

This trail can be followed to the open camp at Denning where the light blue markers of the Long Path are picked up. They lead to Table and Peekamoose mountains. An easier way to climb Slide Mountain, of course, is to drive to Winnisook Lodge on the West Branch road, from Big Indian on Route 28, or from Liberty via Route 55.

South of Slide Mountain—Peekamoose and Vicinity

The area south of Slide-Cornell-Wittenberg is largely trail-less but beautiful; it is interesting and remote, a large bowl drained by the East Branch of Neversink Creek. At its eastern rim are Friday and Balsam Cap mountains. Friday (3694 feet) comes off a shoulder of Cornell and is connected to Balsam Cap (3623 feet) by a ridge. A slide on the eastern face of Cornell occurred in the spring of 1930 and another on Friday in the spring of 1968, both after heavy rains. These may be attractive to the venturesome. Swinging around to the southwest from Balsam Cap are Rocky (3508 feet), Lone (3721 feet), and Table (3847 feet) mountains, all of which are interesting to bushwhackers. As noted above, Table Mountain may be climbed also by the Long Path from Denning or Peekamoose. The view from the north face of Table is one of the finest sweeping panoramas in the Catskills, taking in almost all of the high peaks.

Just to the south of Table Mountain lies Peekamoose Mountain (3843 feet), which together with Table and the lower Van Wyck Mountain (3206 feet) close in the bowl of the East Branch. They also form the northern slope of the Rondout Creek watershed. The road from West Shokan through Watson Hollow goes southwest to Sundown, Grahamsville, and Liberty. It is called the Gulf Road because of the gulf between the headwaters of the Rondout and the head of Watson Hollow. This is interesting geologically as the outlet of the Esopus Creek during part of the last glacial period when the drainage was blocked by a heavy lobe of ice in the Hudson Valley. For a time the dammed waters flowed southwest and west through the Gulf and down Rondout Creek. This accounts for large potholes, heavy glacial gravel beds, and other glacial phenomena to be found there. Later, as some of the water escaped eastward under the melting ice, the creek cut a channel south across the eastern foot of High Point south of Olive Bridge Dam. This cut, known as Wagon Wheel Gap or Goblin Gulch, is conspicuous from Ashokan Reservoir. On its southerly side evidence of a powerful cutting stream is seen, from the top of the gap down to the road from Ashokan Reservoir to Krumville, and even below that road. North of the road two distinct "fossil waterfalls" are evident, with water-worn brinks and a smoothed platform between them. The brink and plunge basin south of the road are larger and more striking. The Long Path on its route from New York City comes around Samson Mountain (2812 feet) and east on the Gulf Road. At a point about 400 feet east of Buttermilk Falls it leaves the road and ascends through open woods to ledges and the fir- and spruce-covered summit of Peekamoose Mountain. There is no one vantage point, but good views are obtainable through the foliage. From the top of Peekamoose it is only a short distance on the LP to the top of Table Mountain.

High Point (3060 feet), or Ashokan High Point as it is often called to distinguish it from similar names, is worth a climb. It can be ascended easily by an old lumber road that takes off from Mountain Road in West Shokan just south of the junction with a black-top road coming in from Rt. 28A just south of West Shokan. Permission to park in the field may be required. There is also a red-blazed trail farther south and one from the Old Kanape trail between High Point and Mombaccus Mountain (3000 feet). The country between Mombaccus and the summit of Samson Mountain may repay a visit and also the area south of Rondout Gulf. The LP north of Kerhonkson passes Vernooy Falls and follows the kill (stream) before going around Samson. There is a deep gorge south of the falls with a series of potholes and basins (warning: there are also rattlesnakes!). The red-marked trail up Red Hill to the fire lookout tower gives a fine panorama of the mountains. It starts 1 mile above Claryville, and the summit can be reached in less than an hour.

North of Slide Mountain—Giant Ledge and Panther Mountain. Length: 8 miles. Blazes: yellow, then red.

The north-south trail over Giant Ledge (3200 feet) and Panther Mountain (3720 feet) offers a series of fine lookouts and a varied terrain. The complete traverse makes a good day trip if a shuttle can be arranged. Starting at the Woodland Valley Campsite, or the parking place 0.4 mile beyond near the Woodland Valley Club, follow the yellow markers on the Phoenicia–East Branch trail to the height of land between Woodland Creek and Esopus Creek (2 miles) where a red trail comes in from the right. In 0.25 mile the red trail reaches the Giant Ledge lean-to, then the top of Giant Ledge with its sharp cliff and view down the valley. From here, after a dip to the low point, the trail climbs rather steeply up Panther with excellent views in all directions. The descent is quite steep, in part through virgin spruce, to the Fox Hollow lean-to and the road to Allaben. The total distance from Woodland to Fox Hollow is 8 miles.

CENTRAL CATSKILLS

Although more populated and with few remote areas, the central portion of the Catskills has many interesting and rewarding climbs. The entrance through Plattekill Clove is spectacular, especially since the eastern wall rises 0.5 mile in a horizontal distance of about 1 mile. The road requires caution, and the clove itself is extremely deep and steep with broken and falling rock. Climbing in it is definitely not recommended even with a hard hat. The Devil's Kitchen, near the top, is accessible and scenic, especially in times of high water, but the rock is very slippery.

To the south of the clove are Plattekill Mountain (3100 feet) and Overlook Mountain (3140 feet). Overlook stands out as the Catskills are approached from the south. As mentioned previously, this was the site of Overlook House, one of the large hotels of the last century. A carriage road was built to it from Saugerties, and part of this is now the yellow-marked trail to Echo Lake and lean-to. It is possible to continue on to Overlook Mountain or it may be reached by an old road from Meads. (It is of interest that the only two places in the Catskills where rattlesnake dens have been found are on Overlook Mountain and Mt. Tremper, but rattlesnakes have been reported in other places, to the south and toward the Shawangunks.)

North of Plattekill Clove is Kaaterskill High Peak, the "High Peak" which, as late as 1870, was thought to be the highest of Catskill summits even though it is only 3655 feet. The top is distinctive, with a cliff on the east side of the summit that marks it as seen from the Thruway. There are various old trails on it starting at the Plattekill Road, all of which in part traverse private land on which permission to hike is necessary. There are several good lookouts on the way up and an excellent panorama of the Hudson Valley from the top. The trail continuing from the top to Twilight Park is hard to follow because of private holdings and because the Indian Trail indicated by a sign in Kaaterskill Clove is nonexistent. Round Mountain or Roundtop (3440 feet), to the west of High Peak, is sufficiently open to bushwhacking without difficulty.

The Devil's Path.

So known because of the rugged country it traverses, the Devil's Path starts from Platte Clove Road 0.5 mile west of the New York Police Camp. It tops Indian Head (3573 feet), Twin (3640 feet), Sugarloaf (3800 feet), and Plateau (3840 feet) mountains and comes out at Devil's Tombstone Campsite in Stony Clove. With these summits and the very considerable drops into Jimmy Dolan Notch, Pecoy Notch, Mink Hollow, and then Stony Clove, it is really a skyline trail with views aplenty. As there is a trail out from each of these notches to the north, and in Mink Hollow one to the south as well, it is possible to do the entire length in sections. The distance from Platte Clove Road to Stony Clove in 12.45 miles. Another climb in this area that is popular because of its views is Mt. Tremper (2720 feet). This may be ascended from old Rt. 28 just over 1 mile south of Phoenicia or from Willow Post Office to the east on Route 212. Neither climb is arduous.

To the west of Stony Clove lies Hunter Mountain (4040 feet), the second highest of the Catskill peaks. There are four trails to the summit. From the east, the Becker Trail (blue markers) starts from Stony Clove Road about 1 mile north of Devil's Tombstone, near Villa Capri and near the old Becker farmhouse. (The Becker family was associated with this mountain for many years. During the 1920s the oldest son was Fire Observer and lived with his family at the tower; the father ran the farm, and the daughter served wonderful meals to boarders and hikers.) At the old tower site (2.05 miles) the Diamond Notch (blue) Trail is joined by the red trail from Devil's Tombstone and then proceeds 0.3 mile to the tower. The Spruceton trail comes up from the Spruceton Road 8 miles east of West Kill on Route 42. This is a fire truck trail with easy grades. At 2.40 miles, 1 mile from the top, the Shanty Hollow trail comes in from Hunter village after passing through the ski slope area. This has blue markers; the Spruceton trail is red to the top. Another way to reach the Spruceton trail is to take the blue trail from Lanesville through Diamond Notch, a very interesting variant. Hunter Mountain, especially from the tower, gives an all-encompassing view of the Catskill peaks though the cleared top is not inviting.

In Spruceton valley, to the west of Hunter, there are some excellent trailless climbs, but access to them is mostly over private lands and permission to cross should be obtained. On the north side of the valley is Rusk Mountain (3680 feet) while on the south are Westkill Mountain (3880 feet), North Dome (3610 feet), and Sherrill Mountain (3540 feet). Sherrill is to the west of North Dome.

NORTHEASTERN CATSKILLS

The State of New York now owns the entire area immediately to the north of Kaaterskill Clove and Rt. 23A. This was once the property of Laurel House, Hotel Kaaterskill, and Catskill Mountain House. All are gone, but in their flourishing days these hostelries constructed many miles of trails so that their guests might see the falls, the lakes, and the vistas. It is said that during the latter part of the last century these trails were more used than any others in the United States. The Conservation Department has wisely preserved and marked them. The focal point is North Lake, a pretty lake where there is a public campsite with fireplaces, tent sites, and picnic spots, and an access road from Tannersville. To the east is the ledge with the view that brought thousands to Catskill Mountain House and close by are the remains of the Otis Elevating Railway which once carried them up to the view. A loop trail from the lake leads

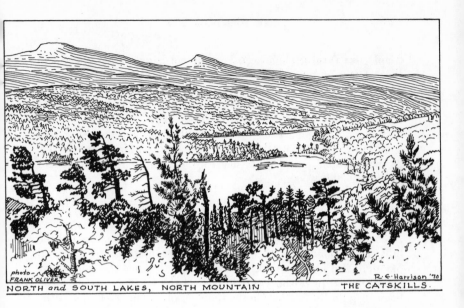

photo - FRANK OLIVER   R. E. Harrison '70

NORTH and SOUTH LAKES,   NORTH MOUNTAIN   THE CATSKILLS.

to the many vantage points along the rim and then returns through Mary's Glen.

The Conservation Department has now completed the Escarpment Trail which follows along the top of the cliffs and ledges from North Lake to Blackhead Range. These ledges show glaciation. Evidently the Hudson Valley lobe of the ice sheet, as it deepened and spread out of its confinement within the walls of the Catskills and Taconics, ground smooth the ledges around North Lake and north of Catskill Mountain House up to about 3000 feet elevation. The trail starts from the north side of Rt. 23A in Kaaterskill Clove at a sharp bend in the road below Haines Falls. There is a parking place on the south side and a sign indicating the trail. It extends 24 miles over varied terrain with considerable climbing. The lower portion provides access to Kaaterskill Falls, with fine views down the Clove, and then along the ledges up to North Point. From there it climbs North Mountain (3180 feet), and Stoppel Point (3420 feet), drops to Dutcher Notch, and then goes up the long ridge to Blackhead Mountain (3940 feet). The entire trail is marked in blue.

From the top of Blackhead Mountain follow the yellow-marked trail to the red Blackhead Range trail, which goes over Black Dome (3990 feet) and Thomas Cole (3945 feet) and down to Maplecrest. These three mountains from the skyline of the Catskills as seen from far up the Northway. Trails to Batavia Kill and out to the

Maplecrest Road are intersected in the col between Blackhead and Black Dome and also farther along the blue trail toward Acra Point (3100 feet). The blue trail goes over Acra Point and skirts the top of Burnt Knob (3180 feet) and on to Windham High Peak (3524 feet). From here the blue trail continues to Rt. 23, 3 miles east of Windham. One mile from the end of the trail a yellow spur trail leads left to Maplecrest Road. The several access roads south of Rt. 23 make posible a number of day trips, each a mixture of excellent panoramas and woods.

WESTERN CATSKILLS

To the west, the slopes of the Catskills become less steep and the hills more rounded as they merge into the dairy country around Stamford and Delhi. As one drives through this area two points may be of interest. In Roxbury, uphill west of the village, is the boyhood home of John Burroughs. On the shoulder of Clump Mountain is the John Burroughs Memorial Field, from which a footpath leads to his "Boyhood Rock," a huge sandstone boulder. Here, from boyhood to old age, he loved to sit and gaze upon an amphitheater of mountains. The rock bears a tablet reading: "John Burroughs 1837 to 1921," and a quotation from his poem "Waiting": "I stand amid eternal ways and what is mine shall know my face." In front of the rocks is a rectangular stone wall marking the grave of the famous naturalist. A few steps beyond bubbles a spring from which he often drank, to the east of the Field is Woodchuck Lodge, his mountain retreat, and to the west is the farm where he grew up.

At Gilboa Dam, north of Prattsville, there is an exhibit of fossil trees that are of exceptional scientific interest. In 1869, as a result of a flash flood that struck the village of Gilboa, there was exposed in the Schoharie Creek a number of petrified tree stumps, with spreading bases up to 11 feet in circumference. They were identified as tree ferns and their age then estimated at 300 million years. This has been revised to 365 million years using present-day test methods. Later, when seeds were found, it was discovered that not only were these forests the oldest in the world but that the trees were remarkable missing links because ferns have spores but not seeds, and these tree ferns linked the older spore-bearing ferns with the later seed-bearing trees. Previously it had been supposed that no seed plants had appeared on earth until some 125 million years after these forest trees at Gilboa.

Three little-known summits in the western area are of interest for their panoramas, as each stands alone and higher than its surrounding ridges. South and west of Prattsville lies Bearpen Mountain (3600 feet). Once developed as a ski slope, it failed for lack of access, not snow. Next to the south is Vly Mountain (3529 feet) and then Halcott Mountain (3520 feet). Bearpen and Vly are private property and permission to hike should be secured.

The country west of Oliverea and Big Indian Valley is almost entirely state land. The main trail with blue markers runs from Pine Hill to the observatory on Bell Ayr Mountain (3360 feet), along the ridge to Balsam Mountain (the Balsam, 3600 feet), on to Haynes (3440 feet), Eagle (3605 feet), Big Indian (3680 feet), and down Biscuit Creek to the West Branch of the Neversink and the highway to Winnisook Lodge or Claryville. There are access trails from both sides, with red markers: Hanley Corners to Big Indian via Lost Clove, Mapledale, and Rider Hollow to McKenley Hollow and Oliverea. In addition, the Seager–Dry Brook Trail with yellow markers comes in between Eagle and Big Indian mountains. Although these access trails are all steep, once the ridge is attained the going is not difficult. The views are limited by the now-dense tree cover. This Seager–Dry Brook Trail bypasses the true summit of Big Indian. Fir Mountain (3625 feet), to the southeast, is trailless.

Dry Brook Ridge Trail, farther to the west, follows high ground, often over 3000 feet, south from Margaretville over Pakatakan Mountain (3100 feet), and along the Dry Brook Ridge, at one place attaining an elevation of 3460 feet. At 11.25 miles there is a junction with the red-marked Balsam Lake Mountain Trail ascending Balsam Lake Mountain (sometimes called Balsam Roundtop, 3725 feet). It passes the lean-to and continues down to a second junction with the blue trail. From here it is 1.9 miles to Quaker Clearing, where yellow markers to the left lead to Round Pond and Claryville, and to the right, along the Beaverkill, to Hardenburg. Graham (3868 feet) and Doubletop (3870 feet) mountains are both in this area but are private property, requiring permission to hike them. Graham has a tote road to the radio tower (now in disrepair) on the summit, but Doubletop is trailless. It is an especially rewarding climb both for its fine panoramas and its unique conifer top.

Part II

INTRODUCTION

 ORTHWARD from the New York City boundary spreads the expanse of Westchester County. Here the earth has been differentially eroded into valleys opening southward or southwestward, the ribs between rising in rounded ridges or knobs 200 to 600 feet higher. However, even though Westchester is in general a landscape nearly tamed and netted with a maze of roads, thanks to an expansive park acquisition program, wild stretches are still to be found and good open woods and steep ledges, fine rocks, and tall trees are not lacking.

It is a region that has supported generations of Americans, who have left the impress of their various lives, much of it associated with Colonial and Revolutionary history. This was the "Neutral Ground" of mixed loyalties in the years after 1776. The restored home of Frederick Philipse, who made money trading with the Indians at Tarrytown, the Manor House of the Van Cortlandts at Croton-on-Hudson, and "Sunnyside," Washington Irving's country retreat at Irvington, are all just a few moment's walk from the Croton Aqueduct.

Geologically the whole Westchester area is quite complex, belonging to the so-called "Manhattan Prong" of the New England Upland

Province, although running down to sea level. In the southern part of the country the underlying rock consists of highly metamorphic schists and gneisses with limestone inclusions, while in the north intrusive granite and pegmatite as well as gneiss predominate. The much older, Precambrian Highlands of the New England Upland show rather definite boundary along Peekskill Creek, which was developed along the same system of faults that formed the front range, the "Rampart," of the Ramapo Mountains in New Jersey and New York. The two parts are topographically uneven, but the northerly one is much more elvated and rugged. In common with the rest of the metropolitan area, this region was subjected to glaciation, evidence of which is everywhere seen in deposits of gravels or boulders and in ponds whose outlets were dammed up thereby.

One can hardly fail to compare the country on the two sides of the Hudson, especially below the Highlands, where the differences are most pronounced. In contrast to the abrupt slopes and cliffs of Westchester County is the undulating terrain of Rockland County with its rim of high Palisades—a diabase intrusion, seemingly, against the Hudson. The Newark sandstones of the Triassic Period in Rockland contrast with the schist and gneiss of Westchester, and the trap rock of the Palisades with the gneiss of the eastern hills. In contrast again is the sandhill character of Long Island, where the glacial sheet dropped a major part of the load that it had taken up in traversing the mainland. That the Hudson flows in the space between the two diverse areas is no doubt due to the fact that the line of cleavage or of contact between the two was also the line of least resistance. So efficient was the river in cutting its bed that it now rests in a rock trough whose lower surface is some 600 feet or more below the present water level. Sinking of the land has resulted in the filling of this trench with gravel and silt.

SPRAIN LAKE PARK

Grassy Sprain Reservoir, which supplies water to the city of Yonkers, is bounded on the west by an area of woods about 0.5 mile wide and 3 miles long. At the northern end is a picnic area, open in summer only, for which a Westchester resident permit is required; the rest of the park is undeveloped and can be entered without permit at any season. The northern end can be reached by public transportation. Take a bus from Woodlawn station of the IRT north on Central Avenue (Rt. 100) to Fort Hill Road; then walk west on

Fort Hill Road 0.5 mile. The southern end can be reached by car from the south from Sprain Road by turning east on a bridge over the New York Thruway just before the toll booths; parking is available on the left, on a service road. Enter the park by a right fork of the road closed by two boulders.

It is possible to make a loop walk of about 6 miles. A road through the woods runs the full length of the park near the west side. On the east side, a series of unmarked trails broken by some stretches where bushwhacking is necessary runs along the ridge above the reservoir. The walk may be shortened by using one of several cross trails. Except for a little bushwhacking, the walking is easy. On the east there are views of the reservoir and on the south an unusually fine stand of forest trees.

BLUE MOUNTAIN RESERVATION

The Blue Mountain Reservation south of Peekskill is a park of some 1600 acres which includes a network of bridle paths and walking trails that aggregate about 15 miles. A circuit over the two principal summits, Blue Mountain and Spitzenberg Hill, can be traversed easily in a half day.

An unusual feature of the Reservation is the Blue Mountain Trail Lodge, which provides men's and women's dormitory accommodations, central dining and living room facilities, and a well-equipped kitchen, for the use of organized groups of up to thirty people. Reservations may be made through the Westchester County Department of Parks, White Plains, N.Y. Applications must be made many months in advance of the desired date.

The Welcher Avenue exit from Route 9 in Peekskill leads east about 0.5 mile directly to the Reservation entrance. During the summer, a parking fee is collected from day visitors; after passing the guard post, bear left onto the road past the Lodge and continue to the parking lot at the end. The "Peekskill" sheet of the U. S. Geological Survey shows the Blue Mountain Reservation and several of its principal trails; a more detailed map may be obtained from attendants at the park.

Blue Mountain and Spitzenberg Circular.
This walk is a loop of about 5 miles, including short spur trails to the two summits. It can be accomplished in approximately three hours; alternative trails, however, may be used to shorten or extend it as desired. A yellow-blazed foot trail starts directly across the road

from the Trail Lodge; follow this in the direction indicated by the "Blue Mountain" sign on a tree. Soon bear right, avoiding a well-worn branch which continues on across a stream. Beyond this, about an eighth of a mile farther, turn left onto a sharply ascending orange-blazed trail (obscurely marked) which shortly joins a blue-blazed bridle path. Here turn right, and in a few minutes reach an unmarked spur trail to the left (group of large hemlocks on left, prominent boulders opposite) which leads to the summit of Blue Mountain. An open viewpoint near the top provides a good outlook to the northwest; just beyond is a ruined stone shelter and the actual summit, which is wooded and without views.

Returning to the bridle path, continue following the blue markers, shortly passing a green-blazed trail to the left and just beyond crossing a pipe line slash and the unpaved Montrose Station Road. Upon reaching a "T" in the path, turn left on a white-blazed trail leading to Spitzenberg Hill. In less than 0.25 mile, bear right up steep stone steps to an abandoned stone building at the summit. Here is a fine panorama of the Tappan Zee and the mountains to the west and north. Retracing, return to the junction of the blue trail and continue straight ahead, leaving the white blazes. Next, bear right on a red-blazed bridle path which leads back to the Lodge parking lot, after recrossing the Montrose Station Road and passing a small pond.

CROTON AQUEDUCT

A pleasant level walk for generations of hikers, the old Croton right-of-way in recent years has become disjointed, and a once pleasurable hike has become difficult. However, because it runs near the Hudson River and has fine views, it still is a favorite for short walks. Efforts are under way by the Taconic State Park Commission to restore the right-of-way so that its entire length can be enjoyed without interruption, and to extend a trail from its northern terminus to join the Appalachian Trail in Fahnestock State Park. Until this plan materializes, it is suggested that those wishing to hike along the aqueduct start at its source at Croton Lake Dam and proceed south as far as is desired. To reach the dam from the Croton-Harmon station (Penn Central Railroad), proceed up the hemlock-shaded west side of the Croton River and cross over the Quaker Bridge to intersect the level aqueduct route.

WARD POUNDRIDGE RESERVATION (see map)

The Ward Poundridge Reservation, consisting of 4172 acres of forest preserve, is the largest recreational area maintained by the Westchester County park system. It is located east of Route 121, with an entrance near the settlement of Cross River. Of roughly elliptical form, measuring some 3.5 by 4.5 miles, and with a circumference of 15 miles, the Reservation consists of rolling farmlands traversed by the Cross River—Boutonville highway and along the vale which Michigan Road follows south into the wooded hills, which rise to 700 and 800 feet. Its roadways generally are narrow two-laned ones; some are gravel-surfaced and some are paved. A farmhouse at a jog in the approach roadway just south of Cross River serves as the Reservation headquarters and the home of the chief ranger. Here maps of the Reservation can be obtained without charge. An additional 72 acres north of the headquarters, along the Cross River, was donated to the Reservation for a memorial arboretum to be known as the Meyer Arboretum. Development of this is proceeding along with the creation of a lake which will be the first within the Reservation. A small but well-equipped trailside museum is maintained with a naturalist appointed by the Westchester County Park Commission. On request, he will conduct nature tours for groups. The museum also serves as a "naturalist school house." Projects in nature study with exhibits and displays appealing to both children and adults can be observed without charge. Some are located on Pell Hill south of the Trailside Museum; others are situated near Michigan Road.

The Reservation can be reached by car from New York by Rt. 22 to Bedford Village and from there by Rt. 121 to Cross River, or by the Saw Mill River Parkway to Katonah, then east on Rt. 35 to Cross River. By train, take the Penn Central to Katonah, then taxi.

There are twenty-four Adirondack-type open-face lean-tos, each accommodating approximately 8 persons. Moderate fees are charged for daytime and overnight use. Fireplaces are installed in or in front of the lean-tos. No tent camping is permitted. There are seven picnic areas, which will accommodate thirty-five hundred persons.

Even during the summer months, however, it is easy to escape the crowds and find solitude along the seldom-used trails. The Reservation is honeycombed with some 35 miles of trails, which can be followed by using Reservation maps. A relief model of the Reserva-

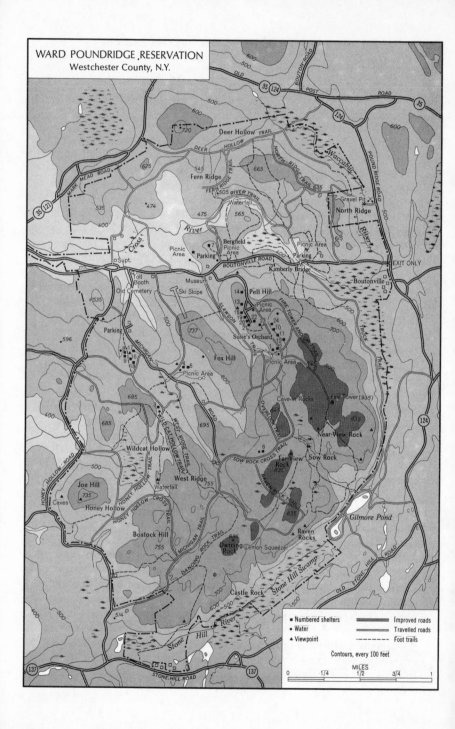

WARD POUNDRIDGE ,RESERVATION
Westchester County, N.Y.

tion, located in the Trailside Museum, also is useful in planning walks. Of particular interest are such trail objectives as: the fire tower, Raven Rocks, Wild Cat Hollow, Honey Hollow, River Trail, Deer Hollow, and Stone Hill River. Two ski trails offer descents of 234 and 430 feet. There is also opportunity for cross-country skiing and snowshoeing, including an excellent 6-mile trail. Although administered as a park, the Reservation is maintained as a "wilderness area." Virtually all of its trees, plants, and flowers are the product of natural ecological change.

From the fire tower observation platform more than twenty-five bodies of water are visible, including reservoirs, lakes, ponds, and distant Long Island Sound. Useful U. S. Geological Survey maps are: "Poundridge, N.Y." and "Peach Lake, N.Y.," which show the total reservation acreage as well as the countryside and waterways which surround it. Seventy-five percent of the trail system is fully or partly within the woods. Trails are varied, through hemlock groves and pine groves, interspersed with numerous varieties of deciduous trees. Mountain laurel is a major attraction in June. Water is generally available at shelter locations, which are scattered throughout the Reservation.

Approximately 5 miles from the Reservation on Rt. 22, between Bedford Village and Katonah, is the John Jay House, which has been restored by the New York State Education Department. This thirty-room home was the birthplace of John Jay, an influential member of George Washington's staff during the Revolution, a delegate to the Continental Congress, and the nation's first Chief Justice. The house is situated on a thirty-acre scenic plateau. Its historical treasures include, in addition to authentic colonial furnishings, two thousand old books and six thousand manuscripts, letters, and mementos.

MIANUS RIVER GORGE WILD LIFE REFUGE AND BOTANICAL PRESERVE

This 227-acre area extends approximately 1.3 miles along the gorge and banks of the Mianus River in the townships of North Castle and Pound Ridge, New York. It has been maintained since 1953 as a nature preserve under sponsorship of the Mianus River Gorge Conservation Committee of The Nature Conservancy.

Access is by car only. From the Merritt Parkway, exit 34, go north 7.7 miles on Long Ridge Road (Rt. 104) to Miller's Mill Road.

Turn left here for 0.1 mile over the bridge to Mianus River Road and then turn left again (south) for 0.7 mile to the entrance sign and to parking on the left.

A foot trail with several side loops runs south along the west bank of the gorge, from the visitors' entrance to the upper end of the Greenwich Water Company Reservoir, which has been formed by damming the Mianus River. The gorge is rugged and spectacular, and drops sharply below the trail, where the roar of water can be heard. Much of the path consists of a carpet of needles from giant hemlocks. Mineral outcrops occur (one side trail leads to an abandoned mica and quartz mine), and over five hundred species of flora and fauna have been cataloged by naturalists. A round trip on the main trail requires 2 hours or less, but considerable additional time can and should be devoted to the exploration of the various side trails. Detailed trail maps are available at the entrance. Lunching in the preserve is not permitted.

BYRAM RIVER TRAIL

The Byram River Trail in Connecticut, between Glenville and North Greenwich, affords a 5.3-mile walk, mainly on bridle paths that follow the course of a narrow river. A 2-mile section between Sherwood Avenue and Cliffdale Road is through the Wildlife Refuge of the Nature Conservancy. Near the northern terminus the trail passes through the National Audubon Society Wildlife Refuge. Residential development threatens both the southern and the northern ends of the trail.

At its southern end the trail is reached by car from the Hutchinson River Parkway, exit 30, King Street (Rt. 120A), and then onto Glenridge Road for 1 mile to Glenville. The trail begins at Glen Plaza (Grand Union parking lot) at Glenridge Road and Glenville Street. From the Plaza to the Merritt Parkway it is 1.5 miles by trail. The trail first ascends Glenridge Road 300 feet to a telephone pole where it turns right, and passes across a stone wall to a foot trail. Because the trail is not maintained, it is overgrown and its yellow blazes are hard to find for approximately 0.3 mile. The trail enters a bridle path, follows a paved road (where residential construction may be in progress) and at 1 mile reaches the Byram River, where it follows the bridle path once again. At the Merritt Parkway it passes close to the toll booth, turns right over an iron mesh footbridge to Riversville Road, and follows this road to Sherwood

Avenue. This is a point of access to the trail; cars can be parked under the Merritt Parkway Bridge on Riversville Road.

The trail follows Sherwood Avenue for 0.4 mile and turns right into the woods on a bridle path, where shortly thereafter boundary markers of the Nature Conservancy Wildlife Refuge are posted. Here the trail passes through hemlocks, rhododendrons, and tulip trees, edges the river for a stretch, climbs its steep banks, and then veers from the water into the quiet woods again. Be attentive to the yellow markers, as the bridle path has many forks.

After crossing Cliffdale Road (no parking here), the trail enters a dirt service road and follows it past a pump station (for the adjacent golf course), where it enters the woods, again on a bridle path. A sign on a tree indicates the National Audubon Society Wildlife Refuge. At 5 miles a side trail leads right 75 feet to a rock at the river's edge with a plaque dedicated to Bayard Read for his donation of 22 acres of the Hemlock Wildlife Sanctuary. Reaching Audubon Lane, the trail turns right and follows the road 0.2 mile to Bedford Road, the northern terminus. This point may be reached by car, 1 mile from the Junction of Bedford Road and King Street (Rt. 120A). This junction is 4 miles north of the Hutchinson River Parkway, exit 30, King Street. The Westchester County Airport is 1.8 miles from the trail terminus at Bedford Road. Walk left (west) on Bedford Road to King Street, left on King Street 0.5 mile to Rye Lake Avenue, and then right 0.6 mile to the airport. Here are refreshments, telephones, and taxi service.

SMALL PARKS AND SANCTUARIES
IN WESTCHESTER COUNTY AND
WESTERN CONNECTICUT

Scattered through the outlying reaches north and east of New York City are numerous areas set aside for conservation purposes, generally under the sponsorship of a foundation, nature organization, or, in some cases, a private owner. For the most part, these tracts are open to walkers, although for some of them advance permission is required. Such sanctuaries are too small to be of interest to those seeking a full day of vigorous exercise, but they do offer retreats of great charm and beauty and opportunities for nature study and observation. It should not be assumed that the visitor will find only well-maintained paths over gentle gradients. Rough terrain abounds so be prepared to encounter any of the hazards and obstacles normally expected in "unimproved" areas.

Marsh Sanctuary and Leonard Park, Mt. Kisco.

Southeast of the business center of Mount Kisco is a roughly triangular area of a few hundred acres that contains the Cornelia V. R. Marsh Memorial Sanctuary of Wildlife Preserves, Inc., Leonard Park, and certain private property. Throughout are bridle paths of the Private Lanes Association which are open to walkers. The area is bounded on the northwest by Rts. 117 and 172 (Bedford and South Bedford roads) and on the southwest and east by Byram Lake Road and Sarles Street, respecively. Two trail entrances about 500 feet apart on the west side of Sarles Street just north of the Byram Road intersection are marked by signs "To Leonard Park via Marsh Sanctuary."

The Sanctuary itself, at the southern point of the triangle, is closed to walkers; however, the southerly of the two entrances affords glimpses of its wetlands. Numerous trail branches offer a wide choice of circuits within the area bounded by the highways; to reach Leonard Park bear consistently left from either entrance to a parking area adjacent to Rt. 172, at about 1.5 miles. A right fork at almost any point leads into a network of bridle trail loops which may be explored to multiply this distance several-fold. Since the area is relatively small, and circumscribed by highways, there is no danger of becoming lost.

Westmoreland Sanctuary.

A 105-acre tract containing a small pond and several miles of foot trails near Bedford Village, New York, is maintained by Westmoreland Sanctuary, Inc. A wide variety of terrain, it includes open grassland, stands of both hardwood and evergreen trees, a brook valley, and one or two modest rocky summits. The varied habitat produces an abundance of flowers and birds. A peripheral trail of about 4 miles provides a pleasant half-day loop, with a network of several interior trails making longer or shorter tours possible. A map obtainable at the entrance shows the trail layout; the paths are identified by tagged posts at junctions.

Westmoreland Sanctuary is located on the east side of Chesnut Ridge Road, about midway between Rts. 22 and 172 (1.5 miles from each). Coming from the west, Chesnut Ridge Road leaves Rt. 172 on the right about 2 miles from Mt. Kisco. From the south, on Rt.

22, it is the next left road after passing Baldwin Road beyond Windmill Farms, a few miles north of Armonk.

KITCHAWAN FIELD STATION
AND TEATOWN LAKE RESERVATION

These scenic natural areas in Westchester County have been acquired by the Brooklyn Botanic Garden. They are both in the Ossining-Kitchawan area, south of Croton Reservoir, about 1 mile east and west, respectively, of the Taconic Parkway. The Field Station property, to the east, comprises 223 acres. It has about 6 miles of trail and a direct connection with the old Putnam Railroad right-of-way. This latter, however, is slated for obliteration by a relocation of Rt. 100. The Teatown Lake Reservation, to the west of the Taconic Parkway, is located on Spring Valley Road. The tract includes some 213 acres and the 33-acre Teatown Lake. There are about 8 miles of trail here offering variety for the hiker.

Routed redwood signs direct the traveler on both properties. Guided tours can be arranged for groups of ten to thirty persons. Labeled trails offer self-instruction in plant identification and nature study. Both properties can be included in a hike, although private property in between necessitates a rather indirect route. From the dam at Teatown Lake a county-owned corridor extends about 2 miles northwest to Croton Reservoir. A path follows this along the lake outlet to Applebee Road, which it crosses, continuing to Croton Reservoir.

Croton Lake Road, which borders the Reservoir, is dirt and may be followed east under the Taconic Parkway and past the New York City water supply pump house to Arcady Road (about 1 mile). Follow Arcady Road up a steep hill to the Field Station property on the left. A trail leaves the road about 100 yards beyond a stand of hemlock and proceeds downhill to a footbridge over a small stream. Most of the trails and property are across this stream to the east and south.

Groups must obtain permission before planning a walk on the Field Station property. The Teatown Lake Reservation is open without appointment. There are facilities for picnicking there as well.

There is no public transportation in the area between Ossining and Mt. Kisco. To reach Kitchawan Field Station, follow Rt. 134 approximately 2 miles east from Taconic Parkway (exit W16) to the entrance on the left, just before Pinesbridge Road on the right. The same Parkway exit is used for Teatown Lake Reservation; here,

however, go west on Rt. 134 for about 0.5 mile to Spring Valley
Road on the right, then follow the latter for about a mile to the
parking area on the right.

VALERIA HOME PROPERTY; DICKERSON
AND SALT HILLS

A mile or two to the southeast of the Blue Mountain Reservation
is the property of the Valeria Home, encompassing Dickerson Hill,
the highest point in Westchester County (810 feet), and Salt Hill
(755 feet). The Valeria Home is a residence for persons of limited
means, a gift of Jacob Langeloth. Permission to use the foot trails
on the property may be obtained by writing in advance to the Manager, Valeria Home, Oscawana, N.Y. 10561. It is recommended that
walks there be scheduled only during the cooler months of the year
in order to minimize any possible disturbance to the occupants, who
may be using the grounds during the other seasons. (It is also reported that copperheads have been found in the area during the
summer months.)

The area is awkwardly covered by the map sheets of the U. S.
Geological Survey, being at the junction of the "Peekskill," "Mohegan Lake," and "Ossining" quadrangles.

To reach the Valeria Home property, leave Rt. 9 at the Montrose-
Buchanan exit south of Peekskill, and drive a short distance west
to old Rt. 9. Here turn right (south) a few yards to Furnace Dock
Road on the left (Chimney Corners Restaurant is at the intersection); turn into Furnace Dock Road and follow it about 3 miles to
the Valeria Home gates on the right. Here permission to enter will
probably have to be shown to a guard, who will give parking
instructions.

A blazed trail starting at the Valeria Home provides a loop walk
of 3 or 4 miles over the two summits. About 2 hours should be
allowed, plus extra time for lunch and view stops. The distance may
be considerably extended, however, by following other, unmarked
trails on the property.

The white-blazed trail up Dickerson Hill starts from the roadway
near the parking lot and climbs steeply to the top; about a half hour
is required for the ascent. Although the summit is wooded, there is
a view during the "leafless" seasons. A sharp right turn is made for
the descent down the southerly slope of the hill. Follow the white
blazes to a double blaze, which indicates a right turn into the trail
up Salt Hill. Follow this, keeping to the left. At the top, a lookout

CROTON RESERVOIR・BEYOND THE SADDLE・SALT HILL・WOLF DEN
KEG MOUNTAIN   VALERIA HOME・THE CLUB・THE LAKE
CROTON RESERVOIR
Road to Oscawanna →
Road to Peakskill
Rose Ave

tower provides extensive views of Croton Reservoir and the surrounding country. The marked trail continues west, then north to the descent of Salt Hill. At the bottom, the white trail merges with a white and yellow marked path that leads back via a woods road to the parking lot.

NEW YORK CENTRAL FORMER RIGHTS-OF-WAY

Portions of the abandoned line of the old New York Central's Putnam Division afford semirural walks in northern Westchester County, as does the former Mahopac Branch which once served as a connecting link between the Putnam and Harlem divisions of the railroad. Rails and ties have been removed, leaving a level but often weed-grown cinder path for walking.

Little convenient public transportation exists now in the areas once served by these lines. Consequently, most access points can be reached by car only. Use two or more cars to avoid backtracking.

Millwood to Croton Reservoir.

Between New York City and Millwood, a distance of some 30 miles, the Putnam division route closely parallels major arterial highways, and in some stretches has actually been obliterated by new road construction. Hence, few if any opportunities for enjoyable walking exist south of Millwood.

A 3-mile walk north to the Croton Reservoir on the old rail line (see "Ossining" sheet of the U. S. Geological Survey) may be started at the former Millwood Station, which is on Rt. 133, 0.5 mile east of the Millwood-Briarcliff Manor exit of the Taconic Parkway. Near the northerly end of the walk, a car may be left at Kitchawan, on Rt. 134, reached by driving north about 2.5 miles from the same Parkway exit on Rt. 100, then west on Rt. 134 about 0.2 mile to a bridge over the old right-of-way.

From Millwood station, the rail route bears north across Rt. 133, shortly leaving the built-up area of Millwood and passing through mixed open areas, thickets, and woodland. Cross Rt. 100 at 1.5 miles, with a gravel quarry on the left. Half a mile beyond, the line passes beneath Kitchawan Road (Rt. 134), with remains of the old Kitchawan station platform just beyond and an arm of Croton Reservoir on the right. Signs indicating the Kitchawan Field Station of the Brooklyn Botanic Garden are soon seen; the walk may be pleasantly extended by exploring the paths and trails of this conservation area, some of which cross the line within sight of the iron bridge over the reservoir. This bridge, at 3 miles, forms the northern terminus of the walk, although it may be crossed by the adventurous who are undeterred by airy exposure some scores of feet above the water.

Former Croton Lake Station to Lake Mahopac.

This 10.5 mile stretch of the former Putnam Division is shown on the "Ossining," "Mohegan Lake," and "Croton Falls" sheets of the U. S. Geological Survey. The starting point, at the site of the old Croton Lake station, is on Rt. 129, which is 2.2 miles east of the Taconic Parkway exit at the north end of the parkway bridge over the Croton Reservoir. Mahopac station (now an American Legion hall) is located on the south side of Rt. 6 at the lower end of Lake Mahopac.

From the former Croton Lake station and across Rt. 129, the right-of-way first runs westerly, initially obscured by weeds and dirt piles. It quickly becomes evident, however, after crossing Birdsall Drive at 0.3 mile and then bears north, paralleling Rt. 118 to Yorktown Heights at 3.1 miles. Here, the hiker should follow Railroad Avenue for a few hundred feet to avoid obstructions, regaining the roadbed at Yorktown Engine Company No. 1 (3.3 miles). The remainder of the route traverses areas of scattered population, abandoned farms, orchards, and pasture land, with occasional road crossings and now and then unsightly collections of discarded remnants of civilization. At 10 miles, the abandoned Mahopac Branch enters from the right, for the last half mile to Mahopac.

Goldens Bridge to Lake Mahopac.

This is a 7.2-mile former connecting line between two branches of the old New York Central. As is the case with the Putnam division, the tracks have been removed except for a few brief sections where old ties remain. The "Croton Falls" sheet of the U. S. Geological Survey shows the route. Goldens Bridge may be reached by trains of the Harlem Division, but a car or taxi service will be required at the Mahopac end of the walk.

Starting at Goldens Bridge station, walk north on the west side of the tracks to a point 300 feet south of Green Street (Rt. 138), where the overgrown Mahopac Branch right-of-way will be seen angling off to the northwest. Following this, reach an arm of the Croton Reservoir, crossed by a low iron bridge and causeway at about 0.6 mile. From here the route traverses mostly attractive rolling countryside through fields and woods and past small bodies of water. The stone Lincolndale Station is passed at 3.3 miles; slightly beyond, the route parallels Plum Brook for some distance, crosses the county line at about 5.2 miles, and reaches Union Valley Road bridge at 5.7 miles. Just beyond this, it makes an easterly detour around a bulldozed area through a new residential section, rejoining the right-of-way at 6 miles. From here, the way follows more open country to the junction with the former Putnam Division line at 6.6 miles, from which point the latter is followed for the final half mile to Lake Mahopac.

9 · FAHNESTOCK STATE PARK
AND ADJACENT CONNECTICUT

(Map 15)

ᴀʜɴᴇꜱᴛᴏᴄᴋ Pᴀʀᴋ is situated in the northern part of Putnam County about 8 miles east of Cold Spring. It is under the direction of the Taconic State Park Commission, with headquarters at Staatsburg. The park originally consisted of about 3600 acres which were given to the state in 1929 by Dr. Alfred Fahnestock in memory of his father, Dr. Clarence Fahnestock. Between 1960 and 1966 several additions were made so that the total is now nearly 6200 acres. The park is shaped somewhat like a U, with the base at the junction of Taconic State Parkway and Rt. 301 and the sides running southeast and southwest along these highways. There is a ski area on the east side of the Parkway 0.5 mile north of Rt. 301, and picnic and camping grounds extending along the east side of Rt. 301 for 1 mile south of its junction with the Parkway. There is free parking on Rt. 301 opposite Canopus Lake, and on small turnouts on the gravel roads in the southwest section. Cars can also be left under the bridge which carries the Taconic Parkway over Peekskill Hollow Road, for access to the southerly section of the Park (formerly known as Roaring Brook State Park). The Park can be reached only by car.

There are two high ridges in the western portion of Fahnestock Park, one culminating in Candlewood Hill in the south and the other in Mt. Shenandoah (1282 feet), a little north of the Park boundary. Canopus Creek flows through a beautiful rugged ravine in the southwest. Much of the remaining portion of the Park is rolling country covered with second-growth hardwood forests and a few old hemlock groves. Throughout the younger forests can be seen traces of early settlements such as overgrown wood roads, cellar holes, stone fences, charcoal pits, and mine cuts. Canopus Lake lies just west of Rt. 301, with Pelton Pond opposite it; Stillwater Pond is west of the Parkway, and there are several small ponds in the southwest area. Many portions of the Park, although not very rugged, are difficult to penetrate because of swamps or dense undergrowth of laurel. The best time to see this in bloom is around the second week in June.

Deer are numerous in the Park, and there is intermittent beaver activity in many swamps. All the usual woodland birds, including

ar Pond, north end. granite blocks & mountain laurel.   XXII June 14 1969 REH

partridges, are abundant, and hawks can often be seen riding the updraft at the face of Candlewood Hill.

Drinking water can be obtained in summer but not in winter at the picnic grounds opposite the north end of Canopus Lake. There are springs in various parts of the Park, but they are usually dry in warm weather. In any case, springs and streams should be considered unsafe for drinking. It is much colder in the Park than in many neighboring districts, and deep snow may be found until the end of March.

There are three main trails in the Park: a bridle path on the east side running from Dicktown Road at its junction with the Parkway north to Rt. 301; a broad trail originally planned as a bridle path running a little west of the Parkway from Wiccopee Road north to Hortontown Road and not now maintained in all sections; and the Appalachian Trail (white blazes) which enters the Park from Bell Hollow Road in the southwest, crosses Rt. 301 at Canopus, and runs along the west ridge through the northern boundary of the Park.

WALKS IN FAHNESTOCK STATE PARK

Walk 1. Length: 5 miles.

Park at Canopus Lake and enter the AT at the double white blazes on the east side of Rt. 301 at the north end of the parking lot. Note an old mine cut on the left. Follow AT for 0.3 mile, then continue straight where the trail turns right (east), and follow unmarked footpaths north through the hemlock grove on the east side of Pelton Pond. Continue through the picnic grounds, avoiding the swamp on the east, to the junction of Rt. 301 and the Parkway. Cross Rt. 301, and look for the obscure entrance to the trail between a small cliff and the Parkway access ramp. Follow this open but unmarked trail for 1 mile as it runs north parallel to, but out of sight of, the Parkway. After climbing a small rise, begin to watch for a yellow blaze and cairn on the left. At the cairn, turn left on an abandoned wood road (yellow blaze) over a brook and up a steep rise to the junction with the AT (white blaze). Bear right (north) on the AT for 1.5 miles to Mt. Shenandoah. This is a good place for lunch when it is not too cold; the view is unobstructed in all directions, and the Catskills are visible in clear weather. (If a longer walk is desired it is possible to reach Mt. Shenandoah by following the unmarked trail to Hortontown Road instead of turning off at the yellow blaze. A left turn on the road leads after 0.5 miles to the

AT about 1 mile north of Shenandoah. This route is not very interesting, and, since it crosses private lands, should not be used in the hunting season.)

To return to Canopus from Shenandoah, go south on the AT to its junction with the yellow blaze. Turn right here at the double blaze (white), and continue on the AT to where it crosses Rt. 301, 0.2 mile below the parking lot. The trail follows the ridge to a rocky knob, where there is a good view of the lake and a register which hikers are invited to sign. The trail then descends steeply (difficult in icy weather) through a ravine where the Torrey Memorial Shelter is situated, skirts the lake through a fine hemlock grove for a short distance, and returns to the ridge. From the ridge there is a gradual descent through a dense stand of laurel to the road. This is about a 9-mile walk, if the Hortontown route is taken, and it is moderately strenuous. (If the northeast end of Canopus Lake is developed for public use, as proposed, the route of the AT around the lake will be changed; watch for white blazes.)

Walk 2. Length: 5 miles.

Park at Canopus and enter the AT as in Walk 1, but continue on the AT 1.5 miles until the upper end of Stillwater Pond is in sight on the left. Turn left (east) off the trail here, and bushwhack 0.5 mile to Taconic Parkway. (There may be some difficulty in crossing a brook at the head of Stillwater, especially when the beavers are active.) Cross the Parkway. This is usually practicable, since the northern and southern roads are divded here. Turn left (north) on the bridle path at the junction of Dicktown Road and the Parkway, and follow it 2 miles to Rt. 301. Watch for foundations and other signs of an old hamlet along the way. At Rt. 301 turn left (southwest) and go 0.4 mile, crossing over the Parkway on a bridge. Turn left into the picnic grounds, and follow paths near Rt. 301 to Pelton Pond. Follow the east shore of Pelton Pond to the AT, and descend to the parking lot. This is about a 5-mile walk and is easy, except for a short stretch of bushwhacking.

Walk 3. Length: 7 miles.

This can be done only if more than one car is available. From Canopus, drive 2.5 miles southwest on Rt. 301; turn left at Fahnestock Corners, and follow an unmarked narrow asphalt road 0.8 mile to a fork. Here take the left fork marked Sunken Mine Road, and follow this narrow gravel road 2.1 miles, past the bridge over Canopus Creek, to an unmarked junction with Bell Hollow Road. Leave one car here, and return to Canopus. Start walking on the AT, as in walks 1 and 2, but at about 2.5 miles be careful not to miss a sharp but well-marked right turn to a gravel road. Jog right here, and follow the AT blazes across another gravel road and up Candlewood Hill. Have lunch here and enjoy the view. Descend steeply to Bell Hollow Road, and turn right north, leaving the AT. Follow this primitive road with views into the gorge of Canopus Creek on the left for 1 mile to where the car was parked. An alternative is to cross the road to the creek and work up through the bottom of the gorge to the bridge. There are several beautiful cascades here, and the trip is rewarding, but it is exceedingly rough. It goes over boulders, blowdowns, and wet moss and should be attempted only by experienced hikers. This walk is about 7 miles and is a moderate hike without the gorge; strenuous if the gorge is included.

Walk 4.

Although not a main trail, for a fourth walk park under the bridge which carries the Taconic Parkway over Peekskill Hollow Road. Walk northeast along this road for about 0.5 mile, cross Roaring Brook on the highway bridge, and turn left on the road which parallels the brook (avoiding a right turn onto private property). Walk uphill about 0.5 mile to a fork in the road and a ruined wooden culvert; there, turn sharp right on a footpath. Going uphill, pass to the right of an old stone wall, and 150 yards farther on take a faint left fork, keeping at the left of another stone wall as the trail winds uphill.

About 0.5 mile farther on, a side trail at the right leads to the summit of Moose Hill (about 1 mile round trip). Views from the top are rewarding. Return to the junction of the side and main trails and continue on the main trail. After crossing a brook, turn left on an old road. Follow this road for about 200 yards, and at the point where the stone wall at the right disappears, follow the right fork upgrade along the trail. Next, bear left on a wood road. Very shortly a partly obscured trail leaves the wood road at the right to circle the heights to the north and return to the wood road just beyond the crossing of Roaring Brook. As this trail is now obscure, it should be considered as a side trail (about 0.75 mile).

Follow the wood road downhill to a bridge across Roaring Brook, cross the Parkway and a brush lot, and turn left on the bridle path which parallels the Parkway. After about a mile on the bridle path, there is a spring on the left (sometimes dry in late summer) and some distance beyond a shelter with a developed spring on a trail immediately to the east. The trail divides beyond the shelter, but soon both branches join. From this junction follow the trail downhill through beautiful hemlock woods, with Roaring Brook far down on the left. After about 2 miles the trail returns to the highway junction.

EASTWARD FROM FAHNESTOCK STATE PARK

Leaving the Park, the AT follows the northern edge of the highlands. Continuing along undulating territory in the midst of old trees and occasional ponds, the trail route leads northeast across the Harlem Valley to the summit of Schaghticoke Mountain and the Connecticut state line. (For details of the Appalachian Trail, see *Guide to the Appalachian Trail in New York and New Jersey.*

Housatonic Range (Map 10) Trail. Length: 8 miles. Blazes: blue.
The Housatonic Range Trail follows the route of an ancient Indian path. The trail affords a fairly rugged hike, from Gaylordsville south to New Milford, Connecticut. It roughly parallels the Housatonic River, and both ends of the trail are easily accessible from Rt. 7. Along the trail are a few short but challenging rock scrambles, and several clear views of the river valley and hills to the east.

Because of many small ascents and descents, the trail is more difficult than its maximum elevation of about 1000 feet would suggest, in some places climbing between boulders and ledges. Allow approximately 4.5 hours; if the two side loops are taken, add another half hour. The trail is delineated on U. S. G. S. topographic maps for "Kent" and "New Milford," Connecticut.

The southern starting point is on Rt. 7, about 1.5 miles north of the junction of Rts. 7 and 25. A cutout on the west side of the road has room for about six cars, and the trail begins immediately to the south of this cutout, on a narrow road that quickly disappears over a small knoll. Just ahead of this cutout, two concrete railings straddle Rt. 7, where a tiny, usually dry, stream called Rocky River runs underneath.

The northern starting point is from Cedar Hill Road, which leaves Rt. 7 about 1 mile south of the junction of Rts. 7 and 55 in Gaylordsville. The blue blazes begin about 200 yards to the west, up Cedar Hill Road. A few cars can be parked right alongside the first blue blaze, but more space is available on a shoulder cutout on Rt. 7, a few yards north of the junction with Cedar Hill Road.

From the origin at Cedar Hill Road, the Housatonic Trail (north to south) climbs steeply amidst elephant-sized boulders to the Pinnacle (about 800 feet), which has a fine view to the north. The trail then follows a ridge before descending to Squash Hollow Road at about 1.4 miles. It travels along this road a short way, returns to the woods, and climbs steeply up a hill that has a good lunch spot at the top. The trail dips a bit, then begins a moderate ascent of Boardman Mountain. Near the top of the Boardman ridge, a loop trail (blue blazed) swings eastward to Tories Cave, which contains several rooms. From Tories Cave, a side trail (also blue blazed) leads to Rt. 7, where several cars can be parked. Each leg of the loop is about 0.3 mile, and the leg to Rt. 7 is a few hundred yards long. The loop returns to the main trail, which continues to another intersection with Squash Hollow Road at about 3 miles. The trail follows the road for a short distance, then veers into the woods, where it follows a series of old charcoal roads. It goes up Suicide Ledges, which is short but steep, and soon winds through a jumble of boulders and ledges which are good rock scrambles. However, these can be avoided by circling to the west. At approximately 4.5 miles, the trail crosses Rt. 37.

The next and final section, about 3.5 miles long, follows the ridge of Pine Knob and Candlewood Mountain. Climbing steeply from Rt. 37, the trail twists through the "Corkscrew," a short scramble for which the hiker needs both hands and feet to negotiate, before approaching the summit of Pine Knob. Candlewood Cave is several hundred feet down the steep side of Pine Knob, but there is no visible or marked trail to the cave. Continuing over Candlewood Mountain, the trail passes a side loop that turns steeply downhill to Kelly Slide for a fine view to the east. The loop rejoins the main path not far from its earlier departure point. Some 0.75 mile farther south, another good lookout point, with an eastern exposure, is reached. The trail makes a hairpin turn to the northeast about 0.4 mile ahead. From here, hikers can see an arm of Candlewood Lake, from which an aqueduct transports water to the New Milford powerhouse and thence to the Shepaug Reservoir. Follow a wood road to the end of the trail on Rt. 7 in New Milford, 0.5 mile north of the powerhouse.

POOTATUCK STATE FOREST

Pootatuck State Forest is an undeveloped state woodland area, bordering Squantz Pond in western Connecticut. The area is reached by way of Rt. 39 where it crosses the causeway that separates Squantz Pond from an arm of Candlewood Lake.

The forest trails are not blazed or otherwise maintained. However, a wood road runs through the forest, generally in the shape of an inverted U whose base is at the north end of the forest. One side of the wood road, for the most part, parallels the lake, and the other side follows a southwesterly direction, eventually reaching the western boundary of the forest. The wood road makes a good departure point for exploring the sometimes-overgrown trails in the higher, middle-core part of the forest. From the picnic area near the lake, the wood road can be most easily reached by following Beaver Bog Road a few hundred yards to the west from its junction with Rt. 39. The wood road turns northward off Beaver Bog Road. There is also a path that follows the shore closely and that can be used in conjunction with the wood road to make an all-day hike.

(Map 11)

INTRODUCTION

ELDOM DO large cities have anything to match the gorge of the Hudson through the Highlands. From Dunderberg north around Anthony's Nose to Storm King and Breakneck the Hudson is narrow and winding and flanked on either side by hills of a thousand feet or more. What we have now is merely the remnant of a gorge two, three, or more times that depth. During the Ice Age the glaciers shaved off the tops of the mountains and filled the gorge with debris.

During the Revolution in 1777 a chain was stretched across the river from the foot of Anthony's Nose to Fort Montgomery, opposite. Just across the river, south of Popolopen Creek, is the site of Fort Clinton (now occupied by buildings of the Bear Mountain Nature Museum) and, on the north side of the cove, the remains of Fort Montgomery. These log and stone ramparts were the scene of a brave defense by Orange County militia, on October 4, 1777, against an assault by British troops under Sir John Vaughan. The British finally took the posts and, with the aid of ships, broke the chain across the river. After the enemy had made a raid up the river in a vain attempt to save Burgoyne at Saratoga, the Americans fortified West Point and built outlying redoubts on several summits east of the river, on Fort Defiance Hill and Fort Hill, east of Garrison, and elsewhere. A new and heavier chain was stretched from West Point to Constitution Island, where the river is the narrowest. This island, now under the administration of West Point, can only be reached by special launch from the Military Academy. The sites of the chain-fastening and the redoubts are marked by bronze tablets.

On the east end of the ridge of Anthony's Nose are the extensive dumps of the old Manitou Copper Mine. The ore was chiefly iron pyrites, with a small amount of copper. This mine was originally opened about 1767 for iron ore by no less a person than the famous Peter Hasenclever, but it was not one of his successful operations because the ore, smelted in one of his furnaces at Cortlandt, south of Peekskill, proved too sulfurous to be satisfactory. Years later, the mine was operated for the sulfur content of the ore rather than for its iron or copper.

No more striking scenery is to be found east of the river than the Highlands of the Hudson. These hills are much like the Highlands west of the Hudson; they are geologically similar, although the granites and gneisses include infolded limestones, slates, and quartz-ites not so much in evidence as on the other side of the river.

A striking feature of the topography of these eastern Highlands is the bold escarpment running along the northwest front of the Fishkill Mountains. This abrupt rise, from sea level at the Hudson to 1200 to 1600 feet, is a part of the great fault which bounds the Highlands on the north, on both sides of the river. The southern boundary of the eastern Highlands is not so well defined topographi-cally, as several fault lines extend northeast into the hills along the valleys, the main one in Peekskill Hollow.

South Beacon, rising as it does over 1600 feet above the country to the north and dwarfing the other hills and mountains to the west and south, commands a superb view. One has to see that view to appreciate fully the significance of the following story of the first land purchase in the Fishkill region.

On February 8, 1682, a license was given to three New Yorkers—Francis Rombout, a distinguished merchant, Jacobus Kipp, and Gulian Ver Planck—to purchase a tract of land from the Indians. Under this license they bought, on August 8, 1683, from Nimham, sachem of the Wappingers, all rights to a huge tract afterwards known as the Rombout Patent. In the preliminary bargaining the Indians agreed to transfer to Rombout all "the land that he could see." Accordingly, Rombout led them to the summit of South Beacon Mountain. With a sweep of his arm northward and eastward he laid claim to a vast expanse of land covering some 85,000 acres. The Indians held to their bargain for many years. However, in 1740, Chief Daniel of the Wappingers sought, in a celebrated but belated and unsuccessful lawsuit, to recover the ancient lands of the tribe.

Gulian Ver Planck died before the English patent was issued. Stephanus Van Cortlandt then joined with Rombout in the deal, while Jacobus Kipp married Ver Planck's widow, thereby neatly tying his share with that of his deceased co-partner. On October 17, 1685, letters of patent were granted by King James II to Rombout, Kipp, and Van Cortlandt.

The view from South Beacon is a beautiful combination of urban, rural, and mountain features. Beacon lies below and Newburgh is to be seen across the widening of the river in Newburgh Bay. In the middle ground are the farms and fields, with interspersed woodlots, of Dutchess and Orange counties; beyond them, across the Wallkill Valley, is the long level-topped line of the Shawangunk Mountains, and, on the far horizon, on a clear day, the sharper outlines of the Catskills. The night view, with the lights of the cities and towns and the bridge, and of automobiles on the highways is no less interesting. The view northeast is partly blocked by the extension of the ridge in Bald Hill, over which is another interesting trail, by wood roads and cross country, down to Fishkill village.

The monument on the summit of North Beacon was erected by the Daughters of the American Revolution to mark a place where beacons were lighted during the Revolutionary War by the American troops encamped below. It was badly damaged by lightning but was reconstructed in 1928. Coursing up the northwest face of the ridge is the Mt. Beacon Incline Railway, one of the steepest in the world. It connects the outskirts of the city of Beacon below with the Casino on top of the mountain.

Mt. Taurus is situated north of the town of Cold Spring and opposite Crows Nest on the side of the Hudson. Its name, as every Latin student knows, is merely the highbrow version of its original name, Bull Hill. How it came by its present high-toned name is of no great concern; it is more interesting to speculate how it got its original name. One version, which has the virtue of explaining the origin not only of Bull Hill but also of Breakneck Ridge, is that in pioneer days a fierce wild bull that roamed the woods and fields of the area fell from a cliff, during a chase, and broke his neck on what is now called Breakneck Ridge. The mountain, which is still sometimes called Bull Hill, is one of the finest elevations at the northern end of the Hudson Gorge.

DOWN THE HUDSON FROM COLD SPRING TO BEAR MOUNTAIN & WEST POINT

On the southern face of Mt. Taurus is an unsightly scar, the result of a quarrying operation which began in the early 1930s and ceased several years afterward. For years lovers of the scenery of the Hudson hoped that eventually the State of New York would acquire this property to protect it permanently. Partially through the efforts of the New York–New Jersey Trail Conference, this was accomplished. In 1970 the Taconic State Park Commission formally assumed the operation of Hudson Highlands State Park. This tract safeguards 2500 acres including Mt. Taurus, Breakneck Ridge, and Sugar Loaf (immediately north of Breakneck Ridge).

South of the park area and north of the Bear Mountain Bridge are several smaller peaks which provide interesting rambles, including another Sugar Loaf. This little mountain is made by the uptilted end of a fault block, such as may be found throughout the Highlands, but this one is more cleanly defined than most.

At the east end of the Bear Mountain Bridge the Appalachian Trail turns left (north) on Rt. 9D. It leaves the highway at the Westchester-Putnam county line, climbs steeply around the northern flank of Anthony's Nose. Crossing over rolling terrain in a forested region, the trail passes near the former hunting grounds of the Wappinger Indians. Sites of old Revolutionary War encampments can still be found throughout the area. For details of the AT from the Hudson River east to the New York–Connecticut boundary, see the *Guide to the Appalachian Trail in New York and New Jersey*.

MT. BEACON–BREAKNECK RIDGE–
MT. TAURUS REGION

Three Notch Trail. Length: 8 miles. Blazes: blue on white.

The Three Notch Trail extends between Cold Spring and the town of Beacon, crossing the shoulders of Mt. Taurus and South Beacon Mountain, which are separated by the valley of Lake Surprise. To reach the Cold Spring end of the trail, go northeast on Rt. 301 from its junction with Rt. 9D in Cold Spring to Cedar Street, on the left; then proceed along Cedar Street one block to Mountain Avenue. Here cars can be parked. The trail markers begin near an old cemetery.

In 0.3 mile or less the Washburn Trail (white blazes) turns off to the left to go over the summit of Mt. Taurus. At 1 mile, Three Notch Trail crosses the Catskill Aqueduct (drinking water on right). In another mile, it ascends more steeply through the woods on an old carriage road, and a spring is passed on the right, with good water. Shortly beyond, at top of Bull's Notch (2.3 miles from the start) is the northern end of the Washburn Trail. At this point, Three Notch Trail turns sharp right, descends 2 miles to and across Lake Surprise Road, and, just beyond, crosses a brook (not for drinking). Almost immediately, it turns left (where the red-blazed Casino Trail goes off to the right) and continues around South Beacon to the Casino Trail on North Beacon. The Three Notch Trail, after a gradual climb of less than 1 mile from that point, joins the Breakneck Ridge Trail (white blazes), which climbs from the tunnel on Route 9D (at Breakneck Point) up Breakneck Ridge to South Beacon. Follow Breakneck north for a very short distance and turn left. The Three Notch Trail levels off, then descends

gradually, skirting the side of South Beacon Mountain, and in 1.5 miles from Surprise Lake Road crosses Squirrel Hollow Brook. Three quarters of a mile farther on it crosses Gordon's Brook on a bridge, then follows an old road bordered by stone walls for slightly over 0.5 mile, passing a view of the Hudson and the Beacon-Newburgh Bridge. The marked trail then bears right, away from the road, passing a few yards to the rear of private houses. At 3.5 miles from Lake Surprise Road (7.3 miles from the start) the trail arrives at the base of the famous Mt. Beacon Incline Railway, 1540 feet high

Newburgh and Beacon from Stormking on the Hudson looking north

and 2384 feet long, built in 1901 with a 64 percent grade. The Dutchess ski area has been developed here, and offers a natural and scenic bushwhack off the mountain from the Casino area. The remaining short stretch of the trail follows the driveway out to the main highway, ending at the intersection of Rt. 9D, Howland Avenue, and Wolcott Avenue in Beacon.

Allow 4 hours for this walk at a moderate pace; fast walkers may do it in 3 hours, since there are few steep climbs.

Washburn Trail. Length: 2 miles. Blazes: white.

Washburn Trail forms a side loop from Three Notch Trail, going over the summit of Mt. Taurus.

It starts at a point about 0.3 mile from the southern end of the Three Notch Trail, as described above. At about 0.2 mile, go through a gap in an old stone wall, passing cellar hole ruins. Climb steeply, coming in about 1 mile to beautiful views of Cold Spring, Constitution Island, and West Point to the south and Crow's Nest, Black Rock Forest, and Storm King to the west. Soon after, at flat rocks from which the summit of Mt. Taurus is visible, descend to a brook (doubtful for drinking), and climb steeply again. At 1.3 miles, there is a view to the west, and a little beyond is a large table rock with excellent views south and east. At the summit (1.5 miles) there is no view, but slightly farther on are beautiful views north and west, including Breakneck Ridge and the Beacons. The remainder of the trail continues downhill, crossing and recrossing a winding carriage road until it ends at the Three Notch Trail at 2.1 miles. The latter may then be followed to the right, to complete the loop back to Cold Spring. The approximate walking time is 3 hours, but additional time should be allowed to enjoy views along the way.

Breakneck Ridge Trail. Length: (?). Blazes: white.

Breakneck Ridge Trail, which follows an open ridge from the Hudson River to the top of South Beacon Mountain, is one of the most rugged and beautiful trails in the Hudson Highlands. The southern end of the trail starts at the north end of the Rt. 9D tunnel, about 2 miles north of Cold Spring, where Breakneck Point juts out to the Hudson River. There is a large parking area just north of the tunnel.

The beginning of the trail ascends the west embankment of the highway and crosses over the tunnel. (Watch out for poison ivy.) Here begins a very steep climb (extreme care is necessary, if descending) to what appears to be the top; however, another false summit follows, and another, until eventually an elevation of 1300 feet is reached. Each successive rocky knob is a little higher than the one before, revealing ever-widening panoramas. After about 2 miles of skipping from knob to valley and valley to knob, turn right onto a descending wood road; in another 0.5 mile (2.5 miles from the start) the Three Notch Trail (blue on white) enters from the right but quickly branches off to the left. In another 0.3 mile are the ledges at Sunset Point, with excellent views. Shortly, a steep descent leads to Squirrel Hollow Brook crossing, where the trail briefly follows a wood road which climbs to the right. The trail soon turns left and climbs sharply via Devil's Ladder to ledges with exceptional views. The fire lookout tower at the summit of South Beacon (1635 feet) is about 1.3 miles from the Three Notch Trail. At the tower the trail turns right and descends past the ranger's cabin. At a 0.3 mile from the tower, the Breakneck Ridge Trail ends at its junction with the red-on-white blazed Casino Trail, which leads northwest to the Casino on North Beacon or south to Surprise Lake Road.

Because of the roughness and steepness of the terrain, at least three and a half hours should be allowed for the Breakneck Ridge Trail, not including the time required to get off the mountain.

Casino Trail. Length: 2.3 miles. Blazes: red-on-white.

This short trail affords the easiest means of reaching the Mt. Beacon summits on foot, since its eastern end is accessible by car at a point 700 feet above the river level—nearly half the vertical distance to the top. The ascent is gradual and provides an excellent snowshoeing or cross-country ski route in winter. In summer, at least half the trail is shaded.

The Casino Trail begins at Lake Surprise Road where it is crossed by the Three Notch Trail. To reach this point by car, from Rt. 9 at North Highland (a hamlet about 13 miles north of Peekskill), turn south at North Highland on Fishkill Road for about 0.5 mile to Lake Surprise Road. Go west on this road for about 1.5 miles and park near the blue-on-white Three Notch crossing, just beyond a roadway to Cold Spring Reservoir on the right.

The Casino Trail forks to the right from the Three Notch Trail almost immediately after crossing the brook northwest of the road. Bearing north, it skirts an 1180-foot knob and then climbs Schofield Ridge, which provides a beautiful view of Lake Valhalla and the surrounding country. In about 1.5 miles, pass the northern end of the white-blazed Breakneck Ridge Trail (left a quarter mile to the fire lookout tower on South Beacon). The Casino Trail continues straight ahead, passing a trail up North Beacon on the right and then joining the service road from North Beacon to the Casino, where the trail ends.

Miscellaneous Walks in the Beacon Range.

Various sections of the marked trails already described can be combined to provide long or short walks or loops which avoid the need to spot cars. The Surprise Lake Valley affords a good return walking route to Breakneck Point after climbing the Breakneck Ridge Trail. The descent to the valley may be made via the Three Notch Trail, Casino Trail, or by bushwhacking down from the ridge at almost any point.

In addition, there are unmarked trails on Fishkill Ridge north of the Beacon summits: a route up the valley on the north side of Dry Brook from the eastern end of the town of Beacon leads between Lamb's Hill and Schofield Ridge; bearing northeast around the contour, the old roads and unmarked trails may be followed east to Rt. 9, to a point about 3 miles south of the village of Fishkill.

CATSKILL AQUEDUCT

Mt. Taurus to Philipse Brook. Length: 3 miles.

This area can be reached at points where the Catskill Aqueduct crosses under Rt. 301, 1 mile northeast of Cold Spring, and on Philipse Brook Road, 0.8 mile east of its junction with Rt. 9D, north of Garrison Four Corners. An intermediate crossing point is at Indian Brook Road. Public transportation to this area is provided by infrequent bus service along Rt. 9D.

For maps of this region see the U.S.G.S. "West Point" quadrangle. This section of the aqueduct provides a pleasant walk which can be combined with a climb to the summit of Mt. Taurus if a longer outing is desired. The characteristic pumping station structures on the hillsides north and south of Rt. 301 indicate the location of the aqueduct at the north end; it is a short climb southeast from the highway to the nominal aqueduct grade. From this point south to Philipse Brook Road there is only one brief interruption, 1 mile south of the start, where the aqueduct pierces a hill, necessitating a scramble over the obstruction, some hundred feet high.

In the next 4 or 5 miles, from Philipse Brook south to Oregon Road in Peekskill Hollow, the aqueduct makes only brief appear-

INDIAN HEAD 530 FEET. HIGH GUTTER PT. PARK END
FOREST VIEW   GIANT STAIR   NEW JERSEY BOUNDARY SNEDENS LANDING PIERMONT

North of
Odell Ave
north Yonkers
Broadway and
the Hastings
trolley and the
R.R are below

Dickinson
October 1924

old Croton Aqueduct

ances, running largely underground and beneath two normally impassable streams. This stretch, therefore, provides no suitable walking route for any but the most avid aqueduct follower.

Oregon Road to Croton Reservoir. Length: 6–7 miles.

By car, numerous points can be reached at aqueduct crossings between Oregon Road, 1.8 miles northeast of Bear Mountain State Parkway at Peekskill, and Baldwin Road east of Taconic Parkway, just north of Croton Reservoir. For maps of the region, see the U.S.G.S. "Peekskill" and "Mohegan Lake" quadrangles.

This stretch passes through populated areas and borders and crosses some major highways at its northern end, but the lower half becomes more remote and secluded. About a dozen road crossings along the way make possible short walks, up to the full distance. The remaining mile, from Baldwin Road to Croton Reservoir, is not recommended for walking because here the aqueduct crosses the Taconic Parkway and penetrates a shoulder of Turkey Mountain.

Croton Reservoir to Hardscrabble Road. Length: 4.5 miles.

Any number of road crossings can be reached by Rt. 134, 1 mile west of Kitchawan, and Hardscrabble Road, 1.5 miles north of Pleasantville Road. The map for this region is the U.S.G.S. "Ossining" quadrangle. The first emergence of the aqueduct south of Croton Reservoir is at the southeasterly base of Stayback Hill, just north of Rt. 134. From here the aqueduct can be followed 2 miles south to Millwood, from there another 2.5 miles to Hardscrabble Road on top of a plateau northwest of Pleasantville. Midway along this latter stretch, a 150-foot ridge intervenes, between Campfire Road and Chappaqua Road, requiring the walker to follow for some distance a rough trail under a power line.

From Hardscrabble Road southeast to Kensico Reservoir, the aqueduct is largely inaccessible because of housing developments and posted areas. Below the reservoir, the assiduous searcher can pick up the route again as it closely parallels the eastern edge of the Sprain Brook Parkway for most of that highway's distance south to Tuckahoe Road in Yonkers. Beyond this point, the Parkway crosses, decisively interrupting the aqueduct path. One or two relatively secluded stretches remain near Ardsley and Elmsford, where the aqueduct briefly diverges from the sight and sound of the Parkway and enters woods. But for the most part, the encroachments of civilization (including transmission line towers, highway crossings, and an ever-increasing population density) rob this part of the aqueduct walk of any charm it once had.

CANADA HILL, WHITE ROCK, AND SUGAR LOAF
Map 1

East of the Hudson and immediately north of Anthony's Nose lie the ridges of Canada Hill (840 feet) and White Rock (885 feet). Beyond, the prominent cone of Sugar Loaf Hill (765 feet) rises close to the river south of Garrison.

Canada Hill and the adjoining ridge of White Rock are interlaced with a network of graded trails in a forest of oaks, laurel, and hemlocks. Several small ponds are in the area. The trails are unmarked, but wide, and are particularly fine for snowshoeing. They have been used by horsemen and walkers for many years without objection by the landowners. Both are expected to continue to show regard for this tract of private property and to respect the privacy of the owners. Some day, it is hoped, this will become park land. By using the Canada Hill–White Rock trails, moderate 5- to 7-mile circular hikes can be made from several starting points. Some of the trails connect with the AT, which runs below the ridge to the east. Access to these trails can be made from: Rt. 9D at Sugar Loaf (see below); from Rt. 403 immediately north of its intersection with Rt. 9 and farther north, opposite the driveway of the Osborn estate; and from South Mountain Pass, formerly Manitou Road, 100 feet north on the AT after it leaves the road.

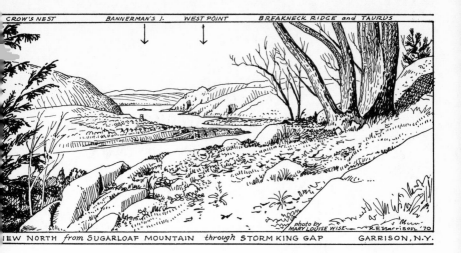

CROW'S NEST   BANNERMAN'S I.   WEST POINT   BREAKNECK RIDGE and TAURUS

photo by
MARY LOUISE WISE   R·E·Garrison '70

IEW NORTH *from* SUGARLOAF MOUNTAIN *through* STORM KING GAP   GARRISON, N.Y.

The base of Sugar Loaf is circled by a 2.3-mile trail which connects with trails from Canada Hill and White Rock. An easy bushwhack from the Sugar Loaf Trail to the summit offers a rewarding view of the Hudson and the Highlands. In order to reach this trail, either park across the road beside the picket fence of St. Francis Retreat House, or walk from Garrison station of the Penn Central Railroad 0.5 mile east on the blacktop road to Rt. 9D, then turn south (right) 1.5 miles on 9D and enter the woods where an open field meets the woods at the roadside. Walk up a slope through the woods for about 75 feet to the wide trail. It is best to follow the trail to the right, with Sugar Loaf on the left. Halfway around the base, at 1 mile, and just before reaching Osborn Pond, leave the trail and ascend left through brush to the wooded summit, where an overgrown trail extends along the ridge to the southern outlook. Return to the trail at the foot of Sugar Loaf, circle the hill by turning left into the trail, passing the pond on the right; bear left at a fork, and return to the starting point beside Rt. 9D.

It was here, in the open field at the foot of Sugar Loaf, that the Beverly Robinson House stood. During the American Revolution the house was used as headquarters by Benedict Arnold, then in command at West Point. On September 25, 1780, while at breakfast, General Arnold received word of the capture of Major John André. Arnold fled immediately and ordered his boatmen to row him downriver to the safety of the British ship *Vulture*, which was lying in the Hudson at Tappan Zee.

THE TACONICS

MBARKING on the main road leading east from the railroad station at Copake Falls, the road winds past the church of St. John's into a steep notch, its narrow walls dark with a hemlock forest. The road climbs steadily, and the mountain streams run below, and there is the feeling of a deep mountain wilderness. For here, where the New York, Massachusetts, and Connecticut boundaries meet is a region superb for the hiker and climber, known topographically and geologically as the Taconics.

"Taconic" is a modern rendering of an Indian name, elsewhere spelled as Taghkannock or Taghkanic. On the U.S.G.S. sheets the name is limited to the range along the New York side of the Massachusetts border, but in common usage it applies to the high plateau topped in the southwestern corner of Massachusetts by Mt. Everett (2602 feet), and extends into New York and Connecticut, including in this last state its highest summit, Bear Mountain (2316 feet). Actually, for those interested in such details, a shoulder of Connecticut's Mt. Frissel (1.5 miles to the northwest) is 34 feet higher.

Although the name Taconics is sometimes applied to the western Berkshires such as Mt. Greylock and to the region as far south as Ten Mile River, the part of chief interest to the New York walker is the area bounded on the south by the highway between Millerton, New York, and Salisbury, Connecticut, and on the north by the highway between Hillsdale, New York, and South Egremount, Massachusetts. The region consists of two mountain ranges that run to 2000 feet, and more elevation and the elevated valley between the two ranges, which is dotted with several beautiful lakes and ponds. The valley is more properly known as Riga Plateau, and derives its name from a community of ironworkers at Forge, or South Pond. All that remains of this old village is a disintegrating iron furnace and a cemetery. The name Mt. Riga has also been used to denote a rocky little promontory (2010 feet and 0.5 mile north) that was originally marked on old maps as Bald Peak. This splendid little summit, with its excellent view of the wild inner valley, should retain its older name.

Some years ago it was proposed to create a Tri-State Park, consisting of 60,000 acres, to be acquired by the three adjoining states. In 1923 an association was formed toward this end, with Robert Moses acting as chairman. New York has made its contribution, through the Taconic State Park Commission, by acquiring 4685 acres on its side up to the state line on Alander Mountain and other summits. Massachusetts has 4161 acres in its Bashbish Falls State Forest and Connecticut has another 1000 acres or so in the smaller Mt. Riga State Park (unimproved), which lies in the eastern range on the slope overlooking Rt. 41. The remainder of this southern portion, including the beautiful Riga lakes, is held by the Mt. Riga Preserve, Inc., of Salisbury, Connecticut. Fortunately, this section still remains as intact wilderness. The Connecticut chapter of the Appalachian Mountain Club has leased 1500 acres of it from the Preserve and has located its "Northwest Camp" in it. This cabin is restricted to use only by members and their guests. An adjacent tract of 90 acres just across the Massachusetts line is owned by the A.M.C. and has been designated as the Edward H. Lorenz Memorial Area, given in memory of one of the founders of the Connecticut chapter. Open to the public, this area lies in Sages Ravine and contains a very beautiful and remote section of the Appalachian Trail.

It is of historical interest that a triangle of land—including Boston Corners, now in New York State—formerly belonged to Massachusetts. This triangle was bounded on the south by a continuation westward of the southern boundary of Massachusetts and on the west by a line runing approximately southwest from the present jog in the New York–Massachusetts line on Alander Mountain. In the 1850s, Massachusetts deeded this land to New York, but the necessary approval of Congress delayed for three years New York's taking over the land. During this time, the area was so neglected that it was nicknamed "Hell's Acres." A historical novel by that name was written by Clay Perry and John L. E. Pell (published by Lee Furman, New York. It gives much local color of the region of that time, although it is none too accurate. Another volume, *Yankees in Connecticut* by W. Stoors Lee (published by Henry Holt & Co.) provides excellent reading on the Mt. Riga area.

The Taconic region is approximately 90 miles from New York City and is as accessible by automobile or railroad, as are the Catskills, which are opposite to the west. Kaaterskill Clove and the north-eastern giants of the Blackhead Range stand out most prominently from viewpoints here. Seen from the Catskills, looking 30 miles east across the Hudson Valley, the Taconics seem to have a fairly level top, but a closer inspection shows them to be rugged, with abrupt fault escarpments on the west and east, and otherwise affected by considerable folding and fracturing. Whereas the Catskill region is not geologically one of these mountains, the Taconics, like the Hudson Highlands and Green Mountains, have a history of extensive crustal deformations in the geological sense.

In addition to the map in this book, there are four U.S.G.S. quadrangles: "Bashbish Falls," Massachusetts; "Copake," New York—Massachusetts; "Egremont," Massachusetts; and "Sharon," Connecticut (scale 1:24,000, 7½ minute series). Although these maps are reliable as far as roads and natural features are concerned, it must be pointed out that many of the secondary trails are obscure and difficult to follow, and others are not shown at all. The Taconics can be reached on the west by the Penn Central to Copake Falls, and by the Resort Bus Line from New York traveling along Rt. 22, parallel to the park and thence east along Rt. 23 to South Egremont, Massachusetts. There is also bus service available from New York via Rt. 44 to Salisbury, Connecticut. All of these services, however, operate on a limited basis, and it is best to check schedules before planning trips. The best way to reach the Taconics from New York is by car, which takes 3 hours. Furthermore, the location of the best walks is such that a car is almost essential for reaching them.

For spending the night in the Taconics, there is a choice of inns or of camping in Taconic State Park. Cottages are available in the Copake Falls area, and tent camping is permitted both there and in the Rudd Pond section near Millerton. For reservations, write to the Superintendent, Taconic State Park, Copake Falls, N.Y. The season usually runs from mid-May to mid-October. Accommodation are also

available in Salisbury, Connecticut, and South Egremont, Massachusetts. The Jug End Barn, a ski resort two miles southwest of South
Egremont, is open all winter.

In 1969 the Taconic State Commission gave its approval to the
redevelopment of a trail system in the park and asked the New
York—New Jersey Trail Conference to do this. For the most part,
the plan is to try to redefine those trails which were originally
scouted and blazed as long as thirty-five years ago. Generally the
trails will continue to follow some of the wood roads through
the park area. The trail plan at present calls for the re-creation of the
State Line Trail from Rudd Pond in the south, following the ridge
line to the northern part of the park, south of Hillsdale. In 1970 trails
were open ascending Alander Mountain and going to Sunset Rock.

In planning walks, the essential thing to remember is that there
is a roadway (the combined Mt. Riga and Mt. Washington roads)
running north between the two ranges of mountains. This is a true
wilderness road of hard-surfaced dirt, and is not recommended for
automobiles in winter, and in muddy weather. Rts. 22 and 41, which
run along the western and eastern sides of these two ranges, are
good all-weather roads. From the Mt. Washington Road, there is
also a side road nearly to the summit of Mt. Everett, with parking
facilities available at Guilder Pond. Picnic sites and sanitary facilities
are located here, and a short trail leads to the fire lookout tower on
the summit. It should be pointed out that the only well-marked and
well-kept trails are the Appalachian Trail and some of its approach
trails, although old trails are now being re-established as described
later in this chapter. In the western range of mountains are numerous old trails and woods roads. Unfortunately, these routes are sometimes so overgrown that they are often obscure and difficult to follow.
Nevertheless, there may be some delightful exploring here for those
who do not expect well-manicured trails and who rejoice for lack
of them. In planning longer trips, be prepared to exercise a little
"wood sense" and to use a compass frequently.

Because these mountains rise up steeply from the lower plains,
the views from either range are outstanding. To the west is an
unobstructed panorama of the distant Catskills, and to the northeast, looking up the great valley of the Housatonic, are the two
peaks of Mt. Greylock, the highest summit in Massachusetts. One
of the most interesting features of the region is the gorges that go
down the outer sides of the two ranges. The most outstanding and
scenic of the gorges is Bash Bish Falls. Others worth visiting are

Sages Ravine and the Race Brook and Roberts Brook ("Blow Hole Brook") gorges.

For the botanically minded, Bingham Pond is well worth a visit because of its bog-lined shores and dark waters lined with aquatic plants and surrounding tamarack and black spruces. The summit of Mt. Everett is of particular interest because here can be found the mountain or three-toothed cinquefoil (*Potentilla tridentata*), a sturdy alpine plant that is common on the high summits of the Adirondacks, the northern Green Mountains, and the White Mountains, but is found only scatteringly southward. The plant can be found not only on Mt. Everett but also on many if not all the exposed summits of both the east and west ranges of the Taconics. Wild azalea and mountain laurel are very plentiful in this region, and in May and June the trails and roads of the Riga Plateau are veritably lined with these lovely plants in full bloom. Autumn brings the flaming crimson and yellow of the hardwood forest into dramatic contrast with the dark steepled conifers.

For maximum enjoyment of these trails, allow an hour for every mile:

Appalachian Trail. Length: 14.8 miles. Blazes: white.

This trail is the longest and best maintained of any in the Taconics. Traversing the entire eastern range from Lions Head to Jug End, it offers both remote-woods walking and a constant variety of spectacular views over the inner plateau as well as over the Housatonic Valley. For its entire length here, the AT is a rough wilderness trail. A number of trips can be made by connecting shorter sections to its feeder trails, listed below. Few roads are crossed and miles of comparatively level walking alternate with several short, steep pitches.

The Taconic portion of the AT begins on Rt. 41 (Under Mountain Road) 0.5 mile north of the junction at Salisbury, Connecticut. Turn left on the side road, and then right, into the woods. Ascend a steep little promontory, which offers a fine view of the lesser ranges and valley to the east. After continuing west through an old pasture, the AT next climbs steeply to the summit of Lions Head (2 miles, 1738 feet). From here the entire range to the north can be seen, including the shadowy bulk of Mt. Greylock in the distance. A blue-blazed trail seen diverging left at the base of Lions Head merely avoids the summit and rejoins the AT again after 0.2 mile. After another 0.5 mile, the blue-blazed Bald Peak Trail diverges left (Bald Peak, 1 mile, Mt. Riga Road, 1.2 miles). The main trail continues north

over fairly level terrain for 2 miles until the intersection of the blue-
blazed Under Mountain Trail is reached coming in from the right
(4 miles). Beyond this point the trail becomes more steep and rough
up to the summit of Bear Mountain (2316 feet, 4.8 miles). The view
is excellent, including nearly all of the Riga Plateau as well as the
Twin Lakes of Washining and Washinee lying far below to the east.
From here the trail drops steeply, then more moderately, crossing
into Massachusetts and the Edward H. Lorenz Memorial area owned
by the Appalachian Mountain Club. A brook is reached 0.8 mile
from the summit and is crossed about 0.5 mile farther down (6.2
miles). Drinking water is available here. This is the heart of the
beautiful Sages Ravine and ample time should be allowed to enjoy
several fine waterfalls and cascades. From the brook, the AT continues east, climbing gradually, and after about 0.5 mile turns
abruptly north and passes along a small bog in another 0.2 mile. A
steeper climb begins here, crossing Bear Rock Stream in another 0.5
mile. Here the grade moderates somewhat and soon the trail passes
along the southeast corner of Plaintain Pond (7.7 miles). Here begins the steep climb up Mt. Race, reaching the summit (2365 feet
at 8.9 miles). The views are superb to the north, east, and south.
From Mt. Race the AT descends steadily for 1 mile until its junction with the red-blazed Race Brook Trail (diverging right) at 9.9
miles. Now begins another steep climb to the summit fire lookout tower
on Mt. Everett (2602 feet, 10.5 miles). Leaving the summit, the trail
begins the long descent, crossing the Mt. Everett Road in nearly 0.5
mile. Nearby are drinking water, sanitary facilities, and a parking
area as the trail continues ahead, passing near the southeast corner
of Guilder Pond in another 0.3 mile. The route now heads northeast,
descending gradually, and then turns north with little change in
elevation; it goes past the top of Mt. Undine and at 13 miles comes
out on Mt. Bushnell (1834 feet). The descent continues for another
mile over Jug End, and after a short, steep drop, followed by a more
gradual one, the AT joins Jug End Road at 14.8 miles.

Under Mountain Trail. Length: 2 miles. Blazes: blue
This trail provides the shortest and probably the easiest access from
the east to Bear Mountain and the entire Riga Plateau. It is a rough
woods path for its entire length and is fairly steep throughout its
middle section. This route makes an excellent approach in winter,
when the Mt. Riga Road approach to the AT via Bear Mountain
Road is impassable for automobiles.
Beginning on Rt. 41 (Under Mountain Road) at a point 3.5 miles

north of Salisbury, Connecticut, the Under Mountain Trail starts at the edge of a pasture on the left side, almost directly opposite the beginning of Beaver Dam Road. A few cars can be left here. Heading west across the pasture, the trail soon enters the woods and begins climbing moderately. After about 0.5 mile the grade steepens and continues thus for more than another 0.5 mile. At about 1.7 miles is the first fork of Brassie Brook, and the second is 0.2 mile later. Drinking water is not always dependable. By continuing left where the AT turns right up Bear Mountain a short distance farther on, the overgrown Bear Mountain Road may be followed quite easily, coming out on the Mt. Riga road 1 mile from the AT.

Race Brook Trail. Length: 1.7 miles. Blazes: red.
This trail provides access from the Under Mountain Road (Rt. 41) to either Mt. Race or Mt. Everett via the AT, which it joins at its upper end. It is extremely steep and rough throughout much of its length, but its wild character and the magnificent falls and cascades of Race Brook make the trip entirely worth while.

Race Brook Trail begins at a stone culvert on Rt. 41, 7.4 miles north of Salisbury, Connecticut. A rest area on the west side of the road allows for the parking of a few cars. Heading west across a small pasture, the trail enters the woods and follows Race Brook for nearly its entire length. The moderate climb begins here, and then the steep section around Race Brook Falls, at about 0.7 mile. Good drinking water is available at the falls. Extreme care should be taken on this part of the trail, as the going is very rough and the trail poorly marked. After about 1 mile the grade becomes less severe and the trail passes the headwaters of Race Brook (a bog, right) in about 1.5 miles. About 0.3 mile beyond is the AT.

Brace Mountain to Riga Lake. Length: 3.5 miles. Blazes: faint blue.
Ascend Brace Mountain (also known as Monument Mountain) via an old wood road from the Mt. Riga Road, and then continue by Riga Lake Trail to the northern corner of Riga Lake. This trip is not an especially difficult one, as the footing is generally good, and the climbing, except for short portions going and returning to Brace Mountain, not at all strenuous. The views are superb from both the north and south peaks of Brace Mountain and the remote shore of Riga Lake conveys a sense of wilderness found in the more northern forest of New York and Maine. This is a fine hike for a long afternoon.

At a point on Mt. Riga Road, 2 miles north of the dam at South (Forge) Pond, a good wide wood road, though somewhat overgrown, leads northwest straight into the forest. One or two cars can be safely parked here. Start here, descending very gradually along the road, crossing Monument Brook at 0.5 mile. Drinking water is not always dependable. Beyond the brook, the road climbs slightly to a fork 1.3 miles. (The New York boundary is very near this point, and the tristate marker itself is only 0.3 mile to the north.) The right fork of the trail is obscure. Take the left fork, climbing steeply over loose stones for about 0.8 mile, reaching the top 1.8 miles (2311 feet). Here the summit of Brace Mountain on the left is surmounted by a large stone monument. The views are superb of Alander Mountain to the north, Stissing Mountain with its chain of lakes to the southwest, the vast Hudson Valley, and the distant high Catskills. The prospect northeast of Mt. Frissel, Mt. Everett, and Bear Mountain is no less grand. Continuing south off the peak, the road soon runs out. However, with a little care, a rough trail can be found leading first through the low woods and then up the westerly side to the summit of the south peak (2.3 miles, 2304 feet). From this point there is an exquisite view of the Riga lakes and South Pond lying below just to the south. From here the fine little wilderness Riga Lake Trail leads down a moderately steep slope to the inlet of Riga Lake, where it ends abruptly (3.5 miles).

Sunset Rock Trail and *Gray Birch Trail*. Length: 4.75 miles. Blazes: red; yellow.

These trails start within the main Taconic State Park camping and recreation area in Copake Falls. From Rt. 22 cross the railroad tracks; you will immediately see a sign to the camping area. Here there is a contact station where tolls are collected. In order to park a car inside the area, a fee must be paid.

Both trails start at the southwest corner of the camping area. The Sunset Rock Trail is blazed red, and ascends gradually in a generally northeasterly direction to the top of North Mountain, a distance of about 1.75 miles. The view to the west from Sunset Rock over to the Catskills is very fine.

Gray Birch Trail starts from the Sunset Rock Trail about one half mile from the bottom. It is marked with yellow blazes and follows an old road in a generally northerly direction for about one mile, where it reaches the North Mountain Road. It turns right, east, on the road to the Massachusetts boundary line, a distance of about 1.5 miles. Just at the Massachusetts line it connects with the old Massachusetts—Sunset Rock Trail, and turns westerly for about one half mile to Sunset Rock, where it rejoins the red trail. This makes a circular walk of 4.75 miles.

The best way to make the circular would be to get to the top of Sunset Rock by the red trail and return by the yellow, Gray Birch Trail.

Alander Trail. Blazes: blue.

This is the most interesting of the recently reopened trails. The approach is on the old Under Mountain—Rudd Pond Road which starts at Rt. 22 just to the north of Boston Corners. This road does not have a turnoff sign, but is just about 1 mile above the Boston Corners turnoff sign. Go in on this second-grade road for about three quarters of a mile, passing a farmhouse on the left. At the end of this farm property the Alander Trail starts on an old wood road. It is marked with blue blazes. In about three quarters of mile cross brook, turn in an easterly direction, and pick up a rather steep piece of cut trail. This leads to an old road which follows up the north side of Alander Brook to the Massachusetts line. Just before the road turns south and crosses the brook, the Trail turns northeast and ascends fairly steeply to the New York—Massachusetts boundary marker on the Alander Ridge line. Here it follows cairns for about 400 yards to the top of Alander Mountain, where there are foundations of a former fire tower. The views from the top are very spectacular, particularly to the west and south.

It has been the fond hope of many hikers that at some time there would be a boundary trail running north and south along the New York, Massachusetts, and Connecticut boundaries. This plan is again being worked on. Now it is only a bushwhack.

If you would like to try it, you can start north along the Ridge, descend a short distance into the col between Alander and the Bash Bish Mountain Ridge, and in 2 miles of very rugged bushwhacking, you will reach the top of Bash Bish Mountain. Here you can descend, still bushwhacking, through a magnificent stand of hemlock. Your route off the mountain should be a compass direction just very slightly east of north. This would take you to Bash Bish Brook, and by following the brook downstream to the bottom of the Falls, you can cross over to Rt. 344 which descends to Copake Falls in about 2 miles.

Bash Bish Falls. Length: 0.8 mile. Blazes: none.

Beginning in a small parking field on the south side of Rt. 344 (Falls Road), 0.9 mile east of Copake Falls, New York, a broad well-traveled footway leads along the north side of Bash Bish Brook for

0.8 mile to the base of the spectacular Bash Bish Falls. These falls drop nearly 200 feet in a series of magnificent cascades.

Northrop Trail to Cedar Mountain. Length: 1.3 miles. Blazes: yellow.

Cedar Mountain, an attractive peak (1883 feet) which forms the northern wall of Bash Bish Gorge, provides the finest views obtainable of the entire notch and surrounding peaks. It may be ascended from Bashbish Falls first by the Northrop Trail and then by bushwhacking west along the crest to the ledges which form its southern face.

The Northrop Trail begins on the north side of Rt. 344 (Falls Road), 1.8 mile east of Copake Falls. A small parking area, marked by a sign, "Bash Bish Falls Scenic Area," erected by the Massachusetts Department of Natural Resources, is directly opposite. A trail from this point descends 0.3 mile to the bottom of Bash Bish Falls. Thus by using the Bash Bish Falls approach described above, the hiker may include both the Falls and Cedar Mountain in a single trip.

To ascend Cedar Mountain, follow the faded yellow metal markers on the trees. The trail here is consistantly steep and great care must be taken since the way is poorly marked in places. The height-of-the-land is reached in about 0.8 mile. The trail ahead continues to Northrop's Camps, 0.3 mile. For Cedar Mountain turn sharply west (left) and bushwhack through fairly open hardwoods 0.5 mile to the ledges. Again, extreme care must be taken to remember the way back as it is easily possible to cross this trail without being aware of it.

From the ledges, with the Bash Bish Falls in full view, looms a magnificent prospect of the entire notch. Directly opposite, one behind the other, stand Bash Bish Mountain and Alander Mountain. Southwest, beyond the flattish crown of Washburn Mountain, is Stissing Mountain. To the west lie the Hudson Valley and the Catskills, and to the south, the fire lookout tower on Mt. Everett is visible.

STISSING MOUNTAIN

East of the Catskills, about midway between the Hudson River and the Housatonic Highlands of Connecticut, and some 90 miles north of New York City in Dutchess County, lies the 1500-foot-high profile of Stissing Mountain. Composed predominately of gneiss of Precambrian age that rises boldly above the surrounding lowlands and valleys of Cambrian to Ordovician aged limestone and Ordovician aged shale and slate, the Precambrian geology of Stissing Mountain is, in this sense, distinctively similar to the Precambrian Housatonic Highlands to the east.

Stissing Mountain does, however, reveal at least one peculiarity in its geology. Unlike the other regions of Precambrian geology—the Housatonic, Hudson, and Jerry Highlands—which comprise sizable sections of Metropolitan New York's landscape, geographically limited Stissing Mountain lies completely detached from these other broad regions of Precambrian geology. To explain such singular geologic isolation, it appears, in all probability, that during past mountain-building episodes, older sections of the earth's crust containing rock of Precambrian age were overthrust onto younger crustal sections containing post-Precambrian sedimentary strata. With subsequent long-term erosion, such detached, overthrust crustal blocks became singular isolated remnants of Precambrian rock so that today they are surrounded on all sides by much younger rock types. Since gneiss is, of course, differentially much more resistant to erosion, Stissing Mountain stands boldly as a conspicuous element in our modern landscape.

Reached by way of the Taconic State Parkway and Rt. 199, Stissing's setting is more pastoral than rugged, with forest and pasture land about equal. Yet the mountain and its three lakes do convey a sense of wildness that makes this a unique area well worth the time and distance involved. The New York State fire tower on the summit commands one of the most superb views east of the Hudson.

In 1959 the Nature Conservancy of Washington, D.C., together with the Dutchess County Bird Club and a committee of interested citizens led by the *Register-Herald* of Pine Plains, succeeded in purchasing and preserving in its natural wild state all of Thompson Pond at the base of the mountain. This area, abounding in wildlife, now enjoys the same protection already given to such preserves as Bergen Swamp in Genesee County.

To reach the red-blazed loop trail to the summit of Stissing Mountain, drive south 1.46 miles on Lake Road from its junction with Rt. 199 1 mile west of Rt. 82A. Cars can be left on Lake Road at the start of the trail, which begins at a small brook, often dry in summer.

Stissing Mountain Circular. Length: 1.7 miles. Blazes: none.

This summit loop trail can be traversed in 2 hours or less; however, a much longer time should be allotted to enjoy the exceptional views from the fire tower and other outlooks. The exploration of abandoned wood roads on the ridge, and paths along the east and west shores of Thompson Pond just off Lake Road are also rewarding.

The summit trail ascends steeply for a short distance to a saddle, then turns south to a fork, either branch of which may be followed. The one to the left provides a direct ascent via the north ridge of the mountain. At the top of this long pitch is the Conservation Department's fire lookout tower (manned during fire seasons); the 360-degree view from here includes the Catskills in the west and the Taconics toward the northeast. In clear weather the buildings of Albany can be seen with binoculars. An open grassy spot just north of the observer's cabin affords an attractive lunch site, with a striking view of Little Stissing Mountain adjoining.

From the summit, the return branch of the trail continues down the westerly slope, following a telephone line in a series of zigzags. Leaving the wires, it passes through a beautiful hardwood forest to rejoin the main trail at the fork passed on the ascent.

Part III

Part III

CORES OF New Yorkers seeking green space by means of subway or ferry ride, yet with rather more country air than is available in Prospect or Central parks, will find it on the perimeter of the city. The upper western rim of Manhattan, the Botanical Garden and Pelham Bay in the Bronx, the larger parks in Queens, and portions of Staten Island offer quick escape from noise and pollution.

Fortunately most of these parks are interesting both geologically and topographically, so that the rambles are quite rewarding. Moreover, most of the parks in the Bronx, Manhattan, and Richmond have the added lure that they were the sites of skirmishes during the Revolution. When scrambling over the summits of the ridges it is not hard to imagine that these locations served as lookouts and encampments, which they were.

FORT WASHINGTON, AND FORT TRYON AND INWOOD HILL PARKS

Take a No. 4 bus to Fort Tryon, or the Independent subway A express to 190 Street. From early spring to late frost the flower gardens display a lovely procession of bloom. At any time of year the broad views of the Hudson River are a reasonable substitute for wide open spaces. Several paths run north through the Park to The Cloisters, a branch of the Metropolitan Museum, with magnificent medieval art. Other paths descend to the river around the base of

THE
INDIAN
CAVES
ON
MAN·
·HAT·
·TAN

SHORAKAPKOK
·INWOOD·

Dickinson
1923

NECK
ORNAMENT
(STONE)

ARROW
HEAD
(FLINT)

PIPE
BOWL

HARPOON
POINT; BONE

PIPE STEM WITH TOOTHMARKS

George Washington Bridge. The old name for the river shore at this point was Jeffries Hook. Here, during the Revolution, a line of sunken ships and chained logs was anchored in an attempt to prevent the passage of British ships. The spot is marked by the little red lighthouse still standing beneath the bridge.

Inwood Hill Park is at the junction of Spuyten Duyvil Creek with the Hudson River. Paths north from The Cloisters lead to Riverside Drive. From here it is only one block to Dyckman Street, and not much farther west on Dyckman to the river and Inwood. Access is also available by IRT subway to Dyckman Street. One of the three main centers of Indian population on Manhattan Island was on Spuyten Duyvil Creek. Here there was shelter from the icy winds which made the rocky ridge of Manhattan so inhospitable, a good freshwater spring, and level planting fields, open to the morning sun. There was an ample supply of fish from the river, including the famous Hudson shad, and the surrounding forests provided good hunting for bear, deer, and beaver. Wolves and bear, in fact, were to be found on Manhattan until 1686, when a hunt to clear them out was organized on Washington Heights. As the Inwood Indians were not consulted about the "sale" of Manhattan Island to the Dutch, they resisted the northward advance of the white men from the Battery. It was not until 1715 that the Freeholders of New Harlem, by special tax, raised a fund with which Colonel Stephen Van Cortlandt made a final settlement with the few survivors who had clung to their favorite planting grounds at Inwood.

To reach the Indian rock shelters from the top of Inwood Hill, follow the ravine down the east side of the ridge, past the great glacial potholes in the exposed rock, and through the grove of spice bush. The quantities of oyster shells found here are the most obvious evidence of Indian habitation. (Pottery and spearheads and other artifacts found here may be seen at the Museum of the American Indian, Broadway at 155 Street.) The village was called Shorakapkok, meaning "as far as the Sitting-Down Place." The Indians have been gone for over two hundred years, but here are real woods to walk in— a climax forest within the boundaries of New York City.

VAN CORTLANDT PARK

A mile or so north of Inwood Hill, via the Broadway IRT subway, lies one of the largest and possibly the most varied of New York's parks. On one side a steep ridge wanders up and down, rising nearly

200 feet, but each visitor must choose for himself which of the myriad trails he wishes to explore.

From the subway station one may wind past the swimming pool to the Van Cortlandt Manor House, built in 1748. Its grounds are worth exploring. To the north lies the immense Parade Ground and beyond Vault Hill, where the early Van Cortlandts are buried. Beyond, cross the valley of Tibbets Brooks with a parkway and continue north on a bridle path, ultimately ascending on a wood road to reach the level Croton Aqueduct on the park's eastern ridge. Turn south on the adqueduct and then, when a paved path is met, follow it past Van Cortlandt Lake and the beginning of the walk. An alternative route, when the aqueduct is reached, is to continue in a southeasterly direction on the bridle path. In less than a half mile a clearing on the left leads to an underpass crossing the Major Deegan Expressway. East of the roadway, an abandoned road leads to Indian Field, where Chief Nimham and seventeen other Stockbridge Indians who fought and died in the Revolution are commemorated by a monument. Head in a southwesterly direction to Jerome Avenue and continue on it over nearby park paths to reach the IRT Lexington Avenue subway at Woodlawn.

NEW YORK BOTANICAL GARDEN

The New York Botanical Garden is accessible either on the Penn Central R. R. to the Botanical Garden station, or on the Independent subway (Concourse line) to Fordham Road and then east by bus. Here are the conservatories containing botanical specimens from all over the world, a museum, library, and herbarium, as well as forest paths and rock ledges. The rock garden and rose garden are well worth a visit. Particularly in late spring, the laurel, rhododendron, and azalea plantings are spectacular. Near the south center of the Garden is the old Lorillard Snuff Mill (1840), beside the Bronx River. It is now an attractive restaurant, open from Palm Sunday to Columbus Day. A few minutes' walk on a path winding north from the mill brings one past a high arching bridge to the Hemlock Falls, which furnished power to the mill. Although the path continues north, go across the bridge to enter the 40-acre hemlock forest, one of the Garden's great attractions. Although the many paths are worth exploring, follow the path near the river, but high above its gorge, which is sometimes 75 feet below. When the main drive is reached, about 0.5 mile from Snuff Mill, a path along the east bank of the river continues north. To the left, the drive leads

to the main entrance to the Garden, but re-enter the hemlock forest
to explore further.

PELHAM BAY PARK

This park lies chiefly between the Hutchinson River and Long
Island Sound. From south to north it includes Rodman Neck, Orchard Beach, and Hunters Island, an area of over two thousand
acres. Access is from the Lexington Avenue IRT subway to the end
of the line at Pelham Bay Park, or by car to Orchard Beach by way
of Pelham Parkway or the Hutchinson River Parkway.

The park contains two sanctuaries for plants and wildlife. Hunters
Island, the area north of Orchard Beach, is of interest to students
as well as to hikers for its great trees and jutting rocks, as well as its
tide pools, salt marshes, and glacial boulders. It is no wonder that
this island was a favorite place for Indians. Their conference rock,
"Mishow," located near a cove at the eastern end of the beach
boardwalk, is now almost buried. When following the "island's"
circumferential trail be sure to observe Gray Mare, an unusually
formed erratic off the northwestern part of the "island."

The second sanctuary, Thomas Pell, encompasses all the park
land north and east of the Hutchinson River to the Penn Central
tracks, excluding the golf course. Following the road west from Orchard Beach past Glover's Rock, in a half mile follow the path north
beside the Hutchinson River Parkway with the salt marshes beyond
along the river itself. In another mile one passes the site of the
Battle of Pell's Point, which started at Glover's Rock and finished
at the Hutchinson River Bridge in Mt. Vernon. In 1776 Colonel
Glover, with 750 men, held off Lord Howe and the British long
enough for General Washington and his troops to withdraw toward

White Plains. Split Rock, a huge cracked boulder, is located on a rise above the main path as it continues north. Nearby was the home of Anne Hutchinson, who had fled from religious persecution in New England. Here she and her children were murdered by the Indians in 1643. In 1654 the land was bought by Thomas Pell from Fairfield, Connecticut. He is reported to have bought it from the Indians who killed Mrs. Hutchinson. Since the Dutch, as well as the English, claimed the land, Thomas Pell became a Dutch citizen to make good his claim. Included in his purchase was City Island, which later owners hoped to develop as a rival of New York. Today its shipyards and seafood restaurants still provide a nautical flavor. From Split Rock turn south along the bridle path to the golf club-house. In the lawn across the road is the circular fence which once enclosed the Pell Treaty Oak (destroyed by lightning in the early 1900s); this is the spot where Pell signed his pact with the Indians. Nearby is the old Pell burial plot. The "Greek Revival" Bartow Mansion beyond the lawn is now the home of the International Garden Club, and is open Tuesdays, Fridays, and Sundays.

QUEENS

North of Grand Central Parkway.

From Jamaica take a bus at the Long Island R.R. station, at the Sutphin Avenue station of the BMT subway, or at the Parsons Boulevard station of the Independent subway. Get off at Springfield Boulevard and walk north uphill a few blocks to the north side of Grand Central Parkway. Walk northeast on the pedestrian path of the Parkway to Alley Pond Park (0.5 mile). Note the huge kettle hole before cutting across the picnic grounds and then north across the parking field to the Nature Trail, and follow this to a pond. North of this pond the park is little developed but is crisscrossed by trails and bridle paths. The topography is irregular, with many small depressions typical of a terminal moraine. Walk north along the ridge above Cross Island Parkway to some old fields which, years ago, were farms producing corn, tomatoes, and melons (1.5 miles). East across the valley is a place where sand has been removed from the terminal moraine for almost two decades. The enormous pit thus created is a useful landmark. Here cross Long Island Expressway and continue north along the ridge 2.5 miles, with Cross Island Parkway on the right. Turn left across the fields to the summit of a hill (3 miles) for an excellent view north across Little Neck Bay

Park and Long Island Sound to City Island (Bronx), and West-chester County. Continue north downhill to Oakland Lake. Just ahead, at Northern Boulevard (3.5 miles), take a bus to Flushing and the IRT or BMT subways.

A short distance to the east of Oakland Lake is the beginning of the pedestrian path on Cross Island Parkway along the west shore of Little Neck Bay. Here, in the late fall and early spring, can be seen thousands of wild ducks, which stop here on their migration between Canada and the southern United States. On the left a footbridge over Cross Island Parkway leads to Crocheron Park, which affords views of Little Neck Bay, Douglaston, and Great Neck. This walk (about 4 miles) passes old Fort Totten and gives a view of the graceful Throggs Neck Bridge, and the State University's Maritime College at the tip of Fort Schuyler, across the Sound. The walk ends at Willets Point Boulevard, Beechhurst. From here, across the Parkway, buses run to Flushing.

As an alternative, turn right downhill at the crossing of the Long Island Expressway, instead of continuing parallel with Cross Island Parkway. On the right is a bird sanctuary, on the left is Alley Pond. Follow the curves of the Expressway to Douglaston Parkway and walk north through a suburban area to Shore Drive. There is a delightful circular walk on the edge of Little Neck Bay and around the Douglaston Peninsula.

Forest Park and Highland Park.

Forest Park is on the Harbor Hill moraine, one of the two great glacial dump heaps on Long Island. Much of it is covered by golf courses, but considerable portions of woods remain. On its south front, 100 feet above the outwash plain below, there are views south toward Jamaica Bay and the ocean, 8 miles away. Some of the kettle-hole depressions have been preserved in the landscaping of this park.

Access to Forest Park (by way of Highland Park) is by BMT-Jamaica line to Norwood Avenue Station. Walk north from the station to Force Tube Avenue and then northeast along this avenue to Jamaica Avenue. Here a road curves up the front of the moraine to Ridgewood Reservoir (1 mile). Walk around the west and north sides of the reservoir and go eastward along the footpath of Inter-borough Parkway to Forest Park Golf Course (3.5 miles). Walk right along a park road and then left, keeping on top of the moraine front, to Woodhaven Boulevard (5 miles). This section is also accessible from Forest Parkway station of the BMT-Jamaica line. At Woodhaven Boulevard turn north to Myrtle Avenue and then south-

Forest Park

The glacial kettle hole as golf hazard

east to the railroad bridge (5.3 miles). The section of Forest Park lying east of this point is heavily wooded and has many paths. Follow any of these in a generally northeast direction to the point where the Interborough Parkway leaves the park (6.3 miles), and then go northeast along the parkway to the Independent subway station (Kew Gardens on Queen Boulevard) (7 miles).

Jamaica Bay Wildlife Refuge.

Jamaica Bay Wildlife Refuge consists of twelve thousand acres of tidal water and marshlands in and on the edge of the Bay. For centuries migratory waterfowl have stopped here to rest and feed. The Park Department has impounded a pond on each side of Cross Bay Boulevard. The west pond, about forty acres, has a walk around it. The larger east pond has no path but is more popular with the birds. The dikes surrounding the ponds have been stabilized with various types of vegetation.

Hundreds of thousands of birds come to the sanctuary. The breeding water birds include great egret, snowy egret, glossy ibis, as well as colonies of terns and skimmers. In the spring the sanctuary attracts migrant shore birds and land birds. Birds are attracted to the sanctuary partly because of its location at the junction of the Hudson River and Atlantic Coast flyways and partly because the Refuge management has by skillful clearing and planting made food and cover available. Ecologists, botanists, and birdwatchers will find a day spent in this wildlife refuge most rewarding.

Permits to visit the Refuge are required, and are issued on request, without fee, to individuals, groups, or clubs: write to N.Y.C. Park Dept., 830 Fifth Avenue, New York, N.Y. 10021. By car the Bay area is accessible on the north and northeast from the Belt Parkway,

and on the south from Beach Channel Drive. From the Belt Parkway turn south on Cross Bay Boulevard. The parking lot is on the
west side. By subway take the Independent, Rockaway Division, to
Broad Channel station, then take a bus or walk 0.5 mile to the
Refuge.

STATEN ISLAND

This "forgotten" borough of New York, dotted with many communities, has developed rapidly since the opening of the Verrazano-
Narrows Bridge, but it still has territory for walkers. The ferry ride
across the Bay from Battery Park on Manhattan to St. George is in
itself a rewarding trip. Bus information and maps are available at
the ferry terminal. A 5-minute walk past the Borough Hall and a
jog to the right on Stuyvesant Place leads to the Staten Island Institute of Arts and Sciences; its Natural History section schedules
monthly walks. The *Staten Island Walk Book* is on sale there.

Take a bus along Victory Boulevard to reach most of the borough's
parks and green space. At Louis Street there is little Hero Park with
a large glacial boulder—Sugar Loaf Rock. Diagonally across the street
is Silver Lake Park, part of New York's water supply system. Farther
along Victory Boulevard is Clove Lakes Park with lakes (and row-
boats), paved walks, and bridle paths. There is a pleasant walk
through the woods around the lake. Across Clove Road is Barrett
Park and the Staten Island Zoo, one of the finest small zoos in the
country. It contains one of the largest snake collections in the world.

Staten Island's proposed greenbelt was visualized by Frederick Law
Olmsted nearly a hundred years ago. His farm was south of the
ridge the Olmsted Trailway will follow, and he enjoyed that inland
view. He became the chief architect of Manhattan's Central Park,
but never had the opportunity to develop the park near home. It
seems appropriate to give his name to it now. Todt Hill is the highest tidewater elevation on the Atlantic seaboard south of Mt. Desert,
Maine. Although three roads cross it, it bears forests and swamps
which still harbor some raccoon, opossum, pheasant, muskrat, and
heron. The Olmsted Trailway will follow this ridge for nearly 5
miles and will provide bikeways and bridle paths as well as 10 miles
of hiking trails, and family picnic facilities.

On Victory Boulevard opposite Clove Lakes Park is the approach
to the Olmsted Trailway route. Proceed along Renwick Avenue,
under the Staten Island Expressway, and bear right past the Staten
Island Community College to woodland. Turn uphill past Reed's

Basket Willow Swamp (1.5 miles) to reach Todt Hill (417 feet). A never-dry "kettle hole" pond is at the top. At the intersection of Todt Hill Road and Ocean Terrace follow the latter 1 block and turn left to woodland. Continue past a radar tower along the crest of the hill above the Dongan Hills Golf Course, avoiding Boy Scout territory on the right which is not open to the public. Pass a small pond on the right and next skirt the Moravian Cemetery, where the Vanderbilts of railroad fame are buried. It is a beautiful spot, worthy of a visit for its plants, both native and exotic. In winter its warm south slope is a favorite haunt of song birds. Continue on through High Rock Nature Conservation Center to see Figure Eight Lake and other ponds scattered among the swamp maples. Self-guided tours are available here from the Visitors' Center of the Institute of Arts and Sciences. One way to conclude the walk here is to follow Nevada Avenue from the main gate of the Center down-hill to Rockland Avenue and turn left on Rockland Avenue to Rich-mond Road for a bus back to the ferry. Otherwise, continue to Buck's Hollow (about 3 miles) through the woods from the parking lot to the right of the main gate, downhill to Manor Road (along a dimly marked yellow trail). Turn right on Manor Road for a short dis-tance before re-entering woodland on the other side of Manor Road along a trail, which crosses a brook at a concrete platform. Continue uphill along a deeply eroded path through thick brambles, bear left and follow the bridle path across Rockland Avenue and then through swampy lowland. At the right is a steep bluff where a detour from the valley bridle path offers a view of the surrounding woodland and the golf course. Still visible is the foundation of an old house which belonged at one time to an estate engaged in the cultivation of grapes for winemaking. From here return to the valley bridle path or continue on the path beyond the bluff, bear right and end up again at the intersection of Rockland Avenue and Manor Road. The valley bridle path continues through the woods to Forest Hill Road at the west side of La Tourette Golf Course. Bear left to Rich-mond Road and turn left again across the slight valley to the bluff overlooking Richmondtown. From a hillock about 0.5 mile farther west can be seen Fresh Kills, the creek up which it is supposed the original settlers of Staten Island brought their supplies to Richmond-town.

Richmondtown, the historic and geographic center of Staten Is-land, abuts the Olmsted Trailway near its southern end. When the restoration now under way has been completed, Richmondtown's three dozen buildings—from basketmaker's shop to tanning mill and

LIGHTHOUSE & SASSAFRASS from golfhouse Latourette Park. Staten I. (in path of Richmond X prenoy) Jan.27 1968 REH.

toll house—will represent an outstanding example of the evolution of an American village from the seventeenth century to the present. Queen Anne gave the communion vessels to old St. Andrew's Church. Beyond is the historical museum, Voorlezer House (the first schoolhouse in this country), and other old houses gradually being moved here from elsewhere on the Island. The project is under the guidance of Loring McMillen and the Staten Island Historical Society. Farther north again, below the lighthouse on the hill, on Lighthouse Avenue, is the Jacques Marchais Center of Tibetan Art with its beautiful oriental garden. Visiting hours may be ascertained in advance by calling the Center or the Staten Island Museum. From Richmondtown, return to St. George by bus.

On the south shore are two more attractive parks, both of which can be reached from the ferry by bus along Hylan Boulevard. At Great Kills Park are the beach and marshlands for walking and bird watching. At Wolfe's Pond Park are two freshwater ponds, a saltwater beach, a wood, and a bog. Its combination of upland and marine ecology and woodland makes it worth a visit at any time, but particularly when the bathing season is over. An alternative to the bus is to take the train from the ferry to Princes Bay. From the station, walk one block southeast on Seguine Avenue, turn left on Herbert Street, and follow that until it comes to a dead end where a trail enters the woods and the park begins. Continue in a southerly direction for 1 mile, passing on the right of Acme Pond to reach Hylan Boulevard. Cross Hylan Boulevard diagonally to another path through woodland skirting either side of Wolfe's Pond to the beach.

Hylan Boulevard terminates at Ward's Point, the southernmost end of New York State. In addition to its view of Raritan Bay and Sandy Hook, it has a special historic interest because it was the site of encampments of Lenni-Lenape Indians. The Conference House, or Billop House, here was the site of the first peace conference during the American Revolution—September 1, 1776. Bus and train routes both terminate here.

Study of a road map or of Hagstrom's map of Richmond (Staten Island) will suggest other smaller but no less attractive parks as objectives for shorter outings. As mentioned earlier, there is also a Staten Island Walk Book available at the Staten Island Museum and at High Rock Nature Conservation Center.

GEOLOGY

HALE-BACKED PAUMANOK," as Walt Whitman called his beloved Long Island, offers a variety of terrain in decided contrast to the highlands of the Hudson and of northern New Jersey. Instead of rugged rocky hills and hardwood forests, the walker finds, on the South Shore, long barrier islands containing beaches of fine sand backed by dunes and, on the North Shore, beaches of sand, pebbles, and boulders, backed by high morainal bluffs. Between these two long shores, in the north, is a region of rolling sandy hills alternating with deep narrow harbors and promontories extending into Long Island Sound. The woods are generally thin and less rich in species than those on the mainland, and tree associations have been materially changed by the introduction, from farther south during the past century and a half, of the black locust, which now appears as if native.

Southward from the undulating North Shore, the hills taper off into plains gently sloping to Great South and Moriches bays. Much of this strip, with a covering of low pitch pines, stunted oaks, laurel, sweet fern, and bayberry, resembles the Pine Barrens of New Jersey. The forest in this southern half, like the Pine Barrens, has suffered greatly from repeated fires, and in consequence much of it is thin and dwarfed.

The topography of Long Island is governed by geological formations quite different from those in the regions north and west of New York City. Instead of the ancient igneous and metamorphic rocks of the Hudson and New Jersey Highlands, with their flankings of sandstones, conglomerates, shales, and limestones, the underlying formations of the island are strata of unconsolidated sands, clays, and gravels worn off the older rocks of the mainland of New England during the Cretaceous Period. Later, during the Pleistocene Epoch, terminal moraines and associated glacial outwash material left on the surface by the great continental ice sheets of Pleistocene times concealed most of the Cretaceous strata. Other evidences of Pleistocene glaciation include old channels of flow from the ice front, lake-bed deposits, kettle-hole lakes or ponds, curiously eroded bluffs of clay and gravel, and pebble and boulder beaches. Perhaps most striking evidence of the Ice Age are the great numbers of huge boulders of New England granite, gneiss, and other durable rock types, some of astonishing size.

The two terminal moraines of Long Island are the long frontal dump heaps of two different advances of the last of the continental ice sheets, the Wisconsin Glacier. The older one is Harbor Hill Moraine, which extends from the Narrows of New York Bay through Brooklyn (including Prospect Park), Cypress Hills, and Forest Park and northeastward along the North Shore to Orient Point. The second, the Ronkonkoma Moraine, runs from Little Neck southeastward through the middle of the island to Montauk Point. They cross like the blades of a pair of scissors in the Wheatley Hills, north of Westbury. Eastward, as they separate, the area between them widens gradually into a fairly level intermorainal area of pine barrens.

Between the Ronkonkoma Moraine and the Atlantic Ocean to the south follow, in succession, the Ronkonkoma outwash plain, the salt marshes, Great South Bay, the barrier islands, and the outer beach.

At Montauk, the Ronkonkoma Moraine comes to the sea, which has washed away perhaps as much as 4 or 5 miles of its former extension into the Atlantic and carried the debris westward to build up the elongate chain of islands. In this way long strips of what had been previously open ocean have been cut off to form lagoons such as Shinnecock Bay, Moriches Bay, and Great South Bay.

HIKING ON "PAUMANOK"

As a result of the tremendous growth in population of Nassau and Suffolk counties in recent years, few of the walks described in earlier editions of this book are still practical. The remaining dirt lanes in the central pine barrens, in the West Hills, and in the South Fluke (the southern fin of "whale-backed Paumanok") are still there for the walker, but their unpaved days are numbered. Even so, open space available to the walking public is still plentiful and rewarding, despite heavy use during the summer months.

The island offers a wide choice in walking environments, and lends itself very well to those who actively combine walking with some other hobby. Photographers, bird watchers, botanists, geologists, herpetologists, and just plain beachcombers, all find ample scope for these avocations. To be sure, the hiker will no longer find any blazed trails, nor will he be concerned with wandering off the trail and becoming lost. Mostly he will be concerned with finding areas large enough and unpopulated enough to enjoy walking in them. There will be no problem of access to state parks or federal preserves. Gaining access to the park of the village, town, or county in which he is not a resident presents problems, but a person on foot is not apt to be challenged.

Most important of all is knowing when to walk where, for to an unusual degree hiking choices here are influenced by the seasons. In January, Montauk Point offers a rugged walking environment with all kinds of sea birds and land birds, hawks and owls, harbor seal, deer and fox and good beachcombing—and no ticks. February is a good month to trespass. There is no hunting, so the walker is left unmolested. People do not "suspect" the walker, and he can go in places from which he would be chased out at other times of the year. March is a good time for the Fire Island National Seashore. The weather is getting milder, and the mob has not yet arrived. April has a touch of spring; Orient Point is good, as is Shelter Island. In May the spring flowers are out and the bird migration is on. Keep to the morainal woodlands. In June the bogs have orchids; the tern and gull nesting areas are occupied (Quogue Beach, Napeague Harbor's northwestern rim, and the western tip of Jones Beach State Park). The ticks have started, so keep out of dense shrubbery. July is hot. The sun worshippers will stroll, perhaps along the surf to Sunken Forest, or along the beach at Napeague. In August try Moriches Inlet and the islands with their shore birds.

September brings the falcon flights (Tobay, Gilgo, and Westhampton beaches). October is the perfect month for foliage and photography. In November the ducks arrive (Hempstead Lake and Tanglewood Reserve). December sees the jetties (Atlantic Beach, Short Beach), Lake Montauk, and the dunes (Short Beach, Quogue Beach, and Orient Point) alive with winter birds and snowy owls.

Note that wood ticks are thick on Long Island from June to September, and in certain areas they are nearly impossible to avoid. Since Spotted Fever occurs in Suffolk, be alert and flick them off your clothes, and be sure to examine yourself carefully after you get home.

On the pages which follow, the places where walking is still refreshing are identified. They fall into three broad classes: the beaches of both the South Shore and the North Shore, the parks and preserves, and the still unspoiled lands on and around the island's eastern forks. We will cover them in that order. All of them can be found on an automobile road map and the walking distances can be calculated at a glance.

THE SOUTH SHORE BEACHES

The gently sloping plain running almost the length of Long Island, south of the Ronkonkoma Moraine and made from its outwash, has very little interest for trampers, since it is too much built up in towns and villages, or too lacking in relief, to be attractive. However, along the northern shore of Great South and Moriches bays are border zones where the salt marsh, the freshwater creeks, and the pine and oak woods meet. These are interesting botanically and offer a few short rambles.

More importantly, across these great bays are the long barrier islands that provide nearly a hundred miles of fine hiking. Much of this strand remains unspoiled, although more and more of it is losing its earlier character through public and private development. Until 1930, Great South Beach stretched from Fire Island Inlet eastward for more than 55 miles, without a break, to Southampton. A storm in March of that year breached the dunes opposite Center Moriches and made Moriches Inlet, through which the ocean now pours deeply and swiftly. Similarly, the hurricane of 1938 opened the inlet to Shinnecock Bay.

Off season, the ocean beach can be walked anywhere, from Atlantic Beach to Montauk (except for the inlets). In summer, access to some of the beaches is restricted. A few notes will be helpful.

The South Shore of Long Island : dunes, beech grass : arbor : dories : drift-wood fire wave markings : beech pools : wreck : coal barges : sunshine.

Atlantic Beach.

Atlantic Beach and the jetty at the inlet are at their best for the walker and bird watcher when storm or season have driven most people indoors. A good winter walk is west from the Nautilus Hotel.

Short Beach.

At the west end of 2400-acre Jones Beach State Park there is a good winter walk from the West End Parking Field to the jetty at Short Beach. This jetty is as interesting for the bird watcher as the Atlantic Beach jetty, and in addition to the birds that appear on Atlantic Beach, snowy owls, short-eared owls, and snow buntings frequent the dunes, and large flocks of brant come to the inlet.

Jones Beach Fishing Station.

A walk from Parking Field 4 north around the Fishing Station, east around Zachs Bay, and south around the Mall provides one of the most rewarding winter birding walks in the east. The shrubbery (autumn olive, black pine, and holly) attracts the birds, many of them rare and seldom seen.

John F. Kennedy Bird Sanctuary.

Park at Parking Field 9, and walk east through the dunes. Then cross the road and enter the main sanctuary, or with a permit (free from the Town of Oyster Bay) park in the private (town) parking field in the sanctuary near the observation tower. This is one of the finest Atlantic Coast bird sanctuaries.

Captree and Robert Moses State Parks.

These two parks provide good beach walking at any time of the year. The whole stretch from the Babylon Town Park at Cedar

Beach on the west to the Fire Island Light on the east is conveniently close to parking fields in the parks.

Fire Island National Seashore.

Although the Fire Island National Seashore from Robert Moses State Park east to Moriches Inlet can be walked without restriction, it is too long a stretch to cover in a brief trip; several shorter trips are recommended. The western end is served by passenger ferries from Bay Shore, the middle part by ferries from Sayville and Patchogue, and the eastern end can be explored by parking at Smith Point County Park. Particular mention should be made of the famous Sunken Forest, west of Cherry Grove. Reached by a direct ferry, it has a ranger station and is well worth seeing any time the trees are in full leaf. The forest is an area of high dunes, with depressions containing a dense growth of large holly trees, curiously gnarled shadbush, pitch pine, sassafras, and other species—a sanctuary for birds, among which the catbird is surprisingly numerous. Except for scattered summer home colonies, the whole seashore is wild and unspoiled.

Westhampton Beach.

Moriches Inlet can also be approached on the east side. Off season, park in the westernmost parking field at Westhampton Beach and walk west to the Inlet.

Southampton Beach.

The beach from Main Street east to Flying Point (Mecox Bay) makes a fine walk. Ponds just inside the dunes are rich in bird life.

East Hampton Beach.

On the east side of Hook Pond there is a road through the golf course to the clubhouse. Just past this is another road to the beach. From this point walk the beach as far as you want, toward Montauk.

THE NORTH SHORE BEACHES

On the North Shore beaches the pebbles and boulders are interesting geologically. They are from many of the rock formations—sedimentary, igneous, or metamorphic—on the opposite Massachusetts, Connecticut, and Westchester shores and from even farther north. Pebbles from as far as the Berkshires and the Green Mountains, carried hundreds of miles in the continental glacier, have been identified in the shingles of these strands. In the neighborhood of Smithtown Bay are boulders of trap rock from the diabase and basalt ridges running north from New Haven, and, farther eastward toward Wading River and Orient Point, more frequently are boulders, some of immense size, from the gneisses, granites, and schists of eastern Connecticut and probably from central Massachusetts.

Unfortunately, relatively few of the beaches and bluffs in Nassau and western Suffolk are open or accessible to hikers. Nearly all are privately owned, with access to the strand only at the public parks and town beaches. Bayville, north of Oyster Bay, has a fine beach. To the east, on Lloyd Neck, is Caumsett State Park (undeveloped), then Eatons Neck Point, tied to the "mainland" by a long strand, Sunken Meadow State Park, and many lovely beaches (some accessible) in the Stony Brook–Setauket area. From Port Jefferson east to Orient Point, a distance of more than 30 miles, there are continuous high bluffs broken only by inlets at Mt. Sinai and Mattituck. At these, the beaches are rather more accessible for swimming and walking and lend themselves well to botanizing and geological rambles. The views from the high bluffs, particularly at Wildwood State Park, of the Long Island shore and of distant Connecticut across the Sound are impressive. Some private beaches are impediments in July and August or in the duck-hunting season, but at other times the entire beach is available.

Garvies Point Park.

In Glen Cove, Nassau County is making a nature center complex out of Garvies Point (Appleby Beach). This spot is famous for its beds of lignite, its multicolored clays, its large numbers of iron pyrite clusters, and its red shale fossils. (Gray shale fossils are found on Eatons Neck just north of Asharoken Beach.) Also, the most extensive Indian "midden" diggings on Long Island are at Garvies Point.

PARKS AND PRESERVES

Perhaps the greatest amount of hiking land to be found on Long Island is in the state, county, and town parks. These vary greatly in size and character, ranging from converted private estates or narrow strip parks along a stream to huge wooded preserves covering thousands of acres. New ones are being added all the time, mostly as a result of tax pressures on large private landholdings. The areas noted below should serve as a starting point only, for as the years pass the list may well be significantly different.

Valley Stream State Park.

This 100-acre state park has a good walking trail and a good winter population of ducks. Park at the Merrick Road end, and walk the trail north to Southern State Parkway and back to the starting point.

Hempstead Lake State Park.

A famous winter birding spot, this area provides a pleasant walk. Start at the parking field at the tennis courts and walk south along the lake or through the woods to Lakeview Avenue, then through the Swamp Maple swamp to Peninsula Boulevard. On the other side is Smith Pond (a good winter duck pond). On the north side of Peninsula Boulevard is Nassau County's lovely Tanglewood Preserve. Return by the east shore of the lake, around the reservoir on the north side of the Parkway, and back to the starting point.

Meadowbrook Parkway.

Starting close to Nassau County's Eisenhower Park (golf–historical museum complex), the Meadowbrook Parkway provides a narrow walking strip from Stewart Avenue as far south as Merrick Road (Montauk Highway). First there are scrubby fields with wet areas and Japanese black pine plantings, then swamp maple woods and a running brook, and finally a series of ponds. This strip, in part, borders the former Mitchel Field, the last remnant of the Hempstead Plains.

Wantagh Parkway.

Starting at a pond on Merrick Road just to the west of Wantagh State Parkway, walk north along the west side and follow the wooded strip and chain of ponds north to Southern State Parkway, returning on the east side. This is a delightful winter walk.

Tackapausha Preserve.

Nassau County's Nature Trail (and Museum), on Seaford's Washington Avenue, provides a good wet-woods walk from Merrick Road to Jerusalem Avenue. It is a very good preserve for birds and wild flowers in springtime.

Muttontown Nature Preserve.

Nassau County is developing two former estates as a North Shore Tackapausha. The Preserve is on North Hempstead Turnpike (Rt. 25A) in East Norwich, with the entrance opposite Mill River Road.

Mill Neck.

One of the most delightful preserves on Long Island is the North Shore Bird and Game Sanctuary in Mill Neck. Park on the south side of the track at the Mill Neck railroad station; a short distance to the northwest, lovely Beaver Lake is worth a visit. Return to the station parking area, opposite which is the sanctuary gate. Wander around in the sanctuary and in the woods to the south of Shu Swamp Road. Also close by, on Planting Field Road, is the State University at the former Coe Estate, with a fine arboretum.

Massapequa and Bethpage State Parks.

The Massapequa Park–Bethpage Park–Old Bethpage Village complex provides an extremely long walking area. Start at Massapequa Lake on Merrick Road, and take the trail on the east side of the lake, walking north. Across Sunrise Highway is Massapequa Pond and then wet woods to Southern State Parkway. From here Bethpage State Parkway connects Massapequa State Park and Bethpage State Park and has grass and shrubbery borders. Although Bethpage State Park is basically a golf course complex, there are many bridle paths and wooded borders which can be walked with pleasure. Just north of the park is Old Bethpage, a restored historical village.

High Point.

Naturally, the highest point on Long Island (406 feet) is a spot everyone will want to visit. It is in the West Hills area, north of Northern State Parkway, with an undeveloped park (Gwynne County Park) and a Boy Scout camp (Camp Kaufman) in the vicinity. High Point is a good starting place for several hours of rambling (generally south and west). To reach it, climb up just beyond the top of Reservoir Road, South Huntington. To find Reservoir Road, take Rt. 110 south from Rt. 25 to West Hills Road, then west to Reservoir Road.

Caumsett State Park.

This very large undeveloped state park occupies the center of Lloyd Neck and was the former Marshall Field estate. All that can be said at this time is that it provides ample walking space (and no place to park). On Lloyd Harbor Road, east of the park, is an impressive old black oak, said to be the largest in the United States.

Belmont Lake State Park.

This 460-acre state park provides one of the best walks on Long Island. Park in the parking field on the east side of the lake. Walk the trail along the east side, then around the north side. There is also a trail running due north along the brook to the north edge of the park. Returning to the lake, go around the west side and cross Southern State Parkway, picking up the walking trail. Follow this south along the brook under Sunrise Highway, around the west side of Southard's Pond and south to Park Avenue. In the dead of winter, continue south to Lake Argyle on Montauk Highway. This lake is a sanctuary for large numbers of wild ducks, including such rare species as European widgeon and ring-necked ducks. The return trip is by the bridle path which parallels the walking trail.

Sunken Meadow State Park.

This 1300-acre state park is not outstanding as a hiking area, but some good walking is available along the beach.

Nissequogue River State Park and Weld Estate Preserve

Nissequogue River State Park on Rt. 25 (Jericho Turnpike) just west of Smithtown Branch, was a gun club and has an excellent lake and stream forming part of the Nissequogue River headwaters. The surrounding swamp maple woods merge into oakpitch pine on the northern perimeter. The most important feature of this pretty park is that it is across the road from a large new Suffolk County park (formerly the Weld estate) in which is hidden Stump Pond (New Mill Pond), Long Island's second largest lake.

Weld Estate Preserve extends from Jericho Turnpike south to Veterans Highway and is bordered on the west by Old Willetts Path. A good way to enter is from Smithtown Branch. At the Hilltop Diner on the west end of town turn south on Brookside Drive one block to Mill Road—then west into the park. It is a very long walk completely around the L-shaped lake. Also, take exploratory trips into the adjacent woodlands, swamps, and fields. Wood ducks breed here, and the entire area is a natural bird sanctuary.

Heckscher State Park.

The Heckscher Park—Cutting Arboretum/Connetquot River State Park complex affords one of the largest public walking areas on Long Island.

Park at Heckscher (1700 acres) in the parking field at the state troopers' barracks. In winter large herds of deer are fed here. Walk due west through the old nursery to the white pine grove, then south through the lane which goes through the wet hardwoods to the east-west canal. Great horned owls nest here, and across the canal is a large marsh grass–peat bog island rich in flora and fauna. Walk east along the north side of the canal until the main paved north-south road is reached. Then follow the shoreline eastward around the park. At the far east end a return route can be plotted through the salt marsh (risky), or through the woods (rough going), or through the fields (easy going). Or leave the park, walk through the little village of Great River to the Connetquot River, and then go north to Montauk Highway (northwest corner of the Arboretum). Enter the Bayard Cutting Arboretum here or, if the gate is closed, at the main gate a short distance to the east.

Bayard Cutting Arboretum.

This large preserve is a former estate which is beautifully situated on the Connetquot River. It has a number of well-marked nature trails that make it of outstanding interest at any season of the year, although it is at its best in spring and summer. The northeast corner of the Arboretum is across Montauk Highway from state park land (with lakes) that connects it to the Connetquot River State Park.

Connetquot River State Park.

This former hunting preserve is several thousand acres in size. The major part of the preserve runs from Sunrise Highway north to Veterans Highway. On the north side of Veterans Highway a smaller area is already accessible to the public. This portion is a lovely brook-traversed wet woodlands in an excellent state of preservation. Park on the grass on Veterans Highway at the bridge where the headwaters of the Connetquot River run under the highway.

Wildwood State Park.

This 700-acre park has some good walks along the beach but is chiefly interesting because of its spectacular high bluffs overlooking the Sound.

Southaven County Park.

This famous sportsman's club on Carmans River in South Haven has been acquired by the County. It is on the Sunrise Highway service road and is reached from (is west of) William Floyd Parkway. The preserve has walking trails, but much of it is wild brush country and woodlands. Bald eagles still frequent it in winter and scavenge along the long Carmans River basin to the south.

SOUTH HARBOR
SOUTHOLD
1929

Old Mastic (Ranger's Station).

The William Floyd homestead in Mastic is on Moriches Bay, east of Great South Bay. Open to the public under the control of the federal government, it is an old Colonial farm with fields and woodlands running into peat bogs and salt marsh. It is a great bird sanctuary and is noteworthy for its flora.

Peconic River and County Park.

Presumably some day the entire Peconic River Basin may be preserved and open to the walking public. Long Island's longest river starts on Rt. 25 (Jericho Turnpike) opposite Panamoka Trail, in a little, usually dry pond. From here south to Manorville, this new park is a lovely complex of ponds and streams.

As the river travels eastward through fenced woodlands, commercial cranberry bogs, deserted cranberry bogs, and the like, there are spots which are accessible to the public and spots which are not. With a little ingenuity, a way can be worked through this area from Brookhaven Laboratory to Riverhead. One interesting stretch is from Forge Pond (on the Brightwoods Road) east along the south bank of the river to the Suffolk County Government Center at Riverhead, then into the cranberry bog behind the Center south to Wildwood Lake, and finally back across the pine barrens (Big Hill) to the starting point.

THE EASTERN END

East of Riverhead the Peconic Bays (Great and Little), Gardiners Bay, and several islands separate Long Island's two moraines. The two peninsulas, known as the North Fluke and the South Fluke from their resemblance to the two lobes of a whale's tail, provide some lovely and still relatively unspoiled walking areas.

There is a wide triangular stretch of rolling moraine topography, east of the Shinnecock Canal at Canoe Place, between Southampton, Bridgehampton, East Hampton, and the old whaling village of Sag Harbor. Farther eastward, the South Fluke narrows abruptly at Amagansett. Here the moraine was probably once cut through by the sea but is now joined by the wide stretch of dunes and marshes of Napeague Beach. Four or 5 miles beyond Amagansett the bluffs rise again to offer a bit of moraine topography as different as can be imagined from anything else for 100 miles north or south along the Atlantic coast from New York harbor. These hills end in the remarkable spearhead of Montauk Point. This wedge of land, tapering quickly from 3 miles in width to the headland where the tall lighthouse and screeching fog signal stand out into the Atlantic, offers one of the most unusual and interesting fields for walking available within a few hours of the metropolis. The best places to hike in this general area are along the beaches.

Jessup Neck.
Now known as the Morton National Wildlife Refuge, this long sandspit west of Sag Harbor is controlled by the Fish and Wildlife Service. The entrance is on Noyac Road, a short distance west of Noyac. Several hours should be allowed for the hike. Due east of the parking field, hidden in the woods, is a wood duck pond. However, the trail goes north through a cedar woods, then drops to the beach. Over a wooded hill is another level stretch of beach and then the final hill.

Cedar Point County Park.
Due north of East Hampton, on Gardiners Bay, is the newly acquired and wild 600-acre Cedar Point County Park. There are numerous lanes through the woods and several ponds. The long tour would be on the west side and out on the spit known as Cedar Point, then east along the beach to the east end of the park and back through the oak woods to the starting point.

Hither Hills State Park.

This 1800-acre park is largely in virgin wilderness condition and is contiguous to another and larger wild area extending all the way to Montauk village. Here is an opportunity for an all-day dawn-to-dark hike.

There is a rough road going north from Montauk Highway along the east side of Napeague harbor. Park at the end, and climb up to the top of the high dunes (highest on Long Island). To the west, across the harbor, are the flats ending at Lazy Point. Along these flats are found fox dens, hills which appear to be star-nosed mole hills, roseate terns at the inlet, and cranberry bogs.

To the east is an amazing world of shifting sands. Every year the vista is different. The oak forest is being buried; the tops of 50-foot trees stick through the sand like two-year-old saplings. Below the wall of sand are pitch pine parks, well sheltered even in winter, where the deer bed down, and woodland flowers bloom and wild cranberries can be found. Work north and east through this area of buried trees to Napeague Bay on the shore of Block Island Sound. Walk eastward along the bay, through the dunes, and note the *hudsonia,* reindeer lichen, and other beach plants. Beach plum is

Amagansett

Promised Land

The Pond in Hither Woods

abundant. At the center of the curve of the bay there is a lane which runs south to an abandoned road running southwest to Montauk Highway, intersecting it just west of the dunes road, which runs along the ocean front to Montauk village. Walk this lane from the bay almost to the railroad track. Here there is a road running down to Fresh Pond, a beautiful virgin lake, full of largemouth bass.

To proceed east from Fresh Pond, cross the railroad track, and walk the road (once a blacktop road) until it becomes a dirt road. Or walk the beach from Napeague Bay about 1 mile, and then take one of the numerous lanes which lead to the dirt road through the woods to Old Fort Pond Bay village. Then walk south to the ocean, skirting the expanding village of Montauk, and follow the beach and dunes back to the starting point.

Montauk Point State Park.

This 700-acre park at the end of Long Island is world-renowned for its bird life, which is particularly abundant in winter. There are sea ducks and many of the offshore birds such as gannets, kittiwakes, dovekies, and razor-billed auks. Harbor seals are present every win-

Fireplace
Gardiners Bay

Montauk Light and the two forms of cliff
1931 Dickinson.

ter. Deer, red fox, and gray fox are abundant. An interesting walk is westward from Montauk Point along Block Island Sound to Oyster Pond, south on the east shore of the pond to the holly woods and thence to Montauk Highway.

The Islands in the Bay.

Gardiners Island and Robins Island are both private, and trespassers are not welcome. Shelter Island is well populated and its only wild area (the southeast end) is a leased hunting preserve, where trespassers are also not welcome. The remainder of the island does not lend itself readily to hiking.

Orient Point.

Almost at the tip of the North Fluke, there is 350-acre Orient Beach State Park. Park at the New London ferry, and take the long walk along the beach, or drive into the park to the parking field, to take a shorter walk west to the end of the spit, Long Beach Point. There find the wreckage of the old lighthouse. In spring the ospreys nest and the prickly pear cactus and beach plum bloom. In summer there are the roseate terns and porpoises. In fall the monarch butterflies gather in tremendous numbers on their way south, and they hang from the cedars in clusters. In winter there are the sea birds and snowy owls. At all times of the year the park is an outstanding bird sanctuary and a favorite place for beachcombers.

Part IV

INTRODUCTION

ııE RAMAPO MOUNTAIN range anchors its northeastern flank at Tomkins Cove on the Hudson and crosses into New Jersey at Mahwah in Bergen County, just below Suffern. As it heads southwest, the range forms a distinctly different geologic province from the Newark Basin farther east. The Ramapo River channels along the Great Border Fault which separates the metamorphic rock complex of the Ramapos from the Triassic sandstones and shales of the lowlands, out of which rise the diabase intrusion that forms the Palisades and the basalt extrusions that form the Watchungs. In general, the Precambrian crystalline rocks of the Ramapos are sharply distinguishable, both topographically and by composition, from those in the Newark Basin.

Aside from describing trails that traverse the Ramapos, this chapter also includes descriptions of trails west of Greenwood Lake and south of the New York line in the Bearfort Range, consisting again of an entirely different geologic structure of sandstone-and-quartz conglomerate ridges.

Much of this wild land here is privately owned and the persistent encroachment of the real estate developer leads to a frequent trail relocation. There are several tracts of state forests and parks that fortunately are being enlarged under New Jersey's enlightened Green Acres program. The Norvin Green State Forest, a gift of the former chairman of the Ringwood Company, covers some 2260 acres in the Wyanokie section. It will be greatly enlarged if restricted lands surrounding the 6-mile-long Wanague Reservoir are opened for recreation purposes in line with the desires of the New Jersey Department of Environmental Protection. Currently, the Reservoir environs are patrolled by uniformed guards of the North Jersey District Water Supply Commission. The Green Mountain Club open shelter at Blue Mine is within one-eighth mile of a guard station and walkers are warned not to cross the line!

The Norvin Green State Forest occupies barely one tenth of the 34-square-mile Wyanokie wild area, which has the largest concentration of trails in the whole state. Elevations range from 400 to 1100 feet. These trails were laid out in the early 1920s by Dr. Will S. Monroe of Montclair, and his co-workers in the Green Mountain Club. When he retired to his Couching Lion Farm (later willed to the State of Vermont), the property and the trail maintenance were taken over by the Nature Friends, who named the area Camp Midvale. This camp is now owned by the American Ethical Union (AEU). A fee may be charged to park in the camp's lot on Snake Den Road, uphill from West Brook Road. (A group planning to park several cars should telephone the camp caretaker in advance. This central starting point is approached from Rt. 511 north of Midvale over a causeway across Wanaque Reservoir. Other entrance points where parking is available are at the eastern end of Hewitt at the junction of the East Shore Road with Greenwood Lake, and at Haskell for the trail up Post Brook. There is also a parking spot on West Brook Road north of Saddle Mountain in the middle of the Wyanokie area.

Ringwood Manor State Park, a gift of Erskine Hewitt, was enlarged a few years ago to include boating and skiing facilities at Sheppard Lake. In 1967 the adjoining Skylands Farm estate, formerly occupied by Shelton College, was acquired by New Jersey under its Green Acres program. The area includes Mt. Defiance (1040 feet), North Cape off Pierson Ridge, and several small ponds. Its maze of jeep roads could occupy hours of exploration on foot. An offshoot of Ringwood Manor State Park to the west includes public fishing along the Wanaque River, the outlet of Greenwood Lake, and the old Long Pond ironworks with its huge water wheels and furnaces, just off Rt. 511 in Hewitt. This area, once off bounds because of vandalism, is open to hikers from the southern end of the Sterling Ridge Trail.

Toward the end of 1967, a tract of about a thousand acres between the Wanaque River and Rt. 511 was added to the Park. The northern entrance is at Valley Inn on Rt. 511; the southern entrance is on Stonetown Road east of the river crossing.

The Bearfort Ridge area west of Greenwood Lake immediately south of the New York State line is almost wholly within the A. S. Hewitt State Forest. It includes Surprise Lake and is separated by Warwick Turnpike from private land to the south with a trail open to hikers and leading to Terrace Pond. Warwick Stages bus line will drop passengers at Great Oak Inn at the south end of Greenwood Lake or at the New Jersey–New York state line on the lake shore.

In the southern section of the Ramapos, two trail systems struggle for existence against suburban sprawl. One heads southwest from Riverdale, near Pompton, to Towaco, east of Lake Valhalla. The other traverses the Wyanokies from Hewitt to Butler. Leaving the streets of Butler, the trail finds a devious path over scenic ridges and a stretch of power lines to Montville, southwest of Lake Valhalla.

Many of the walks in this area begin and end at railroad stations. They are convenient landmarks, although train service is infrequent or nonexistent, particularly on weekends. Bus routes serve most of the towns.

EAST OF THE WYANOKIES

Suffern-Midvale Trail. Length: 12 miles. Blazes: white.

The Suffern-Midvale Trail begins in Suffern, at the railroad station. Going west, the trail skirts a ball field, crosses the Ramapo River on a railroad trestle, passes a row of houses and crosses Rt. 17 at the New Jersey–New York state line. It ascends Split Rock Road and enters the woods, crosses a pipeline, reaches a viewpoint of Suffern and continues to Split Rock boulder on the summit of Hoevenkopf Mountain. It then descends to Split Rock Road and continues to the Silver Lake development. Here the trail enters the woods again, joining the Cannonball Trail to cross brooks, a pipeline, and pass Spoke Spring. Shortly after crossing another pipeline, it leaves the Cannonball Trail and skirts the northwestern end of Bear Swamp Pond (also called Bear Lake). Turning from the lake, it circles a hill and crosses a brook before ascending left to Butler Mine. After crossing two more brooks, it arrives at Ilgenstein Rock overlooking Bear Swamp Pond and the surrounding mountains. Continuing, the trail crosses High Mountain Brook Trail and ascends High Mountain with a view of the Bearfort Range, Erskine Lake, and the Wyanokies to the west. The trail follows the ridge to Matapan Rock with more views of the Wyanokies. Descending, it crosses Skyline Drive and reaches Conklintown Road. From here, the trail follows automobile roads to the site of the former Midvale railroad station on Railroad Avenue in Midvale.

Cannonball Trail. Length: 4.5 miles. Blazes: red.

The historic Cannonball Trail coincides with the Suffern-Midvale Trail between Suffern and the north end of Bear Swamp Pond (Bear Lake). Beyond this point it passes through posted lands. It follows the east side of the lake and passes between Bear Lake Club homes (guard on duty). The trail crosses a bridge over the outlet at the lake's south end, ascends through woods to another road, and passes several scout trails before crossing Keffer Memorial Dam and reaching the western side of Cannonball Lake. Camp Yaw Paw is operated here by Ridgewood–Glen Rock Council, Boy Scouts of America. After passing a few more scout trails, the Cannonball crosses a pipeline and enters posted property of the Montclair Boy Scouts. A trail bends left across a stream to rejoin the Suffern-Midvale Trail in 0.75 mile, as a Revolutionary-period wood road continues ahead a quarter mile to reach Glen Gray Camp and Fox Brook Road. Caretakers at both Scout camps are inclined to be testy about hikers when the woods are dry. Local history has it that the Cannonball Road was used in the transport of munitions by the Continentals, this mountainous route being chosen for safety from the British.

Sterling Ridge Trail. Length: 8.4 miles. Blazes: blue on white.

The Sterling Ridge Trail traverses the Tuxedo Mountains between the high ridge of Rt. 210, north and east of Greenwood Lake Village, and the junction of East Shore Road with Rt. 511 at the southeastern border of Hewitt, New Jersey, where it connects with the Hewitt-Butler Trail. The New York section is on the property of Sterling Forest (City Investing Co.), and the New Jersey portions are within wild lands of Ringwood Manor State Park. In 1968 "no trespassing" signs were at both ends of the trail, but the trail is open to bona fide hikers, particularly those of member clubs of the New York–New Jersey Trail Conference. The Park is restoring the old furnaces and recently uncovered the Long Pond Iron Works site along the Wanaque River below the falls.

Starting from Hewitt, the trail enters a wood road and soon joins an auto road through a small settlement and passes within sight of the iron works and two 25-foot water wheels before crossing the Wanaque River on an iron bridge. From here it ascends a steep embankment and shortly joins an old road. It passes the Jennings

Hollow Trail, the Hewitt Trail, and ascends Big Beech Mountain, which offers a view of the Bearfort Range. Continuing, it crosses the Sterling Forest Trail and arrives at a view, to the southwest, of Big Beech Mountain, Bearfort Range, and the Wyanokies. In a hemlock forest, it crosses Cedar Pond wood road and ascends to the Sterling Fire Tower. From the tower there are views in all directions. After many ups and downs, the trail reaches an excellent view of Sterling Lake with the mountains beyond. From here, it descends to cross Laurel Swamp Trail and follows a ridge past a power line before reaching Rt. 210 near the summit of Tuxedo Mountain.

Allis Trail. Length: under 2 miles. Blazes: blue on white.

The Allis Trail begins at a sharp left bend on Rt. 210, about two miles west of Sterling Forest Gardens. With a mile of road-walking south, it connects the Appalachian Trail with the Sterling Ridge Trail. The Allis Trail almost immediately crosses a pipeline and a power line before reaching Cedar Mountain, where there is a view northeast. From here, it descends to the Appalachian Trail west of Mombasha High Point. This trail is named for J. Ashton Allis, a pioneer hiker and trail builder in the metropolitan area, and for many years president of the Fresh Air Club.

THE WYANOKIE PLATEAU

Burnt Meadow Trail. Length: 0.8 mile. Blazes: yellow.

The Burnt Meadow Trail starts from Burnt Meadow Road 1.6 miles south of Rt. 511 in Hewitt. It descends to a brook and ascends to the Horse Pond Mountain Trail (white) on Horse Pond Mountain.

Carris Hill Trail. Length: 1 mile. Blazes: yellow.

The Carris Hill Trail begins on the Lower Trail (white) and ascends steeply to an impressive view of Wanaque Reservoir and the mountains. Continuing, it reaches Carris Hill and the Hewitt-Butler Trail (blue on white).

Hewitt-Butler Trail. Length: 18 miles. Blazes: blue on white.

The Hewitt-Butler Trail extends the entire length of the Wyanokie region from Hewitt, at the junction of Rt. 511 with East Shore Road, to Cold Spring Lake on Macopin Road in Butler. In Hewitt, the trail follows an old railroad bed to a gas line, on which it turns west. Ascending into the woods, the trail passes the Horse Pond Mountain Trail (left) before descending to cross two brooks and

Burnt Meadow Road. Continuing, the trail passes under a power line and ascends a ridge which offers an excellent view of Long Hill ahead and another view, southeast, of the Ramapos and Garrett Mountain in the Watchungs. The trail descends from the ridge to the former Huyler Farm before ascending to follow the top of Long Hill, with two westward viewpoints of the valley and Bearfort Range. It now descends to Kitchell Lake Trail and, after many ups and downs, crosses a brook. The trail passes a yellow-blazed side trail to an excellent view of Burnt Meadow, passes West Brook Trail (also yellow), and ascends to Tip-Top Point. Here the Mine Trail (yellow on white) joins, and they descend together to Manaticut Point with superb views eastward. Descending, sometimes steeply, to a brook and beautiful hemlock grove, the trail crosses West Brook and West Brook Road (6.5 miles), then ascends to an easterly view which includes the New York City skyline. Descending past Wolf Den, a jumble of rocks, the trail has several up and downs before crossing a brook and joining the Wyanokie Circular Trail (red on white). Together, they cross two brooks before traversing the three Pine Paddies. Of these, No. 3 offers a north-to-east panorama of the Wyanokies and beyond, and No. 1 a view of Wanaque Reservoir and Wyanokie High Point. The trails separate after crossing a brook west of the AEU (American Ethical Union) camp, formerly the Nature Friends Camp (9.5 miles). Following Snake Den Road west about 0.25 mile, the Hewitt-Butler Trail joins the Mine Trail (yellow on white) a short distance before ascending to views of the Wyanokie region. Passing the Macopin Trail (white) and just below the top of Wyanokie High Point, it joins the Wyanokie Circular Trail again for 0.4 miles. The trail ascends past Yoo-Hoo Point to Carris Hill Trail (yellow) and Carris Hill with a view in many directions. Descending to a pipeline and the end of Post Brook Trail (white), it crosses a brook and parallels Post Brook northwest to Otter Hole Trail (green on white). Crossing Post Brook, it ascends to Glen Wild Road (13.5 miles), which it follows west before entering woods to pick up Torne Trail (red on white) and make a steep ascent of Torne Mountain. The summit offers many excellent views of the surrounding valley and mountains. Continuing past the upper end of Torne Trail, the Hewitt-Butler Trail comes to South Torne and Osio Rock, both with impressive views. Descending steeply, it then follows an old road through the valley, crosses a brook, and traverses a hill before arriving at Star Lake. The trail continues past Cold Spring Lake to Macopin Road. From here it is one mile on auto roads to the center of Butler.

Horse Pond Mountain Trail. Length: 2 miles. Blazes: white.

The Horse Pond Mountain Trail starts from the Stonetown Circular Trail (red triangle on white) on Harrison Mountain. It descends steeply to a brook before ascending sharply to meet the Burnt Meadow Trail (yellow) and traverses the entire length of Horse Pond Mountain. While descending, watch for a spectacular view of the Wanaque River and Ringwood Manor State Park. The trail then passes a power line and meets the Hewitt-Butler Trail south of the gas pipeline.

Lower Trail. Length: 1.7 miles. Blazes: white.

The Lower Trail extends between the Wyanokie Circular Trail east of High Point and the Post Brook Trail east of Chikahoki Falls. At the southern end, it borders the Wanaque Reservoir property line and passes the Carris Hill Trail.

Macopin Trail. Length: 2.5 miles. Blazes: white.

The Macopin Trail begins at the junction of Larsen Road with Otter Hole Road, a short distance south of Mountain Glen Lakes. It crosses two brooks before ascending to intersect the Wyanokie Circular Trail (red on white). Continuing on, it meets and joins the Otter Hole Trail over a brook before ascending to meet the Hewitt-Butler Trail (blue on white) west of Wyanokie High Point.

Mine Trail. Length: 5.4 miles. Blazes: yellow on white.

The Mine Trail begins opposite AEU Camp on Snake Den Road. It passes Wyanokie Falls (0.5 mile), Wyanokie Circular Trail (red

WYANOKIE PLATEAU   MIDVALE
WANAQUE RIVER   THE NEW RESERVOIR

on white), and ascends Ball Mountain (0.8 mile), named for two large boulders shaped like giant balls. From here, there is an excellent view of Wyanokie High Point and its surrounding mountains. The trail continues along the ridge to another viewpoint before descending to Roomy Mine (1.1 miles). It shortly joins the Wyanokie Circular Trail to pass the flooded Blue Mine (1.5 miles) and the Green Mountain Club open shelter. It leaves the Wyanokie Circular Trail east of High Point and follows a low route to the Hewitt-Butler Trail (blue on white) and Snake Den Road (2.3 miles). Continuing on, it passes the abandoned Winfield Farm, Otter Hole Trail (green on white), Stone Hunting House Trail (white), and Boy Scout Lake, where it crosses the Wyanokie Circular Trail again. The trail follows the lake overflow to West Brook Road (4.8 miles). After crossing the road, it ascends, sometimes steeply, to view points and Tip-Top Point on the Hewitt-Butler Trail, which it follows to Manaticut Point.

Otter Hole Trail. Length: 2 miles. Blazes: green on white.

The Otter Hole Trail connects the Mine Trail at old Winfield Farm with the Hewitt-Butler Trail at the Otter Hole. Following an old road from the farm site, it crosses a brook as it intersects the Macopin Trail (0.4 mile). The Wyanokie Circular Trail (red on white) enters from the left (0.8 mile) and joins the Otter Hole Trail for 0.3 mile. At 2.0 miles the trail reaches the Hewitt-Butler Trail (blue on white).

Post Brook Trail. Length: 3 miles. Blazes: white.

The Post Brook Trail begins at the junction of Rt. 511 and Doty Road in Haskell. It follows Doty Road one mile west before entering the woods (right) and passing between hills to a rhododendron grove. After crossing two more roads, it zigzags around boulders through a ravine of hemlocks. Crossing Post Brook twice, then paralleling it, the trail passes the Lower Trail and Chikahoki Falls, and ends at the Hewitt-Butler Trail (blue on white).

Stone Hunting House Trail. Length: 0.5 mile. Blazes: white.

This half-mile trail begins at the Stone Hunting House, a rock shelter said to have been used by the Indians, on the Wyanokie Circular Trail and ends at the Mine Trail south of Boy Scout Lake.

Stonetown Circular Trail. Length: 9.5 miles. Blazes: red triangle on white.

The Stonetown Circular goes over a number of peaks, which classifies it as strenuous, since it totals about the equivalent of a 2500-foot climb. If a car must be parked, a good starting place is at the Ringwood Fire Station on Stonetown Road at Magee Road, one mile north of the reservoir police booth located at the junction of West Brook Road and Stonetown Road.

Going counterclockwise from the fire station, the trail follows Stonetown Road south and turns left into the woods (0.5 mile). From here it leads up Windbeam Mountain, a climb of about 600 feet. At a lookout point on the way up and from the fire tower on top (1.2 miles) are good views. Windbeam Mountain, 1026 feet, is a landmark, not only on account of its height, but because of its isolation from other high points. (Miss M. M. Monk's book *Windbeam* has a good deal of interesting material on this mountain and these localities in the days before motor and reservoir brought their changes.)

The trail follows the service road down to a gate in a high fence, ascends 400 feet to the precipitous craggy peak of Bear Mountain (2.7 miles), and then drops down again before its easy ascent of Board Mountain, with its broad views of Wanaque Reservoir and the hills beyond. From here the trail descends steeply and crosses three brooks, then leads up to a housing development. Next it follows White Road to Stonetown Road 3 miles north of the police booth. Here it turns south and follows Stonetown Road 0.3 miles, then turns right on a dirt road. After crossing a brook, the trail turns right into the woods and ascends to a beautiful panorama of the Wyanokies before reaching Harrison Mountain and the southern terminus of Horse Pond Mountain Trail. Descending, it passes a housing development on Harrison Mountain Lake and crosses Sawmill Brook on a bridge on Burnt Meadow Road (6.2 miles). At the end of the bridge it turns left into the woods for a short distance, and then follows Burnt Meadow Road; again enters the woods (6.5 miles) and leads up to Tory Rocks, so named because they were used as a hideout by some Tories during the Revolution. These are 40-foot cliffs, with a view of Windbeam Mountain. From here the trail descends, crosses a brook, and ascends to Signal Rock (8.2 miles), with a view of the Ramapos framed by Windbeam and Bear mountains. Descending, it parallels Stonetown Brook to Magee Road (9.2 miles) and turns left to the Fire Station on Stonetown Road.

Torne Trail. Length: 1 mile. Blazes: red on white.
The Torne Trail begins on the Hewitt-Butler Trail (blue on

white), south of the Otter Hole and Glen Wild Road. It ascends to a point between North and South Torne mountains.

West Brook Trail. Length: 1 mile. Blazes: yellow.

The West Brook Trail begins on West Brook Road 0.7 mile east of Kitchell Lake. Ascending on several old roads, it reaches a shoulder of West Brook Mountain and meets the Hewitt-Butler Trail (blue on white) west of Tip-Top Point.

Wyanokie Circular Trail. Length: 8.7 miles. Blazes: red on white.

The Wyanokie Circular Trail begins at the AEU (American Ethical Union) Camp, formerly the Nature Friends Camp, on Snake Den Road, approached from West Brook Road over a causeway. East of the camp, on Ellen Avenue, the trail passes between houses, enters woods, and intersects Mine Trail (yellow on white), which it later joins to pass Blue Mine and the Green Mountain Club open shelter. Leaving the Mine Trail, it ascends steeply to Wyanokie High Point (1032 feet), (1.6 miles), where there is an excellent panorama of the surrounding countryside with New York City skyline on the horizon. The trail joins the Hewitt-Butler Trail (blue on white) for 0.4 mile as it descends to join the Seven Husbands Trail and later the Otter Hole Trail (green on white) for 0.3 mile. Continuing on, it intersects the Macopin Trail (white), the Stone Hunting House Trail (white) and a cave, Stone Hunting House, an Indian name which gave its name to the Trail (4.1 miles). After crossing two brooks and passing another cave, the trail ascends to several viewpoints before reaching Black Rock (5.4 miles) with a view of Kitchell Lake. The trail descends, sometimes steeply, and follows Snake Den wood road to Boy Scout Lake (owned by the West Essex Lions Club) (6.2 miles), where it crosses a dam, again intersects Mine Trail, and traverses Saddle Mountain to a brook and the Hewitt-Butler Trail. From here, it follows the Hewitt-Butler Trail over two brooks, the three Pine Paddies, each with varying views of the Wyanokies, crosses a brook, and turns left from the Hewitt-Butler Trail. Shortly, it reaches Snake Den Road which it follows left 0.6 mile past the AEU Camp to the beginning of the trail.

SOUTH OF THE WYANOKIES

Butler to Montville. Length: 7.8 miles. Blazes: blue on white.

This trail previously began on Rt. 23 just west of Butler; it crossed Kiel Avenue and then ascended Kakeout Mountain. Due to extensive residential development, the trail now begins just north of Old Reservoir. From the shopping center at the intersection of Rt. 23 and Kiel Avenue, travel south on Kiel Avenue and immediately take the first left turn on Kakeout Avenue. Proceed 0.5 mile and turn right on Reservoir Road. After 0.1 mile, the beginning of the trail is marked on the right by three blue blazes. Reservoir Road is narrow, but has space on the shoulder for three or four cars.

The trail begins with a moderately steep ascent of 450 feet to the summit of Kakeout Mountain (1050-foot elevation). After about 0.3 miles from the beginning, it skirts a housing development and then turns sharp left on the original blue trail. (Many of the markers in this area are on rocks on the ground.) After several scenic views of Butler Reservoir, the trail descends, crosses the inlet brook (crossing the brook is a problem in high water) and in 1.7 miles from the start turns left on Fayson Lakes Road. In a hundred yards, the trail re-enters woods at the right along an arm of the Reservoir. In front of a church, it turns right on a blacktop road which it follows for half a mile uphill.

The trail leaves the road on the left and follows an old wood briefly. A sharp lookout, because of recent housing developments, will reveal a right turn off the wood road into the woods toward Bear Rock. This landmark, an unusually large single rock rising from level ground, is 1.5 miles from the macadam road. The trail turns sharply left at this point and circumnavigates a swamp area before a fairly steep 200-foot ascent through a stand of laurel to a ridge. A short side trail goes left to Tripod Rock. A sharp right turn begins a gradual ascent of 100 feet to the summit of Pyramid Mountain (930-foot elevation), 1 mile from Bear Rock. At the ruins of an old wooden fire tower there is an exceptionally good view south to Deer Lake, Boonton Reservoir, and the valley. If the atmosphere is clear, the New York City skyline is visible.

A very steep descent in 0.2 mile ends at the power lines where the trail turns left toward the east. It follows the clearing beneath the power lines for one mile, dropping 300 feet to Boonton Avenue (Rt. 511), then rises 300 feet where it turns right (south) into the woods and leaves the power lines. (But here again the land has been purchased by a developer.) The following mile is pleasant woodland walking to the top of an abandoned quarry. A steep descent leads to a wood road which reaches Taylortown Road in 0.4 mile, where three blue blazes mark the trail's end. There is space for four or five cars at this point. Taylortown Road is between Rt. 202 and Rt. 511 (east and west) in Montville.

This trail is rewarding for its variety of trees, shrubs, and wild flowers (in season) such as: dogwood, ironwood, maples, oaks, tulip trees, hickories, birches, red cedar, maple-leaved viburnum, sumac (staghorn), solomon's-seal, goldenrod, striped wintergreen, asters, pokeberry, butter-and-eggs, partridgeberry, Christmas fern, and star moss.

Towaco-Pompton Trail. Length: 8 miles. Blazes: yellow.

The Towaco-Pompton Trail goes west from the railroad station in Towaco, off U.S. 202, turns right on Waughaw Road and right on Indian Lane to the pipeline (1 mile). The trail turns left on the pipeline and enters woods. Crossing several roads and several brooks, it ascends Waughaw Mountain. Near the top (887 feet) it meets and follows a power line, with excellent views backward of the valley and of Lake Valhalla. The trail descends into woods, crossing the power line twice before crossing a brook and reaching Brook Valley Road. It follows the road 0.1 mile and enters woods west of a YMCA camp. Here, it follows a dirt road past a stream, a pool, and several old roads. A side trail goes left to Camp Aheka just before the ascent of Mine Hill. On top, there is a magnificent view to the southeast of Pompton Plains and the New York City skyline. Descending, there are views of the Wyanokies before the trail crosses two brooks and reaches Sawmill Pond Road. Crossing the road, the trail ascends a hill, crosses another brook, and passes a swamp before traversing a wide pipeline. The trail goes over a hill before joining the pipline to Rt. 23. Continuing on the other side, it comes to a view of Pompton, skirts a quarry, and descends to the Paterson-Hamburg Turnpike. It follows the road 0.7 mile to Riverdale railroad station.

NEW YORK–NEW JERSEY BOUNDARY WALKS

A way to exercise one's skill in woodcraft is to trace portions of the New York–New Jersey boundary, the southern boundary of Rockland and Orange counties. The dot-and-dash line, which, on the map, separates New Jersey and New York, runs for many miles through the deep woods of the Highlands. At the end of every mile, measured from the Hudson River, there is a small and inconspicuous stone marker. It takes some skill in the use of the topographic map, the compass, and the pace counter to find these markers—in fact, to find even the position of the boundary itself. Unlike Mason and Dixon's Line between Pennsylvania and the South, the New Jersey–

New York boundary is not marked by a wide swath in the woods. To the public, the only sure evidence of its existence is an occasional and inconspicuous stone marker, unnoticed by most travelers, marking the place where the boundary crosses a public road or a railroad.

All the other boundaries of New Jersey are natural shorelines or river courses. Its northeastern boundary was first defined in 1664, when James, Duke of York, sold the Province of New Jersey to Berkeley and Carteret. The terminal points were defined as the mouth of "the northernmost branch of the said bay or river Delaware, which is 41° 40′ of latitude [there is no such point], and the intersection of latitude 41° with Hudson's River." The actual positions of the terminal points were not agreed upon until 1769. In 1770 a joint colonial boundary commission tried to locate the line, but was discomfited by a show of weapons and other evidence of unfriendliness on the part of residents of the coastal plain section and consequently took to the woods to do what it could toward defining the boundary there. The cause of all this, one may surmise, was local satisfaction with a state of affairs which made taxes difficult for either colony to collect. The job was finally completed, however, and mile markers were set in 1774. Most of them can still be found down among the leaves and bushes, with their antiquated and amateurishly carved lettering.

A survey with more modern precision was made just one hundred years later, in 1874, and was followed by a joint state resurvey in 1882, when new markers were set alongside the old stones. The new ones are of granite, with dressed tops six inches square projecting six inches out of the ground. Even these are a little difficult to find, particularly under a heavy snow.

The 1874 and 1882 surveys, made with reference to astronomically fixed positions, revealed that the boundary of 1774 had the general shape of a dog's hind leg, for a reason unsuspected by the pioneers. The 1774 survey was done with the magnetic compass and, since the Highlands are full of magnetic iron ore, the compass line rambles accordingly. At Greenwood Lake the marker was 2415 feet, or nearly half a mile, southwest of the "straight line" (great circle) between the termini. Since the land in the Highlands was of little value, the commissioners, being practical men, left well enough alone and did not disturb the mileposts of 1774. New York State thus retained, through magnetic attraction, a good many acres which the Duke of York intended to convey to the proprietors of New Jersey.

The most interesting walks begin with Stone No. 15 in the town of Suffern, and continue approximately north 60° west for 33.5 miles to Stone No. 49, near Port Jervis. No. 21 is about 0.1 mile east of the old unused road leading north from Ringwood Manor to the Snyder iron mine. No. 23 is about 0.1 mile northwest of the woods road that leads southwest from the vicinity of Sterling Furnace. No. 26 is on the northwest shore of Greenwood Lake. The distance between Nos. 22 and 23 is just under 0.9 mile; evidently someone accidently dropped 10 chains (660 feet) from his count in 1774. In some sections the boundary is hazily indicated by dim dark-red blazes on the trees, deviating from the true course as if marking surveyors' gores. The best time to follow the boundary is in the beginning of winter after the lakes and swamps are frozen, but before the snow has become too deep to permit finding the markers.

GREENWOOD LAKE REGION   *Map 21*

Bearfort Ridge Trail. Length: 2.5 miles. Blazes: white
The Bearfort Ridge Trail begins on Warwick Turnpike in Hewitt about 0.5 mile west of Great Oaks Inn, at the south end of Greenwood Lake (Rt. 511). The trail ascends a dirt road, turns left in 100 yards to enter the A. S. Hewitt State Forest in a hemlock woods. After crossing a stream, the trail makes a strenuous ascent of Bearfort Mountain, from which there are partial views of Upper Greenwood Lake and Greenwood Lake. From here the trail follows picturesque conglomerate rock ridges north to the Ernest Walter Trail. En route, there is a view of the New York City skyline.

Firehouse Trail. Length: 1.67 miles. Blazes: red on white.
This trail begins at a firehouse by Upper Greenwood Lake at the junction of Lakeshore Drive East with Papscoe Road. It follows housing development roads, then enters woods and ascends, crosses a stream, passes Ernest Walter Trail and reaches West Pond (Smoothing Iron Pond). After following a rocky ridge, it ends at the State Line Trail, on top of Bearfort Mountain.

State Line Trail. Length: 1.15 miles. Blazes: blue on white.
The State Line Trail begins at the New York–New Jersey state line on Rt. 511. It ascends steadily to the top of the ridge, passing, en route, the Ernest Walter Trail and a "red" trail, both trails going to Surprise Lake. On top, it meets the end of the Firehouse Trail and continues along the ridge north to the Appalachian Trail.
Ernest Walter Trail. Length: 1.4 miles. Blazes: yellow.
The Ernest Walter Trail was named in honor of a dedicated hiker and trail worker of the Cosmopolitan Club. It connects the State

GREENWOOD LAKE *seen from near* TERRACE POND

Line Trail and the Firehouse Trail. From the former it ascends left to superb views of Greenwood Lake, passes Ernest Walter Shelter and reaches Surprise Lake. From here, it passes through a rhododendron grove, meets Bearfort Ridge Trail and ends at the Firehouse Trail.

Mountain Spring Trail. Length: 0.75 mile. Blazes: blue.
The Mountain Spring Trail begins south of Greenwood Lake Village beside a bowling alley on Rt. 210, just south of a 90-degree bend in the road. It ascends to meet the Appalachian Trail 1.7 miles south of Mt. Peter.

Terrace Pond and Newark Watershed Property.
Bearfort Mountain south of the old Warwick Turnpike is now open to hiking clubs of the New York–New Jersey Trail Conference. The area around Terrace Pond is the most attractive part of this region. This wild gem of water lies at an altitude of 1380 feet, surrounded by high cliffs of puddingstone conglomerate and massive rhododendron and blueberry swamps. Individuals not affiliated with hiking clubs must secure permission to hike in this region by writing to the owner, Sussex Woodlands, Box 338, Hewitt, N.J. Fires, camping, and hunting are prohibited in this privately owned wildlife sanctuary. Swimming in the pond is not encouraged, but is tolerated at the swimmer's risk. The future status of the area is presently insecure, but it is hoped that the State of New Jersey will eventualy add this property to its park and forest system.
A parking area is located on Clinton Road, 1.8 miles from its northern terminus on Warwick Turnpike, and 7.5 miles from its southern terminus at Rt. 23. Here maps and other information about

the area are displayed. On the east side of Clinton Road, across from the parking lot, a "blue" trail leads to the northwest corner of Terrace Pond in 1.5 miles, with several outstanding lookouts. A "yellow" trail leaves from the same place and follows a more circuitous route to the southern end of the pond, terminating in 2.5 miles at a junction with a "white" trail which encircles the pond in 1.2 miles.

At this same junction, a "red" trail takes off in a southeasterly direction and travels 3 miles to Stephens Road where a slight jog to the left will lead to the jeep road to the Bearfort Fire Tower (0.6 mile). Here are fine views in all directions. The easiest approach to the Bearfort Fire Tower for the casual walker is from Stephens Road, which runs for 2 miles between Clinton Road (at 6.5 miles north of Rt. 23) and Union Valley Road (at 4.5 miles north of Rt. 23). Stephens Road is not passable by car. Walk in 0.8 mile from the eastern terminus or 1.3 miles from the western terminus and then south 0.6 mile to the fire tower.

An "orange" trail leaves the Warwick Turnpike at telephone pole No. 25, 1 mile west of the junction of Rts. 210 and 511. This trail follows high ridges with fine views to the northern end of Terrace Pond, where at 3 miles it terminates at a junction with the "white" trail which travels around the pond.

The Newark Watershed to the south of Stephens Road and the Bearfort Fire Tower contains some attractive hiking territory, although there are no marked trails. At the center of the area lies Clinton Reservoir, which can be reached by Clinton Road. An old abandoned footpath leads along the west side of Clinton Reservoir and circles the seldom-seen Buckabear Pond. Also hidden in the area are Cedar Pond, Hank's Pond, and Dunker Pond, all of which can be reached on old abandoned roads. This territory is posted, and parked cars will be ticketed. However, permission to hike in the area may be obtained at the Newark Watershed office in Charlotteburg or by telephoning 201-697-3921.

WAWAYANDA REGION

Wawayanda State Park.

Wawayanda State Park, in the northeastern corner of Sussex County, embraces almost six thousand acres of forests and waters in the rough hilly country of New Jersey's Highland Range. The name "Wa-wa-yanda" is the phonetic redition of the Lenape Indian name, said to mean "water on the mountain." The Appalachian Trail traverses the breadth of the Park, skirting the more developed parts of the region; other trails are planned.

Wawayanda Lake, the focal point of the Park, is a mile and a half long, has five and a half miles of wooded shoreline, and covers 255 acres. Four islands of varying size dot the lake, some with cottages and cottage sites dating back several generations.

This lake was once called Double Pond and was two bodies of water separated by a narrow strip of land which still shows, in part, on the west side of Barker Island in the center of the present lake. In the middle of the last century the Thomas Iron Company built the earthen dam at the northeastern end of the lake. A wing dam also was constructed on the eastern shore over which the waters spill to help feed Laurel Pond. These dams raised the lake level about seven and a half feet.

Laurel Pond, east of Wawayanda Lake, is about ten acres in extent, and is mostly spring-fed. It is a fairly deep lake and is free from contamination. At the southeast end of the Pond, on a steep slope, is a stand of hemlock which is probably the only virgin timber on the mountain. Bear signs have been found in this wild area.

Toward the eastern part of the Wawayanda "Plateau" (it is not a plateau in the geological sense), on which the park is situated, various old wood roads and paths lead southward and penetrate one of the finest jungles of this kind in New Jersey. The cedar swamp and rhododendron, whose great glossy leaves present a tropical display at any season, are glorified in July by the handsome flowers. The extensive stand of southern white cedar (*Chamaecyparis thyoides*), here far away from and above its usual stands along the seacoast marshes, is interesting to students of plant distribution.

Three hundred feet beyond the northeast end of Wawayanda Lake, along the Wawayanda Road, are the remains of a charcoal blast furnace where iron was produced. Oliver Ames and his sons William, Oakes, and Oliver, Jr., constructed it in 1845–46. William supervised the work. His initials "W.L.A." and the date 1846 are still visible on a lintel in the main arch of the old furnace. Shovels and wheels for railroad cars were produced here. During the Civil War, the Ames factories filled government orders for shovels and swords.

The Wawayanda iron mine is 2.5 miles northeast of the iron furnace along the east side of the Wawayanda Road, and consists of five openings or shafts. The largest was a hundred feet in depth, and traveled along a vein of ore twelve to fifteen feet wide. Mules worked in shifts in the mines, hauling the ore and tailings to the

springtime
hillside

Vern

surface. The "Mule Barn" was directly opposite the most south-easterly shaft, across a small creek on the west side of Wawayanda Road. The foundation of the barn still exists. A story told by old-timers in the area claims that several men and one or more mules were buried in a tunnel cave-in.

West of Wawayanda State Park.

After descending from the plateau of Wawayanda Mountain, the Appalachian Trail follows woodlands, fields, and ridges to the Vernon Valley. From here it crosses lowlands to Pochuck Mountain, an isolated block of gneiss of the highlands (8 miles). Much of the adjacent area consists of rolling kames of glacially deposited gravel and some woodland. West of Pochuck, use back roads to reach High Point State Park some 20 miles from Wawayanda.

NORTH OF WAWAYANDA

Adam and Eve.

Two outstanding knobs are Adam and Eve, situated between Florida and Pine Island, N.Y., on the edge of the onion farms. Eve is the higher, and provides excellent views south and west. Adam has an abandoned, water-filled quarry.

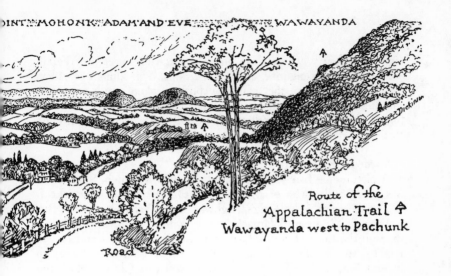

Route of the
Appalachian Trail
Wawayanda west to Pachunk

Road

The best approach is from Warwick. Go north on Rts. 94 and 17A through Florida. At the intersection where 94 and 17A separate, take a hard left into Meadow Road. In 0.5 mile take another left into Roe Street. In 0.1 mile go right into Round Hill Road. Continue south, with onion fields on the right for 2 miles, then jog left and right onto Mt. Eve Road. After 1.5 miles, the road starts uphill. There is a parking area on a woods road just below the height of land.

Mt. Eve

Two minutes walk south from the parking area, take the woods road on the left. The road climbs steadily and easily for ⅞ mile and ends several hundred feet past an old quarrying operation. (Triangulated bench marks can be found on the rocks above the abandoned quarry.) A few steps beyond there is a rock outcropping providing views over Mt. Peter, Bellvale, Bearfort and Wawayanda mountains. Returning to the end of the wood road, follow a faint trail continuing upward and bearing slightly left and then right to another outcropping with views over Walkill Valley, Pochuck Mountain, the Kittatinnies, and High Point.

Mt. Adam.

From the parking area, proceed on the main woods road to the right to a quarry, where there are excellent views over the Walkill Valley, the Shawangunks, and the Catskills. The summit of Adam can be reached from the quarry by bushwhacking south for a few minutes. A more challenging route can be found by walking south on Mt. Eve Road for 0.2 mile to a faint trail, quite overgrown, leading to the quarry. Walk south to the summit.

Sugar Loaf. Length: 1 mile each way.

A picturesque bare knob slightly over 1000 feet high, Sugar Loaf lies 4 to 5 miles west of Monroe, east of the town of Sugar Loaf.

The approach is by King's Highway from Warwick or from Rts. 6/17 and 17. From Warwick follow King's Highway northwest through the town of Sugar Loaf. The road swings right and crosses L.&H.R. tracks. Take the next right turn (Well Sweep Lane) to its end, where there is room to park several cars (do not block the road). From Rts. 6/17 turn left into Well Sweep Lane before crossing the railroad tracks.

From the parking area, go through a gate and follow the main woods road through a stand of red cedar. Continue on the woods road with Sugar Loaf visible on the left; the road follows around Sugar Loaf approximately 180°. After reaching the col between Sugar Loaf and the adjoining 900-foot mountain, follow the woods road left, which finally becomes a trail. Keep left, climbing gradually. The final ascent up the southwest side of Sugar Loaf is steep, with a short rock scramble to the summit. The reward is an outstanding panorama of nearby and distant country.

SUALLY the area extending southward from the Wawayanda Plateau is similar to the northern highlands of the state but more open. Where rough topography has preserved forested valleys and summits, there are worthwhile walks, and there are a number of state parks in this region which have these characteristics and are worth exploring. Due to their scattered locations, however, access can be only by automobile.

JENNY JUMP STATE FOREST

This forest of 966 acres is situated in Warren County, along the Jenny Jump Mountain, between Hope and Great Meadows and lies to the north of the Pequest River at Buttzville. It is about 12 miles southeast of the Delaware Water Gap. Typical of the mountain country in northern New Jersey, elevations range from 399 to 1108 feet. The park presently consists of six detached parcels extending some 8 miles along the ridge, ultimately to be joined as part of a proposed statewide trail. The main tract is immediately south of Rt. 80. Marked trails lead over the ridge tops to the dry east side. The trails on the west side lie lower, but lead through a rich variety of plants, ferns, and lichens. The park portion, 5 miles south, near Mountain Lake, rises to a summit with fine views.

To the hikers, the main features of Jenny Jump State Forest are the spectacular views from forest roads and trails. Toward the west, on clear days, there is an unbroken view of Kittatiny Valley and of Kittatiny Mountain, from Wind Gap, Pennsylvania, to the west, to the highest peak in High Point State Park far to the north. This also includes an unusually fine view of Delaware Water Gap. To the east, the views include Old Silver Mine Valley and the Great Meadows, six thousand acres of rich black muck soil used for intensive truck farming. The contrast of black soil with rows of green vegetables between the hillsides sprinkled with farms and woodlands provides a striking and pleasing panoramic view.

Several picnic areas with sites for family-size groups have been provided. Near the forest headquarters two camp shelters may be rented between April 1 and October 31. The shelters are completely enclosed buildings, each with fireplace-type stove for heating, an out-of-doors fireplace for cooking and bunk facilities for four people. A number of campsites are available for tents or small camp trailers. For further information write to: Forest Officer, Jenny Jump State Park, Hope, N.J. 07844.

A self-guiding trail has been laid out near the Notch picnic area. Along this trail grow five kinds of oak, three kinds of maple, including the striped maple (*Acer pennsylvanicum*), three kinds of pine, three kinds of birch, wild cherry, the slippery elm (*Ulmus ruba*), hornbeam, red cedar, aspen, beech, hemlock, ash, sumac, tulip tree, spruce, walnut, and sassafras. Other species of trees grow nearby as well as a large number of shrubs such as arrowwood, witch hazel, silky camel, and fox grape. Wild flowers and ferns are abundant in season, and the bird life is plentiful and easily observed.

STEPHENS–SAXTON FALLS STATE PARK

Hackettstown, reached by Rt. 46, can be the start of an interesting day's journey. A couple of miles south of the highway is the world's largest freshwater fish hatchery. Returning by car, cross Rt. 46 and continue along Waterloo–Willow Grove Road, or pick up a path northward along the Musconetcong River to Stephens–Saxton Falls State Park. Used primarily as a camping and picnic area, the wooded hillsides and small fields of this 228-acre park were donated in part in 1937 by the late Marsena P. and Augustus W. Stephens. Continue north by the road or the stream for 1 mile to Saxton Falls. This area of varied topographical features and the remnants of the old Morris Canal make the Muscontecong River one of the most interesting streams in New Jersey. At the Falls are the well-preserved remains of one of the twenty-eight locks of the Canal, and directly below the lock structure is a section of the canal and adjoining tow path.

ALLAMUCHY MOUNTAIN STATE PARK

Immediately to the north of Stephen–Saxton Falls State Park, this potential 15,000-acre park embraces both banks of the Musconetcong River and Allamuchy and Deer Park ponds. This fine wooded area will provide miles of hiking. Near Rt. 80 is the restored village of Andover Forge, once a busy port along the Morris Canal; earlier, it was part of the Andover iron forge, which produced cannonballs for the Colonists. For half a century, beginning in 1832, the Morris Canal was the chief means of conveying coal, iron, and zinc across New Jersey. It was 90 miles long, and the trip from Newark to Phillipsburg required five days. Lake Hopatcong State Park, where other reminders of the canal may be seen, is several miles east on Rt. 80.

MUSCONETCONG STATE PARK

This 343-acre park is located in Stanhope, just north of Netcong, on Rt. 206. The State owns the 315-acre Lake Musconetcong and 24 acres of approaches, which gives the public access to the lake. Facilities are available for bathing and fishing.

HOPATCONG STATE PARK

This park is located in Morris and Sussex counties at the lower end of Lake Hopatcong, 9 miles long with over 60 miles of shoreline. Except for the park, it is quite completely built up with hotels and private cottages. It can be reached from Rt. 80 by way of Landing or from Rt. 206 at Netcong. The park includes 107 acres of land and a section of the old Morris Canal. The dam and gate house which control the lake level are in the park, which has been designated as a wildlife sanctuary. Activities such as fishing, bathing, boating, and picnicking are available. The park is open during daylight hours throughout the year.

HACKLEBARNEY STATE PARK

Lying about 3 miles southwest of Chester, and the intersection of Rts. 24 and 206, this park will eventually contain 1500 acres. Situated along the deep gorge of the Black River, the park is traversed by a system of winding footpaths. Its topography, with its ridges of gneiss, is rather rugged. An elevation of 804 feet is attained on the west side of Black River.

One story about the origins of the park's name states that a quick-tempered iron ore foreman in the vicinity was persistently heckled and soon "Heckle" Barney, as he was called, became Hacklebarney. Another theory is that the name is of Lenni-Lenape derivation. A feature worth noting is "Indian Mill"—a pothole in the stream.

VOORHEES STATE PARK

This park is situated in the rolling hills of Hunterdon County along the High Bridge–Long Valley Road (Rt. 513). The entrance is 5 miles north of Clinton, via Rts. 31 and 513. The park covers 437 acres, and drives make the area accessible to motorists. Well-marked trails take the hiker through several miles of the park. Along the nature trails beside the brook are hundreds of flowering plants in season and many species of hardwood trees native to north-central New Jersey. Deer, small mammals, and many species of birds are plentiful.

Picnic areas have been developed on various sections of the park and campsites for family use are available in an attractive wooded area. For further information write to: Voorhees State Park, R.D., Glen Gardner, N.J. 08826.

ROUND VALLEY RECREATION AREA

Annandale, reached by either Rt. 78 or Rt. 22, is the center for a number of pleasant jaunts. A couple of miles to the north, at Highbridge, is the picturesque Raritan River gorge. Named for the railroad trestle, the town is still the site of an operating iron works which made cannonballs for Washington's army. A few scenic trails extend up the valley. North of Highbridge the road continues to the rugged terrain of Voorhees State Park, and about a mile to the south of the park is Spruce Run, a recreation area.

Another possibility is to go southeastward from Annandale a couple of miles to the Round Valley Recreation Area (Cushetunk Mountain), a curious horseshoe-shaped ridge encircling a reservoir. The trap rock is similar to the diabase of the Palisades of the Hudson and part of the same outflows of Triassic time. The rocks of this curving ridge had their origin in an intrusion of diabase between strata of the Brunswick shales and sandstones of the Triassic formation. They were eventually exposed by erosion, which wore down the softer shales above and around and left the harder igneous material standing 800 feet above sea level and 400 feet above the surrounding Hunterdon countryside.

A hiking trail almost 10 miles in length completely circles the reservoir and there are various campsites for use by hikers. At the northern end of the horseshoe, descend in a northwesterly direction to Cherry Street to travel back to the cars, using the reservoir area instead of walking the road. The Cushetunk Ridge, never having been glaciated as were the Palisades, has more residual soil than the latter. A good second growth of hardwood covers most of its upper portion. The region is particularly attractive in spring, at the time of the blossoming dogwood, which is plentiful on the slopes of the ridge. There are good views eastward over the plain of the valley of the Raritan, bordered on the south by similar trap ridges, which are also southwestward extension of the Palisades intrusion. Half a mile west of the south limb of the Cushetunk horseshoe, in abandoned limestone quarries, are the remains of the kilns where the rock was burned. The rock has a peculiar blue color, possibly due to its manganese content. Four miles north of Round Valley Reservoir a smaller horseshoe of diabase shows a curious topography. The Brunswick shales of the interior valley are open, while the contact with the trap rock and border conglomerates is generally indicated by the forest which covers the ridge.

16 · THE WATCHUNGS
AND CENTRAL NEW JERSEY

INTRODUCTION

o HILLS of any height appear in northern New Jersey west of the Hudson River until the Watchungs—"Wach Unks" (high hills) of the Indians—are reached. It was for that reason that they played such an important part in the Revolution. A double line of ridges from one to two miles apart running southwest into Somerset County, where they both turn west and finally northwest, they served both as fortifications and as outlook points for Washington and his armies. As outlook points they are still of interest. In fact, the views obtainable from the First Mountain are its chief attraction.

The northern end of the First Watchung is Garret Rock (533 feet) overlooking the City of Paterson. From there the ridge runs southwest to Eagle Rock Reservation (620 feet) and then to South Mountain Reservation (589 feet), both of which are in Essex County. The First Watchung continues southwest into Union County, where, between Summit and Scotch Plains, is the Watchung Reservation (487 feet). At Bound Brook the ridge swings west and then northwest, its southern end having an elevation of 589 feet.

At the northern end of the Second Watchung are High Mountain (879 feet) and Beech Mountain (866 feet), the latter at the northern end of the Preakness Hills. From there southwest the only public areas along the Second Watchung are in South Mountain Reservation and the Watchung Reservation, both of which reservations straddle the two ridges.

These two ridges are not high, the highest elevations, except at the two ends, being under 600 feet. Moreover, they run through a densely populated area, with the result that the principal areas with pathways available for hiking are those in the various county parks and reservations. Suburban developments have inundated all but isolated sections just as a rising tide submerges all but the highest points of a rocky reef running into the sea.

These outstanding walls of basalt (commercially, "trap rock") form natural ramparts which could not have been better designed by a military engineer for General Washington's needs and purposes. Washington knew nothing of their geological origin, but he was a good military engineer.

The double line of the Watchungs was further engineered by nature in that its flanks recurve, from Bound Brook back to Bernardsville on the south and from Paterson around to Oakland on the north, right up to the older, solid mass of the Precambrian granites and gneisses of the Ramapos. Cross faulting of the Watchung ridge at Paterson, Great Notch, Summit, Plainfield, and Bound Brook made convenient and easily defended sally ports from this great field fortress, with its front of fifty miles. The fronts of the ridges were steep and easy to protect and afforded numerous watching posts from which to spy on movements of the British in the lowlands to the east.

The British never passed the great double line of the Watchungs in force. They marched along the foot of the columned cliffs of First Watchung on their way to Trenton, in December 1776, but, when Washington turned and captured the Hessian garrison and fought the British at Princeton, he eluded the superior forces that soon gathered, and escaped into his hill fortress to Morristown, via the north branch of the Raritan, where the enemy feared to pursue him. The only occasion when the British penetrated the Watchung barrier was in December 1776, when a small cavalry patrol surprised General Charles Lee and his aides in a tavern at Basking Ridge, and it would have been better for the Americans if Lee had remained a prisoner. Never afterward did any British or Hessians pass these ridges. Washington made his main camp at Morristown and its outposts stronger every month, and it served as a rallying place and source of supplies for the rest of the war.

During the winter of 1779–80, the rugged hill country around

Morristown again sheltered the main encampments of the Continental Army while Morristown was Washington's headquarters. The (Jacob) Ford Mansion, which was Washington's headquarters, is now part of the Morristown National Historical Park. The Mansion and the Historical Museum are both worth visiting. The encampments were located in Jockey Hollow about four miles south of Morristown. About a thousand acres of this land, including all but three units of the military camp site, are within the boundaries of the park. In its generally wooded and rural appearance, Jockey Hollow today closely resembles the conditions existing when the Continental troops arrived there in December 1779. Many of the camp grounds have remained relatively undisturbed, and observing visitors can still see physical evidences of army occupation. Careful historical and archeological research has led to the reconstruction of several log huts, typical of hundreds once used as quarters for officers and men.

About a mile from Morristown on the way to Jockey Hollow is a reconstruction of Fort Nonsense, erected in 1937. Most of the army supplies for the 1777 spring campaign were concentrated in Morristown and their protection became essential. On May 28, therefore, Washington issued orders for one detachment to remain in the town "to Strengthen the Works already begun upon the Hill near this place, and erect such other as are necessary for the better defending it, that it may be a safe retreat in case of Necessity." How the works came to be called Fort Nonsense is not yet known but there is some evidence to show the name was of Revolutionary War origin.

JOCKEY HOLLOW

Jockey Hollow is the beautiful hilly area where our Continental Army encamped two winters during the Revolution. It is part of the Morristown National Historical Park and abounds with huge oak and tulip trees and is enriched with reconstructed buildings of the Revolutionary era. Nearby Morristown is easily reached by train from Hoboken or bus from New York City. A taxi can be taken the 3 miles to the park; or you can use the parking lot provided at the lunch area.

A maintained trail completely encircles the Park, allowing a hike of 6.5 miles. Starting at the south end of the lunch area parking lot on Jockey Hollow Road (Western Avenue in Morristown), follow the Wildflower Trail east for 0.3 mile. At the top of the hill, take the left fork (short loop), and descend to the brook. Turn right, and follow the path and brook to a dirt road.

Turn left, and follow the dirt road until a small bridge is crossed. A hundred feet beyond, turn right and proceed in a northeasterly direction. Maintain this direction past another dirt road coming in from the left, and then past a small artificial pond on the right.

At the next intersection make a sharp left turn, and proceed west up a hill. Continue across the paved road, down a slope, and then up Sugar Loaf. If you hike quietly, you may see deer in this area.

Continue on the trail along the northern side of Sugar Loaf to the view point. Watnong Mountain is on the far side of Washington Valley, 4 miles north of the Park. The trail gradually veers south through a handsome stand of birch and then on down to a paved road.

Turn left (south) and walk along the road. Shortly a field will appear on the left and on the far hillside a number of cabins. These cabins were reconstructed by the National Park Service and are typical of the quarters provided the officers and enlisted men of the Revolution.

Following a visit to these cabins, proceed down the hill to the southwest to the hospital and the graveyard. After inspecting these, continue 100 yards farther on the paved road. Here, either continue on the paved road to the Wick House, or take a path to the right through the woods. If the path is taken, keep bearing left at all the trail intersections, eventually coming to the same paved road again. Turn right, and head south on the road until the Wick House is reached. The Wick House was built about 1750 and has been restored and furnished. It served as military quarters for Major General Arthur St. Clair during the Continental Army encampment of 1779–80.

After leaving the Wick House, hike west down the paved road past the ranger station. About 300 yards on the left, pick up a dirt road which winds up a hill in a southerly direction. At the next intersection, keep left, as the road to the right goes into a Girl Scout camp.

Follow this trail as it wends its way east and then gradually turns back north. At any intersections encountered, take the left fork. Cross over the paved road, and continue approximately 1 mile. After crossing over two bridges, watch for the Wildflower Trail on the left with steppingstones to cross the brook. Follow the trail and brook back to the starting parking lot.

Much work has been completed on the development of the Patriot's Path. When completed, it will be an excellent access route from the center of Morristown, along the Whippany River, to Jockey Hollow. Many historical sites lie on the path, making it well worth a hike itself.

Boy Scout Jockey Hollow Trail. Length: 17 miles.

Some of the most beautiful country in Somerset and Morris counties is seen on this hike between Gladstone and Morristown, a hike taken by thousands of Boy Scouts each year. Railroad service is available to both towns from Hoboken.

Although the route is over roads for almost the entire length, the roads are very infrequently used, so car traffic is no problem. The hike begins at the corner of Rt. 512 and Mendham Road in the town of Peapack-Gladstone. The Ellis–Tiger Hardware & Lumber Co. on this road junction will be the most prominent landmark. Proceed in a northwesterly direction on Mendham Road for 0.4 mile. Turn right on Mosle Road (Mount St. John Academy sign); although it is paved at first, it soon becomes a dirt road leading to the Union School House, built in 1851. Turn right on Pleasant Valley Road; at 0.3 mile is the main entrance of the Schiff Scout Reservation, the National Training School of the Boy Scouts of America.

Although the scouts go through the Reservation as part of their hike, it is suggested that others continue along Pleasant Valley Road. At the next intersection, turn left on Hilltop Road. Continue north 0.5 mile to Cherry Lane, which turns off to the right (east). Follow Cherry Lane to Hardscrabble Road (dirt), turn right, and travel as far as Jockey Hollow Road. Here make a left turn, and walk for 1.8 mile to Tempe Wick Road. Turn right, and hike up the hill past the Wick House. Just beyond is Jockey Hollow Road–Western Avenue, which traverses the Morristown National Historical Park to Morristown, 4 miles distant. Continue past this road and in 0.25 mile turn left onto a yellow-blazed trail which goes east and then northward along a stream. After ascending Mt. Kemble, and about 1.75 miles after entering the path, a park road leads downhill to the left, intersecting the road leading to Morristown. (For those so inclined, a trail persists along the mountain ridge to Fort Nonsense.) Swing right toward Morristown. Before the center of the town is reached, a street on the right leads to Fort Nonsense. This side trip is well worthwhile. Return to the main road (Western Avenue) and continue to its end at Washington Street (Rt. 24). Here turn right, and go down to the center of town. There is a large green, with streets emanating from each of its corners as they did when Washington and the Continental Army were camped in the area. At the end of the green, turn left (north) and continue down Morris Street past the post office to the railroad station. If time permits, continue several blocks to the Ford Mansion (George Washington's headquarters). Here the National Park Service has a marvelous display of Revolutionary furniture, clothing, and equipment.

GREAT SWAMP NATIONAL WILDLIFE REFUGE

The Great Swamp, a "postage stamp wilderness," is located in Morris and Somerset counties, thirty miles west of Manhattan Island. It occupies most of a basin which is a vestige of prehistoric Lake Passaic. About eight thousand acres are in marshland, meadows, and dry woodlands. The Passaic River flows through the westerly section. Converging climatic zones in the swamp produce an unusual variety of plant life, which in turn supports a wide range of animal and bird species. The yellow marsh marigold in early April, blue iris in May, and the magnificent display of pink and white mountain laurel in June are great attractions. There are three varieties of ground pine (*Lycopodium*) in the woods. Many woodland mammals live here, as well as 180 species of birds. The Great Swamp is unique today because of the scope of its ecology in the most populous area of the United States.

In order to preserve the natural environment, the U. S. Department of the Interior established a National Wildlife Refuge in the Great Swamp. Subsequently, under the Wilderness Act of 1964, the Department designated a larger portion to be included in the Wilderness System. Permission has been given the Morris County Park Commission to use the land for nature walks. The Commission operates a nature education center off Jay Road in Chatham Township. A boardwalk and series of paths enter the swamp at this point and penetrate into it for a short distance.

To reach this area, drive from the center of Chatham over Fairmount Avenue to Southern Boulevard. Turn right on the Boulevard, and drive about 1 mile to where there is a school on the right and Jay Road on the left. Turn into Jay Road. The Nature Center is at the end. There is a circular 1-mile nature trail from the Center. A map and description of the whole area are available at the Center.

WATCHUNG RESERVATION

The Watchung Reservation, maintained by the Union County Park Commission, is a 2000-acre wooded tract in the Watchung Mountains where animal and plant life are protected. Although there are footpaths and bridle trails throughout, most of it remains in a natural wild state.

High spots of the park include Surprise Lake, the Deserted Village, Trailside Nature and Science Center, the plant nursery, an observation tower, Seeley's Pond, and numerous picnic areas. The dogwood and rhododendron displays in May and early June are outstanding.

Drive or take a bus west along Rt. 22 to the traffic light at New Providence Road, just west of Mountainside. If going by bus, there is a 2-mile walk up the hill to the Lake Surprise parking area. Whether walking or driving, follow the signs marked "Lake Surprise" until a large traffic circle with a refreshment stand in the center is reached.

From this point an interesting 5-mile walk can be taken, the Deserted Village Circular. Take the path down the hill past the restrooms to the boathouse at the edge of the lake. Turn right, pass the Girl Scout cabin above, go around the end of the lake, by the Boy Scout cabin on the hill, and then onto the dam. Cut back across in front on the dam, and follow the path along the brook to the bridge. Cross the bridge, bear left at the fork, and walk to the blacktop road to the deserted village. Turn left, passing houses built in 1840. A bulletin board on the right tells something about the

Summit   Hospital   Hook Mountain in distance

Summit

The Watchung ranges from Summit Observatory tower

Watchung
Ranges
Plainfield

village. Follow this blacktop road until you come to the third road on the left (going downhill). The road has hemlock trees on the right and there are ruins of an old mill. Cross the bridge to see the Glen, then bear right up an old dirt road with the Hemlock Gorge on the right. Follow this until a trail on the left is reached. Take

Second Mountain   First Mountain with Quarry and Washington Rock   The Oranges   Balustrol

all Oranges

links

Looking North to First & Second Mountain & the Oranges

this trail, bearing left at the fork and going on down to the Trailside Nature and Science Center. After browsing through the museum and zoo, follow the road through the nursery back to the traffic circle.

At the museum are a map of the Reservation, a guide to the museum, and a book containing the story of the deserted village. The map shows enough trails to make a 10-mile hike.

SOUTH MOUNTAIN RESERVATION

South Mountain Reservation, which is maintained by the Essex County Park Commission, is a beautiful hilly wooded area north of Millburn. There are many footpaths and bridle trails throughout. In the northeastern section, Turtle Back Rock is an interesting rock formation, and the Turtle Back Zoo displays animals from many parts of the world. The Deer Paddock and Hemlock Falls, a beautiful natural waterfall, are in the southeastern portion. There are numerous picnic areas throughout, and fine views may be had from several spots along Crest Drive.

The Reservation can be visited by car, bus, or train to Millburn. The Locust Grove picnic area is across the road from the railroad station. Following is an outline of the "Hemlock Falls Circular" walk from there.

POND – SOUTH MOUNTAIN
RESERVATION NEAR MILBURN

Starting at the Locust Grove picnic area, take the footpath past the old quarry on the right. Go up into Sunset Trail where, on the left, take the footpath to Maple Falls, Lilliput Knob, Beechbrook Cascades, Mines Point, and Balls Bluff. Then go down the Balls Bluff Trail to River Trail—right into the footpath between the hemlocks to the Falls. Return along the River Trail, passing the Balls Bluff Trail and taking the next trail left up the hill, and then take the first right, which is Bear Lane. This goes past the Deer Paddock to Crest Drive. Turn right into the footpath following the Drive to Washington Rock. This is the spot where George Washington surveyed the countryside during the Revolution. Follow the footpath down the hill from the Rock and left back to Locust Grove.

PREAKNESS RANGE AND HIGH MOUNTAIN

Geologically, the Preakness Range north of Paterson is a continuation of the second Watchung Mountain, although the Passaic River flows through a considerable gap between them. Similar to the Palisades far to the east in that its composition is resistant igneous rock and composed of basalt as at Packanack Mountain to the west, Preakness is the middle of a three-layer basalt series lying roughly parallel to one another.

Much of this range is occupied by Paterson State College, a golf course, Urban Farms Development, and private estates. At its northern end, however, there is an area of wild wooded country, about 3 to 3.5 miles long and 2 to 2.5 miles wide, which is still available for hiking. The main attraction is the wonderfully unobstructed and extensive view from High Mountain (879 feet). Northwest and north lie the range of the Ramapo Mountains with Suffern and the gap of the Ramapo River slightly east of the north point. To the east the horizon is bounded by the Palisades with Hook Mountain at the northeast. Southeast the skyscrapers of Manhattan are visible, with the towers of the George Washington Bridge north of them. Nearer are the towns of Wyckoff and Ridgewood (northeast), and Fairlawn (east), with Paterson lying in the bowl of the valley. Directly opposite is the long slope of the "Goffle" or ridge of the First Watchung Mountain. The eastern cliff is almost vertical, but this cannot be seen. To the south is the abrupt drop of Garret Mountain.

To reach High Mountain from Paterson, get off the bus at Park Place and climb steadily, up the east slope, to the summit. A gate closes off the road for private cars, but so far no objection has been raised to its use by pedestrians.

Those desiring a longer walk should leave the bus at Overlook Avenue. There is a trail from the garage at Overlook Avenue, marked in yellow, which runs first west by an old sandstone quarry. This quarry supplied stone for many of the old houses in the area. Buttermilk or Bridal Veil Falls is formed by a brook dropping into the quarry. Although these Falls are dry most of the year, they frequently freeze in winter into a beautiful cone. On the face of the cliff the contact between the sandstone below and the trap rock above is visible. An 8.2-acre tract comprising this area has been added to the 250 acres of Paterson State College, which lies directly west and south of here.

The yellow trail swings north from the quarry, and in the next depression notice the southern terminus of a red-marked trail which winds northwesterly to end at the spring, mentioned below. The yellow marks next lead around Pennyroyal Hill and, in a little more than 1 mile farther, over High Mountain. Continuing west for about 0.8 mile, the trail crosses a small stream and then turns left onto a wood road and uphill to an excellent spring (0.3 mile). This is the location of the northern terminus of the red trail mentioned above.

Proceed westward on the yellow trail over a low ridge, and descend into a cleft in the hills running north and south. Notice here not only that the yellow trail turns right but also that a white trail coming from the left terminates on this spot. This white trail goes south, past the reservoir and the fairways of the North Jersey Country Club, for a distance of about 0.5 mile. Here it turns left and then crosses a brook and starts uphill, eastward, finally to end as it reaches the red trail, referred to earlier, on the height of land.

The yellow trail winds along the bottom of the gully until it turns westward and climbs steeply up to the crest of Beech Mountain, by way of a wood road. Proceed along the crest, but be aware of a yellow-marked spur trail that leads in a large loop to a marvelous view over Franklin Lake to the distant Bearfort Range. A short distance beyond the spur trail the main route curves westward and downhill. Before descending too far, however, there is a rewarding lookout from a bare rise, just off the rout eon the left. This view affords a sweeping panorama over Point View Reservoir and across Wayne to the Pompton Hills. From here the yellow trail winds its way down to the new road established through Franklin Cove to Franklin Lake. The triple symbol of the western terminus of the trail is painted on a utility pole on the north side of Hamburg Turnpike, a short distance east of the traffic light at Valley Road.

Geologically, the clove and lake are interesting. Franklin Clove is a fault zone, or area of crustal displacement, about 0.5 mile long in the trap rock ridge through which a considerable stream must have flowed during the retreat of the ice. This deep shady pass is similar to many seen along the trap ridges but is much the deepest and longest. It has its counterparts in Long Clove and Short Clove below Haverstraw.

Franklin Lake is the largest of a series of ponds occupying depressions among the kames of the glacial drift covering the plain to the north. Along the ice front more or less stratified sand and gravel were deposited. With the retreat of the ice, the glacial drift settled into the irregular knolls, called kames, which are characteristic of glaciated lowland.

MILLSTONE VALLEY

Few of North America's rivers flow northward. One of the exceptions is the little Millstone, the axis of a charming valley of modest hills and green prairies. The river, from Carnegie Lake at Princeton to its junction with the Raritan near Bound Brook, provides a delightful canoe trip when the rains have been adequate and if one is willing to portage occasionally.

Parallel to the river is the Delaware and Raritan Canal, which extends all the way from the Delaware River at Trenton to New Brunswick on the Raritan River. This was a functioning canal from 1834 to 1933, but now it is owned by the state and used for recreational purposes only. Fishing is a common pursuit, and canoeing, again with portages, can be enjoyed, combining a southward stretch along the canal with a downstream paddle on the river to make a round trip. Ordinary road maps or the Hagstrom Somerset County map will furnish adequate guidance for access to the towpath.

Most of the towpath provides excellent walking. At Princeton the path follows the shore of Carnegie Lake. Three miles from the start, a huge red mill and abundant water at Kingston form an impressive picture. In another 2 miles is Rocky Hill; here at the Berrien House, overlooking the canal, General Washington drafted his Farewell Address. The locks, the little swing bridges, and the canal tenders' shacks are characteristic of the route. From Griggstown on, the scenic beauty is especially notable. One caution: watch for poison ivy.

From Blackwell's Mills north, the road on the east side of the canal to the village of East Millstone is little traveled and provides an attractive alternate route to the towpath to Millstone. Between

Millstone and Bound Brook, the religious community of Zarephath is of interest. The path continues along the Raritan Valley, another 7 miles beyond Bound Brook to New Brunswick.

Another attraction in the Millstone valley is a 136-acre forest tract, of which 65 acres are virgin forest, long known as Mettler's Woods. Widespread contributions, capped by a major one from the Carpenters' Union, have preserved this as the William L. Hutcheson Memorial Forest. It is used for teaching and research by Rutgers University. The Forest, located on Amwell Road (Rt. 514) about 2 miles east of East Millstone, is open to the public only on guided tours. Information can be secured from the Forest Director at Rutgers University, New Brunswick.

INTRODUCTION

PORT JERVIS to Delaware Water Gap is a 40-mile span that runs along the Delaware River. Paralleling the river is the long, rocky, wooded ridge of Kittatinny Mountain, the Indian name for "Big Mountain." The elevations range from 1400 to 1800 feet at High Point at its northern end. The ridge continues on the Pennsylvania side of the Water Gap southwest to Wind Gap and beyond. Northeast, the ridge continues into New York State as the Shawangunk Mountains.

The New Jersey Department of Environmental Protection long sought to acquire as a State Park or Forest the whole of Kittatinny Mountain and its borders. While this has not proved possible as a whole, a continuous stretch of mountain extending nearly twenty-five miles south from the New York line has been acquired. This stretch includes High Point State Park and Stokes State Forest.

The Stokes State Forest, north and south of Culvers Gap and west of Branchville and Beemersville, now comprises 13,630 acres. High Point State Park, extending from the New York line southward for ten miles and comprising 12,270 acres, was given to the state in 1923 by the late Colonel Anthony R. Kuser of Bernardsville, New

Jersey. It includes Lake Marcia, the highest lake in the state (1570 feet elevation), and Colonel Kuser's former residence on the western ridge.

The views from the Kittatinnies are spectacular. That from High Point is the most extensive, in view of the unbroken panoramas to the east, west, north, and south, as well as along the mountain ridges to the southwest as far as Mt. Tammany, overlooking the Delaware Water Gap. Sunrise Mountain in the northern part of Stokes State Forest has a view second only to that from High Point. In addition, there are innumerable outlook points along the Appalachian Trail as it follows the crest of the Kittatinny ridge southwest to the Delaware Water Gap.

In 1930 a tall monument, modeled after the Bunker Hill tower, was erected on High Point (1803 feet, the highest elevation in New Jersey) as a memorial to the soldiers, sailors, and aviators of the state in all previous wars. It is one of the most conspicuous landmarks for many miles around.

The Appalachian Trail runs through both High Point State Park and Stokes State Forest. Detailed trail descriptions for the Appalachian Trail in this section and south along Kittatinny Mountain to the Water Gap may be found in the *Guide to the Appalachian Trail in New York and New Jersey*. Some suggested trips using portions of the trail in the Kittatinny area are described later in this sectoin.

HIGH POINT STATE PARK

Colonel Kuser's residence—now known as the "Lodge" and located more than 1600 feet above sea level—is maintained by the New Jersey Department of Environmental Protection for the convenience of visitors. Sleeping accommodations are available for from one night to a full week at reasonable rates throughout the summer, and on weekends only in the winter. Restaurants are available not too far away. The view from the broad veranda which encircles the Lodge includes the winding Delaware and the ranges of the Kittatinnies, Poconos, Shawangunks, and Catskills, as well as the hills and mountains of northern New Jersey to the east. For further information, write or telephone the Park Superintendent, Sussex, N.J. 07461.

The Lodge makes an excellent base for weekend trips on the Appalachian Trail over the mountains to the south.

Naturalists will also enjoy a visit to a swampland area about one mile north of the Lodge, for its unusual association of plants. Southern white cedar, common to the Pine Barrens of southern New Jersey, and red spruce, usually found growing farther north and at higher elevations, grow side by side in a unique combination that has few counterparts in the East. The area is easily accessible by a road that encircles the swamp and is banked high with great masses of rhododendron, tall hemlock, and pines. Moisture-loving plants grow in great variety and profusion.

A pleasant 3- or 4-hour walk (about 6 miles) on the Appalachian Trail may be arranged by spotting cars at two trail-crossing points. One is at Williams Corners on Mountain Road (Rt. 519) 1.5 miles north of Rt. 23. The other crossing point is at Mashipacong Road (formerly Deckertown Turnpike). This is reached by returning to Rt. 23 (here 23 and 519 are on the same route), going east on 23 to a short distance below Colesville, then south following 519 for 1.5 miles to Mashipacong Road, right at this point for about 0.5 mile to where the trail crosses at the top of the ridge.

Starting southward, at Williams Corner, the trail enters an open field, then shortly begins to climb sharply through woods which parallel a brook. After a short level stretch the trail passes High Point shelter No. 1, an open lean-to pleasantly situated by another small stream. After a second short steep ascent, the trail reaches the ridge crest near Lake Marcia, and follows a roadway south to Rt. 23. This first portion of the walk shows the striking transition between the valley farmland and the oak and scrub growth characteristic of the heights of Kittatinny ridge.

After crossing Rt. 23, the Appalachian Trail essentially follows the ridge crest south, although with several dips to transfer from one subsidiary spur to a parallel one. Outlooks to the valley lands east and west are frequent, with Lake Rutherford to the east a prominent feature for some distance. About 3 miles south of Rt. 23, a side trail leads left to High Point shelter No. 2. After passing this point, the main trail follows a rough roadway through the woods for its final half mile before coming to the Deckertown Turnpike crossing. This concludes the walk. To visit shelter No. 3, continue on the trail beyond the Turnpike for another few hundred feet, near the southern boundary of High Point Park.

STOKES STATE FOREST

No public accommodations comparable to the Lodge at High Point (see above) are available in Stokes State Forest to the south. However, a number of public campsites as well as several shelters on the Appalachian Trail afford overnight facilities for suitably equipped parties. For information, write the Superintendent, Stokes State Forest, Branchville, N.J. 07826. Descriptive brochures and local trail maps may also be obtained from the Superintendent. Park headquarters are located on the north side of Rt. 206 about 1.5 miles west of Culvers Lake.

A system of foot trails in Stokes State Forest, mostly north of Rt. 206, offers many possibilities for walks of various lengths. Since marking and maintenance are sometimes substandard, however, it is advisable to obtain up-to-date information from the Superintendent or the ranger on duty before planning a specific walk on any of the lesser trails.

The Appalachian Trail continues south through Stokes State Forest after traversing 2 or 3 miles of private property below the southern boundary of High Point Park. By using two or more cars to reach the end points, the length of the trail within the Forest (approximately 8 miles) can easily be walked in a day. From Rt. 206 near Culvers Gap, automobiles may be driven north on Sunrise Mountain Road to a parking area at the end of a spur road to Sunrise Mountain, and south past Kittatinny Lake on Woods Road to Brink Road, where there is a trail shelter. If a somewhat longer walk is desired, the northerly spotting point may be placed at Deckertown Turnpike, reached by a circuitous continuation of Sunrise Mountain Road.

A large stone rain shelter on Sunrise Mountain, much used by picnic parties, is strategically located for valley views in all directions; High Point monument is prominent to the north. To the south, the Appalachian Trail parallels the Sunrise Mountain Road, passing through woods and scrub growth with occasional views. The Gren Anderson Shelter and a spring (not infallible in exceptionally dry seasons) are located on a short side trail leading to the Sunrise Mountain Road, about 2 miles from Sunrise Mountain. The Trail passes a fire tower after another mile, and beyond this descends steadily for the better part of a mile to the Upper North Shore Road of Culvers Lake, which it follows for a half mile to Rt. 206.

Crossing the highway, the Appalachian Trail ascends sharply to the summit of the opposite ridge, following the crest for three miles to the Brink Road, where the Brink Road Shelter is located 0.2 mile to the west. The Brink Road is not the actual boundary of Stokes State Forest; to reach this boundary, continue across the road on the Appalachian Trail for another mile, climbing 300 feet to a ridge with fine views toward the Delaware Valley, then retrace the route to the Brink Road.

One outstanding feature of Stokes Forest is Tillman Ravine at the southern end; this is easily accessible by a well-used path leading off the Brink Road. The steep banks of the ravine are covered with hemlock and rhododendron and there are, in seasons of high water, fine cascades near its upper end.

Paralleling the Appalachian Trail in Stokes State Forest, 0.8 mile to the west, is the 4-mile Swenson Trail. To reach it, turn west from the AT at Crigger Road. It is a level walk until Crigger Brook crossing, where it begins to ascend. Portions of the area were logged fifty to seventy-five years ago, and the oak forest, which is typical of such conditions, is in evidence. The remains of the chestnut forest that blanketed this region before the 1920 blight, introduced from Europe, can be graphically seen at Stony Lake, where the trail ends. Large chestnut stubs stand, now gray and bare of branches, as mute evidence of the ability of man to make gross ecological changes.

The Tinsley Trail is one of three connecting the Swenson Trail with the AT. It is about 1.5 miles south of Crigger Road. This trail passes through typical hardwood forests of oak, maple, hickory, birch, and stands of mountain laurel. A mile farther south is another connecting link, the Stony Brook Trail, a moderately steep descent, but interesting for its fungi and lichen. A final connection, about a mile beyond, is the Tower Trail.

DELAWARE WATER GAP NATIONAL RECREATION AREA

On September 1, 1965, President Lyndon B. Johnson signed into law the Act authorizing establishment of the Delaware Water Gap National Recreation Area. This National Recreation Area, to be developed as an integral part of the Tocks Island Dam and Reservoir project, includes the Kittatinny Mountain from the southern extremity of Stokes State Forest southward across the Water Gap to Totts Gap in Pennsylvania. It also includes the former Worthington (New Jersey) State Forest which extended approximately seven miles north along the ridge and included about five thousand acres of the surrounding mountainous terrain. The beautiful glacial lake, Sunfish Pond, was recently restored to the state by the public utility which had planned a pumped storage project there, after a long and stubborn fight to save it by conservationists and hikers.

This National Recreation Area will complete the link of public ownership from the New York–New Jersey state line through New Jersey and about three miles beyond the Water Gap into Pennsylvania.

The Appalachian Trail is included within the area to be acquired for the National Recreation Area. The Area, when it is in full operation, will consist of about 60,000 acres of land surrounding the 12,000-acre multiple-purpose Tocks Island Reservoir. The Recreation Area will also encompass about six miles of river below the dam and numerous scientifically and recreationally significant lands including the Delaware Water Gap itself. The Recreation Area, like the reservoir, is scheduled to be in full operation by 1977. Some recreation facilities, not dependent on the reservoir, have been provided since 1968.

Upstream from the scenically famous Delaware Water Gap surrounding a man-made lake extending for almost thirty-seven miles along the Delaware River Valley, the National Park Service will offer recreational opportunities for an estimated ten million visitors annually. Since much of this visitation will occur between June 1 and September 15, it is estimated that on weekends and holidays as many as 150,000 visitors may be in the Area at one time. Through careful planning and management it is hoped that this heavy load can be absorbed without damage to area values or overcrowding of some sections and underuse of others.

Future developments will provide opportunities for almost every type of outdoor recreation associated with the natural, historical, and recreational resources of the area. Twenty bathing beaches of varying sizes are planned, with long stretches of undeveloped scenic shoreline between them. Four major boating centers will have facilities for launching, docking, and servicing of boats.

Camping and picnicking facilities will be developed, maintaining the proper atmosphere. For hikers there will be three interconnected systems of trails. These will consist of:

(1) a system of short, easy interpretive trails originating from roadside parking areas,

(2) a system of longer trails originating from beaches, picnic areas, camp grounds, and other facilities, and

(3) a circumferential trail making it possible to hike completely around the Recreation Area. This latter trail will have small overnight campgrounds and trail-head parking areas. Preservation of the wildland mood of the twenty-five miles of the Appalachian Trail within the Recreation Area will also be an objective.

Wayside museums, on-site exhibits, and campfire programs will be used to present the natural and cultural history of the area. These

DELAWARE WATER GAP

TAMMANY

will explain the formation of the area's outstanding geological features and will tell of the uses man has made of this environment. Archeological evidence indicates that the Indians came to the valley almost ten thousand years ago, and early written records reveal that Dutch explorers began building here even before William Penn founded Philadelphia. By 1664 the Dutch are believed to have transported copper dug from the Pahaquarry Copper Mines some 104 miles to Esopus (now Kingston, New York). Portions of the Old Mine Road, possibly the first road over a hundred miles in length in America, and traces of the mines are still evident. Descendants of these early settlers participated in the Indian Wars of the eighteenth century, and during the American Revolution their valley was a vital link in the line of communications between New York and Philadelphia.

Construction of the Tocks Island Dam and development of the National Recreation Area will mean continually changing conditions throughout this area for possibly the next decade. Its completion, however, should guarantee preservation for future public benefit.

INTRODUCTION

NCE the province of the Lenni-Lenape Indians and the first Dutch and Swedish settlers in the early 1600s, the Upper Delaware has always been rich in history. Population seeped northward by river and Indian trails. Gradually the English Quakers were displaced by the Germans in the middle 1700s and the era of New Sweden, as this part of New Jersey was once called, was but a memory.

The Durham Iron Furnace was established, just south of Riegelsville in Pennsylvania, as early as 1727. It was supplied by ore from nearby mines, being an empire in the wilderness. Charcoal was burned for the furnace. Here Robert Durham designed and built the first Durham boat at the mouth of Durham Creek. The Durham boats became the workhorses of the eastern rivers and later the canals. They are historically important because of the strategic part a Durham boat played in ferrying Washington's troops across the Delaware on Christmas Eve, 1776, for the Battle of Trenton the following morning.

Canals came to the Delaware Valley in 1831 when the Delaware Canal was completed along the Pennsylvania side. It was one of the great commercial arteries of its time, used principally to bring coal and other products to coastal markets. In 1834 the equally famous Delaware and Raritan Canal was completed across New Jersey, including its feeder canal. This latter artery began at Raven Rock and continued south along the east bank of the Delaware River to Trenton, where it joined the main canal. The canals eventually became obsolete and in 1931 the Delaware Canal and a year later the Delaware and Raritan Canal ceased operations. (See Chapter 16 for hiking along the Raritan Canal.) Subsequently each of the states acquired the respective canals and maintains them primarily for historic and recreational purposes.

A functional reminder of the past are the dozen or so covered bridges that are still in existence. New Jersey's solitary survivor of these bridges and many of those in Pennsylvania will be visited on these walks coursing the rural roads and paths of the region.

Riegelsville to Easton and Return on the New Jersey Side. Length: 18 miles.

For this hike, use U.S.G.S. maps "Easton," Pennsylvania, and "Riegelsville," Pennsylvania. This is an 18-mile hike if done in a circular fashion; otherwise it can be split into a 9-mile level walk from Riegelsville to Easton along the Delaware Canal or 9 miles return on the Pennsylvania side if cars are shuttled. It is level walking with splendid canal scenery, old locks and houses along the way.

The cars can be parked on the New Jersey side of Riegelsville. There is an area for parking a few feet north of the old iron bridge that crosses the Delaware Canal. Cross the bridge on foot (good views of the river), find the canal towpath in Riegelsville, and proceed north along the canal to Easton. There are many fine views of the Delaware and also if you look sharply goldfish can be seen in the Canal. How they got there is a mystery, but they are there in numbers. In about 9 miles arrive at Easton, and see the beginning of the Delaware Canal. It is interesting that the Canal is filled with water from the Lehigh River, where the latter is dammed just before it empties into the Delaware. From here observe the green iron traffic bridge that crosses the Delaware at Easton. Head for it, cross it to Phillipsburg, and begin the return half of the hike.

The return portion is different, featuring rural scenery and several tiny villages with colorful houses. As soon as the bridge into Phillipsburg is crossed, proceed immediately south along the railroad. Follow it through the railroad yards, and keep on as it follows the curves of the river for about 3.5 miles until a small blacktop road crosses the railroad. Take the road, and follow along it, as it never wanders far from the Delaware. There are old houses and the quiet village of Carpentersville.

Where the road forks south of Carpentersville, take the right fork, and follow the road along the railroad. About 1.5 miles before the end of the hike there is a delicious cold spring on the left side of the road, which should revive tired hikers enough to complete the hike in good style.

Hexenkopf Rock. Length: 11–12 miles.

For this hike, use the U.S.G.S. "Riegelsville," Pennsylvania, sheet. Hexenkopf is a peculiar rock that emerges from a woodland plateau. The literal translation of the name from the Pennsylvania Dutch means "Witch's Head." It is best visited in winter because at other times the view from the top is obscured by the leaves of the trees.

Park the cars at the intersection of the two blacktop roads where the map is marked Durham Furnace, 2 miles southwest of Riegelsville. The Durham Furnace produced chains, cannon balls, and small shot for the Revolutionary army, and also made the famous "Sally Anne" stove. Follow Rt. 212 generally westward for 1 mile. At the fork, take the northernmost of the two roads 2.5 miles into Durham, and turn north on a blacktop road by the old mill. At the first intersection go left (west) on a blacktop road until a dirt road leads off northwest. Take this uphill, and when it bends near the power line switch over to the power line, also going northwest, for a steep climb and views at the top. Continuing on the power line, descend to the dirt road into a nice little glen with a pond. Stay on the power line until another is reached leading northeast.

This power line is then followed as best as possible (some detours are necessary due to private properties) until the intersection of the power line with the blacktop road at Stouts is reached (about 2 miles). Follow this blacktop road northeast a short distance then leave the road at any likely spot, and travel by compass in a north-northwest direction to the peak of the ridge. This will be Hexenkopf Rock, the highest point.

Descend via a path to the same road at a point on the road due east of Hexenkopf Rock. Go southwest on the road 0.3 mile to a blacktop road leading southwest and stay on it 0.5 mile to a fork. Leave the roads behind here, and strike out in a direction slightly north of east. This direction is calculated to go over the two knobs of Burgher Hills if good judgment and a compass are followed. The two hills are separated by Bought Hill Road leading north and south. The second hill is about one-third mile west of the Delaware.

When the hill is reached go southeast to a small blacktop road in about 0.3 mile. Follow this road with its quaint houses 0.5 mile west to a T-intersection with the main road. Go southwest on this for 0.75 mile to another paved road which is followed 1.25 miles southwest back to the cars at Durham Furnace.

The Delaware Palisades and Ringing Rocks. Length: 8–9 miles.

For this hike, use the U.S.G.S. "Riegelsville," Pennsylvania, sheet. This walk has three main points of interest: the palisades near Kintnersville, Ringing Rocks, and the breathtakingly beautiful gorge near Ringing Rocks.

A good place to park cars is by a small road leading southwest from Rt. 611 about 0.5 mile from the river, south of the intersection of Rt. 32 and Rt. 611 at Kintnersville. Follow this road about 0.5 mile, and then as the stream that had been beside the road leaves the road, follow it eastward about 0.5 mile (bushwhacking, no trails) until Center Hill Road is reached. Follow this latter road through rural scenery toward Rt. 32 and the Delaware River. However, after about 1.5 miles on Center Hill Road, come to a fork. Take the right fork (east) for about 0.5 mile to where a small stream crosses. Leave the road here, and follow the stream downhill (northerly, no trails) to Rt. 32. Go east (downriver) on Rt. 32 for about 0.5 mile until another small stream is reached. Leave the road, and follow the stream uphill (south). Pick your way along the water through one of the most beautiful gorges found anywhere.

The gorge ends at a solid wall of rock about 15 feet high over which the water falls. Go to the top of the wall, and follow the stream to a road; go right about 0.3 mile to a sign pointing to Ringing Rocks, and follow the path eastward to the Rocks. This is a large (about 3.5 acres) barren field of conglomerate stone and mineral formations. The rocks produce bell-like sounds when struck with a hammer. The phenomena is caused by interior stress of the rocks due to weathering. Return to the road and go northwest on it about one-eighth mile to a small dirt road leading off to the left. Follow this in a westerly direction until another road is reached in about 0.3 mile. Take this road south to the power line in about 0.3 mile. Go northwest on the power line, crossing a road in about 1 mile to reach the Delaware Palisades in about another 0.3 mile. Here, from atop the sheer cut, look down at the canal and the Delaware River, 500 feet below. There are fine views at various points of about one-eighth mile along the cliffs, hedaing in a westerly direction. There is a path at one point leading right down to a small balcony of stone overlooking the canal far below.

Leaving the Palisades, come south for a short distance to a power line which goes off to the west-southeast, and follow this to the right back to Kintnersville and the cars, about 1.5 miles away.

Uhlerstown to Upper Black Eddy. Length: 10 miles.

A pleasant one-day circular hike is from Uhlerstown, Pennsylvania, to Upper Black Eddy, Pennsylvania, and return along the Delaware Canal. Use the U.S.G.S. map "Frenchtown," New Jersey. Uhlerstown, formerly called Mexico, was once a boat stop in the heyday of the Delaware Canal. Located directly across the river from Frenchtown, New Jersey, and about 0.5 mile inland on the Canal, it is a quaint village of about five Spanish-type houses. A rare and old covered bridge overlooks the Canal and a set of locks that were once used to raise and lower the boats.

Cars can be parked in the yard of an abandoned schoolhouse, and this circular hike can begin from there. Cross the covered bridge, bear right, upstream, and in about 100 yards the road forks. Take the left fork, and follow the narrow dirt road steeply uphill, away from the river, about 0.5 mile, and turn on a blacktop road. Heading northward, pass the Upper Tinicum Union Church and at the next intersection go right on a blacktop road for about 0.5 mile to where an old woods road leads off to the left. Take this road to the crest of the ridge overlooking the Canal, and follow the crest of the ridge northwestward to a power line. There is a good view overlooking the Canal, the Delaware, and the rolling Pennsylvania countryside. The cliff is steep here.

Continuing northward, follow the ridge above the Canal about 0.5 mile and descend to a blacktop road at the Canal. Head southwest through the glen, away from the river, for almost 1.3 miles to where the road takes a northerly turn at a small bridge over an intermittent stream. (This point is 0.5 mile north of the Upper Tinicum Union Church.) After about 2 miles of fine plateau scenery a small road leads off to the right in an easterly direction. Take this, and in one-eighth mile go left (north), where in another one-eighth mile there is a strong spring off to the right of the road with plenty of watercress available for the picking.

Try to find an old woods road a short distance north of the house which is north of the spring. Follow this old road northwest to the blacktop road about five-eighths mile (some bushwhacking). Go northeast on this road to the Canal towpath. At Upper Black Eddy there is an old grocery store right on the towpath. Follow the scenic towpath from Upper Black Eddy back to Uhlerstown.

Uhlerstown Circular. Length: 12 miles.

For this hike, use the U.S.G.S. maps "Frenchtown," New Jersey, and "Lumberville," Pennsylvania. Erwinna is the next village along the Delaware Canal south from Uhlerstown and there are two covered bridges on this hike.

Park the cars in the yard of the old abandoned school at Uhlerstown. Cross the old covered bridge spanning the canal, bear right, northward, and follow the dirt road as it ascends the hill, leaving the river behind. At the top of the hill turn south off the road, and follow the crest of the cliffs in a general fashion for about 1.5 miles until a descent begins. At a point about 0.5 mile west of Erwinna, on the south side of the road there is a strong spring.

Turn right in slightly less than 0.3 mile beyond the spring, where the road forks. Go left, and follow this dirt road southwesterly, ignoring side roads, for 1 mile or perhaps a little more through very nice pastoral scenery until a blacktop road is reached. Go right (southwest) on this road, and pass through the village of Sundale, and go left on the first dirt road to the left about 0.5 mile from Sundale. Follow this road southeast, and ford Tinicum Creek where the road does, and proceed southeast on this road for about 0.8 mile from the ford to where the road ends as it meets another dirt road. Go northeast on this road, and in 1 mile meet Erwinna Covered Bridge spanning the Tinicum. From here, leave the road and ascend to the height of land on the southerly side of Tinicum Creek, and, using ingenuity and intuition, follow the general course of the Tinicum from the ridge with its ravines through the woods until the canal is reached in about 2 miles.

Here there is one of those interesting aqueducts the canal system employs to carry the canal waters over those of the Tinicum far below. (The aqueduct is passable to the sure-footed!) Go north for about 3 miles on the canal towpath to Uhlerstown and the cars.

Ralph Stover State Park. Length: 10-11 miles.

For this hike, use the U.S.G.S. map, "Lumberville," Pennsylvania. This hike features fine rural scenery, two old covered bridges, and an outstanding view of the horseshoe of Tohickon Creek from the cliffs near Ralph Stover State Park.

Drive to Point Pleasant, Pennsylvania, about 8 miles south of the

Frenchtown bridge, and northwest uphill, away from the river, to the Tohickon Hill School about 1 mile from the turn. (This is an old one-room schoolhouse now privately owned; this is shown on the map.) Park the cars at or near the crossroads, go southwest to Meetinghouse Road, and proceed to the first intersection, 0.25 mile farther, and bear right (northwest) on Stump Road to Smith's Corner, 1.25 miles distant. Turn left (southwest) for another mile to Wismer, and turn right, generally northwesterly, on the blacktop road for about 1 mile to Loux Covered Bridge.

At the south side of the bridge, a small woods road near some structures proceeds across the stream. Take this across, and here a path follows the stream northeast. When the path turns uphill in 0.5 mile, leave it, cross the stream, and find the path on the south side of the stream, which will lead to Cabin Run Covered Bridge, a little more than 1 mile from the first covered bridge.

Take the little road northwest for about 0.3 mile, and cross an old iron-frame bridge spanning Tohickon Creek. Take the dirt road northeast for 0.8 mile to the crossroads, bear right (southeast) for about 0.5 mile, and then go left (northeast) on a wood road. In about 0.3 mile, unseen from the road, are the cliffs, Boileau ("High") Rock, a few hundred yards southwest from the road (a good place for lunch). Here the view of the perfect horseshoe of the Tohickon, 200 feet below, is impressive.

After lunch follow the wood road to the blacktop road, and take it for about 1.3 miles to the crossroad. Go left (north) about 0.8 mile to a small crossroad. Take the dirt road right (northeast) down through a gorge and in less than 1 mile downhill arrive at the Delaware Canal.

The scenic Canal towpath can then be followed south about 2.5 miles to Point Pleasant where there is an acqueduct allowing the Canal to pass over the Tohickon Creek below. Leave the Canal at Point Pleasant, and follow the blacktop road uphill about 0.8 mile to the cars.

The Devil's Tea Table. Length: 11 miles.

For this circular, use the U.S.G.S. map "Lumberville," Pennsylvania. The Devil's Tea Table is a peculiar pedestal-shaped rock formation high above the Delaware which affords an outstanding view across to Pennsylvania and for miles up the river. It is roughly 5 miles south of Frenchtown, New Jersey, and is marked on the map.

Take River Road from Frenchtown. About 0.5 mile south of Rush Island on the Delaware River a dirt road leads off to the east, under the south face of the Devil's Tea Table. Park the cars here-abouts. Hike along this road in a northeast direction for about 1.5 miles to a blacktop road, then turn right, south, for about 0.8 mile to where a dirt road leads off to the west. Follow this back to the parked cars where a small stream goes under River Road. Immediately on the north side of the stream at River Road an unmarked trail ascends steeply to the Tea Table, which is a pleasant lunch spot.

Descend the same way to River Road, and follow it south for about one-third mile; take a dirt road slanting uphill to the southeast away from the river, and then continue generally eastward for a good mile to another blacktop road. Go south 0.8 mile, turn east on another small road, and in 1 mile take a fork to the north-northeast. After about 0.8 mile a small road leads to the northeast and Milltown, a quaint little community nestled in a glen by Lockatong Creek. After bypassing a house on the east bank, a footpath can be followed along the creek to Idell.

At Idell go west on the blacktop road about 0.5 mile to the intersection with a similar road. Go northward about 1 mile past the intersections of two roads seen earlier before lunch to where a small dirt road leads west. Follow this past several houses to where it bends sharply in the woods to go downhill. Here either go downhill to River Road, turning left to reach the cars, or go left to the plateau, head southwest to the cliffs and the Devil's Tea Table once more, and thence to the cars.

Stockton Circular and Green Sergeant's Bridge. Length: 12–14 miles.

For this hike, use the U.S.G.S. map "Stockton," New Jersey. The cars can be parked along a convenient street in Stockton. Go along the main street in a northwesterly direction for about 0.5 mile to where Wickecheoke Creek passes under the road. On the near (southerly) side of the creek a little dirt road heads northeast. Follow this for about 2 miles to a blacktop road. Here bear left, still continuing northeast, 0.5 mile to another road. Follow this, ultimately bending west, and observing the distant rural landscape, until another road is reached in about 1 mile. Turn right (north) on this road and in about five-eighths mile reach Green Sergeant's Bridge, the only covered bridge in New Jersey.

From the bridge, go east on the blacktop road 0.3 mile to a road branching off to the left (northeast); follow this, and after about 1 mile come to a little covered spring, Indian Springs, by the side of the road. Continue to a blacktop road; go northwest on this for 0.3 mile to a road headed west. Take this 1 mile to a scenic dirt road, and go right (north) through some nice woodland. This latter road parallels Wickecheoke Creek and then crosses Plum Brook and continues in a generally northerly direction to the town of Locktown (famous for its sweater shop), 2 miles from the northerly turn.

At Locktown go west on a small blacktop road to the first blacktop road leading south (by Wickecheoke Creek). Follow this for 1.5 miles to an intersection; go right (west) for 0.3 mile. Turn left on another road, and follow this road for about 1.5 miles south through some nice rural scenery and a few beautiful old homes, arriving back at Green Sergeant's Bridge.

Cross the bridge and go south (the first half mile retraces what was covered on the first leg of the hike) on the dirt road following the creek about 3.5 miles to the road leading to the town of Stockton. At this point you are now on the west side of Wickecheoke Creek, opposite from where the hike began. Follow the blacktop road 0.5 mile back to Stockton and the cars.

New Hope to Washington Crossing State Park and Side Trip to Bowman's Hill. Length: 8–9 miles.

For this hike, use the U.S.G.S. "Lambertville," New Jersey, map. This hike along the Delaware Canal involves a car shuttle. Cars can be parked in Lambertville, New Jersey, across the Delaware, on a quiet side street and again near the canal in the southern section of Washington Crossing State Park.

Cross the Delaware via the traffic bridge, and be sure to hike along the interesting sidewalks of New Hope with their various quaint old shops and taverns. Find the canal towpath, and follow it south for about 3 miles to Washington Crossing State Park. (This is the upper section; the park is in two sections.) Here can be seen the tall, ruggedly constructed Bowman's Tower. Bowman's Hill is renowned as an important observation post during the Revolutionary War. The tower is worth a visit, and if the canal towpath is left at one of the bridges crossing the canal, it can be reached by a short hike. There are many interesting nature trails, particularly the Azalea Trail, in the area at the foot of Bowman's Hill, and an extra mile or two of walking along these short trails is rewarding. One of the trails follows the contours of Bowman's Hill, and at a point about 100 yards below the tower the trail can be left and an ascent without a trail can be made to the tower.

Do not forget to visit the old grist mill dating back to 1740, with

its original water wheel, near the intersection of Pidcock Creek and
Rt. 32 in the Park to the west of Rt. 32, in the shadow of Bowman's
Hill. Also worth exploring is the nearby Thompson-Neely House,
which served as a command headquarters during the Revolution.
After visiting Bowman's Hill, the scenic towpath can be followed
another 4 miles to the southern section of Washington Crossing
State Park and the cars. This section of the park is worth a little
"walk around" to see the points of historic interest, old dwellings
and the point of embarkation where George Washington is reputed
to have crossed over to New Jersey.

Those who desire a longer hike and who prefer not to shuttle
cars can return to Lambertville by crossing the Delaware via the
bridge at Washington Crossing Park and using map and instinct
pick their way back on the New Jersey side. This is quite feasible if one
never ventures more than a half mile inland from the river. Straw-
berry Hill on Baldpate Mountain offers an excellent view of the
Delaware Valley, as does Belle Mountain and Goat Hill. The last
2 miles are best done on the strip of land west of River Road (Rt.
29), between the railroad and the shores of the Delaware, in order
to avoid houses.

*Washington Crossing to Trenton, and Return on the New Jersey
Side.* Length: 15 miles.

For this hike along two famous old canals, use New Jersey Atlas
Sheet 27, issued by the New Jersey Department of Environmental
Protection. This circular and level hike which can be done as two
separate hikes if desired, one on the Pennsylvania side and the other
on the New Jerse yside if cars are shuttled. The return on the New
Jersey side is adventurous and devious; some ingenuity and perserver-
ance is necessary, but this part of the hike is too interesting to be
excluded.

The cars can be parked near the Delaware Canal on the Pennsylvania side of Washington's Crossing State Park, very near the
same blacktop road that crosses the Delaware into New Jersey.
Follow the canal towpath southward about 7 miles to Morrisville.
Shortly before Morrisville, there is a large swamp off to the left where
beaver houses have been seen. This is unusual inasmuch as they are
so close to civilization. Cross the Delaware on the bridge at Morrisville. Rather than attempt a detailed description of how to return,
and thereby thoroughly confuse the reader, a few simple hints can
be given. Find the Delaware and Raritan Canal on the map as it
passes through Trenton and head for it by the shortest route after

crossing the Delaware. Follow its *eastern* bank northward. This is possible for about 4 miles. Do not give up! When in doubt, after this (because of roads following near the canal), take the railroad, and follow it northward instead of the canal towpath. It is never necessary to go far from the canal. Eventually the iron structure of the bridge at Washington Crossing comes in sight, and then the rest is easy. For something very different, this is the hike to try.

Delaware Canal, Washington Crossing State Park.

In addition to the circular walks on the Pennsylvania side of the Delaware River, there are 60 miles of towpath along the Delaware Canal, paralleling the river, which offer an easy trail suitable for hiking or bicycling. The canal and towpaths are now formally known as Theodore Roosevelt State Park, a linear park stretching from Easton to Bristol. Although accessible by train or bus from Philadelphia to Bristol, and from the New York metropolitan area by car, it includes stretches of woods, marsh, and farmland out of sight of habitation. Fishing, birding, and canoeing also are available. Picnic grounds and camp sites provide trips of one day or more, and there are small inns for overnight accommodations.

At Washington Crossing State Park, south of New Hope, history is reenacted each Christmas Day. On Christmas Eve in 1776 General Washington and his army crossed the river to surprise and overcome the Hessians at Trenton. In a reproduction of one of the old Durham boats, which were commandeered by Washington, a crew of eighteen crosses from Pennsylvania to New Jersey in the style of the famous painting by Emanuel Leutze. A copy of the painting is displayed, accompanied by narration and music, in the impressive Memorial Building. Many landmarks of those times may be visited on both sides of the river. One of these is the old McKonkey Ferry House (once a tavern and now a museum), on the New Jersey side. The New Jersey section of the park contains 714 acres of deciduous woods, meadows, and red cedars. In springtime, the masses of pink and white dogwood are magnificent. A hiking trail leads from the museum along Steele Run; other trails follow a tributary to the more remote northern portion of the park. Several campsites also are available.

INTRODUCTION

EW Jersey's Pine Barrens are a broad expanse of relatively level land covering approximately one and two-thirds million acres, roughly 80 miles long and 30 miles wide, on the coastal plain between Piedmont and the tidal lands. The Barrens include most of Ocean and Atlantic counties, much of Burlington County, and portions of Cape May, Cumberland, Gloucester, and Camden counties. Fringes of the pine area extend also into Salem and Monmouth counties.

This remarkable physiographic and biologic province is far from being botanically barren. Temperature maps for the winter and spring months show that it has a climate nearly as mild as that of Virginia and the Carolinas, 200 to 400 miles farther south. The region is entirely unglaciated; there are few substantial hills, and rock outcroppings are absent.

The first white men to enter the pine lands of southern New Jersey undoubtedly followed the few established trails of the Lenni-Lenape that led to the shell fisheries on the coast. The peculiar wildness of the region, empty of human life, must have impressed these early explorers, accustomed as they were to the massive deciduous forest trees and the grass meadows of the uplands, and the river valleys and the coastal marshes where an occasional Indian village could be found. Although these trails through the pine represented a long day's journey, there is no evidence of any permanent Indian camp or village within the area. The red men apparently held the deep pine lands in certain awe and shunned them as much as possible.

There is a strange wild beauty in the region, even today, that both attracts and repels. It is not unlike a desert in this respect. "Unique" properly describes the Pine Barrens, but those sensitive to the appeal of open space prefer the word "incomparable" in visualizing this block of wilderness. The average citizen flying over it or driving the long straight highways that transect it is likely to think of it as wasteland. And those persons always eager to exploit undeveloped open areas see only what they consider a great potential for profit and tax revenue. Botanists, foresters, naturalists, biologists, and many outdoor recreationists, however, will quickly challenge any views that threaten the status quo of the pinelands.

There are places in the pine barrens—for instance, Bear Swamp Fire Tower in the middle of Penn State Forest—where the outlook to the four horizons is an apparently unbroken carpet of forest with a glimmer here and there of small ponds and only a distant hint or two of human intrusion. And this amazing wilderness is less than a hundred miles from New York City at the north and from Philadelphia to the west! Attractive at all seasons—spring and summer with the beauty of countless bog flowers and the fragrance of sun-warmed pines and cedars, autumn with a colorful palette on a background of green, and winter with its snow-streaked, almost stark and lonely aspect—the region has a continuing appeal the more striking because of its geographic setting.

The white sandy soil of the barrens, developed on what is known to geologists as the Cohansey formation, is largely infertile. With the exception of blueberry and cranberry culture and isolated truck farms, it is not suited to commercial agriculture. The natural forest covering the bulk of the region is predominantly pitch pine (*Pinus rigida*) with scattered stands of shortleaf pine (*Pinus echinata*). In no other region in North America does the pitch pine cover such an extended area of country as the dominant tree. Oaks of several species are common where the pines have been removed, and oak becomes the climax type where firmly established. In the swamps and along the streams southern white cedar, sweet and swamp magnolia are very common, with sour gum, red maple, and gray birch on somewhat drier soils nearby.

The forest understory and thicket consists of a variety of woody shrubs and subshrubs such as blueberries, huckleberries, sweet pepperbush, buttonbush, winterberries, chokeberries, poison sumac, shadbush, staggerbush, greenbriers, and Virginia creeper. There is also an abundance of sweet fern, sand myrtle, sheep laurel, Hudsonia, bearberries, viburnum, and azalea. Well over a hundred species of herbaceous plants, some exceedingly rare, are found in the bogs, the wooded swamps, and dry woods, and along the roadsides. In areas of fire-ravaged woodland, the underbrush is often very dense and furnishes protection for the young pitch pines that sprout profusely from the burned stumps of the parent trees.

In the east-central part of the region, north and northeast of Bass River State Forest and Penn State Forest, there is a tract of about 15,000 acres popularly known as the "Plains." This tract supports a growth of unusually scrubby oak and pine which scarcely reaches an average height of four feet. Scientists have published several theories accounting for this stunted forest, the consensus pointing to a combination of factors: fires, infertility, exposure, and aridity. But under the trees grows a fairly heavy ground cover, mostly heath types, with a generous mixture of herbaceous plants. Typical of Plains flora are carpets of the Conrad crowberry (*Corema conradii*) and the bearberry (*Arctostaphylos uva-ursi*), both plants reminiscent of the cold barrens in the North. In spite of repeated fires which have swept the Plains since before white settlement, an interesting variety of plant life continues to thrive there.

Extensive acreages of swamp land in the pine region have been cleared over the years for cranberry growing, and large tracts of drier ground are cultivated for blueberry production. In a few sections, as in the vicinity of Tabernacle and Indian Mills, considerable truck farming is carried on. An interesting industry of the pine barrens which has disappeared in many sections is the gathering and drying of sphagnum moss for sale to nurserymen and for packing and insulation. In former days, local inhabitants augmented the family income by gathering laurel, misletoe, arbutus, and medicinal herbs for sale in Philadelphia and other cities.

The cranberry lands were established in cut-over white cedar swamps. Where cranberry growing has been abandoned the bogs have gradually changed to savanna types with grasses, other herbaceous plants, and seedling deciduous trees and shrubs moving in. Where conditions have been favorable, a few pines will also enter the bog edges. Students of natural phenomena find here an excellent example of plant succession and the attempt by nature to vegetate an exposed area.

Under the mats of vegetation and layers of sand is a fairly constant water table, the top of a great "reservoir" underlying the whole region. It was this tremendous water resource that influenced the late Joseph Wharton to make widespread land purchases in the last century. This area of about 100,000 acres, now owned by the state, is called Wharton State Forest. Mr. Wharton estimated that the water from his holdings would furnish nearby cities with up to 300 million gallons daily. Politics, however, dictated that he could not export water from one state (New Jersey) into another (Pennsylvania) and the water enterprise was abandoned.

The principal streams which drain the Pine Barrens are the several branches of Rancocas Creek at the west; Great Egg Harbor River at the southeast; Westecunck, Oyster, and Cedar creeks, and the Toms and Metedeconk rivers at the east and north; and the Mullica River and its tributaries (Wading, Bass, and Batsto rivers, and Nescochague and Landing creeks) easterly. Oswego River and Tulpehocken Creek flow into Wading River.

Other state holdings in the Pine Barrens region include Bass River State Forest, a tract of almost ten thousand acres located immediately east of Wharton State Forest. To the northeast of the latter is Penn State Forest, whose thirty-three hundred acres are covered mostly with young pine, and with young cedar along the streams. About 8 miles to the north is Lebanon State Forest, consisting of about twenty-seven thousand acres of interesting bog and upland. The Lebanon Glass Works, which were located here, gave the area its name.

Long before Wharton saw water sale possibilities in the massive aquifers of the pinelands, Jersey men, who were not impressed by Indian Pine Barrens folklore, were using the region for whatever profitable ventures the Barrens afforded. First to move in were the loggers, who cut clean. Pine and cedar lumber moved steadily to shipyards and nearby towns for years before, during, and after the Revolution. Roads to the coastal communities followed the loggers and charcoal burners, and hostelries were established at a number of places along the sand roads. Bog iron was discovered in the Barrens, and forges and furnaces were built on the major streams and branches. Iron proved a fairly profitable venture for a generation or so but shortly after the mid-nineteenth century the Jersey iron industry practically disappeared, overwhelmed by competition from the Pennsylvania furnaces with their superior ore and coal fuel; the bog iron works were forced to rely on the uncertain qualities and limited availability of charcoal for fueling their forges.

Glassmaking, using the fine silica sands of certain areas, followed the iron era and flourished for a time; a few large glassworks still prosper on the southern edge of the pines, around Glassboro. Paper mills were built on several of the streams, with salt hay used for fiber, but they, too, were short-lived. By the turn of the twentieth century, however, the cranberry industry was full-fledged, and a few years later blueberry culture became a business of great promise, continuing to the present day. Although cranberrying has declined to some extent, these are the only extensive and profitable industries now active in the pine lands.

Aside from the berry growing, in recent times the Pine Barrens have been put to practically no productive or consumptive use. Over the years there have been many attempts by individuals and land promoters to settle the area with homes and farms. Most were complete failures, resulting in property abandonment, tax sales, removal of names from assessment lists, selling and reselling, subdividing, and a general confusion of ownership. Clear titles were often difficult to obtain; the land was found to be "worthless" to many hopeful owners, and the attempted move to populate the uninhabited Barrens slowed to a halt.

Where the ironworks once stood, nature has practically obliterated all traces of once-busy communities. Ghost towns now dot the pines with only the remains of a structure or two, or none at all, as vague reminders of the places where people once lived and worked. A number of the ponds that were built to power sawmills and grist mills and to furnish water for other purposes still remain. The shores of these ponds provide fertile ground for typical Pine Barrens flora. Likewise, the abandoned cranberry bogs and the old clearings have become ideal propagation grounds for the characteristic growth of the barrens.

Although the region has remained wild and primitive—a forbidding land to most people—it claimed the attention of the early naturalists and became especially well known as a locality for unusual plants. To botanists, the Barrens were a natural wilderness recovered from its early clear-cutting and slashing by lumbermen and charcoal burners. A number of such areas have become major botanical meccas and many have historical and sentimental value as well. The combination of natural history and human interest associated with those places gives them an intellectual aura and educational status that many concerned persons would preserve.

One of the principal communities of the iron days was Batsto, established in 1765 in Burlington County a few miles from the salt reaches of the lower Mullica River. Although fires and neglect left their destructive marks on the village, which later became a glassmaking center, the core of the community has remained. Protection and restoration by the state has resulted in an attractive and authentic early Pine Barrens village. Open to the view of visitors now are the "big house" where the master lived, several workers' cottages, the general store and post office, sawmill, gristmill, and a number of other old buildings. Restoration is continuing.

In the Batsto vicinity a nature area has been set aside for those who wish to know more of the flora of the region. Tours of this area, as well as of the historical structures and village layout, are available.

It is reasonable to suppose that other forms of wildlife would be present in the barrens in addition to the much-publicized plant life. To some extent this is so. Where underbrush furnishes browse and protection and the savannahs support desirable grasses, the white-tailed deer is plentiful. The local herds do not seem to have been decimated to any appreciable extent by the heavy hunting pressure in this intermetropolitan area; deer may be seen on almost any excursion into the pine woods. Throughout the region where once the black bear, panther, timber wolf, and bobcat were found, there is now only the deer, the gray fox, skunk, raccoon, rabbit, and opossum. Muskrats thrive on many of the creeks and rivers; mink are found here and there; otters are known to be present in a few places; and beavers are increasing to the point of being a nuisance in some areas on the edge of the barrens. Smaller mammals such as a few species of mice, red squirrel, gray squirrel, common mole, shrews, little brown bats, and the weasel are more or less common.

The last of the big mammals to disappear was the black bear. Not wholly carnivorous, the bear subsisted in season on the abundant blueberries and acorns. Bruin was said to be so common that he would sometimes be seen sharing a blueberry patch with a lone human berry picker.

Seventy species of birds are known to breed in the pines, some regularly and others occasionally, including those kinds that follow the clearing of the woods and the establishment of homes and farms. Little concentrated study of the bird life of the Barrens has been made, although ornithological research is much needed in such an unusual environment.

Reptile and amphibian species in the Pine Barrens are represented by thirteen frogs and toads, nine salamanders, three lizards, eighteen snakes, and ten turtles. Two of the frogs are rare: the Pine Barrens tree frog (*Hyla andersoni*) and the carpenter or sphagnum frog (*Rana virgatipes*). The former has its principal habitat here, and is known elsewhere only in isolated colonies in the South. The carpenter frog lives in cool, mossy bogs elsewhere than in New Jersey, but nowhere is it a common species. It is undoubtedly the peculiarly acid waters of the habitat that have localized these two amphibians.

The unusual soil and water acidity and great areas of sand have truly made the New Jersey Pine Barrens an "island" habitat for several species of plant and animal life not found in other parts of the state. As an outdoor laboratory and museum for biologists and ecologists, the pine lands have no equal in the state.

The vegetation in general is an old and relict flora which has occupied this area since prehistoric days. Existing essentially in the same circumstances as in its original state, it provides most unusual opportunities for plant research. There are areas here that are visited regularly by students from Eastern schools and colleges for teaching and special projects. Many of these special areas are in the protected state lands within the Barrens, but there are other sites of equal ecological significance presently outside of state ownership that should be protected from future disturbance.

The multiacred pine and oak natural areas of southern New Jersey are among the last of these biologically important types. Much basic information is available here in the study of structure, function, and development of mankind's natural environment. Ecologists look to the Pine Barrens with its oak interludes as a significant segment of a continent-wide biological reserve, a concept now under consideration by a number of the nation's scientists.

The white cedar swamps still in existence approach their primeval condition and appearance in every way except in size of trees. The straight trunks of the southern, or Atlantic, white cedar (*Chamaecyparis thyoides*) grow in thick stands, rising from the soggy ground where their buttress roots are matted with sphagnum mosses. Shade-tolerant ferns, vines, and shrubs thrive in the dark and humid surroundings, and a few moisture-loving flowers find a home in the brandy-colored cedar water. The mossy hummocks and fallen logs also carry their little colorful gardens of interesting plant life. There is little animal life in these gloomy but intriguing morasses. A few birds call, and the occasional track of a raccoon or fox may be found.

The special wildness of a white cedar swamp is unequaled in this part of the Northeast. It is an attractive remnant of original New Jersey that will continue to flourish and generate its own wilderness atmosphere, provided it is not drained, cut, or opened to the often questionable designs of certain types of planners and developers. Some of the more extensive and typical white cedar swamps within or bordering the Pine Barrens include the excellent forest at Double Trouble on the upper reaches of Cedar Creek, the exceptionally photogenic stand on Rt. 539 near Warren Grove, and the swamp downstream from Lake Oswego in Penn State Forest. Other cedar swamps of note and worth visiting are found along the streams in the northern part of Lebanon State Forest and in the Batsto River drainage in Wharton State Forest, particularly a couple of miles northeast of Atsion. A small white cedar bog (as well as a cross section of typical Pine Barrens pine and oak woods) is traversed by the Lake Absegami Nature Trail at Bass River State Forest.

Human activities in the Barrens at present are not incompatible with their generally natural aspect and condition. Hikers, canoeists, campers, hunters, fishermen, nature students, history buffs, solitude seekers—all find them a rewarding place to pursue their interests. Forest management practices, such as selective harvesting of timber in special plots, experimental planting, and controlled burning to combat wildfire and maintain the dominance of the pines, have little effect on the Barrens as a whole. The culture of cranberries and blueberries contributes to the appeal of the area; these are basic earthy occupations that fit the environment and add the human touch which a certain segment of visitors seems to need.

However, any use of the barrens beyond the current extent and tempo of activities could well have a negative effect not only on the surface environment, but, more importantly, on the quality and yield of the tremendous "reservoir" of water beneath the pines. This underground reserve is now the largest potential source of fresh water in the state. The disturbance which would be caused by industry, housing developments, airports, stadiums, and more access highways is incalculable. It is to be hoped that the greater part of the pine region may be preserved from exploitation, whatever the reason.

SUGGESTED WALKS

Trails and old sand roads used by hikers interlace the pines and cedar swamps. Every now and then along these roads, one sees ghost towns of one or two structures—vague reminders of a flourishing past. The Batona Trail is the longest footway, connecting Wharton and Lebanon State forests. Several canoe routes are popular on the bigger streams. The most frequent routes follow stretches of the Oswego, Wading, Batsto, and Mullica rivers. Lengths vary from 1 mile or so to 12 miles. Some courses are easy paddling; others, especially on the less-traveled branches, require carrying, poling, or dragging, and forcing the canoe through overhanging underbrush. There are no "white-water" stretches, however, nor dangerous "sweepers" to upset the canoeist. A number of campsites are available to canoeists and hikers on the major streams and hiking trails.

Routes from Lake Absegami, Bass River State Forest.
A circular hike of less than 15 miles for the seasoned hiker or naturalist who wants to explore the hinterland is toward Munion Field. This route northward, at times on old wagon ways and white sand roads, leads toward the Eastern Plains—the region of stunted trees.

An easy 7-mile walk is toward Martha, where the overgrown ruins of an old furnace built in 1793 may still be seen on the Oswego River. The route is through upland forest, savanna, and swamp. In summertime the river's nearby bogs display rare beauty and color from wildflowers, particularly the river bogs north of Martha. The walk can be extended another 6 miles along a charming stretch of the Oswego River to Oswego Lake, passing cranberry bogs en route.

Routes from Oswego Lake, Penn State Forest.
A circular walk over any number of sand roads to Bear Swamp Observation Tower and back again makes an enjoyable 5-mile outing. The tower is 165 feet above sea level. From its deck, for miles in all directions, there is an exciting view of unbroken forest wilderness, with an occasional winding white sand road. To the north and northeast of the tower lie the "Plains"—the wilderness of the dwarf trees; on the eastern horizon is Barnegat Bay, and to the southeast the Tuckerton radio towers. The circular walk can be increased by 3 or 4 miles by going north of the tower and swinging east across the "Plains" before turning south.

Batsto to Atsion, Wharton State Forest.
There are several varied routes leading to the site of the Atsion Iron Works, less than 10 miles distant to the northwest, where a small restoration is in progress. From Batsto swing west to intercept the nearby Mullica River. The sand road along the near bank follows the riverbank to Atsion. A road on the far bank also parallels the river but tends to drift away from it from time to time. A third alternative is to go north and follow the west bank of the Batsto River. About 2 miles north of Batsto Lake a road branches left to

N. J. PINE BARRENS
Mullica River w. of Batsto looking downstream.

Dec. 13 1970

Atsion, or the river can be followed to Quaker Bridge 2 miles farther, where another road goes to Atsion.

Batona Trail (Map 16). Length: 30 miles. Blazes: pink.

This longest of blazed hiking trails in southern New Jersey extends for 30 miles through the heart of the pine lands between Batsto and Carpenter Spring in Lebanon State Forest. It was established in 1961 by the Batona (Back to Nature) Hiking Club in Philadelphia. In order to pierce the genuine wilderness of the area, this pink-blazed trail avoids the sand roads as much as possible, producing a firm yet resilient footpath.

From Batsto village proceed north to the Batsto Fire Tower, where the trail begins. Continue north, generally following the Batsto River, playing tag with a sand road that also parallels the eastern bank of the stream. At Quaker Bridge (6 miles) the sand road is followed for a mile and then the trail veers right through the evergreen woods on a northeasterly course. At 12 miles, cross the Central R. R. of N. J. tracks and reach the Carranza Memorial, a monument to Emilio Carranza whose plane crashed at this spot in 1928 while returning to Mexico City after a good will flight to New York.

A half mile to the north is the Batona Camp, designed for those hiking the trail. The Skit Branch, a stream, is now followed for about a mile and then several hummocks are crossed before reaching Apple Pie Hill Fire Tower (16.5 miles). Still following a northeasterly course, the next 6 miles generally follow sand roads until Rt. 72 and Lebanon State Forest is reached. Swinging past the site of the Lebanon Glass Works, the direction is now northwest to the Lebanon Fire Tower (27 miles). A mile later, Deep Hollow Pond is reached on the way to the trail's terminal at Carpenter Spring at the western end of the state forest.

Pakim Pond (Lebanon State Forest) Circular Routes.

An infinite number of routes over the many sand roads can be used for an interesting day's walk north from Pakim Pond. Go northeast past the former glass works site and head for the area near or north of the Penn Central R. R. tracks. Here the bogs of cedar trees are at their best. Return via one of the many alternate roads; the entire trip is about 10 miles. Several additional miles can be added if the walk is extended to Whitesbog. A shorter objective is Field Bridge, due north from Pakim Pond, where several sand roads traverse the 3-mile distance.

 HERE ARE extensive salt marshes, bays, sand dunes, and sand barrier-beach islands flanking New Jersey's coast from Sandy Hook southward. Salt-loving plants (halophytes) fringe the beach, and in season the back marshes are brave with the showy marshmallow (*Hibiscus moscheutos*). The air teems with birds of the shore.

CHEESEQUAKE STATE PARK

The hiker accustomed to the rocky hill country that is characteristic of so much of the metropolitan area will find a strikingly different terrain in Cheesequake State Park, northwest of Matawan. To some degree, the park is a northern outpost of the Pine Barrens. The park can be entered either from the Garden State Parkway (Exit 120) at the east edge, or from Rt. 34 on the southwest side. From any of the picnic grounds, walks of 1 or 2 hours can be improvised over trails which skirt the edges of low piney knolls overlooking broad marshes and savannas.

From late fall to early spring is preferable for walking here, when summertime crowds of picnickers, swimmers, and mosquitoes are absent and the calm beauty of the plant life's muted yellows, browns, and greens can be appreciated. Little Hook's Creek Lake provides contrast and a center of interest.

THE ATLANTIC HIGHLANDS

This area to the east of Cheesequake State Park has the highest elevations so close to the seashore, south of Maine. It forms the southern border of New York harbor and is easily visible on clear days from the shore areas of Brooklyn and Staten Island. The Highlands are a high peninsula between Sandy Hook Bay (a portion of New York Bay) and the Navesink "River." There is still much old-fashioned charm along the byroads and in the streets of the little towns, and many wooded areas remain. Red maples in bloom in the early spring are especially fine here. Rambles along the side roads will reveal many fine views. The so-designated "scenic road," which extends a few miles eastward from the town of Atlantic Highlands, and the historic Twin Lights high above the town of Highlands, just south of the bridge, provide exceptional views over Sandy Hook, New York harbor, and the sea. The Twin Lights, whose brownstone towers are connected by a building with a 300-foot façade, were built in 1826. They are no longer in operation, but a museum, open during the summer months, tells their story. An old stone church at Navesink and many lovely and distinctive homes, old and new, add to the interest of the area.

SANDY HOOK STATE PARK

Located at the northern tip of New Jersey's coastal plain, this 470-acre, 3-mile-long park is most interesting. Access is via Garden State Parkway to Matawan; then proceed on Rt. 36. Composed chiefly of sands eroded from the nearby Atlantic Highlands, this long and strongly curved hook is the result of currents in Sandy Hook Bay. Built up in stages, each stage results in a cove on the inland side, such as Horseshoe and Spermaceti coves. In spite of sea walls, Sandy Hook is in constant danger of erosion.

To the north of the park, on the government reservation, is Sandy Hook Light, reputed to be the oldest in the nation. A "sea" walk along the length of this barrier beach is an enjoyable experience, but a walk along the bay side will be of particular interest to the hiker. Following a marked trail through this wildlife sanctuary, notice the holly forest that has trees dating back to 1700. Nearby are prickly pear cactus (*Opuntia compressa*), whose brilliant yellow flowers in late June cover large expanses of dune. The beach plums (*Prunus maritima*) are famous, and their blossoms are everywhere in June; by Labor Day the cherry-sized plums are purple and ripe. A persistent legend holds that a huge pine tree is supposed to mark the spot where the famous pirate Captain Kidd buried a handsome treasure, but the treasure has never been found.

ISLAND BEACH STATE PARK

Located some 30 miles south of Sandy Hook, access is via the Garden State Parkway. Exit at Toms River, and proceed east. Here, south of South Seaside Park, is the most desirable area on the Jersey coast for an extensive hike through unspoiled dune land. Purchased in 1953 from the Phipps family, this 2694-acre, 10-mile strip extends as far south as Barnegat Inlet. Across the inlet is the beautiful Barnegat Lighthouse (172 feet). For those willing to climb its spiral staircase (open in season), there are fine views over the bays and ocean. The light is at the north tip of Long Beach Island, with access from Garden State Parkway or Rt. 9 by means of Rt. 72 across Manahawkin Bay. Besides the light itself, the nearby dunes and beach are well worth a short ramble. Bathing, picnicking, and fishing are permitted.

All along the eastern edge of the park, great breakers roll in from the ocean to constantly reshape the beach and to tear at the high dunes which protect the park area from invasion by the sea. On the western edge of the park, the land slopes gently toward the bay and becomes interspersed with areas of salt marsh. Here reeds, ivy, dense thickets of green briar (*Smilax rotundifolia*), occasional cedars, clumps of holly (*Ilex opaca*), bayberry (*Myrica pennsylvanica*), and other shrubs form an almost impenetrable barrier to the bay shore. Open areas on relatively dry dunes are occupied by *Hudsonia,* a heatherlike plant that has tiny butter-yellow flower blooms in late May and early June.

While traversing the dunes notice that beach grass (*Ammophila breviligulata*) helps to stabilize the sands. Many songbirds use the briar thickets as a summer nesting ground, and birds of almost all species common to eastern North America use the park as a rest area during migrations. For variation, follow the beach on the return leg back to the start.

MONMOUTH BATTLEFIELD STATE PARK

Located a dozen or so miles inland from the northern Jersey shore is Freehold, an area for the historically inclined which is reached via Rt. 9. Opposite the county courthouse stands a 94-foot shaft commemorating the Revolutionary Battle of Monmouth. The monument is surrounded by five bronze bas-reliefs depicting scenes of the battle, one of which shows Molly Pitcher manning a cannon. One mile northwest, on the Freehold-Englishtown road, brings one to the 1000-acre battlefield park. The orchards, woodlands, and fields must be very similar in appearance to that torrid day in June 1778. Today, the visitor can wander past the sites of the major breastworks and military encampments of years ago. Along the eastern border of the park, at Wemrock Road and Rt. 552, is the spring from which Molly Pitcher drew water to wet the swab of her husband's cannon during the battle. Perhaps the most picturesque relic of the fight is the old Tennent Church, about 1 mile west of the spring. The straight-backed wooden pews of this church were stained with the blood of dying British and American soldiers, when the church was a field hospital just back of the line that Washington and Lafayette held firmly after the confusion caused by Lee's dastardly retreat. The graves of soldiers of both armies lie under the old oaks in the courtyard.

THE NEW YORK–NEW JERSEY
TRAIL CONFERENCE

Although numerous clubs and individuals had been hiking for years over the Hudson Highlands and on the Wyanokie Plateau in New Jersey, regular trail systems were lacking until about fifty years ago. In 1920 Major William A. Welch, General Manager of the Palisades Interstate Park, called together representatives of the hiking organizations in New York to plan with him a system of marked trails to make the Bear Mountain–Harriman Park more accessible to the public. The meeting resulted in an informal federation known as the Palisades Interstate Park Conference. This name was adopted from the first tract acquired for this system of interstate parks: the Palisades of the Hudson River. Among the charter members were Raymond H. Torrey, Professor Will S. Monroe, Meade C. Dobson, Frank Place, and J. Ashton Allis. These pioneers and their friends planned, cut, and marked what are now the major Park trails. The first to be completed was the Ramapo-Dunderberg Trail from Jones Point on the Hudson to Tuxedo, 20 miles west. In 1923 the first section of the Appalachian Trail to be finished was constructed through the Park. In that year, the organization changed its name to the New York–New Jersey Trail Conference, with the intention of including trails in New Jersey.

The year 1923 also saw the appearance of the first edition of the *New York Walk Book,* published by the American Geographical Society. The plan, the title, the introductory material to the volume, many of the descriptions, and the drawings were by Robert L. Dickinson. Raymond H. Torrey furnished walk descriptions and maps from "The Long Brown Path," his weekly outdoor column in the New York *Evening Post,* and Frank Place, Jr., Librarian at the New York Academy of Medicine, contributed material from his trail notes and outing club schedules. The three again collaborated on the second edition, in 1934. The third edition, sponsored by the New York–New Jersey Trail Conference, was published in 1951. Hikers from the affiliated clubs walked the trails to bring the descriptions up to date, revised the maps, and edited the text.

The Trail Conference has expanded its interests and influence with each decade. In the 1930s it developed a trail maintenance system in which each member club was allotted a share. This service now extends over 600 miles of marked trails from the Connecticut border to the Delaware Water Gap. During World War II a small group, including Joseph Bartha and William Hoeferlin, continued the job as best they could and in addition measured all the Park trails. In the 1950s, under the leadership of Leo Rothschild, conservation activities assumed equal importance with trail work. The constitution adopted in 1938 had stated the objectives of the Conference: "to build and maintain trails and shelters in the States of New York and New Jersey; to assist in the conservation of wild lands and wild life and the protection of places of natural beauty and interest." A major undertaking, still continuing, has been to preserve the beauty of the Hudson Highlands.

In the 1960s there were several new achievements. The Conference reactivated the Long Path which, when completed, will link the George Washington Bridge with Whiteface Mountain in the Adirondacks, a plan first suggested thirty years earlier. During the drought years volunteers from member clubs patrolled the Park trails, on the alert for fires and for hikers and campers who were unaware that the woods had been closed to the public. The Conference publication, *The Trail Walker,* has a growing list of subscribers who depend on it for hiking and conservation news. Since 1965 the spring trail and shelter clean-up has annually drawn increasing members of hikers and Scouts working under the slogan "Leave nothing but footprints."

The Conference has for some time been cooperating with the Regional Plan Association for long-range development of green space to keep pace with population growth in its area of responsibility. Not only hikers, but all those who believe in the need for recreation in surroundings of natural beauty, are invited to join with the Conference in achieving this goal.

NOTE ON THE MAPS

The topographic maps in this book were compiled chiefly from the quadrangles on scales 1:24,000 (2½ inches to 1 mile) and 1:31,680 (2 inches to 1 mile) produced by the Corps of Engineers, U.S. Army and from the quadrangles on scale of 1:62,500 (a little larger than 1 inch to the mile) produced by the U.S. Geological Survey.

In earlier editions of the *Walk Book* similar maps were reproduced on the scales of 1:125,000 (about 1 inch to 2 miles) and approximately 1:75,000. The scales of these maps varied somewhat as they received slightly different amounts of reductions. In the present edition, maps are reproduced on uniform scales: maps 12, 13, 14, and 16 are on the scale of 1:125,000; all other maps are on the scale of 1:125,000; all other maps are on the scale of 1:62,500.

The smaller scale was found to be satisfactory for areas in which there are large mountain masses and no complicated trail pattern. The larger scale is used for southern New York and northern New Jersey where the country is more broken and many of the more popular walking areas carry a close network of trails. On all of these maps, both marked and unmarked trails or wood roads have been plotted and as much detail has been retained from the quadrangles as the scale would permit. In addition, symbols and colors of the marked trails are indicated and hypsometric tints are used to enhance readability.

These maps cover those areas in southern New York and northern New Jersey most easily accessible from the metropolitan area and consequently the most popular for walkers. No maps have been provided for Long Island since the walk directions there are so simple that a detailed map is scarcely called for. To supplement the maps in this book, and for the more distant sections covered by the teext, the U.S. Geological Survey quadrangles are available and can be obtained from any large commercial map dealer or by writing to Washington Distribution Section, U.S. Geological Survey, 1200 South Eads Street, Arlington, Va. 22202. The price of these maps is 50 cents and prepayment is required when ordering. For New Jersey, the sheets of the Topographic Atlas of New Jersey, on the scale of 1 inch to 1 mile, issued by the State Department of Conservation and Development, State House, Trenton, New Jersey, are available. Unfortunately, many of these sheets are now out of print. Hagstrom's Atlases of the counties of New Jersey and southern New York published by Hagstrom Co., Inc., 311 Broadway, New York, N.Y. 10007, are also useful since they not only show roads but name them so that they can be identified. For most state and county parks, reservations, and forests there are maps issued by the authorities in charge.

SUGGESTED READINGS

GUIDEBOOKS AND MAPS

Bear Mountain–Harriman Park.
  Palisades Interstate Park Commission, Bear Mountain, N.Y. 10911.
Catskill Trails and Shelters.
  New York State Dept. of Environmental Conservation, Albany, N.Y. 12226.
Guide to the Applachian Trail in New York and New Jersey.
  Walker and Company, New York, 1972.
Kjellstrom, Bjorn. *Be Expert with Map and Compass. The Orienteering Handbook.*
  American Orienteering Service, New York, 1967, c/o Bjorn Kjellstrom, Honey Hollow Road, Pound Ridge, N.Y. 10576.
New York State Dept. of Environmental Conservation, *The Conservationist.*
  Monthly publication of the Department, with articles and illustrations on all phases of natural history and the outdoors in New York State. Available by subscription only, Albany, N.Y. 12226.
Staten Island Walk Book.
  Staten Island Institute of Arts and Sciences, New York, 1962.

LOCAL HISTORY AND FOLKLORE

Appalachian Mountain Club, New York Chapter. *In the Hudson Highlands.*
  Lancaster Press, Lancaster, Pa., 1945. (Available in the New York Public Library.)

Bedell, Cornelia. *Now and Then and Long Ago in Rockland County.*
The Historical Society of Rockland County, 1968.

Botkin, B. A. *New York City Folklore.*
(Captain Kidd's treasure ship sunk off Dunderberg)
Random House, New York, 1956.

Boyle, Robert H. *The Hudson River.*
W. W. Norton & Co., New York, 1969.

Carmer, Carl. *The Hudson.*
Farrar & Rinehart, New York, 1939.

Cole, David. *History of Rockland County.*
J. B. Beers & Co., New York, 1884. Reprinted, December 1969,
by the Rockland County Public Librarians Association, Nyack
Public Library, N.Y.

Cottrell, Alden T. *The Story of Ringwood Manor.*
Trenton Printing Co. Pamphlet available at the Manor House,
Ringwood Manor, Ringwood, N.J.

Fast, Howard. *The Unvanquished.* (Novel dealing with events of
the Revolutionary War)
Duell, Sloane & Pearce, New York, 1942.

Flexner, James. *The Benedict Arnold Case* (originally *The Traitor
and the Spy: Benedict Arnold and John André*).
Colliers, New York, 1962.

Green, Frank. *History of Rockland County.*
A. S. Barnes & Co., New York, 1886. Reprinted, December 1969,
by the Rockland County Public Librarians Association, Nyack
Public Library, N.Y.

Heusser, Albert H. *George Washington's Mapmaker: A Biography
of Robert Erskine.*
Rutgers University Press, New Brunswick, N.J., 1966.

Howell, W. T. *Hudson Highlands. Diaries of a Pioneer Hiker.*
Lenz & Rieckee, New York, 1933.

Menzies, Elizabeth G. C. *Millstone Valley—History and Natural
History of a New Jersey River Valley.*
Rutgers University Press, New Brunswick, N.J., 1969.

Murphy, Robert Cushman. *Fish-Shape Paumanok—Nature and Man
on Long Island.*
American Philosophical Society, Philadelphia, 1964.

Palisades Interstate Park Commission. *60 Years of Park Cooperation:
N.Y.–N.J. 1900–1960.*
Bear Mountain, N.Y., 1960. Available from the Commission,
Administration Bldg., Bear Mountain, N.Y. 10911.

Pierson, E. F. *The Ramapo Pass.* (Privately printed)
Suffern, N.Y., Free Library, 1915.

Ransom, James M. *Vanishing Ironworks of the Ramapos,* with an introduction by Carl Carmer.
Rutgers University Press, New Brunswick, N.J., 1966.

Roberts, Kenneth. *Oliver Wiswell.* (Novel dealing with events of the Revolutionary War)
Doubleday, New York, 1940.

Sklarsky, I. W. *The Revolution's Boldest Venture—Battle for Stony Point.*
Kennikat Press, Port Washington, N.Y., 1965.

Smiley, Daniel. *The Shawangunks.*
Articles on history and natural history in publications of the John Burroughs Natural History Society.
Daniel Smiley, Mohonk Lake, New Paltz, N.Y.

Sutton, Ann and Myron. *The Appalachian Trail: Wilderness on the Doorstep.*
Lippincott, Philadelphia and New York, 1967.

Ward, Christopher. *The War of the Revolution,* Vol. 2, Stony Point and the Forts on the Popolopen.
Macmillan, New York, 1952.

NATURAL HISTORY

Arbib, Robert. *Enjoying Birds Around New York.* (Includes maps showing where and when to find the birds)
Houghton, Mifflin Co., Boston, 1966.

Bull, John L. *Birds of the New York Area.* (Catalogues by species when and where seen)
Harper and Row, New York, 1964.

Cobb, Boughton. *A Field Guide to the Ferns.*
Houghton, Mifflin Co., Boston, 1956.

Conant, Roger. *A Field Guide to Reptiles and Amphibians of the United States and Canada East of the 100th Meridian.*
Houghton, Mifflin Co., Boston, 1958.

Conrad, Henry S. *How to Know Mosses and Liverworts.*
W. C. Brown Co., Dubuque, Iowa, 1956.

Dunham, Elizabeth Marie. *How to Know the Mosses.*
The Mosher Press, Boston, 1951.

Gleason, H. A. *Plants of the Vicinity of New York.*
New York Botanical Garden, Hafner Publishing Co., New York, 1962.

Goldring, Winifred. *The Oldest Known Petrified Forest*.
New York State Museum, Albany, N.Y., 1927.
Kieran, John. *A Natural History of New York City*.
Houghton, Mifflin Co., Boston, 1959 (Paperback edition: The Natural History Press, New York, 1971)
Krieger, Louis C. C. *The Mushroom Handbook*.
Dover Publications, New York, 1967.
Murie, Olaus J. *A Field Guide to Animal Tracks*.
Houghton, Mifflin Co., Boston, 1954.
Peterson, Roger Tory. *A Field Guide to the Birds*.
Houghton, Mifflin Co., Boston, 1960.
Petrides, George A. *A Field Guide to Trees and Shrubs*.
Houghton, Mifflin Co., Boston, 1958.
Rickett, Harold W. *Flowers of the United States: The Northeastern States*.
New York Botanical Garden, McGraw Hill Book Co., New York, 1965.
————. *The New Field Book of American Wildflowers*.
New York Botanical Garden, G. P. Putnam's Sons, New York, 1963.
Schuberth, Christopher J. *The Geology of New York City and Environs*.
The Natural History Press, New York, 1968.
Teale, Edwin Way. *The Strange Lives of Familiar Insects*.
Dodd, Mead & Co., New York, 1962.

THE CATSKILLS

Haring, H. A. *Our Catskill Mountains*.
G. P. Putnam's Sons, New York, 1931.
Longstreth, T. Morris. *The Catskills*.
Century Co., New York, 1918.
Mack, Arthur G. *Enjoying the Catskills*.
Funk & Wagnalls, New York, 1950.
Van Zandt, Roland. *The Catskill Mountain House*.
Rutgers University Press, New Brunswick, N.J., 1967.

THE PINE BARRENS

McPhee, John. *The Pine Barrens*.
Farrar, Straus & Giroux, New York, 1968.

Pierce, Arthur D. *Family Empire in Jersey Iron—The Richards Enterprises in the Pine Barrens.*
Rutgers University Press, New York, N.J., 1965.
_____. *Iron in the Pines—The Story of New Jersey's Ghost Towns and Bog Iron.*
Rutgers University Press, New Brunswick, N.J., 1957.
_____. *Smugglers' Woods—Jaunts and Journeys in Colonial Revolutionary New Jersey.*
Rutgers University Press, New Brunswick, N.J., 1960.

INDEX

Numbers in italics are main entries
Boldface numbers refer to map section

LEGEND

—— – – –	Boundary, state	⋯⋯⋯⋯	Power line
—— – –	Boundary, county	⋯⋯⋯⋯⋯	Telephone line
++++++	Railroad	⊛	Tower
═⟨9W⟩═	Super highway	▪ ⌂	Town or village
─⟨17⟩─	Main road	⛪	Church
————	Secondary road	⊡	Cemetery
─⟨R⟩─	Marked Trail ⟨R⟩ red ⟨B⟩ blue ⟨W⟩ white ⟨Y⟩ yellow	⚑	School
⋯⋯⋯⋯	Unmarked Trail or wood road	●	Spring or well
P	Parking	————	Aqueduct
⋏	Shelter	⊢⊢⊢⊢	Canal
★	Viewpoint	⟋	Dam
⚒	Mine	⋰⋰⋰	Marsh
✕	Quarry or pit	≈500≈	Contours, every 100 feet
⊤	Airfield	.1029	Spot height, in feet

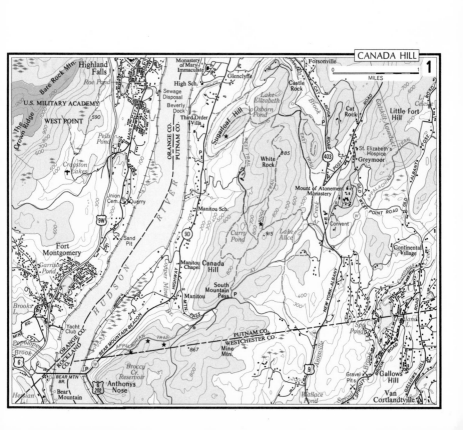

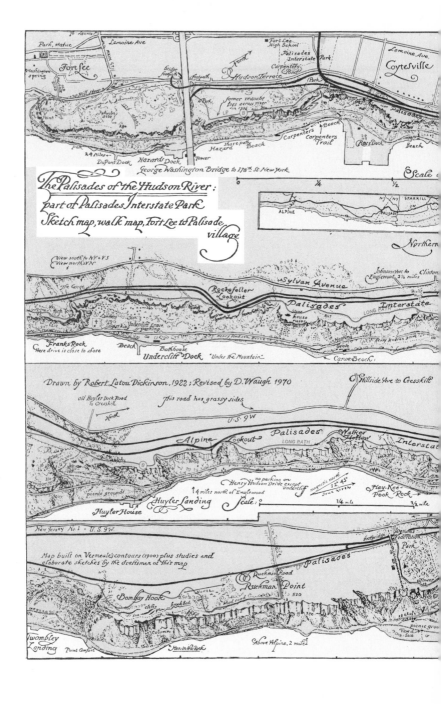

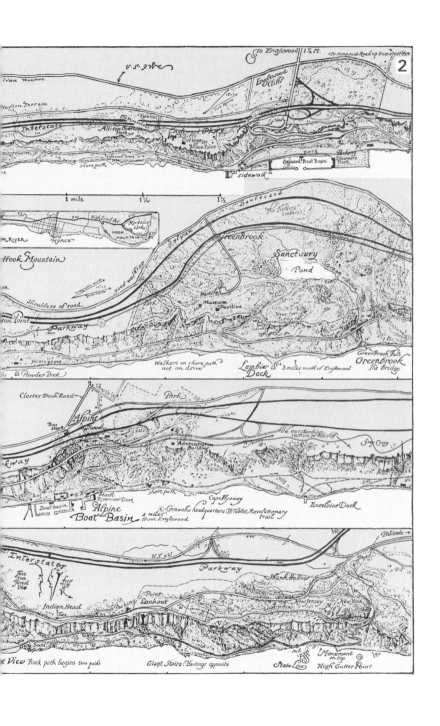

2

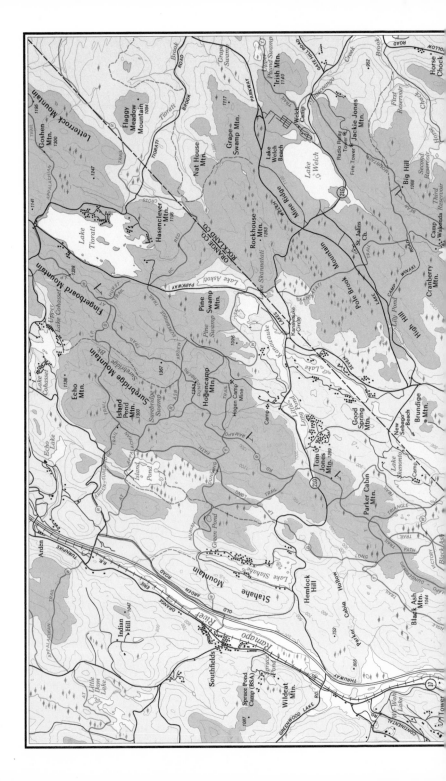

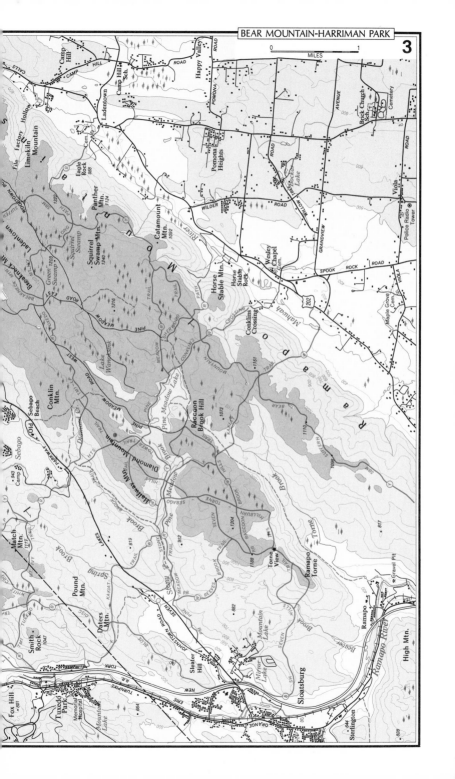

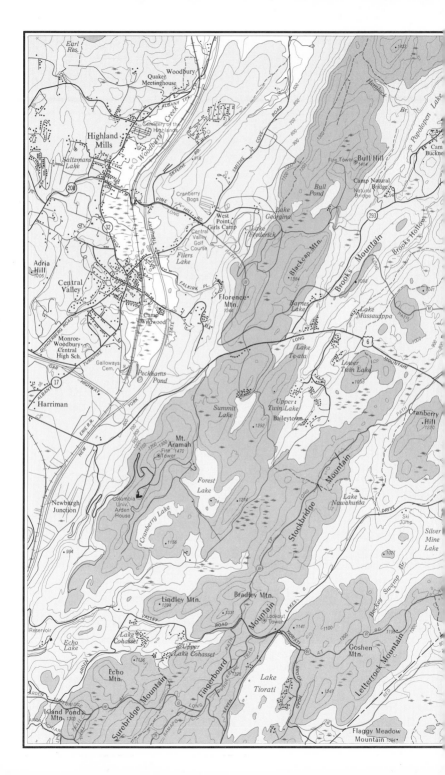

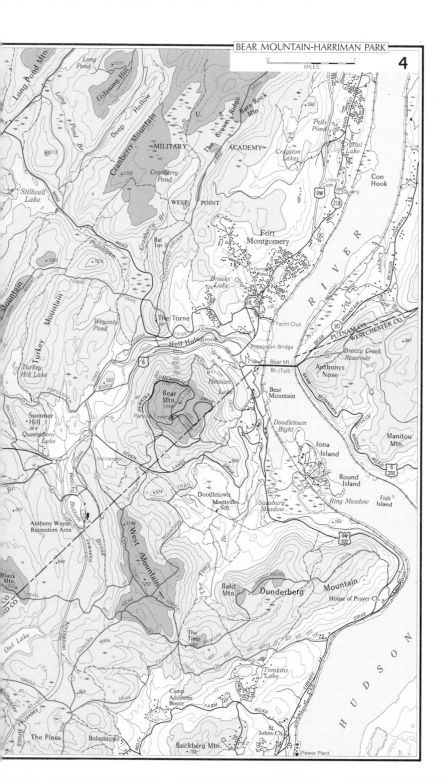

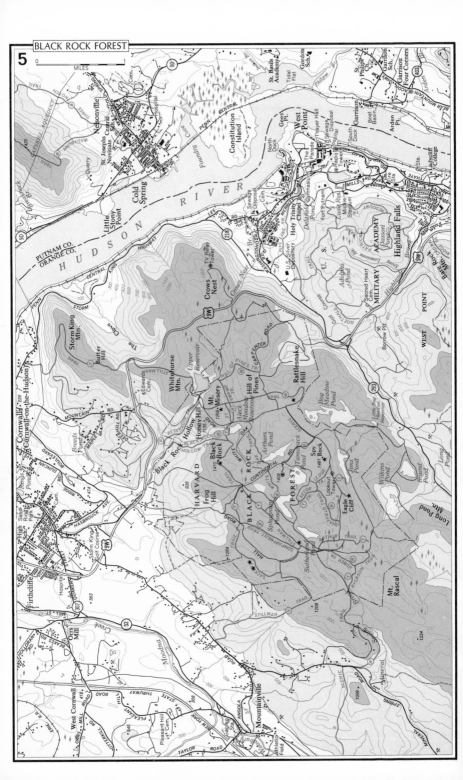

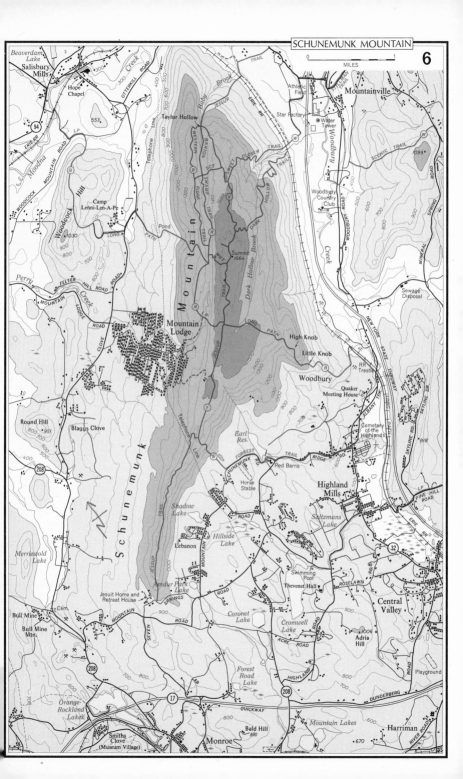

0   1
MILES

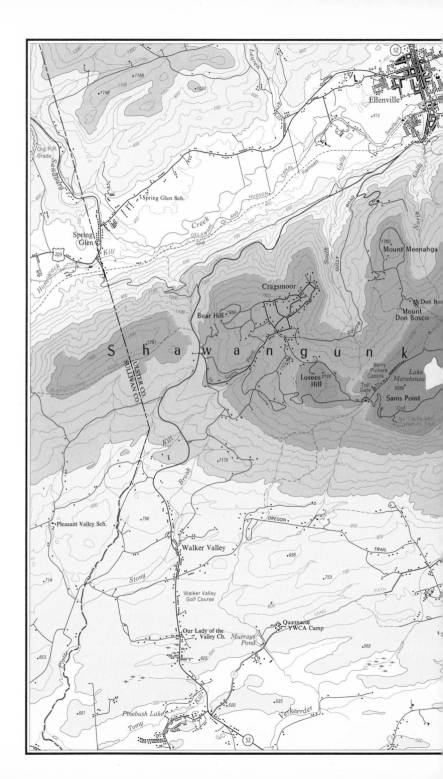

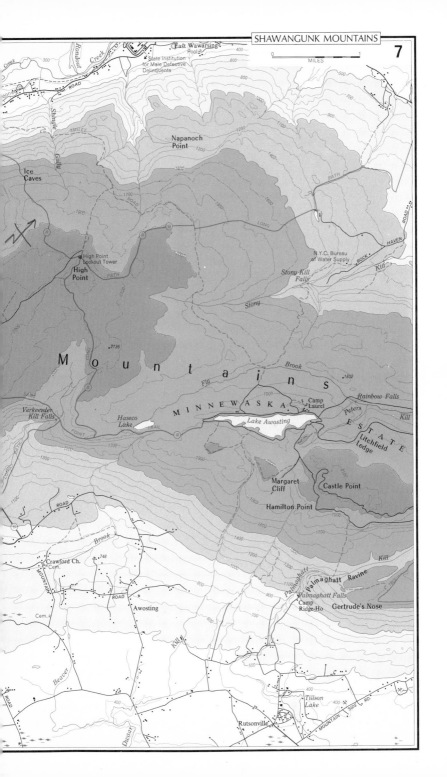

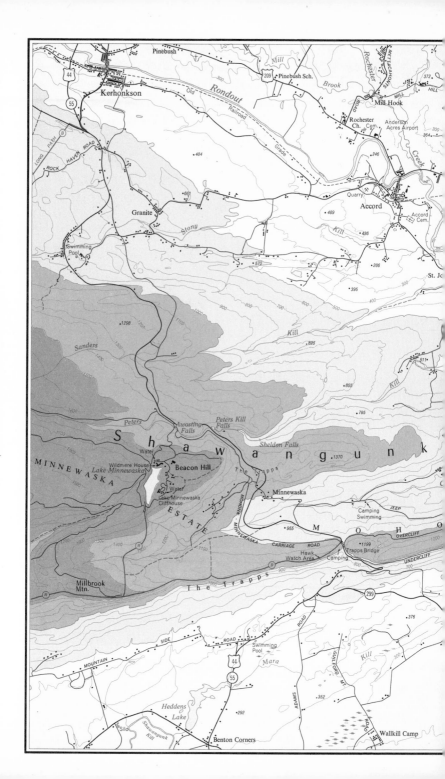

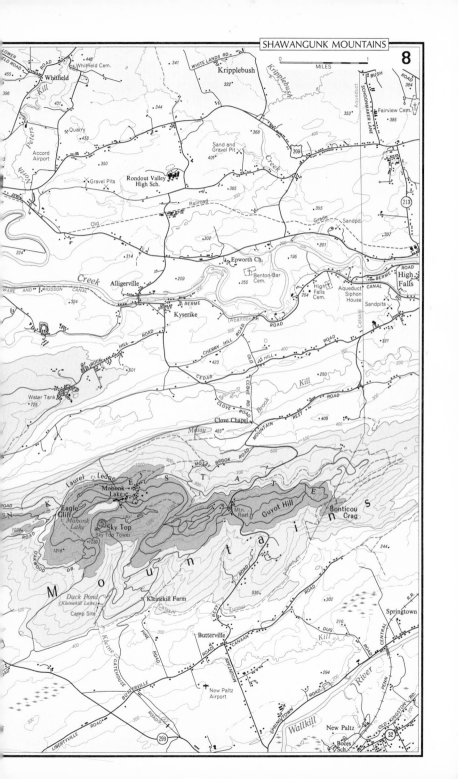

MILES

Whitfield

Whitfield Cem.

Kripplebush

Kripplebush

Fairview Cem.

BUSH
ROAD

SCHOONMAKER LANE

Aqueduct

WHITE LANDS RD.

LOWER
FIELD ROAD

North

Peters

Kill

Quarry

Accord
Airport

Gravel Pits

Rondout Valley
High Sch.

Sand and
Gravel Pit

Creek

Old

Railroad

Grade

Sandpit

213

Creek

Epworth Ch.

Benton-Bar
Cem.

High
Falls
Cem.

High
Falls

Alligerville

WARE AND HUDSON CANAL

BERME

Kyserike

(Abandoned)

ROAD

Aqueduct
Siphon
House

BERME

CANAL

ROAD

Sandpits

Catskill

HILL ROAD

CHERRY HILL ROAD

OLD HILL

ROCK

CEDAR

Water Tank

CLOVE ROAD

CLOVE

Brook

Kill

REST

ROAD

ROAD

Clove Chapel

Mossy

MOUNTAIN

ROAD

MOSSY BROOK

Laurel Ledge

Mohonk
Lake

E S T A T E

Mtn.
Rest

Guyot Hill

Bonticou
Crag

Eagle
Cliff

Mohonk
Lake

Sky Top
Sky Top Tower

Aqueduct

Mountains

OAKWOOD DR.

Duck Pond
(Kleinekill Lake)

Camp Site

Kleinekill Farm

Catskill

Tunnel

REST ROAD

ROAD

Springtown

R.R.

Butterville

PINE ROAD

MOUNTAIN

CANAAN

DUG

Kill

CENTRAL

ROAD

New Paltz
Airport

Kleine

GATEHOUSE

ROAD

BUTTERVILLE ROAD

SPRINGTOWN

Wallkill

River

PENN

New Paltz

OLD KINGSTON RD.

32

Boces
Sch.

LIBERTYVILLE ROAD

299

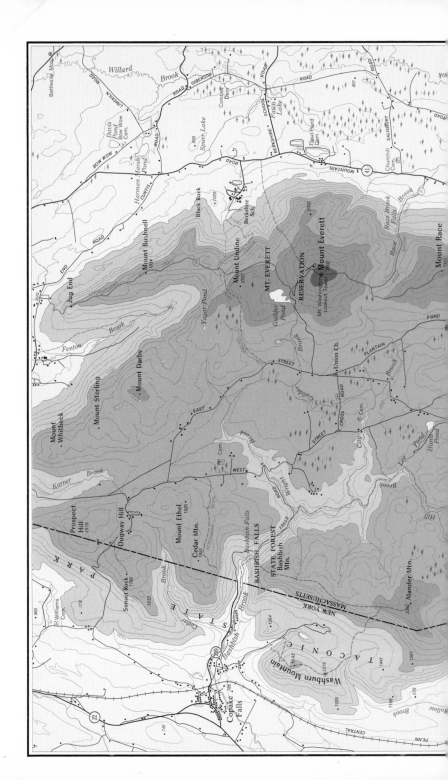

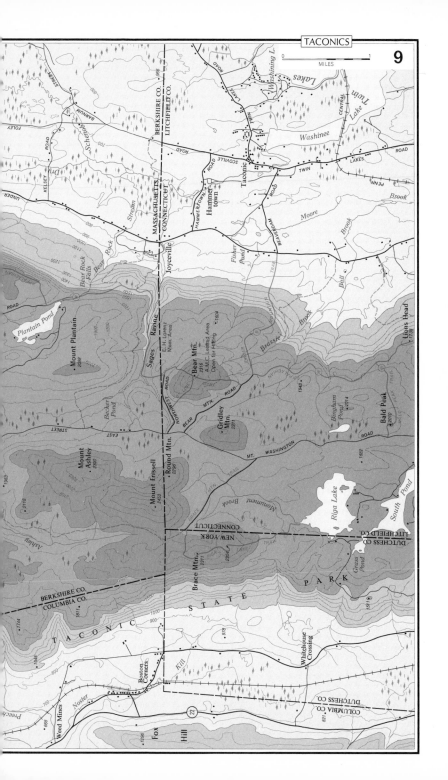

MILES

0   1

Twin Lakes

Wishining L.

Washinee Lake

Washinee

Central

Penn

Brook

BERKSHIRE CO.
LITCHFIELD CO.

Scoville Road

Foley

Barnum

Scheno

Kelsey Road

Dry

Under

Road

Stream

Moore

Bell Brook

Bear Rock

Bear Rock Falls

Hammertown Road

Joyeville

MASSACHUSETTS
CONNECTICUT

Hammertown

Taconic

Twin Lakes Road

Road

Beaverdam Road

Fisher Pond

Bear Rock

Lions Head
1738

Plantain Pond

Mount Plantain
2069

Sages Ravine

E. H. Lorenz
Mem. Area

Bear Mtn.
2316
A.M.C. Leaflet Area
Open for Hiking

Brassie Brook

1946

Bingham Pond
2914

Bald Peak
2010

Road

ROAD

Becker Pond

EAST

STREET

Northwest Road

Bear Mtn. Road

Gridley Mtn.
2211

MT. WASHINGTON

1582

Riga Lake

South Pond

Mount Ashley
2390

2118

1983

Mount Frissell
2453

Round Mtn.
2296

Monument Brook

CONNECTICUT
NEW YORK

DUTCHESS CO.
LITCHFIELD CO.

Grass Pond

Ashley

Brace Mtn.
2311

Road

STATE

PARK

181

BERKSHIRE CO.
COLUMBIA CO.

1811

1744

1746

TACONIC

900

1000

978

Whitehouse Crossing

Boston Corners

Kill

828

COLUMBIA CO.
DUTCHESS CO.

Preechy

Noster

Weed Mines

669

Fox

Hill

22

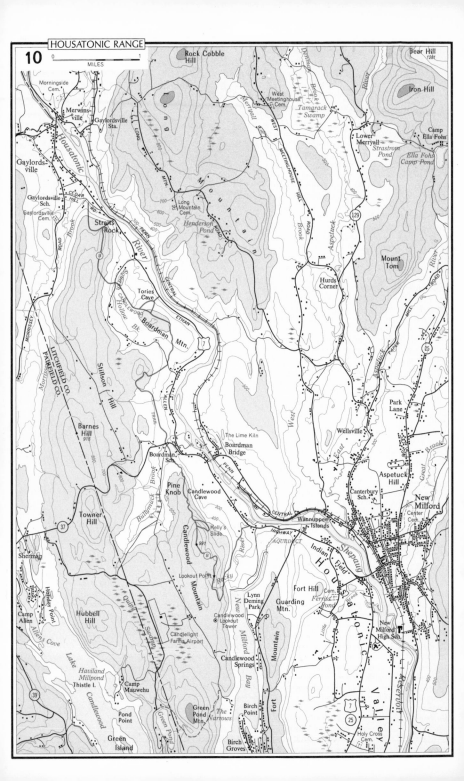

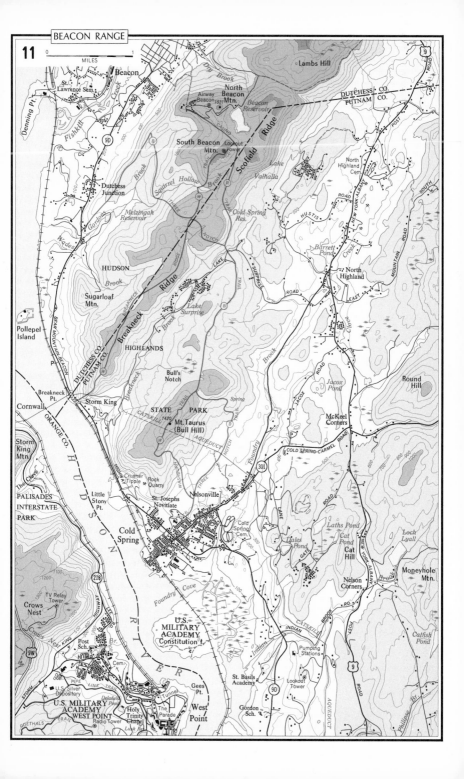

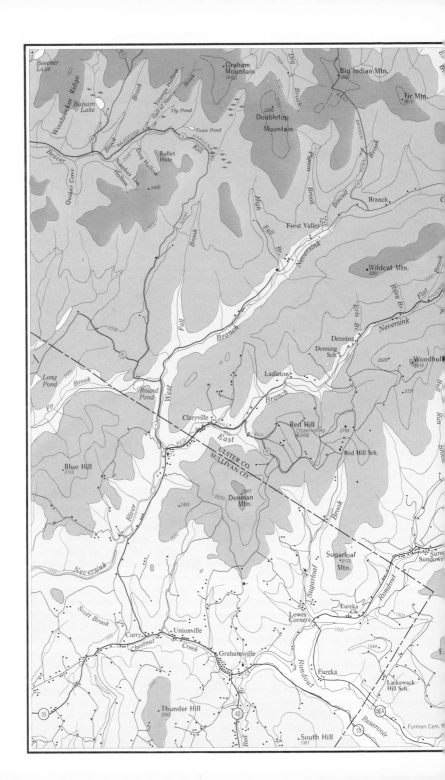

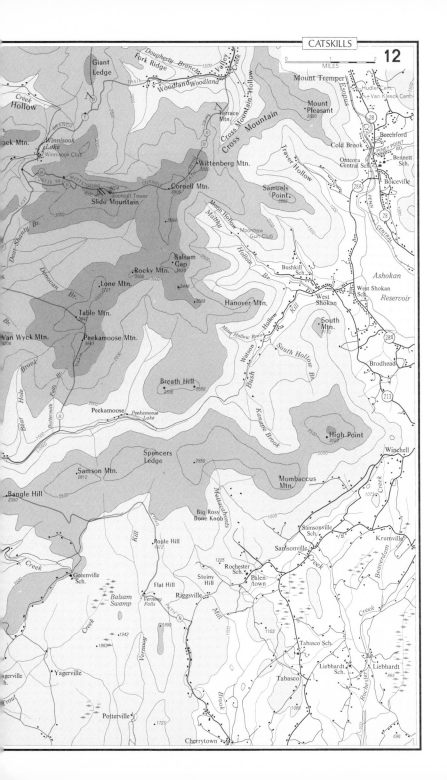

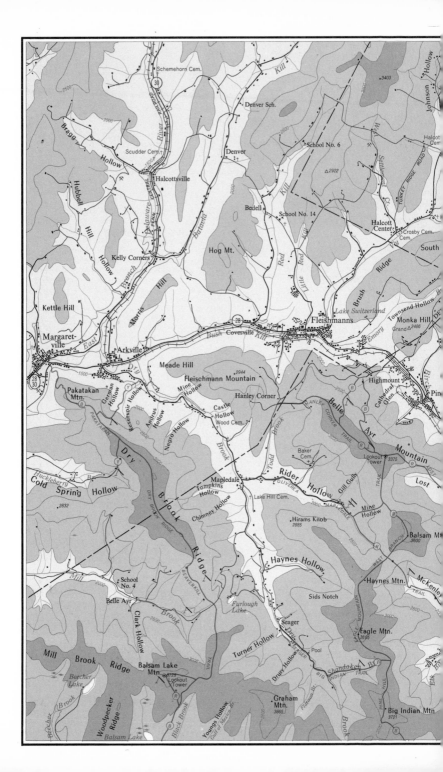

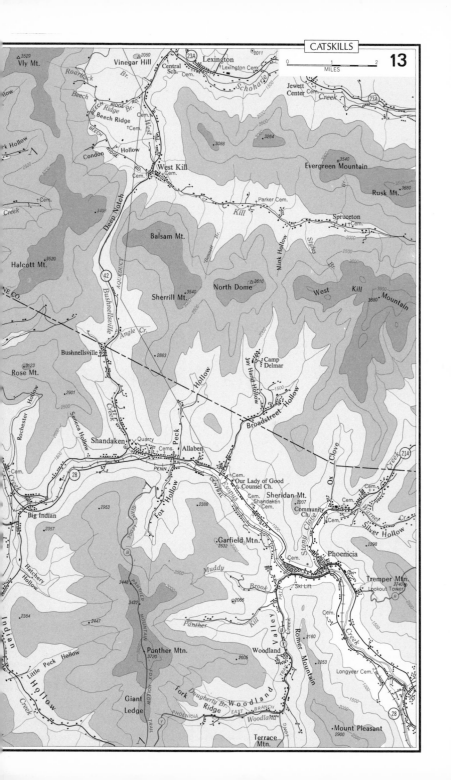

0 1 2
MILES

△3529
Vly Mt.

Roarback

△2050
Vinegar Hill

Central
Sch.

Cem.

23A
Lexington
Lexington Cem.

2011

Jewett
Center Cem.

Creek

23A

Schoharie

Beech
RIDGE
Ridge Br.

Br.

Beech Ridge
†Cem.

Cem.

3088

3264

Evergreen Mountain

3540

BEECH

West

Condon

Hollow

RIDGE
RD.
Cem.

West Kill
Cem.

Rusk Mt. 3680
3600

Parker Cem.

Spruceton
Cem.

Kill

2000

Mink Hollow

Stiles

Deep Notch

†Cem.

Creek

3406

Balsam Mt.

Sherrill Mt. 3540

North Dome

△3610

West Kill 3500
3880 Mountain

2500

Halcott Mt. 3520

AQUEDUCT

Bushnellsville

42

Sherrill Mt.

2500

NE CO.

Angle Cr.

Hollow

2883

Jay Hand Hollow

Camp
Delmar

Broadstreet Hollow

1500

△3123
Rose Mt.

Rochester Hollow

2901

2500

Spruce Hollow

Creek

Shandaken

Quarry

Cems.

Peck

Allaben

Bushnellsville

PENN

28

Big Indian

2953

2357

Fox

Hollow

2388

CENTRAL

Esopus

Our Lady of Good
Counsel Ch.

Cem.

Cem.
Shandaken
Cem.

Sheridan Mt.
2607

Community
Clove

Cem.

Ox

Clove

Cem.

214

Creek

Cem.

Sunny

Silver Hollow

2298

Clove

Garfield Mtn.
2532

Cem.

Phoenicia

2500

Muddy

Hatchery
Hollow

2384

3448

PANTHER

3422

2447

Brook

3066

Panther

Kill

Valley

Ski Lift

Tremper Mtn.
2740
Lookout Tower
8

Cem.

2160

Romer

Mountain

1500

Longyear Cem.

Little Peck Hollow

Panther Mtn.
3720

MOUNTAIN

FOX

HOLLOW

Woodland

2605

Indian

Hollow

Giant
Ledge

Fork
Ridge

TRAIL

Dougherty Br.

PHOENICIA

Woodland

EAST BRANCH

Woodland

Terrace
Mtn.

Mount Pleasant
2900 2500

28

2253

1500

2000

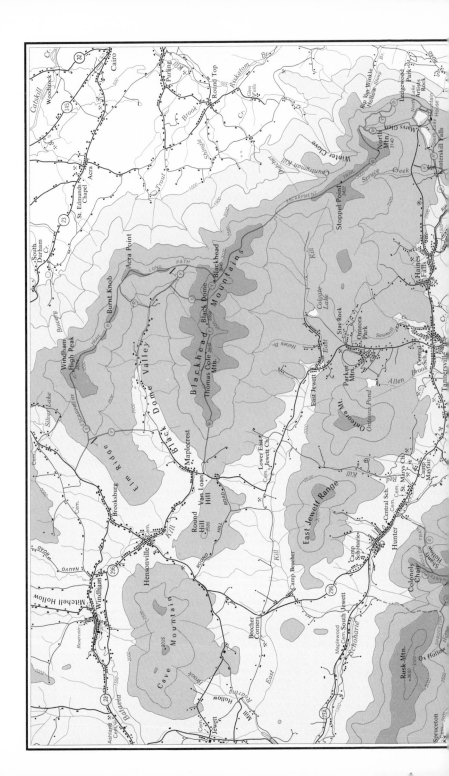

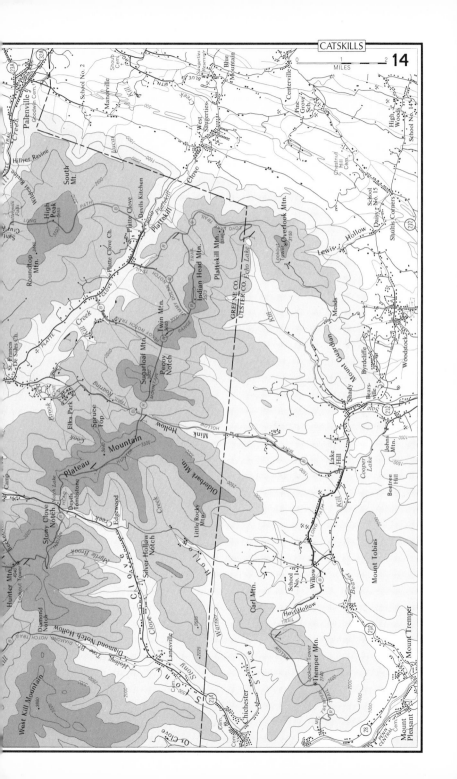

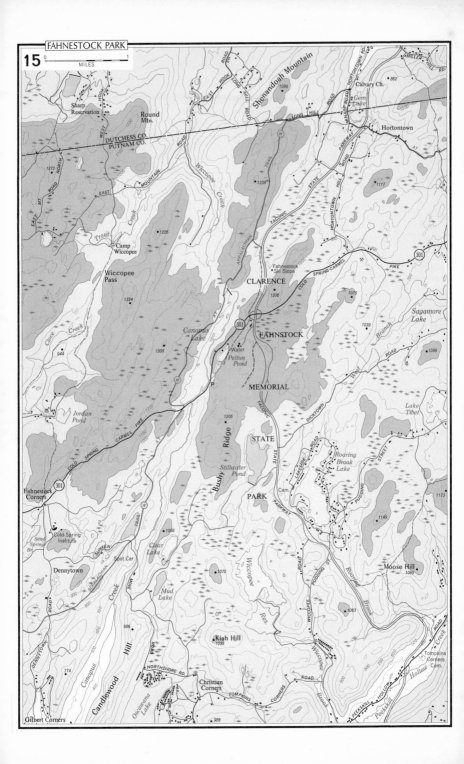

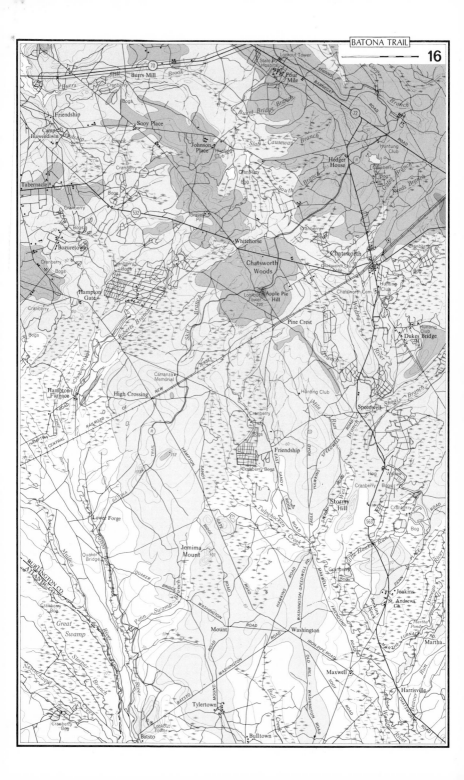

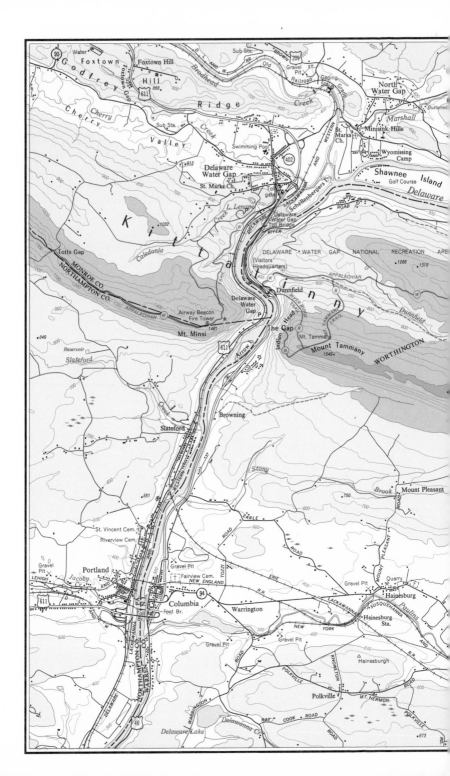

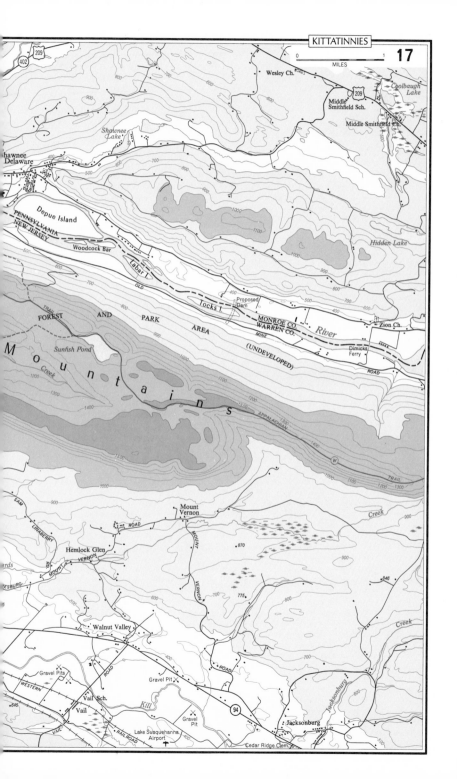

MILES
0   1

209
402

Wesley Ch.

Coolbaugh
Lake

209

Middle
Smithfield Sch.

Middle Smithfield Ch.

Shawnee
Lake

Shawnee
Delaware

Depue Island

PENNSYLVANIA
NEW JERSEY

Hidden Lake

Woodcock Bar

Tabor I.

OLD

Tocks I.

Proposed
Dam

MONROE CO.
WARREN CO.

Zion Ch.

FOREST   AND   PARK
AREA

MINE

River

TRAIL

M o u n t a i n s

Sunfish Pond

Creek

(UNDEVELOPED)

Dimicks
Ferry

ROAD

APPALACHIAN

W

TRAIL

Creek

Mount
Vernon

ROAD

SAM

LINABERRY

Hemlock Glen

VERNON

MOUNT

VERNON

870

846

900

rds

esburg

MOUNT

Walnut Valley

Creek

Gravel Pits

WESTERN

Vail Sch.

Vail

845

Kill

Gravel Pit

ROAD

ROAD

775

Jacksonburg

700

94

Gravel
Pit

Lake Susquehanna
Airport

VAIL

RAILROAD

Jacksonburg

Cedar Ridge Cem.

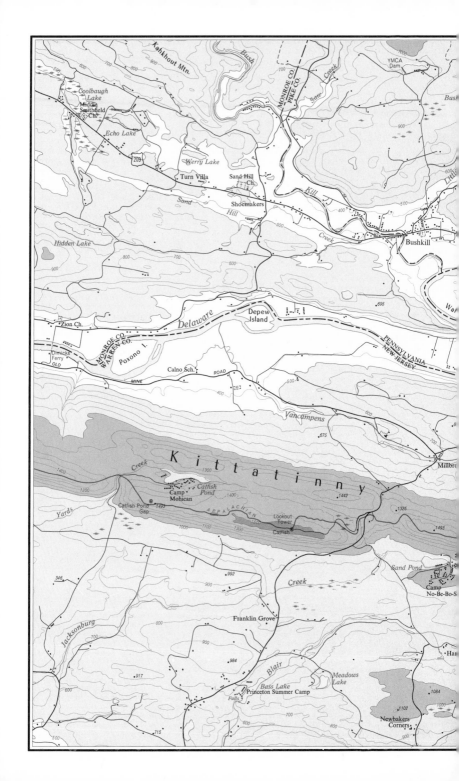

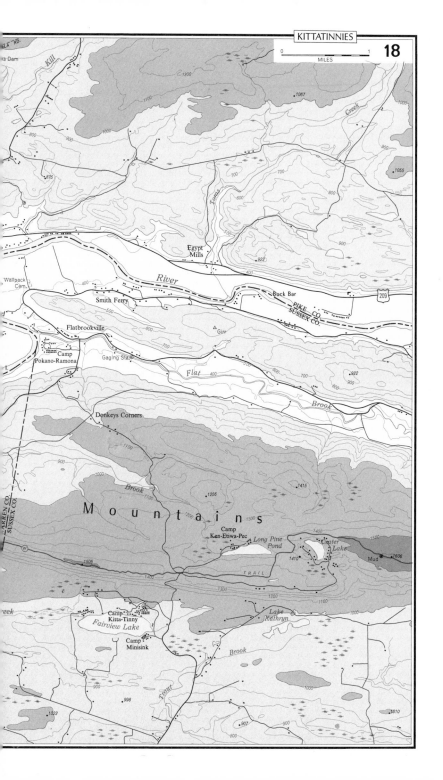

MILES

KILLA RD.

ks Dam

Kill

1067

Creek

1000

1900

1100

800

1000

900

875

1055

700

Tom

700

800

600

900

800

Egypt
Mills

922

River

500

Wallpack
Cam.

400

209

Smith Ferry

Buck Bar

PIKE CO.
SUSSEX CO.

Flatbrookville

500

Girr

Camp
Pokano-Ramona

Gaging Sta.

600

700

922

Flat

400

800

700

900

Brook

Donkeys Corners

1100

900

Brook

1000

1415

1256

1100

M o u n t a i n s

1200

1300

Camp
Ken-Etiwa-Pec

1400

Long Pine
Pond

Crater
Lake

1500

WARREN CO.
SUSSEX CO.

W

1506

1300

1410

Mud

1606

TRAIL

1300

1200

1100

reek

Camp
Kitta-Tinny

Lake
Kathryn

1000

Fairview Lake

Camp
Minisink

Brook

Trout

900

998

1000

1022

907

900

1010

800

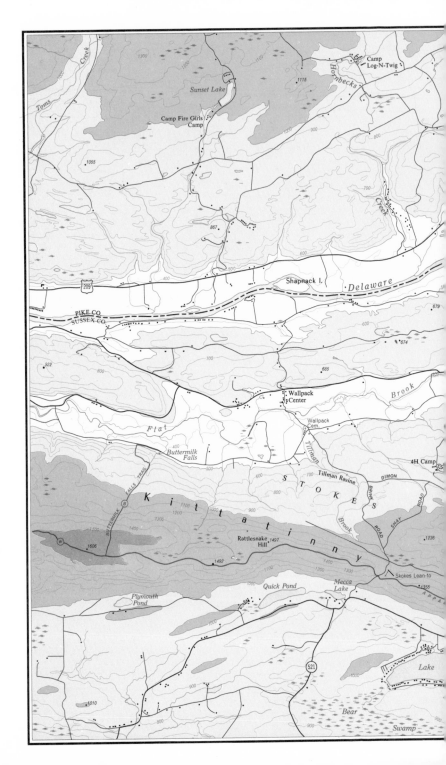

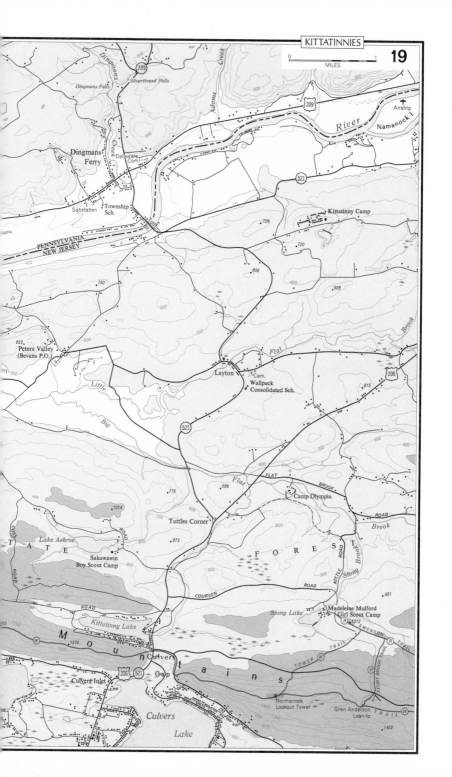

0   MILES   1

739

Dingmans Falls

Silverthread Falls

Adams   Creek

Dingmans   Creek

900

River

209

Airstrip

Namanock I.

Dingmans
Ferry

Delaware
Cem.

521

Kittatinny Camp

Substation   Township
Sch.

726

PENNSYLVANIA
NEW JERSEY

720

400

808

800

928

750

900

700

Brook

653

Peters Valley
(Bevans P.O.)

600

Flat

Layton   Cem.

Wallpack
Consolidated Sch.

206

815

500

Little

Big

521

700

800

900

600

FLAT

Flat   BROOK

775

686

Camp Olympia

ROAD

1014

Tuttles Corner

700

600

800

Brook

873

F   O   R   E   S   T

991

ROAD

Stony   Brook

KITTLE   ROAD

COSS

Lake Ashroe

900

Sakawawin
Boy Scout Camp

1000

900

COURSEN

ROAD

1100

ROAD

Madeleine Mulford
Girl Scout Camp

1012

R

Stony Lake

Kittatinny Lake

1376

M   o   u

1305

Culvers

Gap

SWENSON

TRAIL

R

TRAIL

STONY BROOK TRAIL

206   521

Culvers Inlet

TOWER

W

TRAIL

C   u   l   v   e   r   s

n   t   a   i   n   s

Normanook
Lookout Tower

1400

Gren Anderson
Lean-to

1483

Lake

900

1100

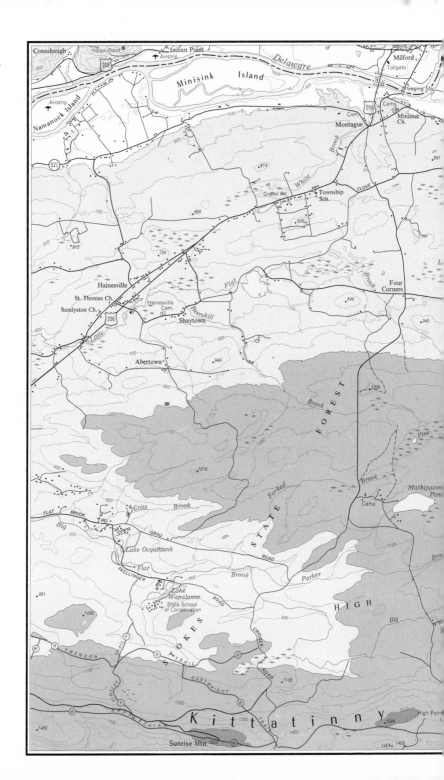

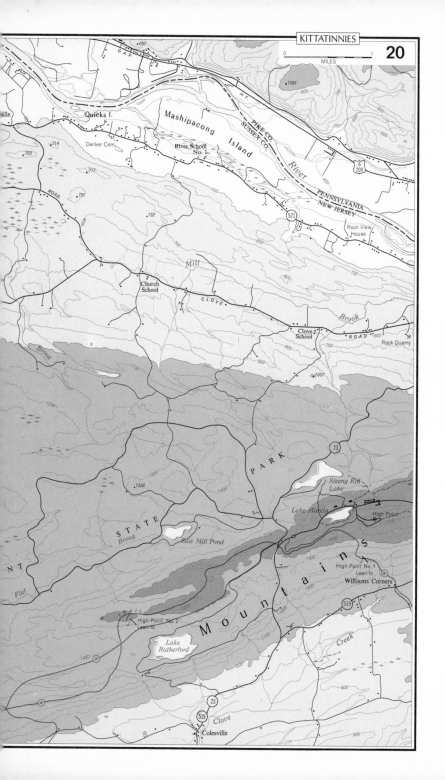

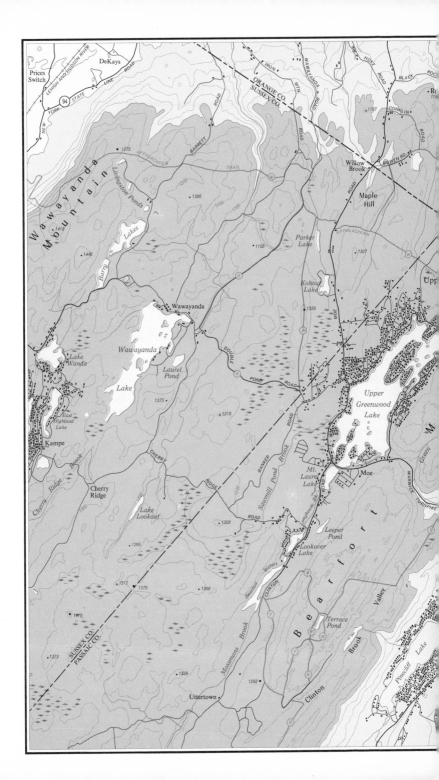

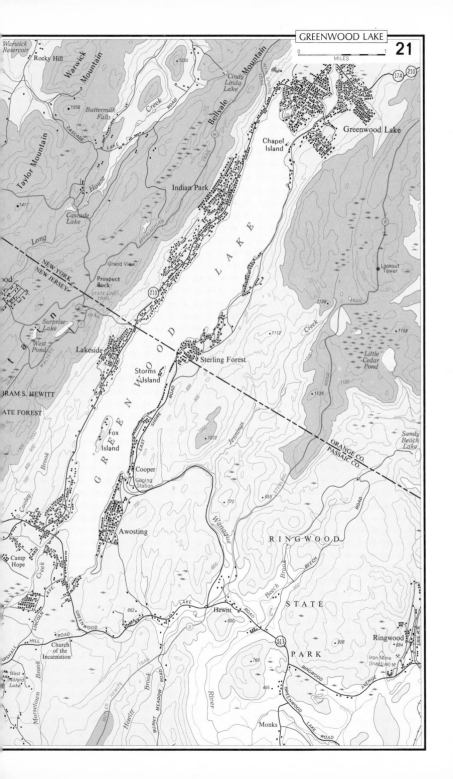

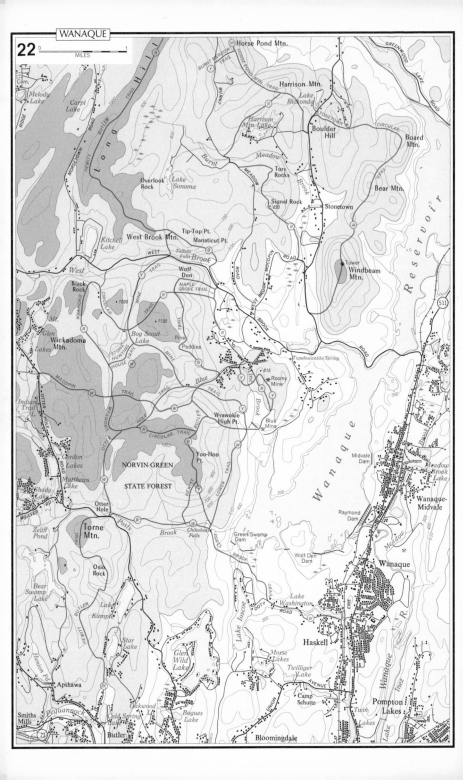

Index Map *(overleaf)*

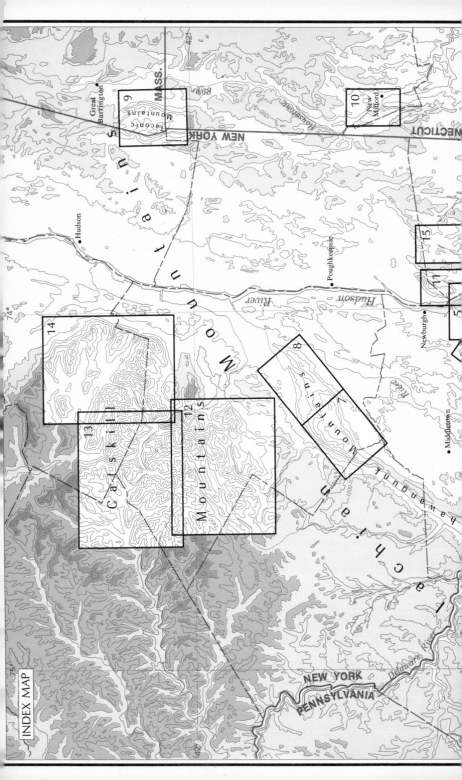

INDEX MAP

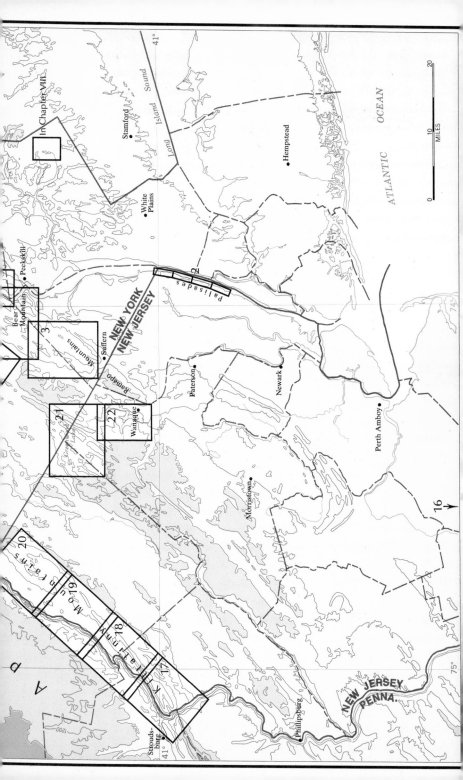